Rehearsing for Life

This work examines the production and performance of theatrical activities aimed at bringing about social change in both development and political intervention in Nepal. If everyday social problems can be both represented and challenged through drama-based performances, then what differentiates street theatre performed in planned development from street theatre performed within social and political movements? This multi-sited ethnography attempts to answer this question by following the works of Aarohan Theatre – a Kathmandu-based professional company, performing both *loktantrik natak* (theatre for democracy) in the context of the 2005–06 popular movement, and *kachahari natak* (forum theatre) for development projects. The analysis then extends to the forum theatre produced by one of Aarohan's partner groups, the Kamlari Natak Samuha – a Tharu grass-roots activist organization based in Deukhuri Valley (West Nepal) campaigning against indentured child labour. The book explores how Maoist cultural troupes moving out of the People's War into the peace process used cultural programmes as a tool to enroll their audience into the changing political project.

Employing a critical perspective and considering theatre as a mode of socio-cultural practice embedded in the wider socio-political reality, the book looks at the groups' organizational structures, the artists' identities and professional aspirations in a context where lack of State support for arts turned development aid into a crucial source of livelihood for theatre artists.

What emerges is an account of what it means to perform theatre and live by theatre. This study explores the challenges of being a professional artist engaged in activism, the pressures felt by Maoist cultural activists to 'professionalize' their productions when performing in the capital after the end of the war, and closely analyzes how a group of theatre workers who are committed to transforming a stigmatized passion into a respectable and glamorous job in contemporary Nepal.

Monica Mottin teaches at Ruskin College, Oxford, and is research associate at the School of Languages, Cultures and Linguistics, School of Oriental and African Studies, University of London. She is a social anthropologist and specializes in Nepal (South Asia at large). Her research focuses on the anthropology of theatre and performance, art and activism, social movements, community mobilization through cultural performance, development and aid.

Rehearsing for Life

Theatre for Social Change in Nepal

Monica Mottin

CAMBRIDGE
UNIVERSITY PRESS

CAMBRIDGE
UNIVERSITY PRESS

University Printing House, Cambridge CB2 8BS, United Kingdom

One Liberty Plaza, 20th Floor, New York, NY 10006, USA

477 Williamstown Road, Port Melbourne, vic 3207, Australia

314 to 321, 3rd Floor, Plot No.3, Splendor Forum, Jasola District Centre, New Delhi 110025, India

79 Anson Road, #06–04/06, Singapore 079906

Cambridge University Press is part of the University of Cambridge.

It furthers the University's mission by disseminating knowledge in the pursuit of education, learning and research at the highest international levels of excellence.

www.cambridge.org
Information on this title: www.cambridge.org/9781108416115

© Monica Mottin 2018

First published 2018

Printed in India at Rajkamal Electric Press, Kundli, Haryana.

A catalogue record for this publication is available from the British Library

ISBN 978-1-108-41611-5 Hardback

Cambridge University Press has no responsibility for the persistence or accuracy of URLs for external or third-party internet websites referred to in this publication, and does not guarantee that any content on such websites is, or will remain, accurate or appropriate.

For my parents, Aldo and Adriana

Contents

List of Tables, Figures and Boxes

LIST OF BOXES

Acknowledgements

Many people have helped to make this book possible; penning the acknowledgements section feels like going back in time to recollect an important part of my life and thinking about all of them. A lot has changed since I started fieldwork for this research. The Kathmandu theatre scene has seen a rebirth in the last decade, but many of the challenges of making theatre a sustainable profession and many of the political contradictions highlighted in the street plays are still relevant. Although the content of this book may not satisfy everyone, I hope that it can bear witness to the creative richness and incessant passion and dedication of the theatre and cultural workers.

I would like to express my gratitude and affection to Aarohan Theatre artists, for the time they spent answering my questions, for their patience, for their friendship and for letting me stay in their 'home', Gurukul: Sunil Pokharel, Nisha Sharma, Basanta Bhatta, Sarita Giri, Aruna Karki, Rajkumar Pudasaini, Rajan, Kathiwada, Suresh Chand, Bhola Raj Sapkota, Yubaraj Ghimire, Mani Pokharel, Saugat Malla, Kamal Mani Nepal, Pashupati Rai, Samuna K. C., Saraswati Chaudhary, Pramila Katwal, Prabin Khatiwada, Mahesh Shakya, Ram Hari Dhakal, Sindhu Pokharel, Rabindra Sigh Baniya, Anoj Pokharel, Anil Pokharel, Jeebesh Rayamajhi. I owe a huge debt to countless scholars, artists, activists and theatre lovers that I had the chance to talk with and learn from in *Gurukul* and in Kathmandu. In particular, I am grateful to Prachanda Malla, Anup Baral and Puskar Gurung for sharing their profound knowledge and experience of Nepali and world theatre, the 'Friends of Gurukul', Professor Abhi Subedi, Shiva Rijal, Prakash Subedi, Asha Magarati, Ashesh Malla, Sarwanam artists, Kirstine Ronnov Due, Usha Titikshu, Bhaskar Gautam, Tatsuro Fujikura and Mara Matta. Extra thanks are due to Samuna K. C. for her assistance in part of this research, Aruna and Mani Pokharel for accommodating me in their home during my shorter stays in Kathmandu, Prakash Subedi for reading a draft of this book and providing precious comments.

I am grateful to the Kamlari Natak Samuha, Krishna Chaudhary and Dhaniram Chaudhary for taking the time to guide me in Deukhuri Valley and introduce me to groups and people. I am grateful to Man Bahadur Chhetri, who offered ample explanations and documentation to understand projects better. I would like to thank Kopila Dangol, Ram Gupta, Baghiram Chaudhary and to all the former kamlaris who shared their life stories since 2005, in particular Shiva Chaudhary, Shivani Chaudhary, Sita Chaudhary, Deepa, Chandrama and Sushila Chaudhary. I owe a lot also to the Kalika Self-Reliance Social Centre from Taulihawa (Kapilvastu), in particular to their *kachahari* team, Mr Pradeep

Singh, Ravi Thakur and his family. The group members did not spare their time in showing me how they work in their communities through theatre.

I wish to thank all the artists who at the time of my fieldwork belonged to Sen Chyang Sanskritik Parivar, Newa Sankritik Parivar and Samana Parivar for their patience in accepting my questions and my presence in their groups. Raj Bahadur Kunwar and Khem Thapaliya have been exceptionally generous with time, documents and books. Thanks to Anish Hyonjan Chayngba and to Laxmi Tamang for welcoming me in their homes.

SOAS has been a stimulating place where I could develop my research and establish friendships that lasted and supported me across the world. Thanks to Paola Prestinoni, Katia Fabbri, Debbie Whelan, Ilana van Wyk and George Kunnath. I owe much of my intellectual development to the Department of Anthropology and to my PhD supervisors, Professor David Mosse and Professor Michael Hutt. Professor David Mosse deserves a special mention for the time and guidance he generously offered during fieldwork and writing process and in the follow-up activities; his enthusiasm about this project over the years and his encouragement helped me overcome the challenges. My grateful thanks are also extended to Professors David Gellner and Alpa Shah for valuable suggestions on my thesis and to two anonymous reviewers for Cambridge University Press who provided insightful and constructive comments on the manuscript. A Central Research Fund (University of London) grant facilitated my fieldwork; a Research Associate affiliation to the SOAS Department of Languages and Cultures of South Asia helped me in turning my thesis into this book. Earlier versions of two chapters of this publication have appeared in press before. Thanks are due to Cambridge University Press and Routledge for permission to reproduce them.

Despite the difficult period of relentless neoliberal pressures, job insecurity, course cuts and industrial disputes, London Metropolitan University has been an inspiring place to work. I was fortunate to discuss ideas and share drafts of this book with Georgie Wemyss, July Scott, Brian Mcdonogh, Sandra Abegglen, Jessie Bustillos, David Blundell, Rossana Perez del Aguila, Anna Paraskevopolou and Peter Cunningham. I also owe a lot to the interest and encouragement of my students, who, through stimulating class discussions, reminded me of the importance of publishing this research and of writing this book in an accurate but accessible way.

Finally, I could start this research thanks to the trust of Lidia Cattelan, Elena Clauser and Patrizia Messinese, who facilitated unpaid leave from my previous job and my return to work between stretches of fieldwork. I will never forget the day when Lidia drove me early in the morning to the Provincial Education Office to have a part-time arrangement exceptionally approved so that I could fly to London on a weekly basis and take up the PhD offer. Having financial security and periodic breaks allowed me the freedom and mental peace to complete the research as I wished. Mark Campbell has encouraged me throughout the publication of this book, and also meticulously edited drafts and patiently checked proofs: I have no words to express what this meant to me. My brother Alessio and Lucia, my parents Adriana and Aldo, have travelled the world to show their support: I thank them for their love, and for keeping a place for me when I return home.

1

Theatre and Life

Theatre at the intersection of art, politics and international development

This book is about social and political theatre in Nepal. In particular, it examines how everyday social problems and macro-political conflicts are both represented and challenged through drama-based performances. How are theatre and social reality (dis)connected? How can reflexivity and ambiguity allow for the aesthetic space to become a transformative place? What differentiates street theatre performed in planned development from street theatre performed within social and political movements? How can performance and dramatic action move communities towards social action? To answer these questions I delve into both aesthetic and social performance contexts of three types of theatre and performance for social change available to Nepali audiences in the mid-2000s: *kachahari natak* (forum theatre/street theatre), *loktantrik natak* (theatre for democracy) and Maoist political cultural programmes that may include *krantikari natak* (revolutionary theatre). In other words, the political theatre for democracy performed by Aarohan Theatre Group, development forum theatre performed by both Aarohan Theatre in Kathmandu and by the Kamlari Natak Samuha, a Tharu activist group, in the rural areas of western Nepal, the political performance of the Maoist cultural groups, all aim to bring about social change, but how are they similar and how do they differ?

Aarohan Theatre Group, a Kathmandu-based professional company and Gurukul, the theatre school associated with the group, is at the core of this ethnography. It is the main field site from which I tried to understand the world of theatre for social change in Nepal. To respond to what they describe as the 'needs of the country' Aarohan performed both political and street theatre in development projects. *Loktantrik natak* (theatre for democracy) was staged voluntarily within the popular movement led by civil society organizations that developed as a reaction to the king's coup and state of Emergency in 2005. *Kachahari natak* (forum theatre) was performed as part of donor-funded development projects. But project-funded development theatre was also a means for Aarohan and other theatre groups in Nepal to survive and continue developing their artistic stage productions. In fact, to develop theatre acting as a full-fledged profession in the emerging Nepali creative industries, Aarohan Theatre also staged high profile proscenium plays at their halls in Gurukul. If *loktantrik natak* represented the 'special', once off response to the urgency of the political threats, *kachahari natak* undoubtedly constituted the everyday, the 'ordinary' NGO-funded project work that financially contributed to the sustenance of Aarohan Theatre as an organization. Understanding the challenges faced by Aarohan Theatre provides powerful insight into the impact that international development funding can have on emergent theatre groups, in particular in countries like Nepal in which the government does not subsidize the arts. But *kachahari* performed in Kathmandu by professionals is different from *kachahari* performed by activists in rural areas. To get a comparative perspective, I have focused on work of the Kamlari Natak Samuha in Deukhuri Valley, west Nepal, one of Aarohan partner groups. The Kamlari Natak Samuha is a group formed by activists who performed in their spare time and in their own communities to fight a form of indentured child labour. The performances were part of the advocacy campaign carried out by local grassroots and national NGOs. Similarly, political street theatre performed in the capital during the movement for democracy finds interesting comparative insight in the work of the Maoist cultural groups. In this case, political cultural work is an 'ordinary', everyday activity for full-time party cadres. Maoist performances in fact are deeply embedded in Maoist organizational and ideological structure, using well-defined formats, images and language. 'Revolutionary theatre' can be considered as a radical form of agit-prop, a militant form of art that is intended to emotionally and ideologically mobilize its audience within a wider political project.

Understanding the contributions and limitations of using street theatre in development intervention or in political and social movements is not possible without understanding the lived experiences, the hopes and the expectations of the theatre 'makers', the relationship between theatre groups, government institutions, political parties and donor agencies, the groups' identities and the process of performance production. Yet, an additional form of performance emerged from the field. The critical years when Nepal moved from the 2005 autocracy to republic, via the 2006 People's Movement, produced a fascinating flurry of contentious street performances: the king deployed a pseudo-theatrical apparatus to legitimize his power including processions, official ceremonies, religious festivals, slogans, radio announcements and metal billboards. Similarly, demonstrators furthered their claims for democracy through slogans, puppets, colourful symbolic actions and cultural programmes including political theatre. I argue that performances do not simply represent, but construct and deconstruct power because of the aesthetic space that is conjured up and the extent to which they capture the essence of 'reality'. Performances also create the moral space to ground and sanction political struggle.

Performance is a notoriously contested and fluid concept. This book is therefore situated at the crossroads between anthropology, politics, theatre and international development. Recent research has moved away from a reductionist theatrical understanding of performance as mimicry, catharsis, or entertainment to embrace a broader, almost all-encompassing notion of performance as a way through which human beings make culture, engage with power and invent new ways of being in the world (Conquergood, 1995; Madison and Hamera, 2006). In particular, Conquergood suggests understanding 'the ubiquitous and generative force of performance that is beyond the theatrical' (Madison and Hamera, 2006, xii). Following this framework, cultural performance is distinguished from social performance. The first includes symbolic and self-conscious acts presented within specific and well-defined spaces, such as plays, rituals, circus, carnivals, concerts and storytelling. Social performance indicates the ordinary day-to-day interaction of individuals in the unfolding of social life, where behaviour is not 'marked' (Turner, 1982). In this study I want to go back to the theatrical and 'marked' performance to understand how social transformation is triggered at the blurred margins when the cultural fades into the social, where performance is actioned into performativity and back. Drawing from anthropological contributions to performance studies (Turner and Bruner, 1986; Schechner, 1993, 2002; Schechner and Turner, 1985), the work of Victor Turner (1969, 1974, 1982, 1987; St. John, 2008) concerning the interplay between ritual, theatre and everyday life, his theory of 'social dramas', concepts of the liminal/liminoid and communitas as well as his last works on the anthropology of experience are central to my analysis. They provide a framework within which to observe development theatre, political theatre and performative forms of protest as places in which conflictual practices, relationships and roles may be examined, and where possible resolutions may be articulated. The dramatic metaphor has often been employed to describe social life (Burke, 1945; Turner, 1982, 1984; Goffman, 1959) and anthropologists have documented its spectacular qualities (Cohen, 1993; Geertz, 1980; Turner, 1974). Roles, behaviour and social practices are understood as 'scripts' that are performed every day (Goffman, 1959; Trevino, 2003). However, performances do not simply provide transparent representations of social realities (mimesis), they create 'reflexive', contested representations to challenge both everyday social oppressions and macro-political conflict (poiesis). As Turner (1982) put it, performance is making, not faking. The theatrical space may become a place for reflexive awareness in which the 'actions' that make up the 'scripts' can be distanced, isolated, magnified and, in some cases, questioned, contested and changed, in ways similar to what Turner and Schechner describes as 'restored behaviour', 'twice-behaved behaviour' (Schechner and Turner, 1985, 35–37). 'Reflexivity' rather than 'reflectivity' can trigger agency. Schutzman and Cohen-Cruz (2006, 77) highlight that 'reflective images are analogous to looking into a mirror and seeing an '"accurate" representation'; conversely, 'reflexive images are those [...] wherein multiple representations are created through deliberate distortions (such as exaggeration, caricature, resonance) and utilized for interpretative purposes'. In short, reflexions are representations with a distortion, with a focus that can function as a model for some wished for world rather than a mirror of existing practices. This book will explore different forms of collective and public reflexive actions, some spontaneous such as street demonstrations, others planned like theatre for democracy. Conquergood adds a third element to the dichotomy mimesis (imitation) – poiesis (production) and talks about kinesis (rupture) when performance is understood as 'breaking and remaking', unleashing forces that unsettle power hierarchies (Conquergood, 1995, 138). Taussig (1993) also complicates a static notion of mimesis and shows how powerless people represent practices and gestures of the powerful to subvert authority. In this way mimesis opens the way to creation and intervention. Trying to classify performance through categories is limiting as performance is processual, relational and fluid so, as we will see in the next chapters, representation merges into creation and disruption like an ebb and flow, often in relation to the perceived opposition that comes from the surroundings.

Boal's[1] research on theatre for social change and especially his techniques of Forum Theatre (1979, 1992, 1995, 1998, 2006; Cohen-Cruz and Schutzman, 1994; Schutzman and Cohen-Cruz, 2006) offer an interesting perspective through which to study social reality and the way in which real-life conflicts and oppressions are expressed and challenged via the theatrical. *Kachahari natak* is the Nepali adaptation of Forum Theatre. Practised all over the world, forum theatre is a dramaturgical technique that Brazilian director Augusto Boal systematized into a methodology called the Theatre of the Oppressed (1979). It is employed in several kinds of projects such as community development, personal or organizational development, advocacy and therapy. In Nepal, forum theatre is mostly used in international development projects.[2] Boal advocates an aesthetic transformation through theatre. He believed that what makes a performance really critical is neither the plot nor the dialogue but the structure itself: oppression is achieved through the separation between actors vs. audience, lead actors vs. chorus (Ibid., 1979). The process of identification that affects the spectator and generates catharsis does not produce effective changes in reality according to Boal. On the contrary, it reasserts the oppressive condition. What Boal suggests is to turn the spectators in spect-actors, that is actors that not only take part in the dramatic action, but who are also creators of the drama: 'some people 'make' theatre' suggests Boal, but everybody 'is' theatre'. Audience's participation becomes therefore a significant element in order to understand how drama-based work can bring forward social change.

Boal wished to 'activate' the spectators by offering them the chance of entering the aesthetic space. 'Simultaneous dramaturgy' is the first attempt to break the barrier between actors and spectators, between fiction and reality. When the scene reaches a point of crisis, the play is stopped and the spectators can verbally offer alternative solutions that the actors enact on the spot: 'the audience members 'write' and the actors 'perform' (Cohen-Cruz and Schutzman, 1994, 238). However, telling someone to do something and actually doing it are two very different things. Boal recounts a famous example that transformed his theatre towards the even more participatory[3] methodology of forum theatre. A woman in the audience became so outraged by the actor's inability to understand her suggestion that she went onto the stage and demonstrated what she meant through her own actions. Boal argues that

> when the spectator herself comes on stage and carries out the action she has in mind, she does it in a manner which is personal, unique and non-transferable, as she alone can do it, and as no artist can do it in her place. On stage the actor is an interpreter who, in the act of translating, plays false (1995, 7)

Trying to embody real-life dilemmas and enact possible solutions triggers off different involvement and emotions: for Boal 'doing' is different from 'talking about doing', 'representing' is different from 'being'.

During a forum theatre performance, participants and audience belong both to the 'real' world they live in and to the imagined 'representation' created by the play. The performance arena becomes a metaxic space. Boal describes metaxis as

> [t]he state of belonging completely and simultaneously to two different, autonomous worlds: the image of reality and the reality of the image. The participants shares and belongs to these two autonomous worlds; their reality and the image of their reality which she herself has created (1995, 43)

Through forum theatre techniques the boundaries between fiction and reality may become blurred. Words can become actions, but actions that are simultaneously 'real' but not in actual 'real' life situations. Actions are embedded within the assumed 'fiction' of the aesthetic space. While critics see participatory development as concealing power behind representation, and introducing 'real' power into the apolitical theatre of participations, Boal uses a parallel shift between reality/play and on/off stage with the audience themselves in order to challenge power (see Chapter 4).

The anthropological critique of development, in particular the shift from 'whether' to 'how' development works provides the background against which to situate theatrical work as an intervention for social change (Long and Long, 1992; Mosse, 2004, 2005a). This involves revealing the complex agency and interests of the different actors involved in the processes, as well as the necessity of taking into account the 'back stage' of the different agendas. Mosse (2005a, 8) described development as representation and explained how the success of development projects is produced by the control over the interpretation of events that are themselves socially produced and maintained. Theatre, and art in general, occupies a 'special' place within the development discourse: it is often framed instrumentally as a means, as a tool towards the achievement of other development goals, or through which to showcase the success of development projects. The symbolic sphere is privileged over the material. However, Aarohan Theatre's actions, commitments and dilemmas – as well as the artistic aspiration of Maoist cultural workers – show that the 'theatre-making' is indeed a goal in its own right. Theatre artists call themselves 'theatre workers', thus suggesting that theirs is an 'ordinary' profession and the Gurukul decade de facto ended by creating the basis of Nepali contemporary cultural economies.

The anthropology of power provided the *fil rouge* to understand how theatre and the theatrical mode can undo and expose the invisible workings of politics (Lukes, 2005; Ankersmit, 1996; Kertzer, 1988; Scott, 1985, 1990). Ankersmit (1996) explains that representation is political and always presents us an 'aesthetic gap' between the represented and the representation. In this aesthetic gap legitimate political power and political creativity originates. In fact, an effective use of ritual is crucial in the success of both conservative and revolutionary political groups.

Finally, I take a critical perspective considering theatre making as 'a mode of socio-cultural practice' (Zarrilli, 1995, 1) embedded in the wider socio-political-economic reality rather than a simple tool for behaviour change, and focus on how performance 'affects' rather than on how performance produces 'effects'(Zarrilli, 1995; Thompson, 2009). For these reasons, street drama performed within development projects has not been objectified as a 'product of development' and Maoist cultural work has not been dismissed as propaganda. Rather, both have been analysed as forms of popular culture to be understood within both the political and aesthetic conditions of their performance. Instead of directing primary attention to performance texts, this analysis sheds light on patterns of cultural practices, such as other forms of contentious performances questioning the social order, continuities and innovations upon well-known themes and strategies, as well as artists' changing professional identities. While acknowledging the relevance of reception research and the productive role of any theatre audience (Bennet, 1997), I mostly focus on the production and performance stages – with just a brief incursion in reception. To understand how technical choices allowed for different degrees of audience participation and agency, I focus on Aarohan Theatre organizational development, the artists' identities and professional expectations. Similarly, by focusing on the artists' point of view instead of the audience's, I don't consider theatre as 'literature that happens to be on stage' but rather as a 'moving life force' (Berkoff in Hastrup, 2004, 29) capable of encouraging the audience to collectively fight for democracy or social justice as well as to inspire the artists to overcome their own hardships and turn a stigmatized passion into a respectable job.

Theatre and power in Nepal

The words *natak* and *natya*, 'drama/theatre' in Nepali, have the same root as *nach* (informal) and *nrtya* (formal). They both mean 'dance' and immediately suggest that the two genres are connected. Often *nach* indicates a performance that includes songs, dance and dialogues. Unlike classical western theatre, largely word-based, Nepali theatre is rooted in actions and movements like Asian theatre (Brandon and Banham, 1997). Theatre thus becomes a privileged locus to study cultural practices. For anthropology, culture is not only inscribed and absorbed in the bodies of the actor, or dancer, or the spectator, but it is also contested and created through the body becoming embodied knowledge (Pavis, 2003; Bourdieu, 1990).

Nepali theatre(s)[4] reflects the country's geographical, cultural, religious and linguistic diversity where Hindu and Buddhist religious-cultural traditions mingle with Indic, indigenous and western theatrical practices (Subedi, 2001, 2006). Subedi (2001) distinguishes three theatrical streams. First, folk theatre, diversified according to ethnic traditions; second, heritage performances, blending rituals, festivals and dance-dramas, and linked to folk and shamanic practices; third, proscenium theatre, influenced by Sanskritic and western traditions. For Subedi, 'the traditional forms, the mask dances, ritual dramas, traditional dance dramas, tabloids representing vibrant cultural forms, short dance dramas are participated in and watched by a larger number of people than any modern plays' (Ibid., 11). What's fascinating is the way in which theatre, ritual and performance relate to authority and power, both spiritual and political. Through this short historical background I want to highlight how such relationship has also determined Nepali theatre's ambivalent connection to political power, the Royal Palace in particular,

shaping the types of performances available to common citizens as well as affecting
the establishment of acting as a profession.

Nepali theatre is thought to have begun during the Licchavi period (fifth
to eighth century CE) though little remains of that kind of theatre except for
statues and inscriptions (Subedi, 2006, 25; Malla, 1980, 11; Toffin, 2012; Davis,
2002). Art and architecture flourished thanks to the country's position along
the commercial route linking India to China (Subedi, Ibid.). The Malla period
(1200–1768) is regarded the 'golden age' of drama, theatre and arts (Subedi,
2006, 34). The kings performed as actors on the *dabali* or *dabu*, a performance
platform where coronations also took place. They wrote dramas and patronized
performances. During the seventeenth and eighteenth centuries, kings, courtiers
and common people watched plays performed on the *dabali*[5] situated in the middle
of the *tole* (locality), near the palace and the temple. Until the end of the Rana rule,
guards protected the *dabu* and only kings or artists could step on it.[6] Dramas were
performed for festivals, religious celebrations, pilgrimages and for royal ceremonies
such as weddings, births and coronations.[7]

In 1768, Prithvi Narayan Shah 'unified'[8] Nepal and brought about deep socio-
economic, political, cultural and linguistic changes but this did not lead to significant
theatrical development. The Shah Kings (1768–1846) participated in rituals and
powerfully grounded their authority through performance and festivals but did not
patronize theatre *per sè* (Subedi, 2006, 15). King Prithvi Narayan Shah is believed
to have exploited the power of performance when he conquered the Nepal Valley
(Subedi, 2006, 14; van den Hoek, 1990). The Newar were celebrating the Indra Jatra
festival:[9] the Newar King Jayaprakash Malla fled the chariot, which was supposed to
carry him around the city. Prithvi Narayan himself took his place and was welcomed
by the citizens with flowers (Subedi, Ibid.). Prithvi Narayan then submitted himself
to the Kumari, the virgin incarnation of the Goddess of the Malla Taleju (van den
Hoek, 1990, 149). Political occupation was sanctioned through the appropriation
of ritual practices and reinforced annually in the streets. Though Indra is mythically
associated with fertility and prosperity, the main aim of this public ritual[10] is to
consolidate, renew and preserve the king's power (van den Hoek, 1990; Toffin,
1992, 2010). Through the festival the king is empowered by the *shakti* (power)
of the city (van den Hoek, 1993, 371). The festival is mostly performed publicly
in the streets and symbolically in key places of the capital. Indra Jatra festival lasts
for eight days between the months of *Bhadra* (August-September) and *Ashwin*
(September-October). The month of *Bhadra* is considered a month of contestation
and licence in the Kathmandu Valley (Toffin, 1992). Demons threaten the universe
and dance in the streets (*lakkhe pyakha*); improvised comic sketches (*khyalah*)

involve lampooning politicians and religious personalities (Ibid.). Indra Jatra closes the period, restoring the king's order over disruptive forces.

The Ranas (1846–1950) introduced great changes in theatre practices. They created theatre groups and established exclusive theatre houses inside their palaces for family members, officials and servants, that would sit according to their rank. These performances were influenced by the theatre of the royal courts of India as well as by western and Parsi performances, so-called because they were run by and bankrolled by Parsis in ninenteenth-century India (Malla, 1980). Theatre in the Rana courts had no local connotations and used Hindi-Urdu language (Rijal, 2007, 26). Although confined to the courts, because the Ranas were not interested in creating a theatre public, Parsi theatre nevertheless influenced dramatic productions outside the court and the capital, in towns like Pokhara, Dharan, Dhankuta and Palpa (Subedi, 2006, 77). Artists outside the court tried to emulate the quality of Parsi dramas, by making use of magnificent scenic curtains, melodrama and mixing Urdu and Hindi in songs and dialogues, but their lack of resources and skills made such experiments short-lived (Ibid.). Rijal (2007, 27) suggests that such exclusivity was one of the ways in which the Ranas distanced themselves from the common people and retained their power: they lived in buildings that emulated western architecture, associated themselves with western art, photography, clothing and imported the theatre from India.

At the turn of the twentieth century, exchanges between India and Nepal were common. Dumber Shumsher Rana[11] was sent to Calcutta in 1893 to get training in dramaturgy while Manik Man Tuladhar was the first non-Rana to be trained in India in 1900 (Subedi, 2006, 80). However, during the Rana period, except for Sama's plays, dramas were usually not written in Nepali but translated from Sanskrit and Hindi. Nepali was mixed with Urdu and Hindi (Malla, 1980). While patronizing theatre in their courts, the Rana prevented any attempt to expand Parsi theatre to local tastes as they were worried about public uprisings (Rijal, 2007, 29). When Manik Man Tuladhar tried to perform a play as Indrasabha in Tundikhel, Rana Prime Minister Chandra Shamser stopped him and ordered him to only perform for the people who can sponsor the shows (Malla in Rijal, 2007, 27).

The Ranas brought girls aged 13–14 from villages to their palaces. In every palace there were about 50–60 girls who were taught dance, drama, singing and music by Indian trainers. They resided in separate palaces and also received a salary. Inside the palace, women were responsible for all kinds of art and entertainment activities forbidden to men.[12] Prachanda Malla explains that in many palaces, trainers tuned a women's voice into a man's voice with 'lots and lots of practice'. Others retained their everyday female voice but in performance they could project their voice as a male.

In contrast, beyond the palaces, there were no stages or facilities and women were not allowed to perform. There were also no training facilities. Plays performed in the streets on the *dabali* during the same period were much simpler, without curtains and props. *Jyapunach*, the farmer's dance, was performed for eight days during Gai Jatra or Indra Jatra, provided the actors received permission from the Rana. Bekha Narayan Maharjan (1926–2006) and his group were among the most prominent performers. The audience would sit on straw mats around the *dabali* while street vendors sold peanuts and other foods (Subedi, 2006, 102). Artists were very popular at that time. Master Ratnadas, as Prachanda Malla refers to him, a singer and an actor, was considered a superstar. Having a good voice, in fact, was an essential quality for an actor.

Schools and colleges[13] in Kathmandu became the places where modern drama and theatre in Nepali language could develop. Dramatist Bhim Nidhi Tiwari (1911–73) writes of his play 'The Tolerant Sushila' (*Sahanshila Sushila*) being produced at Darbar High School in 1940, even though Rana officials and spies discouraged them (Rijal, 2007, 33). Balakrishna Sama (1903–81),[14] the most prominent Nepali dramatist, was also a strong supporter of the use of Nepali language in theatre and education (Onta, 1993). *Mukunda Indira* was the first Nepali play written and directed by Sama in 1937. Historians believe that this play marked the beginning of modern Nepali theatre in all aspects, 'language, costumes, story, emotions and feeling' (Malla cited in Rijal, 2007, 33). Prachanda Malla, one of Sama's students and actors, remembers his master's theatrical revolution:

> Balkrishna Sama involved students of Darbar High School to stage this play. Women were not allowed to play, that's why men had to play female roles. He also changed the costumes, because initially, when they did plays in the palaces, costumes were made from very expensive clothes with real diamonds and pearls. But he used normal clothes that normal people wear. He did the play in pure and clear Nepali language. He didn't use painted screens but a black screen.[15]

There was a fracture between the theatre inside the palaces and what was emerging in schools. Rijal remarks that plays in Nepali created by 'teacher-dramatists and student-performers' were 'instrumental in creating a public sphere for theatre in Nepali' (2007, 34). Dramatists writing in Nepali considered Parsi theatre as a 'vulgar and foreign form of art', and emulated modern, in particular western, dramaturgy. The exaggerations of Parsi theatre were abandoned: realistic plots became popular; naturalistic acting replaced both the 'artificial style' of Parsi artists and the grandiosity of Sama's theatre (Rijal, 2007, 36). Despite the popularity of Parsi theatre troupes, after the 1950s the knowledge and techniques mastered by

Parsi practitioners did not transfer outside the palaces. Rijal explains that '[b]oth the patrons and art forms died as democracy and modern theatre in Nepali came into prominence in the country' (2007, 29).

With the restoration of the Shah dynasty in 1951, the theatre was strengthened. King Mahendra himself is frequently represented as a great lover of the arts. He was well aware of the celebrative power of art, requested artists to write plays in his honour, and sponsored the construction of the Nepal Academy (*Pragya Pratishthan*)[16] in 1958 and many theatre halls in the capital. The Nepal Academy aimed to support research on Nepali languages, literature, arts, culture and science, as well as to train and honour artists, learned people and authors and to develop arts and philosophy in Nepal. The National Theatre (*Rastriya Nachghar*)/Cultural Corporation (*Sanskritik Samsthan*) was established in 1972. Focusing only on performing arts, it aimed to promote, preserve and perform music, dance, songs and drama. Unlike the Academy, the Cultural Corporation did not follow the academic side of the performing arts. The Academy was the first institution to provide acting courses, well before the Cultural Corporation, but stopped because of financial shortage. Both the Academy and the Cultural Corporation cast permanent artists to perform in their productions. Independent artists were employed on a short-term basis according to need. The artists of the Corporation performed on official occasions such as welcoming international guests and heads of governments, thus representing the official state sponsored image of the country. The government directly supported also the groups associated with the Police and the Army, that had their own repertory and yearly dance and song competitions. Theatre thus became 'academised', a means through which to popularize the government's social and political projects. Subedi (2006, 52) explains that artists wrote

> poetry on nationalistic topics given by King Mahindra. Performances were managed accordingly. The Academy became an extension of the Royal Opera House that the palace used to house in the past. It became the centre for performances which would please its patron.

While cultural and traditional street performances continued, the 1970s were characterized by popular well-made sentimental and often nationalistic plays (Rijal in Subedi 2006, 142) as well as *gitinatak*, musical plays mirroring Hindi film stories and style. In the 1980s, a theatre of humour and political satire hitting the corrupt practices of ministers, politicians and bureaucrats increased in popularity (Ibid.). Street theatre and poetry festivals, including ethnic and language festivals, expressed 'permitted' resistance to Panchayat rule. The early 1980s also marked the beginning of a new kind of street theatre in Nepal that I will describe in Chapter 2.

From this short historical background, five points are worth emphasizing. First, theatricality helps in conveying the sacredness of the ritual pertaining to the highest levels of power. Political power, the king's power in this case, was reinforced symbolically and publicly through popular participation in the streets. In Chapter 3 I will provide contemporary instances of the royal power's manipulation of symbols and public ceremonies during the Emergency 2005 and describe how theatrical street demonstrations worked to delegitimize it. Second, with the end of the Malla period, royal and popular audiences were separated. Theatre entered the palaces and popular performances developed outside. Some artists like Bekha Narayan Maharjan and Hari Prasad Rimal had access to and performed in both spaces. Subedi (2006, 107) defines them

> bridge between the courts and the public, but they did not act as liaisons between these two worlds represented by the Rana rulers and their feudatory relatives and those of the common mass because there was nothing in common between the entertainment structure inside the courts and the people's powerful traditions of performance culture outside.

Third, Aarohan Theatre was inspired by both Balkrishna Sama and Gopal Prasad Rimal, dedicating their two halls to them. Through these two very different artists arose two important revolutions: Balakrishna Sama popularized theatre and carried out important stylistic changes while Gopal Prasad Rimal powerfully introduced social themes (Subedi, 2006; Hutt, 1991). Fourth, from a caste perspective, theatre emerges as predominantly the domain of Bahuns and Newars. Lastly, theatre could not develop as an independent art outside the palaces until the end of the Rana rule, thus affecting the establishment of professional acting. This also reinforces the apparent fracture between the official, government-sponsored theatre offered by the Academy, the National Theatre and the independent theatre groups that emerged from the pro-democracy street theatre of the 1980s, growing in opposition to the Royal Palace and animating the independent, creative economy emerging in Kathmandu. This vacuum was filled by international non-governmental organizations (INGOs) that acted as 'patrons' for theatre groups (Rijal, 2007). A powerful narrative of lack was common in artists' descriptions of the theatrical scene during my fieldwork: the lack of state policies regarding the arts, the lack of a developed stage theatre circuit and culture, the lack of financial sustainability, a lack of training facilities, an unstable political situation, dependence on development work shaped by development agencies' practices, an on-going process of theatre professionalization, which restricted actors' possibilities of developing their own careers across different groups and a centralization of professional theatrical activities in the capital, Kathmandu.

Aarohan Theatre Group and the growth of theatre in Nepal

Aarohan Theatre Group was established in 1982 under the direction of Sunil Pokharel. Sunil was born in the eastern hills of Nepal but was introduced to theatre in Biratnagar, where his parents had migrated. Situated near the Indian border, at the time Biratnagar was a very active and lively city, full of theatre, literature and poetry. A Brahmin boy who grew up with lots of restrictions, Sunil found in the theatre a means of self-expression and in Badri Adhikari, now a film director, a supporter. As a teenager, Sunil was selected for dance, drama and voice training at the Royal Nepal Academy. However, this was only for two hours per day. After completing the training, Sunil remained for another couple of years as an actor. Despite having facilities, teachers, theatre halls and a salary, he felt dissatisfied with the lack of productions and the fact that they were not free to decide which plays to perform. With Badri Adhikari, who in the meantime had arrived in Kathmandu, and his future wife Nisha's sister, Suryamala, also an artist at the Academy, Sunil established Aarohan. The group soon defined itself in opposition to mainstream popular entertainment. A leaflet from the late 1990s stresses that the main objective of Aarohan was to perform 'meaningful plays in Nepalese Theatre', an objective the group shared with other regional groups active in the 1980s like Janam in India (Hashmi, 1989) or Ajoka Theatre in Pakistan (Afzal-Khan, 1997, 2005). Explaining the ideals that moved them to found a theatre group, Sunil[17] remarked that they were 'young, dissatisfied with Bollywood movies that were very popular in Nepal', and that they 'wanted to change the world'. These words sum up the double soul of the group, committed to artistic proscenium theatre on the one hand, and to political and social street theatre on the other.

Aarohan staged many foreign plays in Nepal for the first time, such as Sophocles' *Oedipus* in 1985. The reviewer of *The Rising Nepal*[18] praised the choice of staging the classics as 'a matter of great cultural value'. Then in 1989–90 Aarohan organized what was described as a groundbreaking programme in Kathmandu. *Aarohan Shanibar* (Aarohan Saturday) scheduled a new play every month, by Nepali and world playwrights alternately. Each drama was performed for four Saturdays in a row, at 3 p.m., for a membership-based audience at the French Cultural Centre. In 1989 the membership fee was 200 Nepali Rupees (NRs.) a year and around 400 members joined the programme.[19] The group performed works by Albert Camus, Jean-Paul Sartre, Bertold Brecht, Mohan Rakesh, Alexander Vampolov, Junji Kinoshita, as well as by Nepali playwrights such as Govinda Bahadur Malla 'Gothale', and Balkrishna Sama. Performing diverse work seemed a heartfelt concern for Aarohan's artists. Documents of the time suggest that the plays targeted a specific audience composed of philosophers, professors, lawyers, journalists and the intelligentsia of Nepal.

Even an information sheet produced by the French Cultural Centre for the 1989 edition highlights the targeting of a restricted audience, emphasizing that 'those plays will be classical texts intended for a learned audience', hinting at a search for a formal and official recognition of the cultural activities organized by the group. The long production was a catalyst for motivating artists and art lovers in the capital. Throughout the year, a poem, a picture and a painting were also displayed, alongside the performance of each play. Commenting upon the project 15 years later, Sunil explained that it failed financially, many spectators did not pay the membership fee and artists had to volunteer, but it created a wave of interest for the theatre. The audience participated, asking questions after the plays, and helping with the organization by sponsoring brochures or tea. The network of connections created at the time is still in existence and includes present-day politicians and journalists. The 1990s were a critical time for Nepali theatre. Aarohan staged some proscenium plays, such as "Dr. Knox', 'Ask the Yogi about his Caste' (*Jat Sodhnu Yogiko*), and 'Oedipus', but they ran only for a few days, as was usual practice at the time because of the high rents of the theatre halls and uncertain audience participation.

From the very beginning, Aarohan's identity was associated with artistic, 'serious' (Subedi 2006, 157) and meaningful theatre work for the capital's intellectuals; therefore, having a positive response from the public was important for self-sustainability. In fact, in the late 1980s, artists strategically used what was considered as 'respectable', 'written' Nepali and foreign dramas, to legitimize not only their productions but also their art itself. Distancing themselves from popular street and traditional performances, they attempted to give dignity and recognition to their work. Although Aarohan performed street theatre since the 80s, both during political demonstrations and for development projects, the label of an intellectual and élite group followed them, as I was occasionally told by some research participants. Artists outside the group criticized Aarohan for staging too many foreign plays. Sunil explained that there were several reasons behind their choice. First, staging foreign plays was important to train artists by exposing them to different artistic styles and forms. Second, there were not many 'meaningful' Nepali plays to stage. And then, by presenting foreign plays, actors aimed at giving 'respectability' to their job. Respectability was perceived as being connected to the 'intellectuality' of the work, through the 'thoughts'. He explains that when they started,

> theatre wasn't a prestigious job. It was a third-rate thing in our families, because we came from middle-class families, Brahmin families. And theatre as a job was like what prostitutes do, or like that, uneducated people, under SLC [school leaving certificate] people, they do theatre. That was the basic idea. At least in my 25 years in theatre I

tried to prove that 'no, theatre is good work'. There are thoughts...[20]
That's why we did lots of foreign plays and [to] shock people actually.
We did Camus and people [said] 'Camus? Wow!'[21]

For some significant time, foreign plays have been strategically used to assert the
actors' value. For example, Krishna Shah Yatri, an actor and director of Jyoti Punja
Theatre, remembered staging plays for Dashain festival in the late 1980s. When he
was a teenager, groups of people in his community gathered to organize the plays.
They joined spontaneously, and staged religious-cultural works. On the contrary,
for Dasain 2006, the youth of his village staged Shakespeare's 'Romeo and Juliet'.
The youth justified their choice saying 'if we do a foreign play, people will say this is
good, people will say he's one who knows'. Krishna commented that in this way the
'typical culture and identity is lost'. Conversely, his observations recall the criticism
raised against Aarohan's choices. There is a hierarchy of 'knowledge' at stake.
'Knowledge' serves to achieve prestige and recognition. 'Foreign knowledge' pays
higher than 'Nepali knowledge'. A more practical issue needs to be considered at this
point though. Staging proscenium plays require funding, which is provided neither
by NGOs nor by international organizations. Artists reported that even the British
Council preferred to fund development projects rather than proscenium plays. It is
often foreign embassies that sponsor the staging of theatrical pieces, providing they
are written by playwrights from their country. Therefore, the relationship between
Nepali theatre and 'foreignness' is controversial, not only a matter of theatrical
identity but also of 'professional identity'. Nepali's relationship with 'foreign goods'
in general is a contradicting co-existence between attraction and rejection (see
Liechty, 1997; Hachhethu, 1990; Onta, 1997). In theatre, staging foreign plays[22] can
simultaneously be a source of prestige but may also attract accusations of lacking
'Nepaliness'.

Performance continuity was a huge problem for theatre groups in Nepal. What
granted continuity to Aarohan was the leading actors' personal involvement and
commitment through decades. From 1984 to 1987 Sunil studied direction at the
National School of Drama (NSD) in New Delhi, India, but he returned to Nepal
every year during holidays to stage theatrical productions. For many years the group
only gathered sporadically as necessary to rehearse stage productions or dramas
for development projects as at that time most of the actors were making a living
through other jobs. In fact, many of the founding members of Aarohan left theatre
for income-generating work because the theatre did not provide sustenance. In the
1980s and 1990s, only artists regularly employed at the government institutions,
and those engaged in television productions or in the upper echelons of the movie
industry could live from their acting. When my fieldwork started in 2004, the only

founding members still actively involved in the group were Sunil Pokharel, Nisha Sharma Pokharel and Basanta Bhatta. They managed to find time for Aarohan rehearsals, and as a source of income took roles in films, tele-serials, radio dramas and produced documentaries for NGOs when not doing theatre. While officially retaining their membership of the group, all other artists were effectively only present as sympathizers. Sunil, Nisha, and Basanta supervised decision-making and group management. Sunil recalls that the group's 'office' was contained in his bag until the establishment of Gurukul.[23] Sunil and Nisha's narratives reveal the great personal effort invested to give continuity to Aarohan. They took personal risks, which resulted in a profound sense of commitment.

Other members did too. Basanta juggled his job at the Home Ministry with his passion for acting for 20 years. His participation in theatrical productions were independent of his professional occupation though he relied on being granted permission to take leave. He recounts that he only joined rehearsals because his managers often allowed him time; they knew he was an artist, and because he was good at his office job they were generous and accommodating of his requests. Even when he was transferred to the Indian border in Karkharbitta he still found time to go to Kathmandu for rehearsals. However, in the subsequent period, when he worked in the Sunauli border in 1994–95, he had to stop acting. His workload was heavy and thus leave was restricted. He therefore asked for an assignment in Kathmandu. At the time, Basanta was working in the immigration office at the Indian border, and his boss was happy with his work performance:

> When I told him, 'Sir, I am an actor, if I go to the western side I could not do theatre and my life is finished. So if you love me, please give me a place here [in Kathmandu]', so that I can do theatre on weekly holidays'...the boss said, 'he's a national actor, please give him facilities.'[24]

It was only in 2004, that Basanta, then in his 40s, was able to finally be employed full-time in theatre. To sum up, Aarohan Theatre Group had been active since 1982. However, such involvement, like that of other Nepali theatre groups, had been discontinuous. The emotional, economic and time investment of the committed members created permanent bonds as the theatre group became the focal point of their lives. But it was only with the establishment of the Gurukul School of Theatre that it developed into a structured and stable organization representing, for the three leading artists, the possibility of fulfilling their dreams.

In 2006 I rehearsed for a month in Gurukul a play produced by another independent theatre group. I experienced first-hand what I had often heard stories of: artists not turning up for rehearsals, or arriving 2–3 hours late, by which time those who had been punctual had finished or left; artists quitting a few days before the opening; dancers coming to only one in four rehearsals. At the beginning I was very committed and I dedicated the whole month to observing 'how a play was built'. But after weeks of disruption, even my enthusiasm diminished. In the end, I also turned up only when I had time, and prioritized my other research work. There was desperation and anger. The director threatened to leave if actors did not behave more responsibly, and then skipped the following day's rehearsal, thus disappointing those actors who were trying to follow the 'agreements'. There were long discussions about the necessity of taking theatre more 'seriously'. An actor expressed their frustration, saying 'This is why *bikas* (development) is not coming to Nepal! People don't take responsibilities'. At that time, we did not manage to do even one full rehearsal before the opening. Because of the lack of a proper sound-check, many voices could hardly be heard. There was a saying, then, that in Nepal the opening was the grand rehearsal.

Creating a formal school of theatre was therefore a response to the needs for improved artistic skills, ownership of the performance space and means of production, offering performance continuity, and the stable employment of full-time actors. These were the main objectives guiding Sunil's ideation of Gurukul, the first independent theatre school in Nepal. Gurukul was established in 2002 in Purano Baneshwor and it took six months of hard work to set up Sama Natak Ghar (Sama Theatre Hall), accommodating around 200 people, which was inaugurated in 2003. A second hall, Rimal Natak Ghar, hosting around 450 people, was set up in 2007. The Gurukul compound comprised the two theatre halls, a main building whose lower floors were dedicated to the group office, a library, actors' and guests' bedrooms (hostel) and rehearsal hall, an open-air canteen situated under a tin roof on the north flank of the hill and the lodgings of the night guard and helper Devi Khatri and his family. The Tarai-based landlord used the top floor of the main building as a residence during his trips to Kathmandu. The thatched roof, wooden gazebo, under which visitors and artists would spend hours talking, was another landmark of Gurukul, together with the Tibetan prayer flags that often decorated the space infusing a sense of peace. For the first two years students got NR 3,000 a month scholarship for living expenses. After graduating, they got a monthly salary of NR. 5,000. At the beginning, the group paid NR. 10,000 rent for the building and seven *ropanis*[25] of land. The rent would be raised up to NR. 60,000 in 2005/06, and continued to increase, creating problems of sustainability that would eventually lead to the closure of Gurukul in 2012. In 2009, the group opened a similar school and arts centre in Biratnagar. Aarohan Gurukul Biratnagar is still active.

Aiming at professionalizing theatre in Nepal, Gurukul had maintained its

foundational cultural and social focus, as defined in both its slogan – Theatre for
Better Reasons – and in its three goals (Fig 1.1 and 1.2):

1. Bringing theatre to the Nepali people

Aarohan develops theatre as a local alternative to the globalized
mass-media. We create stage performances, street theatre, training
and workshops, festivals, as well as telefilms and documentaries. Our
performance group has staged a wide variety [of] plays in Nepal and
at international theatre festivals. We have adapted some of the great
plays of the world to the Nepali stage, including works by Brecht,
Sophocles, Junji Kinosita, Albert Camus and Sartre. We also stage
plays of Nepal's playwrights – Govinda Gothale, Bijaya Malla, Abhi
Subedi and Ashesh Malla among others.

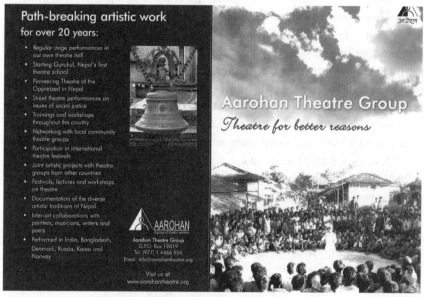

Figure 1.1: Arohan Theatre Group brochure (2005)

2. Exploring a Nepali Theatre Language

Aarohan struggles to preserve, develop, and reinterpret the diverse
artistic traditions of the Nepali people. We have built upon the
artistic traditions our country through reinterpretations in stage
dramas (such as the critically acclaimed *Agni ko Katha*). We also work
to revitalize indigenous performance traditions where they exist. We
pioneered this work with performances of *Dabali*, the traditional
public theatre of Newar Kathmandu. Aarohan now is developing a

resource centre and theatre school, with documentation and training facilities focusing especially on Nepali theatre traditions.

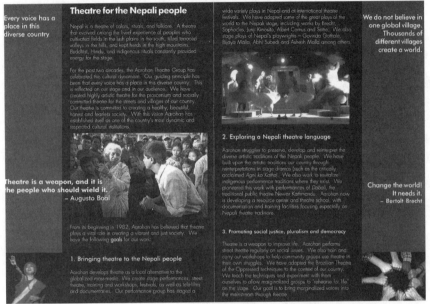

Figure 1.2: Arohan Theatre Group brochure (2005)

3. Promoting social justice, pluralism and democracy

Theatre is a weapon to improve life. Aarohan performs street theatre regularly on social issues. We also train and carry out workshops to help community groups use theatre in their own struggles. We have adopted the Brazilian Theatre of the Oppressed techniques to the context of our country. We teach the techniques and experiment with them ourselves to allow marginalized groups to 'rehearse for life' on stage. Our goal is to bring marginalized voices into the mainstream through theatre.

(From the brochure of Aarohan Theatre Group, 2005)

Gurukul was initially conceived as an integrated art centre, as a traditional school centred around a *guru*:

Before Nepal had western-style schools providing formal education, we had other centres of learning. One was the *Gurukul*, an ashram where a kul guru – a principal guru or sage – would teach in his own way. Classes did not take place in classrooms, nor did they take place through formal teaching. Students lived and worked at the ashram

– cooking meals, serving the guru, and collecting alms. The learning went beyond the boundaries of subjects to educate the entire human beings. (Gurukul's brochure, 2005)

This is how the group itself defines the modern Nepali version of Gurukul in its brochure (2005)

> The Aarohan Theatre Group has adapted the concept of *Gurukul* to modern times. We run a full-time two-year theatre course, with classes ranging from acting and world theatre to yoga and martial art. But we still hold on to the heart of the *Gurukul* concept. The students live at the school and manage the centre themselves, cleaning, supervising various departments, and participating in theatre productions. The school does not teach theatre skills alone. We also believe that theatre is still the strong means of promoting human values. Theatre should always remain close to the aspirations and experience of human life. A good theatre worker is a fundamentally good human being.

Its board members included artists from different fields including photography, painting, and cinema. It was intially intended that they live and work there as artists-in-residence. However, the original idea was not implemented, and, at least for the time that I was there, the board did not meet. Sunil became the centre's de facto director. Gurukul was refocused as a theatre school and other artistic activities were only hosted temporarily. The group's vision is described as follows:

> We seek a theatre that reflects the diverse society, history and cultural traditions of our country. We pursue theatre as politics, as a form or resistance to the passivity induced by globalized consumer-oriented mass-media. We want to create theatre activists – in our school and in communities throughout the country – who know their history and engage creatively and skillfully in the struggles of the people.[26]

The first batch of 10 students who enrolled in 2002, Sarita Giri from Kathmandu, Rajkumar Pudasaini from Nuwakot, Aruna Karki from Dhanusha, Rajan Kathiwada from Bara, Suresh Chand from Salyan, Bhola Sapkota from Hetauda, Saugat Malla from Nawalparasi, Kamal Mani Nepal from Sunsari, Yubaraj Ghimire and Mani Pokharel from Morang all helped with creating the centre. In 2004, the second intake of students started the courses and included[27] Pasupati Rai from Dharan, Saraswati Chaudhary from Bardhiya, Samuna KC, Pramila Katuwal, Prabin Kathiwada and Mahesh Shakya from Kathmandu and Ram Hari Dhakal from Nuwakot.

Field methods

Fieldwork for this book took place during several stays in Nepal: November 2004 to February 2006, July to December 2006, July to September 2007, March to April 2008 and October to December 2008. This analysis mainly focuses on the first three periods and a follow-up carried out in 2012. I returned to Nepal several times as the political challenges had both limited and expanded performance activities. I initially intended to spend the first months in Kathmandu working with Aarohan Theatre Group and then move outside the capital for another two stretches of fieldwork with two of their local partner groups. The aim was to understand how drama-based techniques were adapted and used at the centre and in the periphery. This plan had to be significantly changed once I was in Nepal, largely due to the political crisis that first stopped street performances and then opened up new opportunities of observing performances for social change during the cultural programmes for democracy and through Maoist cultural work. I took a multi-sited stance (Marcus, 1995). In particular, apart from the Aarohan Theatre Group, I carried out significant ethnographic research with a Maoist cultural group, the Sen Chyang Sanskritik Parivar and activist Tharu group, the Kamlari Natak Samuha. I also carried out informal, open-ended interviews with practitioners from other theatre groups working both in Kathmandu and in the Tarai (Deukhuri, Dang and Kapilvastu), cultural workers, NGO staff, activists and government officials to contextualize these accounts. I also observed and recorded the work of other theatre and Maoist groups.

The first part of fieldwork was built around participant observation: living with artists, getting to know them, following their daily work, from physical training to performance creation and production. It involved watching and documenting dozens of *kachahari* performances, acting in some political street plays, and engaging in informal conversations about actors' lives and work. The historical development of the group's productions was traced through newspaper articles and magazines available at Aarohan's archive. Participant observation happened before I expected. Soon after arriving in Kathmandu, at the end of November 2004, Sunil Pokharel, Aarohan Theatre director, invited me to move inside the Gurukul hostel, an 'ideal' field situation. It was supposed to be a temporary arrangement but since we could not find any suitable room nearby, I was allowed to stay for as long as I wished in exchange for a small fee. I shared a room with three artists belonging to the second intake of students that had started the theatre course in 2004. Both the first and second intake of students lived in Gurukul hostel and ate at the Gurukul canteen. Sunil and his wife Nisha lived in a private flat 20 minutes away from the school. So did Basanta, an actor and group manager, and his family. Anil Pokharel, a senior artist from Aarohan also lived outside Gurukul. Anoj, who volunteered in the administration, lived in the hostel as well.

The king's coup on 1 February 2005 profoundly affected the work of both Aarohan and their partner groups. The curtailing of civil liberties (Chapter 3) stopped any *kachahari natak* in the streets. Some of Aarohan partner groups outside Kathmandu were also prevented from working, while others had already stopped their activities because of the civil war. For the three months of the Emergency, Aarohan Theatre performed only proscenium plays. In the meantime, after spending more than six months almost exclusively inside the Gurukul compound, as artists usually did, I felt the need to understand both the wider theatrical and political context. Getting involved with an activist group allowed me to understand the hardship faced by political activists during the king's rule and expand my view beyond the theatre world. Edmondson (2007, 10) highlighted that a single focus can preclude the anthropologist from 'locating' the community/theatre group within other communities of interest and instead reify local narratives. I realized that during the first months I had become closely associated with the group, spending all my time in the compound and occasionally performing. This 'precluded' other strong associations. The grand narrative that circulated inside Gurukul described Aarohan as the only active theatre group in the city. In reality, other groups were working, although not with the continuity and the organization that Aarohan had. Moreover, I felt I would also benefit from more independence in moving around the city to understand how civil society groups were getting organized in the popular movement. Living in a commune system had been exciting and allowed for the creation of friendly relationships with the artists. However, Gurukul was also a 'hyper' public space. From February 2005 performances ran daily and therefore it was visited by hundreds of people. I often sat in cafés outside the compound to find a calm place to write my field notes. In July 2005, I moved into an independent flat but continued to follow *kachahari* performances and visit Gurukul on a daily basis.

In June 2005 *kachahari* performances resumed with a different pattern. Up until January, workshop-based performances were staged together with issue-based plays (Chapter 4). From June 2005, the second modality became almost exclusive, which meant that the same play was repeated in different schools or streets. A significant change in theatre practice was taking place. In order to understand this shift, the initial plan of not doing audience research was reviewed and I conducted a survey among nine schools, involving about 800 students/audience members. A behaviouristic approach, considering if performances brought about immediate behaviour changes, remained outside the scope of my inquiry and is itself fraught with difficulties (see Kershaw, 1992). Some performances may produce immediate effects, such as when political theatre stirs up the audience and for this reason is considered as dangerous by the establishment. But others may provide hints that can lead to change in the long run.[28] The survey simply aimed to understand the relevance of the performance topic to the audiences' real-life experience. In fact, what distinguishes Forum Theatre from other street theatre techniques is its potential for questioning embodied patterns of experience.

In September 2005, this project was reinvested with energy and urgency as a result of the political theatre, which came to the fore in conjunction with the mass meetings organized by civil society (Chapter 3). I had to choose between focusing exclusively on development theatre, which was taking a lower profile at the time, and documenting also political theatre or *loktantrik natak* (theatre for democracy). Paradoxically, the political situation had obliged artists to adopt strategies similar to the political theatre of the 1980s. I therefore decided to follow the topicality of the political plays. All in all, collecting 'variations' of the same *kachahari* play was not meaningful to my research methodology, which focused on the generative aspects of the performances. Historically speaking, *kachahari* represented the 'ordinary' side of theatre work and thus could be revisited and analysed in more depth. Political theatre, instead, represented the 'special', the contingent, and would have been much more difficult to reconstruct at a later stage.

During the second period of fieldwork, from July 2006, I got in contact with Maoist cultural groups, travelled with them, lived in their camps and followed their performances during their party's politico-cultural programmes. Documenting Maoist cultural programmes was important in order to have a more complete picture of cultural performances for social change. Working with Maoist artists was like carrying out a fieldwork within the fieldwork in particular during the transitional, post-conflict period. Although the Maoist's agenda differed from that of NGOs using theatre in development projects, the ways in which theatre was used and the form showed fascinating similarities.

There is an inherent tension in doing participant observation embedded in the technique itself and which has been highlighted by many anthropologists. It is the necessity of being both a participant and an observer; of being both simultaneously. The degrees of participation and of observation change throughout different stages of the fieldwork. Co-performance, in which the ethnographer dances, sings and acts with the local group, is considered basic in order to unveil embodied knowledge about the performance tradition and foster cultural rapport. It is in fact a common feature of anthropological research on performance (Conquergood, 1982; Askew, 2002; Barber, 2000; Cole, 2001; Afzal-Khan, 2005). Edmondson (2007), who opted not to perform with her informants, claims that the methodology of co-performance is outdated, just like the ideal of single-site ethnography. She associates it with the ambiguous concept of cultural rapport that is 'the notion that the researchers finally succeeded in crossing the cultural threshold and were welcomed with open arms' (2007, 10). Marcus remarks that the 'ice-breaking' moments in which the anthropologist crosses the cultural boundaries reify both the boundaries themselves and the binary opposition of self/others, resulting in 'a proper mise-en-scene of fieldwork – a physically and symbolically enclosed world, a culture for the ethnographer to live within and figure out' (1998, 109). Dismissing the symbolic value of participation would equate to a simplification of the politics of the field site. In my case, co-performance did occur. I had not planned it in advance, as I did not want to force my presence in the group, but when asked to perform I usually accepted. Aarohan had a tradition of incorporating foreigners in their plays. I was the third foreigner playing the tourist role in 'Dreams of Peach Blossom', a play written by Abhi Subedi. The first was a visiting American scholar and the second a Danish advisor who had previously worked with the group.

Researching performance through co-performance inevitably exposes the researcher to the public gaze, in particular in transitional scenarios and when working across political boundaries. My own experience with combining both researching and performing revealed that the ethnographer's membership or 'perceived' membership to groups was often intensified, familiarity with the group increase, and showed the gaps between private rehearsals and public performances. In some cases, I received insights as to which questions were worth developing with the artists off-stage. In others, I could distinguish more clearly the differences between what had been rehearsed and what was actually performed in public. After performing in the political street plays with Aarohan, for example, I realized that my perception of the risks involved was much lower than that of the actors, but I wouldn't have felt this had I remained off-stage. Performing together also increases familiarity. For example, the day after dancing with the Maoists artists at the Nepal Academy, I interviewed a theatre actor associated with the Academy for my work on 'mainstream theatre'. He was with a friend, one of the technicians who had worked during the previous day's Maoist programme. Recognizing me, the technician asked me about the Maoist performances. When I explained this research work with them, he commented that it could not have been only 'work'. They must be my 'friends' because I knew everybody. In reality, many of the people he had seen me socializing with I had met only once, but they came to greet me. They 'knew' me as I had joined the dances in one of their previous performances but I did not 'know' them. Visibility, however, allows for subjective and diverging interpretations. I do not even want to claim that during co-performance I 'crossed the cultural threshold' of my research collaborators but on both sides boundaries were certainly softened. There were important moments during the performances in which our separate identities were recognized and accepted as such, and in which both cultures co-created a 'shared history'. Sharing a 'history' is important to create familiarity. Performance creates 'out-of-the-ordinary' situations. They are quickly remembered and referred back to. In both field situations, when I was introduced to strangers, actors mentioned the plays in which I had acted with them. Similarly, while talking with Maoist artists they often recalled the first time I danced with them. Substituting the idea of fieldwork as a contained location that the ethnographer manages to enter, Marcus employs the term 'complicity' to describe the contested negotiation that takes place across the cultural divide in which cultural difference is emphasized rather than elided. Marcus suggests that

> it is only in an anthropologist-informant situation in which the 'outsideness' is never elided and is indeed the basis of an affinity between ethnographer and subject that the reigning traditional ideology of fieldwork can shift to reflect the changing conditions of research (1998:119).

Co-performance also creates membership, as the sharing other daily activities does. I conducted this fieldwork through two, to some degree conflictual sites, e.g., Aarohan Theatre Group and Sen Chyang Parivar. I initially tried to invite artists from both groups to each other's programmes, attempting to create coherence in my dramatis personae. When I understood some theatre people's uneasiness towards the Maoist programmes, I realized my need to talk, to share my experience and make people connect, but was not reciprocated. When I recounted to a Maoist commander, who became my main research collaborator for that emerging new field, that I was in the habit of telling Aarohan artists about the cultural group work, he suggested the opposite, not to tell anybody: the two sites had to be kept apart. Artists in Gurukul were friendly but for the first year of my fieldwork conversation did not move beyond daily problems, food, clothes or rehearsal. When I joined an activist group, I heard and witnessed harsh situations of abuse. But I could not share them with my Gurukul friends for security reasons. Indeed, I had to keep living inside the compound as if nothing was happening, just like the artists in Gurukul who were living through the insurgency without talking about it in public (Chapter 3). My tension grew. I had two panic attacks, leading 'separate' field lives and simultaneously being alone was challenging. I could play with characters on stage, but I could not reconcile my dramatis personae off stage, in 'real life'.

Slowly, I learnt that not talking about my Maoist work with theatre people was not 'faking', it was just another way of experiencing communication. It was only then that I felt I was getting closer to my research participants who had to co-exist amidst different realities, and negotiate the impracticality of exchange between 'front' and 'back' stage (cf. Chapter 3). I had to embody what I felt as an 'oppression'. Whilst avoiding postmodern-style confessionalism (Geertz, 1988) I treated my experience as data (Seizer, 2000), as my reactions, feelings, and fears no doubt affected my collaborators' as much as they did to me.

Ethnographic challenges

> Theatre is not a disseminator of truths but a provider of versions.
> (Barker, 1989, 44)

When I arrived in Gurukul in 2004, I explained I had never acted in professional theatre, just in amateur groups. I ended up acting with the group anyway and thus 'participating'. In 2006, I acted in 'New Nepal' (*Naya Nepal*), a commercial feature film directed by Kishor Dhakal. I got a lead role through my Nepali 'non-theatrical' connections. My partner in the film was Biraj Bhatta, a popular Nepali film hero. I realized then that the degree of my co-performance was 'shallow play'. During the shooting of the film, I had much more agency than when I played with Aarohan. I was free to question directives that I did not agree with, I could refuse to accomplish certain movements to safeguard 'my role' and I was able to express myself. During my fieldwork, instead, I was bound by ethical guidelines that obliged me to accept without questioning too much. My agency was limited. I 'played' the anthropologist, not the actress. In fact, artists in Gurukul greeted my participation in the film with interest and mixed comments. A complaint was about the fact that I got such a big role after having spent only two years in Nepal. It was not fair, an artist claimed, they should have cast his wife instead, as she had much more experience. I realized my acting with Gurukul had been 'safe' and 'guided'. I did not threaten anybody's opportunities, as I had inadvertently done by acting in the film. This unexpected reaction made me realize that despite my 'co-performance', my actual participation had been limited. My position of 'participant' was perceived as 'harmless' to the real management of resources and work possibilities.

Dwyer argues that in ethnographic writing it is fundamental to 'confront rather than disguise the vulnerability of the Self and its society in the encounter with the Other' (1982). Distancing myself from my field 'role' in order to write was a process fraught with difficulties. I realized I had partly incorporated my role. Thus I found myself struggling with how to reconcile the contrasting narratives that were present in the group. When I returned to Nepal and Gurukul after the end of fieldwork, my membership was frequently reinforced in public. I was asked to perform again and I was introduced as a 'group member' rather than a 'guest'. For my collaborators there was no separation between the fieldwork period and the post-fieldwork, it was rather a continuum in relational terms; it was indeed life, as it was for me. I felt challenged by conflicting duties: giving voice to 'the group' that had welcome and opened their lives to me while representing the divergent narratives the emerged in the field. After completing my PhD, I tried to circulate my thesis with the whole group, as is an increasingly standard practice in anthropology. But 'Aarohan', as I had known it during fieldwork, did not exist anymore. Many artists had left to form new groups and Gurukul was about to be closed down. I therefore gave a copy of my thesis to the artistic director, Sunil Pokharel, but could not discuss it with the whole group. Similarly, many of the activists that were members of Sen-Chyang in 2006, by 2012 had taken up other tasks in the party. Even the *kamlari* activists active in 2005, by 2012 had moved on with their lives and were not performing anymore. The 2012 revisit, however, allowed me to further contextualize the work of these groups. I therefore consider this ethnography, like a theatre piece, as 'one' of the possible versions of reality. Though integrity has guided my research project, this account results from my specific social and historical position in the field and from the social relations that developed from it in ways that I will detail in the rest of the book.

Conclusion

So far I have introduced and located methodologically the theatrical performances for social change that will be analysed in this book. I have also situated myself in relation to the theatre communities that I have researched.

Triggered by the similarities between the 2005 Emergency and the Panchayat period restrictions, the second chapter reviews the rich Nepali tradition of contentious cultural performances dating back to the beginning of the twentieth century, the subtle connections between artists and politicians and the place of cultural programmes in political mass meetings. Theatre and cultural performances are analysed as means of entering the dominated public space in 'disguise', of overcoming and fooling the government's control and of amplifying the voices of the speakers in the same ways as mass meetings do. For this reason, artists are conceptualized as 'space brokers'. After having outlined the birth of political street theatre in the 1980s, the chapter provides examples of how theatre artists actively participated in the 1990 popular movement, the tricks they used to avoid censorship, the stage conventions employed to communicate with the audience, the key texts and symbols.

The third chapter jumps straight to the middle of the 2005 Emergency that is hypothesized as a deliberate recreation of the Panchayat environment. By providing ethnographic examples, I explore how the state built up a theatrical apparatus to legitimize the king's power and how the king resurrected the Panchayat spirit, practices and rhetoric. The performative character of the street demonstrations – the dramaturgy of protest – that led to the 2006 People's Movement in which many of the royal symbols were reversed is set against the exploration of the role of the artists in the public cultural programmes for democracy. In particular, ethnographic descriptions of two *loktantrik natak* (theatre for democracy) performances staged by Aarohan in that context will provide details of their critique at different degrees of oppression and explore what artists meant by 'doing theatre from the heart'.

Chapter 4 traces the origin of the genre of 'theatre for development' in Nepal, starting from the experimentation carried out in the 1990s to avoid top-down forms of street theatre that led Aarohan Theatre Group to adopt/adapt the Forum Theatre techniques in *kachahari natak*. The 'Nepalization' and evolution of *kachahari* from workshop-based to issue-based will be described together with the analysis of the process of ideation-production-performance of a *kachahari* play. Cross-cultural comparative examples will substantiate the argument.

Chapter 5 examines the ways in which a Tharu activist group challenged the 'traditional' *kamlari* practice, that is sending girls aged 6–16 to work as house-helpers in the cities, through *kachahari natak* both at local and at national/international levels. I will compare the village performance to the proscenium play that the group staged in Kathmandu in collaboration with Aarohan Theatre Group. The chapter will situate *kachahari* within the other 'development' and advocacy activities organized by a grassroots NGO linked to the group as well as other national and international organizations to eradicate the *kamlari* practice. Two interesting narratives unfold that point towards an appropriation/normalization of the development discourses and practices in Deukhuri Valley: first, despite the programme including theatre being funded by donors, the activists claimed they did 'activism' not 'development work'; second, they believed that what made the dramas effective were the real feelings and pain showed by the former *kamlari* female actors.

Chapter 6 examines the role of revolutionary theatre and cultural programmes as deliberate, planned, structured, systematic and prolonged means of forwarding revolutionary political struggle by creating a shared and cohesive revolutionary imagination. I argue that artists act as mediators between the Maoist party and the masses and cultural performances provide a language through which artists express their sorrows and hopes and talk the audience through the party policy changes in a very simple and captivating way. Artists are not only the storytellers but also the story-makers of revolution and contributed to challenging dominant ideology through affective and aesthetic opposition.

Chapter 7 details the development of Aarohan Theatre Group as an organization, struggling with the co-existence of different and sometimes contrasting identities and expectations, in particular the challenges of developing artistic theatre productions and, at the same time, engaging theatre for social change. The transitional role of the *guru* will be examined in relation to the *guru-kula* practice within a theatre organization. The chapter also narrates the artists' efforts to maintain and strengthen their professional identity against the traditional stigma attached to the profession. Through the life journey of some artists, the chapter explores gender differences within the acting profession.

The concluding chapter will compare and contrast the different forms of theatre for social change explored throughout this book: development theatre, political street theatre and Maoist cultural work to identifying elements of an aesthetics of theatre for social change. This will be informed by analysis arising from a revisit carried out in 2012 aimed at providing perspective to the main narratives.

Endnotes

1   Augusto Boal is a theatre actor, director, and activist born in Rio de Janeiro in 1931. After studying dramatic arts at Columbia University, New York, he engaged in classical theatre and experimented with theatre applied to adult education. He theorized and searched for techniques that could enhance the audience participation in performance, and gathered them in the Theatre of the Oppressed (1979). Tortured for his cultural activities during the Brazilian military regime, in 1971 he exiled first to Argentina and then to France where he remained to live and work for 15 years. In 1992, Boal was elected as *vereador* (city councellor) in Rio de Janeiro. Through his theatre group, he discussed in the streets issues that citizens were facing and their suggestions were proposed as law. Boal thus theorized and initiated the Legislative Theatre Movement. Augusto Boal died in Rio de Janeiro in 2009 (for more on Boal see Babbage [2004] as well as Boal's own writings).

2   Forms of forum theatre were performed in projects run by the Nepal government during the Constituent Assembly elections (Prakash Subedi, personal communication).

3   Boal emphasizes the importance of giving people the chance to 'participate', it is then their choice to actually being involved or not.

4   This section is not meant to provide a history of Nepali theatre. For thorough accounts see Malla (1980, 2009), Acharya (2009), Subedi (2006). For contemporary theatre see Davis (2002, 2009, 2010).

5   A platform for performance said to have originate in the Lichhavi period (Malla, 1990, 11). In southern India the platform – *mandai* – in the centre of the village is the site of the village goddess (*mandaiammal*); the etymology of the term for headman – *ampalar* – also comes from the platform/stage (David Mosse, personal communication). In Nepali, there seems to be no word related to authority linked with *dabali/dabu*.

6   Prachanda Malla, personal communication.

7   The Kartik Nach, a dance-drama of Malla origin is still performed in Patan (Toffin, 2012; Subedi, 40).

8   This is a contested event in the history of Nepal: what is described as a unification under the Shah can equally be regarded as an occupation that ended the rule of the indigenous Newar kings.

9   See Toffin (1992) for more on the festival.

10   For details on the ritual practices, social significance and historical development see Toffin (1992), van den Hoek (1990). The king's power is ritually celebrated also during the festival of Dasai (see Krauskopff and Lecomte-Tilouine, 1996).

11   The grandfather of Balakrishna Sama.

12   Interviewed in November 2006.

13   Education was available only to the ruling elite until the end of the Rana period in 1951.

14   Sama's family background allowed him to receive the best education available in the country. However, he could not bear the inequalities he saw among the ruling class and after experiencing great mental strain he even changed his name. Sama, which means 'equal', is said to have introduced 'real human characters' on stage, moving away from previous productions characterized by historical, traditional and mythological topics and shifted proscenium theatre out of the Rana palaces.

15   Interviewed in November 2006.

16   Founded on 2 July 1957, it was first called Nepal Sahitya Academy and renamed Royal Nepal Academy on 3 March 1958. The institution went through different constitutional changes. After the abolition of the monarchy, the institution was renamed Nepal Academy through the Nepal Academy Act 2007. The Academy annually organized music and drama festival, but was not perceived as supporting independent theatre groups. To further develop music and theatre, in 2007 the government established a separate organization, the Nepal Academy of Music and Drama.

17   Interviewed in November 2004.

18   The Rising Nepal, 5 August 1995.

19   Sunil Pokharel, personal communication, December 2005.

20   Sunil justifies his work through the same 'intellectual' categories that society used to question the value of theatre.

21   Interviewed in November 2006.

22   For a detailed analysis of the successful translation and adaptation of Ibsen's 'A Doll's House' and Camus' 'The Justes' see Subedi 2011, 59-69.

23   Informal communication, December 2004.

24   Interviewed in October 2005.

25   Traditional unit of land measurement used in Nepal, 1 *ropani* is equivalent to 508.72 sq m.

26   Ibid.

27   There were other students in the first batch: Subash left Gurukul before the starting of this research and Krishna during the first period of fieldwork. Some students enrolled in the second batch but did not complete the two-year course: Saraswati (quit in 2005), Om Prakash (quit in 2006), Ganeshyam (quit in 2005) and Sita (quit in 2005).

28 As artists point out (Chapter 4), what distinguishes forum theatre from other forms of street theatre techniques is that artists do not start a performance with a preconceived solution to a problem. It is the audience member, once onstage as spect-actor that engages in enacting solutions and has to persuade the remaining audience that such solution is a possible and plausible alternative. The audience in fact can even reject what suggested by the spect-actor as fanciful and not applicable to a real-life problem. Chapter 4 will detail how the practice of *kachahari natak* changed from standard forum theatre performance.

2

Spacing Out to Speak Up

Resistance, protest and the emergence of street theatre

Universes of worlds as well as worlds themselves may be built in many different ways.

(Goodman, 1978,5)

Listen to other people's opinions about the king but never tell yours.

(Identity withdrawn, Kathmandu, 4 February 2005)

On the first of February 2005, around 10.15 a.m., I stopped by a shop on the way back to Gurukul after a Nepali language class. The king was speaking on the radio: *prajatantra*,[1] 'democracy', was a word he uttered repeatedly. Customers and shopkeepers were listening in silence. I did my shopping quickly and left. In the Gurukul courtyard, Sunil was listening attentively to the radio sitting on a chair under the thatched wooden gazebo. The atmosphere was thick with tension, different from the cheerfulness that had filled the air a couple of hours earlier. Some of the artists were sitting near Sunil. 'It is finished' – said one of them with despair – 'our fight for democracy in 1990 was useless.'[2]

In fact, at 10 a.m., King Gyanendra used the government-run media, Radio Nepal and Nepal TV, to declare a state of emergency under the Constitution of the Kingdom of Nepal 1990, Article 23(7) on the grounds that 'a serious crisis had arisen threatening the kingdom's integrity and security'. He suspended the right of freedom of expression, assembly and movement, press and publication rights, rights against preventive detention, the right to information, the right to property, the right to privacy, the right to constitutional remedy, and formed a council of ministers under his own chairmanship. During his 40 minute proclamation to the nation, Gyanendra severely criticized the political parties for their inability to solve the Maoist conflict and hold elections. Legitimizing his actions through the history of the Shah dynasty and referring to the age-long bond between the king and the Nepali people, he promised to restore multi-party democracy within three years.

Soon after the king's speech, land and mobile phone lines – both local and international – as well as the internet service were cut. The valley remained in total isolation for seven days. Tribhuvan International Airport was closed and the security forces blocked the main roads leading out of the valley. Army soldiers occupied the offices of TV, newspaper and radio stations to censor broadcast and printed information. In the following days, the *bandh* (blockade) was lifted. The newspapers – their pages thinned – showed images of Nepal's wonderful weather and the traffic in Kathmandu. Rumours spread suggesting that hundreds of politicians and activists had been arrested. Subsequently it was confirmed that many were under house arrest, while others were in police custody.

The capital was patrolled by armed police but appeared normal, with most shops open on 1 February. Soldiers in riot gear patrolled the streets but no significant protests were reported, except for clashes between students and police in campuses in Pokhara and in Butwal. People seemed to be leading their lives as if nothing had happened. I was told:

> It is more of a problem for the people in Kathmandu. In most of Nepal, in the villages, they don't have phones anyway so it doesn't make a big difference. All westerners think like this. Here in Kathmandu people are waiting to see what happens and are hoping that the king can improve the situation. Democracy as it was before was no better. Here people are really fed up with the power struggles among the political parties. Many people have gained in the past years. Now the king's men will, what's the difference?

I began to realize there was much more to understand behind this seeming non-reaction. Gyanendra was taking great risks. According to my interlocutors he would either restore peace in the country or risk losing his crown. Sometimes dramatic circumstances require dramatic solutions, a theatre artist stated, quoting the Nepali saying *war ki par*, 'either one way [the parties] or the other [the king]'. When asked about the difference between the 2001 and 2005 state of emergency, another artist explained that the first 'was a democratic Emergency decided by a constitutional king, this one is different. It is a despotic Emergency decided by a despot'. He added 'there were rights here in Nepal. Now we have lost half. We are not men any more. We are treated like animals'. Such opinions were quitely expressed against a background of fearful restraint. Sunil confirmed it was dangerous to talk openly. One evening in a restaurant he had stopped a political conversation with other artists, resuming it later in the private space of Gurukul. There might have been spies;[3] even the phone calls could have been under police surveillance. Talking freely even with the members of their partner theatre groups outside the capital was impossible. Besides, given that Aarohan had been politically active during the People's Movement in 1990, they had to be extra careful.

There was suspicion and fear in Kathmandu but at first I failed to notice it. In Gurukul, life continued around everyday activities: rehearsals, performances and day-to-day conversations. The political situation of the country was not the object of open discussion. I could discuss politics with development advisers who passed information from their INGOs. 'They [Nepalis in general] don't realize the gravity of the situation', I was told once – a remark that reminded me of a phone conversation I had had with an information adviser from an INGO based in Italy in September 2004, just before leaving for Nepal. I was trying to understand whether the conflict would prevent me from carrying out research. 'It is hard to understand' the information officer had said, 'Nepalis never say anything about the war. They say everything is fine. Maybe they don't understand what is happening'.

All in all what emerged was the gap between how reality 'seemed' or was 'talked about' and how it was 'perceived' in private; how it was 'interpreted' by some outsiders and how it was 'lived' by insiders. I did not notice any danger but it was apparently dangerous to talk freely. I did not 'see' any visible reaction in the form of immediate street protests but the following months proved, in fact, that the activists' reaction was prompt and powerful. Most importantly, 'silence' and 'non-reaction' had a significance that needed to be understood. This will be explored in this chapter through flashback, providing a politico-historical context to the Emergency in 2005. In order to give words to the silent reaction and unveil the cracks between 'appearance' and 'reality', I will explore the interface between politics, power and theatre, and trace the specific historically and culturally constructed qualities of the public and private domains in Nepal. What I argue through this chapter is that a long experience of autocratic rule had created and sustained multiple 'stages' in which communication and dialogue between the public and private domains were conditioned and filtered (Burghart, 1993). Because of the experience of 'not being heard', citizens had to follow scripted ways of voicing concerns and objections. This took extreme forms: either secretly through underground activities, or through public 'spectacular' demonstrations in which the streets became highly contested political spaces. Political power, space and artistic performance intermingled in intriguing ways. In Hindu religious tradition, the streets are shared by humans and gods, and their union is reasserted publicly through processions and rituals (Chapter 1). I argue that having the possibility of taking up 'roles', e.g., becoming' gods, actors are endowed with significant transformative power. Folk artists used songs and dances as a medium of subversion, as cultural critique and for the reassessment of dominant ideologies. In such a political culture, artists' transformative and metamorphic skills granted them privileged access to forbidden public spaces and allowed them to engage in creative forms of political resistance and opposition. This will help understand how some artists' previous experience of Panchayat domination guided their choices during 2005 and the 'culture of silence' that *kachahari* theatre aimed at challenging.

Counterfeit worlds

> On 16 December 1960 King Mahendra Bir Bikram Shah Deva assumed emergency powers and dismissed the Nepali Congress government that had been elected with a substantial majority only 18 months earlier. Arguing that parliamentary democracy was alien to Nepalese traditions and unsuited for developing the country, Mahendra also arrested the prime minister, banned all political parties and suspended the constitution. (Burghart, 1993, 1)

Richard Burghart's description of King Mahendra's take-over in 1960 strikingly anticipates the 2005 state of emergency: history sinisterly repeated itself. Burghart introduced two concepts to describe the Panchayat rule: 'public life as counterfeit reality' (1993, 9) and 'the conditions of listening' (1996 , 300). Since these notions will be useful to understanding the 2005 coup and to my analysis in the next chapter, let me begin with a more detailed explanation. Burghart (1993, 1996) illustrates how Mahendra's banning of political parties in 1960 aimed at erasing any 'rival interpretations of the popular will' (1993, 1), thus allowing the king to lead the country through the partyless Panchayat democracy[4] without facing any public form of criticism. The government manipulation of the 'public' and 'private'[5] created what Burghart called 'public life as counterfeit reality' (Ibid., 9). In such a dominated public space, citizens' participation in the country's political life was guided through specific regulations that obliged them to enter the public sphere following specific scripts, often wearing a metaphorical mask. Only unity and harmony were permitted in the public domain in order to not disturb or break the royal fiction of unity (Ibid.). Political parties were considered the expression of the self-interest of their leaders and supporters. So they were outlawed. For example, the government regarded newspapers voicing party opinions to be private. When entering the public space, they had to be subjected to government censorship (Ibid., 8). In contrast, state-run, 'public' newspapers like *Gorkhapatra* and *The Rising Nepal* published news supporting the public image of such a unitary state. Other 'private' institutions – in the form of meetings, publications and public events – were allowed to enter the public space in an 'appropriate' way, only with the government's permission (Ibid.). The state monopolized both the 'legitimate use of force' and the 'performance of public service', a right that is handled by civil society in western democracies (Burghart, 1996, 303). The king's power was exercised by preventing conflictual issues from becoming the subject of open discussion and by determining the agenda of what was public and thus debatable. In this context, the private space was safe and hosted the organization of dissent. Activists were usually arrested only when they entered the public space (Ibid., 1993, 8–9).

The levels of repression varied throughout the 30 years of Panchayat rule. My analysis concentrates on the last decade (1980–90), the period when theatre groups entered the streets and started a street theatre movement. It was such experience that guided senior artists' reaction to the 2005 state of emergency. Burghart argues that a certain gap between the rules governing the system and its practical work is part of the 'fiction' of the modern state (Ibid., 10). Yet, in Nepal, after 1980, this crack became so wide that 'the structures of Panchayat democracy began to acquire a fictional character' (Ibid., 11). For example, the 1980 referendum that confirmed the continuation of the Panchayat system was won by a slim margin. I want to quote Burghart's description at length here because it clarifies popular reaction to the 2005 Emergency and spells out how political resistance was organized underground, backstage, from a 'private' position.[6] What was mirrored to the royal eyes was only what the ruler wanted to see and what the ruler allowed citizens to reveal, at least in the capital – that is unity and order.

> The fact that the political parties were able to mobilise the electorate for the multi-party vote in the referendum meant that although being 'illegal', they were nonetheless tolerated within limits by the state. Both the factionalism among the panchas and the tolerance by the state of the political underground created a half-real political world where things were not what they seemed. By having to fight against political parties to win the referendum, the 'Panchas' – that is to say, the local leaders who were reputedly above politics – had to fully immerse themselves in it. By fighting against the collectively organized parties, the Panchas became effectively a political party of partyless people and Nepal was transformed from a partyless democracy to a one-party state that was run by the partyless party. Meanwhile, despite their illegal status, Congress and various leftist groups were able to operate fairly openly within the country. Congress boycotted the 1981 and 1986 general elections, objecting to the requirement that all candidates be members of one of the 'class organizations'[7] set up under the panchayat system and to the ban on standing avowedly as the representative of a party. It did, however, field candidates (as partyless individuals) in the 1987 local elections and won a number

of seats, including the mayorship of Kathmandu. The duly elected party members, however, were later removed from office by the government upon their refusal to take part in public processions on 16 December. This was the day when, from the government's point of view, Mahendra gave (panchayat) democracy to the people, and when, from the parties' point of view, the government took (parliamentary) democracy away. Meanwhile, some leftist groups campaigned in the national elections, and managed to return candidates in a few cases where their network of activists was particularly strong, as in Bhaktapur constituency in 1981 and 1986 and Chitwan in 1986.

In the minds of the Nepalese intelligentsia the work of the political parties had become an 'open secret' and the hidden work of the state revealed that public life was a 'counterfeit reality' (Ibid., 11).

The outcome of the elections showed that government control was not systematic. Provided the politicians wore the 'official mask' and played the 'role' required by the system, they could win elections. They lost their places only when they refused to acknowledge in public their support for the king, when they went 'out of role'. However, there were loopholes in the system, which were skillfully exploited by political activists. It was not a totally dominated space. In fact, cultural activists took advantage of discontinuities in surveillance to enter the public domain, as I will detail in the next sections.

But Burghart raises another key issue that helps explain the interaction between private and public space, what he calls 'the conditions of listening', that is the 'way one ought to speak if one is to be heard' (1996, 300). Burghart underlines how the conditions of listening are taken for granted in European social thought, following Habermas' assumption of ideal communication being based on a community of speakers having equal access, becoming a moral community, or civil society evaluating the state's action from an external position (Ibid., 301). The scenario is different in hierarchical societies where moral authority conditions the possibility of being listened to.

Because the possibility of speaking and being heard was filtered, theatre, dance, and songs offered masquerade platforms to voice political concerns in the otherwise deaf public space. Under the royal autocratic regime, the public space was not a proper public space, in Arendt's sense, as no plurality was allowed. According to western tradition, modern[8] individuals, at home in their private space, consider the public as their outside. The outside is the place of politics, where the action of the individual is exposed to the presence of others and there seeks recognition; that which Hannah Arendt in 'The Human Condition' (1958) calls 'the space of public appearance'. These arenas are spaces were people and ideas come into public view and worldviews are shared. Arendt's 'space of appearance' is where the plurality of views develops and critically engages in a 'multi-dimensional understanding rather than sublimating private interests to a singular 'public good'' (Donovan cited in Cornwall, 2002, 6). During the Panchayat period, criticism was comparable to disloyalty and could not be publicly uttered but only kept in one's mind, 'expressed in private within the family or among close friends' (Burghart, 1996, 307). Alternatively, criticism was rephrased in the public domain in ways that could be acceptable such as through silence, irony, insincere praise, procrastination, or officially saying yes but then delaying the enactment: 'one has a headache, one's daughter is getting married, etc.' (Ibid., 206–07). Similarly, the government or king's speeches were received with suspicion[9] and could not be taken at face value but had to be tested against the intentions of the speaker, 'the king cannot speak formally to the body politic: rather he must speak formally to everyone, for he represents everyone' (1996, 308). Burghart concludes: 'Public life is the realm of truth, but it must be a truth concealed in its intention' (Ibid., 309). Intentions had to be concealed in the public/non-public space and carefully crafted symbolic street dramas paradoxically managed to keep real intentions hidden while simultaneously communicating a message that resulted unmistakable to the audience. Communication between audience and actors took place in the 'representational space' (Lefebvre, 1991) while simultaneously following the opposite rules that governed the public according to the authority's 'representation of space'. Theatre could thus provide a powerful moral space for political criticism. The 'representational space' turned into a space for social transformation.

Bringing back Arendt's notions, dramatic acting of oppositional plays and songs can be conceived not only as an attempt to defy the regime or 'communicate with the king'[10] but also as a way of finding an audience, of regaining a plurality banned by the rulers, of reestablishing a community by creating an alternative 'space' for dissent; in other words by temporarily 'appropriating' the dominated space. Plurality was found on a different spatial level, not in the banned physical space but on the representational level, engaging in 'cultural remapping as a form of resistance' (Giroux 2005, 25). Elaborating Burghart's concept (1996, 318), I think it is this spatial dimension that makes theatrical forms of criticism such as symbolic demonstrations and street performances, a form of consciousness, both theatrically and critically. They become an embodied and performative consciousness involving the whole being in action while the aesthetics of the actions allow for the intent to be hidden in public.

Cultural activism in Nepal

One day comes once in an age,
It brings overturning, topsy-turvy and change,
The mute and the meek begin to speak, to move their lips of sorrow
(Gopal Prasad Rimal in Hutt, 1997, 191)

Gopal Prasad Rimal (1918–73) composed this poem during the Rana domination. It would be later put to music and sung by *janabadi* (people's) artists during the Panchayat time. The song was sung also during the People's Movement in 2005–06 and the first line became an icon of victory, thus linking rebellions against autocracy across time (see next Chapter). This section explores the undercurrent of political and social critique conveyed through subversive popular art in particular in times of authoritarian rule and controlled space.

The Rana period (1846–1951)

Just like the Panchayat era described in the previous section, the Rana rule cannot be reduced to a uniform pattern as far as degree of freedom of opinion is concerned. The system of internal intelligence with secret agents and spies set up by Maharaj Jang Bahadur Kunwar Rana (1817–77) characterized the whole age, despite periods of varying imposition (Rana, 2001). Jang Bahadur himself is said to have walked in the capital disguised as a common citizen for surveillance. Except for Deb Shamsher (March-June 1901), most of the Rana prime ministers discouraged education as a tool to keep people under control (Ibid.). Chandra Shamsher (1901–29) imposed restraints on poets and writers and established the 'Gorkha Bhasa Prakashini Samiti' in January 1913 (Ibid., 118).[11] While functioning as a censorship board, this organization was also founded to encourage literary publication. From that moment, every literary work, including poems and stories had to be approved by the Samiti board before publication. Suspicion infiltrated religion too. At the beginning of the twentieth century, Chandra Shamsher had Nepali members of the Indian reformist religious movement Arya Samaj arrested, on suspicion of political activity (Ibid., 121). Bhim Shamsher (1929–32) is said to have feared intellectuals as enemies (Ibid., 133).

Political activists assumed 'masked roles', used acting skills and the ambiguities allowed by artistic language to overcome the restrictions imposed by the Rana regime (1846–1951) and to reach the public space. In 1920, several people were jailed as the result of publishing a booklet entitled 'The Cultivation of Maize' (*Makai ko kheti*). Among them, the publisher Krishnalal Adhikari died in prison while serving a sedition charge (Hutt, 2002, 1689; Rana, 1999, 117; Seddon and

Karki, 2003, 5; Upreti, 1992, 25–28). No copy of the booklet exists today. Yet it
contained allegories that the rulers interpreted as criticism and a call for social
and economic reforms, including land reform under the guise of suggesting a new
technique for cultivating maize, from which the title derives (Ibid.). Later, Juddha
Shamsher (1932–45) softened the controls and allowed publication of Nepal's first
literary magazine, 'Sharada', in 1938, although contributions had to be approved by
the Nepali Bhasa Prakashini Samiti before publication.

Yogmaya's non-violent rebellion in Bhojpur, eastern Nepal in the 1930s (Aziz,
2001; Hutt, 2013) offers another, though controversial, example of popular criticism
silenced by the ruling class. Popular tradition describes Yogamaya as a female ascetic
who led a campaign for reform and justice, attacking both caste discrimination
and state oppression, that ended in her drowning along with 60 other disciples
in 1941 (Aziz, 2001; Hutt, 2013). Her means of 'campaigning' were songs, the
banis (utterances), that she sang when she awakened from meditation. These were
collected in a text known as 'Sarvartha Yogabani', that was banned in Nepal for more
than 40 years (Hutt, 2013, 387). Hutt explains that although the historical truth of
Yogmaya's story is difficult to ascertain, her rediscovery in the 1980s, and a loose
interpretation of 'Sarvartha Yogabani' turned Yogmaya into a 'revolutionary icon' of
progressive forces in Kathmandu (Hutt, 2013).

In the early 1940s, activists of the Praja Parishad[12] manipulated religious readings
for political purposes. Hoftun, Raeper, and Whelpton (1999, 7) report that Shukra
Raj Sastri, one of the first martyrs of Nepal, read passages from the 'Mahabharata'
in front of an audience of 400 to 500 people in Asan Tole or Indra Chowk.[13] The
heroic struggles between the people and an unjust ruler were meant to prompt the
audience to political action. Members of the Rana family hid among the spectators
in poor men's clothes to spy. However, this dissident action was ended a few days
after it began. Kedar Man Byathit observes that 'in his lecture Ganga Lal[14] had
overstepped our rules and gone into direct political agitation' (Ibid.). As a Hindu
kingdom, in Nepal authorities used religious festivals to legitimize their own rule
(Chapter 1). However, religious festivals could conversely become a relatively
safe space for staging critiques of oppression and for raising awareness, forging
community bonds and mobilizing collective action, provided they were conveyed
in a veiled way. Political activists could thus voice dissent through forms that were
acceptable by the rulers, providing their 'intentions' remained hidden. Yet, as we
have seen, going 'out of role', or, as I suggest, 'out of space', led to the arrest of Ganga
Lal. As soon as the 'mask' protecting his challenge was lowered, the system could not
allow any public, open defiance.

During the Rana period artists used the aesthetic space to question autocratic power. But when the poet and playwright Gopal Prasad Rimal[15] (1918–73), who directed the monthly magazine *Sharada* around which young democrats (*prajatantrabadi*) gathered, openly shouted slogans supporting democracy in the streets along with other artists, the authorities removed him from his position (Malla, 2007). Rimal, though, then continued to engage in awareness raising artistic actions, inspired by the revolutionary poet Siddhicharan Shrestha (1912–92). Rimal sang revolutionary *bhajans* with other artist friends in different temples of Kathmandu to motivate people to struggle against the regime (Ibid.). Prachanda Malla, a student of Balakrishna Sama's, recounts that when the Rana discovered Rimal's ploy, they sent all those artists to jail. The following is one of the *bhajans* sang at the time by Rimal:

Oh Goddess Durga, mother of the world, open your eyes and look

Can you see the internal situation, how can I say you are blind!

On our condition, on our trouble/bad luck, please look just once

Reform this country, there is hope here, make all brains clear

We are Nepali, Nepal is ours, raise this feeling in everybody (Malla, 2007)

Prachanda argues that after being released from jail, Rimal committed himself totally to politics. Prachanda also remembers that suspicion surrounded public dramatic performances. 'The Ranas were a very big problem for drama players', he explains, adding that if there was any dialogue against them they would cancel the plays. They would censor lines that they didn't like, stop plays and put actors in prison after beating them. For example, Ratnadas Prakash and Bekha Narayan were both jailed.[16] Nepali authorities did not issue specific laws such as the Dramatic Performances Censorship Act (1857) in colonial India (Bhatia, 2004) or Franco's Law on Chamber Theatre and Theatrical Rehearsals (van Erven, 1988, 147) to control theatrical activities. Yet, the presence of officials in disguise and, subsequently, the artists' arrests show that they were well aware of the potential threat deriving from cultural and dramatic performances.

The Panchayat time (1960–90)

During the Panchayat period art entered political culture[17] in a more structured and organized way. Most left parties, like ML (Communist Party of Nepal - Marxist Leninist) or Jana Morcha, had established well-organized cultural fronts. Since political parties were banned and their leaders were underground, the work of these cultural fronts was fundamental to mobilize citizens. Political leaders organized their party work from a 'private' position to avoid arrest.[18] The necessity of exchanging information between leaders and their activists is crucial in sustaining party politics, especially in rural areas. Access to political information took place mainly through personal relations (Whelpton, 2005, 11). At the time, the Nepalese electorate was composed for the most part of illiterate peasants. Whelpton (2005, 94) explains that establishing connections with influential people and groups at local level, as well as creating networks of activists,[19] made the difference among political parties.[20]

Political parties were able to convey messages that could not be openly expressed by politicians and activists through cultural programmes (sanskritik karyakram). Cultural programmes are a malleable format including songs, dances and theatre performed by cultural families (sanskritik parivar). The term 'cultural family' or 'cultural group' (sanskritik samuha) covers heterogeneous groups performing both traditional folk dance and songs, and modern dance based upon pop and Bollywood film music. Cultural groups are still innumerable in the capital and a popular form of leisure activity outside Kathmandu. Since the Panchayat years, schools have been encouraged to prepare annual cultural programmes for Parents' Day[21] and for Saraswati Puja.[22] Moreover, cultural groups can be connected to ethnic communities to religious groups or NGOs, and perform during public events; professional cultural groups perform traditional dances and songs in hotels to entertain tourists.[23] Similarly, cultural programmes displaying ethnic traditions were cosmetically used by the government and by the Panchayat state to sustain the fiction of the 'unity in diversity' national culture (cf. Burghart, 1993) during public and official functions, in particular during national celebrations or royal birthdays.

Cultural workers (sanskritik karmi)[24], artists, and activists aligned with the political parties, travelled the whole country performing in the villages. In a camouflaged way they publicized subversive political messages. Folk songs and dance were said, by cultural workers, to be immensely popular, especially in the villages, where few other sources of entertainment were available. While even cultural workers were obliged to follow the rules of the 'public', their position was highly fluid, like professional chameleons skillfully playing around with 'public life as counterfeit reality'. They managed to survive through disguise, for example having double identities, different names, and changing repertoires according to the context. When police were nearby, cultural workers sang folk or love songs; when the police left, their repertoire switched to 'progressive' songs. Artists with dance, songs and dramas were at the front of political campaigning. If artists were welcomed by the people of a particular area, other activists would later bring in political magazines and books.

Let me return briefly to political songs and cultural programmes. Since the 1950s Gopal Prasad Rimal and other poets/singers replaced lyrics centred on love and nature, or celebratory praises for the rulers with lyrics based on the social reality of the time, depicting the hardships common people had to face or anticipating a better future. Siddhicharan Shrestha's (1912–92) 'Mother I am not mad'[25] or Laksmiprasad Devkota's (1909–59)s 'The golden day will rise one day' represent the seeds out of which grew a very productive stream of political music known as *janataka git* (people's songs) and *pragatisil git* (progressive songs) (Rai, 2060 B.S.; Grandin, 1994, 2005). In 1958, Gukul Joshi and Dharma Raj Thapa started a joint *gitiyatra* (singing tour) taking their songs to different regions of Nepal (Rai, 2060 B.S.). 1967 marks the establishment of Ralfa, a cultural movement including Ramesh, Rayan, Arim and Manjul. Their songs denounced social oppression, injustice, corruption as well as the malpractices of the Panchayat system. Songs that had been composed for awareness-raising, later became popular for their artistic value and quickly spread across the country (Rai, Ibid.). The cultural front was strong in the 1971 Jhapa Revolt[26] led by a group of radical Communists in the attempt to overthrow the Panchayat system that was brutally suppressed by the state. Cultural programmes and progressive songs had a lasting impact on audiences across the country. During the street protests that led to the People's Movement in April 2006, young and old people alike sang many such songs.[27] What is more, they created powerful rhetorical images (Grandin, 1994; Rai, 2060 B.S.) that constituted the core artistic patterns from which Maoist artistic rhetoric developed. What follows is an account of how an artist, who worked as cultural worker for a Leftist party during the Panchayat, subsequently became a theatre actor.

Box 2.1: Bijay and the villagers who thought artists were like gods

Bijay Bisfot[28] is an extremely active, witty and energetic actor. He has experimented with theatre and social commitment for most of his life. When in September 2005 I asked him how he got involved in art and politics, he immediately explained that he was a cultural worker for the Communist Party of Nepal-United Marxist Leninist, unlike other artists who often hid their affiliation or avoided mentioning the exact name of the political party they supported, or had supported. Indeed, he was the first person who openly addressed the usually avoided sensitive issue of the relationship between art and politics. Bijay also made clear that he was still a Communist, although when interviewed in 2005, he was not associated with any political party. Bijay explained that in 1984 he was an active political worker (*karyakarta*). At the time political leaders would ask artists to create songs, poems, or plays to match the different interests of the spectators and to fill political programmes. Cultural workers did not receive financial support from the political parties they belonged to; they were fed and given shelter by the villagers they met along their trips.[29]

Contd.

Cultural programmes took place in open spaces but they were obviously not authorized. Therefore, artists had to be skillful and invent ways of showing an open identity that could be acceptable to the security forces, but at the same time, maintain their political purpose. In their resistance, cultural workers were using the same tools as the government, playing masked games: cultural workers disguised as traditional musicians, secret agents disguised as villagers, in games of reciprocal deception and credulity; just like decades earlier, when political activists read religious texts in public, and government officers mingled in the crowds disguised in rags. Front and backstage were easily interchangeable: multiple identities, multiple roles, multiple costumes and obviously plenty of tricks. For example, Bijay recounts that his group was to provide progressive books to the rural areas. At the time, most Russian books were banned. They had to carry thick volumes by Lenin, Marx, Mao, or Chekhov. But how? Having hidden them inside a drum (*madal*),[30] they managed to pass the police check post without trouble. However, once they reached Therathum (eastern Nepal), they found themselves in an isolated area, in the cold of winter, far from any lodges or houses so they took shelter under a tree. Bijay continues the story with words laced with a sense of risk and danger: 'There was no environment for sleep. We were also hungry, no food... Five villagers came to our tree. They thought we were Damai, so they gave us money and asked, 'please, we like entertainment, give us entertainment'... We laughed, the villagers were CID, secret police'. So, political activists entered the political space through their artistic cover. Their 'invisible theatre' performances, unlike Boal's interventions, were not supposed to provoke society through 'fictitious' theatrical ways; rather, the invisible theatre of the cultural workers protected exactly those who were carrying out a real political revolution in disguise.

Artists' representations depict the affection of villagers for these cultural workers. 'People loved us' is a recurrent refrain in interviews. Moreover, villagers are represented as innocent and honest people unable to grasp the meaning of their cultural groups' representation. Because they arrived from Kathmandu, the centre of power, far away from the village and because of their artistic skills, Bijay says that artists were seen as 'quasi-gods', as those who can 'change the problems'. Having an almost magical halo, they not only received hospitality reserved to the guests but also respect to the point of making Bijay feel 'guilty' for not being able to fulfill such high expectations, and 'for just bringing political messages'. He is still touched by an encounter with a villager in a remote corner of Okhaldhunga, eastern Nepal. Once the cultural programme ended, a 'father' approached him with tears in his eyes. Bijay could not understand the reason. The man replied 'I met a god', suggesting that the cultural workers were like

Contd.

gods because they went to rural areas to change society.[31] 'But I think they didn't know the whole story', comments Bijay bitterly.

Bijay explains that soon after 1990, especially during elections, dramas in particular became monothematic, open and explicit: 'give us votes', 'this is a good party', 'we will make the government'.[32] The social space had changed. There was no longer need for tricks or symbols. 1990 interestingly marked the beginning of a deep crisis in the street theatre movement as well, because of the changed political conditions. Yet, while cultural workers moved towards more open political propaganda, theatre artists engaged in social theatre in connection to NGOs, somehow losing their critical edge in both cases (see Chapter 4).

Some theatre artists started professional careers after performing as cultural workers during the Panchayat period or in the post 1990 years, and somehow detached themselves from what they now consider as a partisan use of art. Nonetheless, political parties constituted a lively cultural and artistic laboratory. Other artists, already popular at the time, joined political parties and supported their ideals but resisted pressure to convey open political messages in order to preserve the 'integrity' of their craft. These experiences are truly valuable to understanding the arts' potential for social change, to understand local forms of cultural critique, to locate historically the present-day politico-artistic practices, and to understand how socio-political performances became traditions/practices out of necessity to resist autocratic state rule. The legacy of these practices still lives on. The second narrative describes the experience of a singer who was a member of Ralfa and travelled Nepal performing 'people's songs' in the 1970s but struggled with the limitations imposed by party membership. Striking the balance between politics and aesthetics was and still is a thorny challenge. If Bijay's narrative illustrates the experience of a cultural worker associated to a political party, Manjul provides a different perspective. A popular singer who for a limited period of time was associated with a political party, Manjul described extensively his experience in his 1988 memoir 'The Footsteps of Memory: Memoir of a Musical Journey' (*Samjhanaka Pailaharu: Giti Yatrako Samsmaran*):

Box 2.2: Manjul and 'art for life's sake'

Manjul started his career as a folk singer. With an independent group of friends, he travelled extensively as a troubadour through the hills and mountains of the country for nearly two years collecting folk songs, singing 'people's songs' and receiving great praise. 'I got such a nice education. I got such knowledge of my land', Manjul tells me with pride, 'I learnt so many good things about my people, I was changed and I think that was the golden time of my life'.

Contd.

Manjul explains that song-writing has a long tradition in Nepal, connected to both folk and political culture. However, in the late 1960s song-writing was considered as a 'lower' form of art compared to writing poetry, and hence less prestigious in society. In Manjul's words, poetry gave 'more honour'. Manjul remembers being discouraged in his desire to write songs. Nonetheless, following the tradition of Laxmi Prasad Devkota (1909–59) and Madhav Ghimire (b. 1919) he started writing 'songs that are not only songs, they are like poetry, but they are not poetry, they are lyrical, they are singable, half they are songs'. Manjul continues explaining that 'the songs were not superficial. We tried to make them very meaningful and with a good message, but we were not interested at all in being sloganist, propagandist. We were interested in creating our real art' (Ibid.). For Manjul, 'real art' is the art that is 'true to life', no matter artists' political association. He provides an example:

> I read my poems with Sarwanam outside Kathmandu. Many people thought that we belonged to the same party but that was not true. I told Ashesh Malla [the director of the group] 'eh, these people are saying….. [we belong to the same political party]', because our art was very close. We were true to the people. One day, I was making a campaign for the Communist party, and I presented a drama written by Ashesh Malla. Later we won in that area, and I said 'Asheshdai, our party won in those many places because of your drama'. And he said 'We [close to Nepali Congress] are singing your songs in so many places and we won'. People sometimes belong to different parties but if they are very true to life, if they are real friends of the people,[33] they are close. Many times they are together.[34]

Both songs and theatre were stigmatized forms of art linked to the lower castes. But both theatre artists and singers often belonged to high castes. Therefore songs were to be 'sanitized', devoid of 'sloganist' connotations, and made 'meaningful', in order to find a place in the world of 'real' art.[35] Manjul is keen to mark the difference between Ralfa and cultural groups connected to political parties. His preoccupations reveal the controversial relationship between artists and the political parties and an attempt to differentiate himself and his group from party cultural workers. Manjul describes how his group, and him in particular, took the decision to become associated with one of the Communist parties of the time.[36] They accepted the invitation to perform in a Leftist mass assembly. Manjul and other three people were arrested. Policemen thought he was a politician, but the Communist people of the area pushed for his liberation on the ground that he was 'an artist'. Manjul remembers them

Contd.

saying 'he is not a politician, he is an artist, he sang our songs, why did you arrest him?' This incident affected their identity:

> Earlier we were not saying we are Communist, or Congress, anything, at the beginning. When we started to sing we were very close to the Congress, but we were not Congress. Later on we were very close to the Communists, but we were not Communists. But that incident encouraged me so much, me, Ramesh and Arim, and so we started to think maybe we need to be their friends, we should not have a separate identity, a separate name. [. . .] The movement that had started from Jhapa, we joined that. We were very close to that but later we took their membership as well but other friends had other groups.[37]

Manjul's experience offers an interesting example of the interface between art and politics, of the blurred space existing between using art as a means of discussing social issues and the easy, real or assumed, association to political parties. In this case the artists' position is ambiguous: it is true that they were not politicians or activists, but was singing political songs and speaking on behalf of the underground leaders not a political activity? Yet, as Manjul suggested, ideological commitment and party politics would not always overlap. Or were artists themselves playing tricks, situationally moving between spaces? This may explain the difficulty of assessing the artists' 'party' membership, questioning whether boundaries could be drawn at all. An example from the time can spell out the problem. There are no recordings of those concerts but storytelling was much a part of the musical performance itself, and it was indeed political. Songs in fact were preceded by an introduction. Manjul explains that as the Master of Ceremony (MC) he would not explain the song but accompany the audience on a proper journey:

> If you are going to New Road, my duty was to take you up to the New Road gate, this way, this way, you are going to this and this kind of place, up to New Road gate. It is your duty to enter New Road gate and to enjoy New Road. So New Road was our song. I could take you up to the gate of our song. After listening you should enter. I was very good. Even now many people say the introductory part was much nicer than the song, the way they used to listen, the way they used to applaud...[38]

The role of the MC was particularly important as there was no freedom of speech and political leaders were banned from talking in public spaces. Since artists could speak, it was them who carried political messages. Manjul remembers,

Contd.

I used to speak as a political leader. I used to give messages and the people used to ask me. If I went to Biratnagar, people used to ask me [to speak in their name]. Our friends were banned, they could not speak, so they said 'please say this and this and this', so I used to speak before singing the song (Ibid., November 2006).

What was therefore the difference between a singer speaking as a political leader and an actual political leader? What boundaries did both Manjul, as an artist in the 1970s, and Ganga Lal as a politician in the 1940s, overstep when ending in jail? The example given above shows that artists lived with multiple identities although sometimes the artistic cover was not enough to spare them arrest, and police officers managed to read beyond the performance, perceiving a threat to the system.

Cultural programmes were important in creating and keeping networks and connections between the political leaders and their potential supporters. Cultural programmes offered opportunities for fund-raising and also functioned as gate openers for subsequent, more in depth political work. Since political parties could not organize demonstrations or mass meeting they used cultural programmes with a double aim. On the one hand, to popularize their messages and for mass mobilization, and on the other, to raise funds to publish political magazines that would be distributed in the countryside by political activists:

> The political workers who were underground used to carry our songs, you know, they used to play them. They could read the mood of the people, the psychology of the people. More than half of the people have become Communists because of our songs, the songs that my group sang, the songs that our friends' groups sang. They were so powerful, it was the only way.[39]

Art's independence from political parties is a much debated issue in Nepal. In politically charged moments, the tendency to categorize people according to their party sympathies is strong and carving a space out of such games is complex. However, the content of poems and drama written by artists close to opposed political groups may have been very similar, if not interchangeable. Ideological position was not always what made the difference in the political parties.[40] Yet, 'differentiation' was remarkable and had consequences in daily relationships. Striking the balance between art, craftsmanship, and message is what the audience normally perceives as the difference between party propaganda and 'art for life'.[41] Manjul explains that any kind of environment is politicized and he also claims that despite what some people may say, 'in Nepal

Contd.

no tradition of independent thinkers, writers, and performers exists'. In one way or another, everybody is 'under some political party'. Manjul does not regret having worked for political parties. He recognizes that as artists they were helped by the parties to reach the people, as they wanted to. It was a reciprocal exchange: 'we helped them, they helped us'. However, when interviewed, he remarked that artists should have an independent space. His position seems at first glance contradictory. He remarks that no independent thinker can survive in Nepal, and at the same time calls for independence. Manjul shifts the focus towards the performance 'space'. It is the different contexts in which even the same songs are sung, that give the songs different meanings. It is as if, now that the climate is different and there is freedom of speech in comparison to the Panchayat times, the 'mask' that was protecting the artist-activist had to be dropped. The game should be over for him, no more time for camouflage. In fact, while supporting the 2005–06 popular movement, Manjul never performed during cultural programmes, not even those organized by the civil society (see Chapter 4). What he advocated for was an independent artistic space where artists could perform their songs independent of political leaders' speeches.

The relationship between artists and political parties is complex and would deserve further exploration. For the moment, it suffices to say that after the artists that formed Ralfa separated, some still continued to produce progressive songs. For example, Ramesh, Manjul and Arym formed Sankalpa Parivar, close to the Jhapa ML. Rayan followed another Leftist group Nirmal Lama's CPN (Fourth Division) and then established Bedana Parivar and ISAS – Indreni Sanskritic Samaj (Rainbow Cultural Society); Ramesh would then establish Astha Parivar (Ghimire, 2005).

Besides political campaigning and mobilization, there are other arenas where deep social and political critique is raised through cultural performances.[42] Each year during Teej festival women compose and sing songs that function both as social and political commentary, e.g., questioning gender ideology or wider political events (Skinner, Holland and Adhikari, 1994; Ahearn, 1999). Skinner, Holland and Adhikari (1994, 279) suggest that in the Panchayat time, *rajnitik* or political Teej songs could not be sang openly but after the 1990 pro-democracy moment they emerged as a predominant type. Revolutionary women also published Teej songs collections with the explicit aim of raising political awareness (Baral, 2007). During Gai Jatra, a festival celebrated in the month of *Bhadra* (August-September) to worship Yamraj, the god of death, the social norms that govern everyday life are momentarily loosened and the improvised political satire and parodic sketches, the *khyaala*, soar in the streets (Grieve, 2004, 481; Widdess, 2006; Anderson,

1971). In addition, Gai Jatra stage shows at the Nepal Academy or at the City Hall gathered comedians who directed pungent satire towards political parties, leaders and institutions alike. During the Panchayat time when freedom of expression was restricted, comedians could thus target political figures and dominant views in ways that would have been otherwise impossible.[43]

Lefebvre claims that etched in every space are the traces of its production, its 'generative past' (1991,116). Religious, political and cultural performances are interwoven to provide a wide range of performative modes, motives and practices that people can draw from. This historical background provides the key to understanding the social and performance context in which both political street theatre originated in the 1980s and re-emerged powerfully in 2005, and the tradition to which Maoist cultural groups belong. In the next section, I will describe the beginning of the street theatre movement in Nepal. Artists describe it as an attempt of performing theatre with a civic engagement, although party politics hovers once again. The beginning of street theatre can also be associated to the growing of a politically engaged and active civil society in Nepal.

Into the streets: Theatre for political change

Ghumdai, phirdai, naachdai, gaundai, ayau, aja ayau (2)
jay jay jay jay Natyashwori (2)
natak gardai, natak bachdai, ayau hami aja ayau
sadak sadakma gardai sadak sadakma puja gardai
khabardari gardai ayo hami, ayo hami khabardari gardai
jay jay jay he Natyashwori

Travelling, returning, dancing, singing, we're here today (2)
glory, glory, glory, glory to Natyashwori (2)
doing theatre, living theatre, we're here today
playing road to road, doing puja road to road
to give a warning we're here, we're here to give a warning
glory, glory, glory, glory to Natyashwori

This is an old song, a prayer to Natyashwori, a call to the god of theatre, created by Ashesh Malla in the early 1980s. Since then, Sarwanam's actors still sing it before starting their street plays to call the people around the square and announce the arrival of the group. It is a song that epitomizes a strong stream in Nepali theatre, a theatre of streets, of journeys, of dances and songs, of religious commitment, of political engagement, a theatre of warning and a lifestyle in itself. Different opinions characterize the beginning of street theatre in Nepal. While some artists claim a

'Nepali origin', as I will detail below, others suggest Indian influences as two Indian theatre groups apparently performed in Kathmandu in the early 1980s. The 1980s represent a very creative period of activist, militant political theatre in India with the emergence of powerful groups like Janam in New Delhi (Hashmi, 1989; van Erven, 1992; Epskamp, 1989). In many ways, the theatre of Sarwanan essentializes symbols in forms that are similar to those practiced by Janam. The beginnings of political theatre in Nepal will be introduced through the narrative of Ashesh Malla, who is considered the pioneer of the street theatre movement that developed in Nepal in the early 1980s. Nepali street theatre is credited with a strong political origin. Malla explains that it developed among university students out of a disdain and anger for the system, the political critique springing out of personal pain:

> At that time, two Nepali Congress activists were hung by the government.[44] I knew one of them, he was from Dhankuta [Ashesh Malla's own home place]. King Birendra had him hung. I felt a great rebellion inside my heart against the Panchayat. That time I wrote the second drama,[45] 'Hands Raised in Protest' (*Murdabadma Utheka Hathharu*)... After writing the drama we performed at the university auditorium in Kirtipur. At that time it was not possible to criticize the Panchayat system, the king, the government [...]. We played for three days, on the third day, the royalist students started beating us harshly and tortured us and the government banned the play. Then I wrote a short play and we performed it at the university as well. But again it was stopped by royalist students...[46]

After playing 'Hands Raised in Protest' (*Murdabadma Utheka Hathharu*), Ashesh Malla wrote and performed several other plays at Tribhuvan University and with some other friends formed a theatre group. Sarwanam (meaning 'Pronoun' in the sense of representing everyone) was established in 1982. Their engagement with political theatre continued and the next hit would be 'From the Street to the Street' (*Sadakdekhi Sadaksamma*) in 1984, performed inside theatre halls. It portrayed the suffering of the country, describing a day in Kathmandu from morning to evening. The director explained that there were no actresses available,[47] no halls, no light systems or technical facilities, no money and, instead, a severe censorship curtailing artists' freedom of expression. The play ended with a plea to the audience: 'Sorry, we could not perform the drama, please come tomorrow'. The actors' strong motivations, however, gave them forbearance in the face of such difficulties. Ashesh Malla continues:

> How to change the political system, how to reach the people, what is the alternative? What can we do? And suddenly we went to the streets.

Then we started street theatre for the first time in Nepal, 1983-84. In Kirtipur, there is a ground, Coronation Garden, we performed 'We are Searching for the Spring' (*Hami Basanta Khoji Rahechaun*).[48] All students were there. Sunil [Pokharel] was also there, I wrote the play and did the direction. The first street play, everybody was surprised because the presentation was very new.

What I did was [place] four artists sitting, like here [he shows me], and I was the *sutradhar*.[49] I told the people [audience] that I was going to start the drama and first thing I would open the curtain and I did like this [hands joint in front of his chest part as if opening a curtain] and two people enter from each side. We did theatre through body movements. We used body movements for the first time in that play. So we discussed about the name to give this kind of theatre, and we said it must be called *sadak natak* (street theatre). So that's how *sadak natak* was born in Nepal.[50]

Sarwanam's artists soon started to perform out of the Kathmandu Valley, in the month-long Nepal *yatra*[51] (journey) that they would establish as an identifying feature of the group. Playing outside Kathmandu was even more difficult because of the police and the censors. They managed anyway because as soon as the play was over, the actors left for the next location by bus. The police would usually come after the play and by the time they arrived the actors had already gone. At times, however, artists were arrested by the police (Davis, 2009, 99). Even back in the capital authorities warned them to stop playing. But they did not. Circumstances also shaped their theatre artistically. What Ashesh Malla is keen to highlight, is that the artists decided to move to the street out of necessity, or 'compulsion', as he says, not out of choice:

> Theatre itself creates the stage, the circumstances. Theatre is inside self-creative of the stage and we performed on that stage. This is street theatre. We could easily perform anywhere and manage to give our message with aesthetic sense. That was not an experiment, that was a compulsion. People say, 'it's experimental drama', but I say 'no experiment, it's my compulsion'. How can it be experimental? I don't have a stage, I don't have money, I don't have technical support. I was searching for alternative theatre and that was alternative theatre for me, it was also easy. We did theatre, [...], moving from one place to the other, it would have also been difficult to bring the set, how to make artistic and powerful drama then. We thought we had to use our body and afterwards we searched and made whatever we needed.[52]

In the 1980s, Ashesh Malla and Sarwanam created regional links and organized exchanges with other people's theatre groups across South Asia, connecting with theatre activists such as Badal Sircar, Subodh Patnaik, Probir Guha and Safdar Hashmi (Davis, 2009, 102). Sarwanam and Aarohan are unique and pioneer theatre groups in Nepal. They are still active, working in and from the capital. Their paths have crossed – for example Sunil Pokharel was a lead actor in Sarwanam before founding Aarohan – but they have profoundly different identities. From its establishment Sarwanam took a clear agitprop, political stance for democracy and based its identity on simple, physical street theatre outlined above by its director. In contrast, Aarohan[53] concentrated more on proscenium theatre, staging plays with social and political values and symbols, while occasionally doing street drama. If the political environment and 'spatial' framework conditioned the development of modern Nepali theatre, theatre artists questioned the disciplined space of the regime and in doing so posed serious threats to its credibility.

Theatre with a mission

As we have seen, during the Panchayat years, government censorship was harsh and did not allow for public challenge. Theatre groups too had to comply with the norms of the system. Before each performance the state administration required actors to submit copies of the script to get permission to perform from the CDO (Chief District Officer), the Nachghar (National Theatre) and the Zonal Administration Office.[54] The officers carefully scrutinized the texts to identify objectionable passages and handed the scripts back, requesting actors to omit or alter the controversial parts. Unlike in British India (Bhatia, 2004, 20), in Nepal officers did not always follow up on the theatrical performances to make sure the corrections were implemented. Artists played around these incongruous practices.

There were in fact several techniques to elude censorship. For example, actors gave one script to the censors and performed a totally different one, or played the same dialogues but imbuing them with different meaning through body language. Sunil remembers an example:

> In a play there was a dialogue in which one intellectual said to a young boy 'you have to support the system', the political system. Of course there was nothing wrong so the censor passed it. Then, when we performed it, what we did was 'you have to support the political system' otherwise [show a choking gesture with the hands], several gestures, so it became clear for the audience that otherwise you would be killed. At that time they hadn't any system to document the performance, you know, so the next day if they called us we would say 'no, we didn't do that'. There wasn't any evidence, any concrete evidence.[55]

Using physical actions to transform the meaning of words in the script was a device Ashesh Malla also used widely:[56]

> At that time 'From the Street to the Street' (*Sadakdekhi Sadaksamma*) was heavily censored, many pages. There was a dialogue marked in red pen, it says... '*Mantriharule hamilai chirchhan*', which means 'the ministers suppress us'. They cut the dialogue. So what I did on the stage was [he mimes a sequence, first pointing the forefinger of the right hand up a few times, to indicate 'those above', the ministers; then he holds the neck a few times with the right hand again, and afterwards with both hands squeezing and turning towards opposite sides mimes the action of strangling; finally he repeats the sequence a few times, adding kicks towards the person being strangled and ends with open hands suggesting there is nothing to do, no hope] and then clap began and the censor could not do anything... .[57]

Another way of avoiding cersorship was using allegories and metaphors that the audience would easily recognize but that were apparently innocuous to the system because the challenge was not open and artists could use metaphors as masks. Coded and allegorical language also characterized the poetry and literature of the 1980s (Hutt, 1993). Similarly, oppositional theatre during Panchayat time made extensive use of coded language.[58] For example:

> Sometimes some words like 'the old tree' or 'the old house' were symbols for the political system, the Panchayat. The 'sunrise', the 'new branch', and sometimes the 'new flower in the spring', 'spring' in particular was the symbol for democracy, so we used a lot of those [symbols].... Sometimes they stopped the play of course. Many theatre groups and people were supporting the old political system and some are still, even in this new political situation they are there, but for the people who wanted to have democracy it was a mission theatre...[59]

Ashesh Malla takes his '"I" means "We"' (*Ma Bhaneko Hami*) as an example of how he used allegorical language to attack the most powerful person in his country. He was inspired to write the play by an accident, when a statue of a god in Bhaktapur was stolen. It was an open secret that it had been taken away by the king. So he used symbolic language to portray a character with two faces to show his duplicity. The play was performed without ever mentioning the keyword 'king', by utilizing a long practiced habit of hinting rather than stating plainly. While affirming that the police did not understand the symbolism, he emphasizes once more that his choice was not at all experimental, rather a 'compulsion'.[60]

Artists mentioned the inability of the police to understand the allegorical overtones of the plays while the audience seemed quick to pick up the criticism. This gap recalls the 'open secret' of the work of the political parties described by Burghart earlier. It is worth asking if turning a blind eye to the coded theatrical messages was, in fact, a deliberate choice by the security forces. Did they tacitly comply with the actors by willingly bracketing the 'hidden transcripts', or did they genuinely not understand? Albert Boadella, from the Spanish theatre group Els Joglars, thus explains a similar situation where the police did not understand the satire in their mime performance: 'They thought it was all part of a real circus act. They were pretty stupid, fortunately. The regime was one big bureaucratic, brutal sometimes, but also terribly idiotic. Everybody shoved responsibility onto the next guy' (van Erven, 1988, 160). Burghart's analysis is once again helpful here. He explained that the objective of the government was not to control people's thoughts, but rather their public expression (1996, 307). It is possible that the police were thus not required to interfere with the speakers' intentions and therefore bought into the 'show'.

Another method of bypassing the policing enforced by the rulers was to move into 'private' spaces. Sunil tells how they performed in the colleges or school compounds because they were regarded as safe places that the police would rarely enter. Afterwards Aarohan chose to perform in the French Cultural Centre, which had a 100-seat hall and a small stage. It was safe because it was a diplomatic space and the police could not enter. Actors also masked their political critique by performing foreign plays to elude supervision. Sunil explains that they chose plays that reflected their present state of mind, that were relevant to them and to the historical moment. For these reasons, they staged 'Men without Shadows',[61] 'The Respectful Prostitute', and 'Outsider' by Camus. Although the plays dealt with all sorts of absurdities, the audience could easily identify their own situation and how helpless they were in it.

Both in British and postcolonial India the choice of the performance space was often crucial for theatre groups and resulted in an escalation of theatrical activity in private residences and clubs (Bhatia, 2004, 65). Even Indian theatre groups, including the Indian People's Theatre Association (IPTA) made use of European dramas to tackle political topics forbidden by the government especially in the 1960s and 1970s (Bhatia, 2004, 51–75) – mostly Shakespeare and Ibsen. Foreign plays became both a means of elitist distinction and a means of resistance (Ibid.). In Nepal, Aarohan Theatre in particular opted for this choice.

Stories of creative tricks to fool the system are told with pride by many artists. But there are also narrations of the real danger they were constantly living with, such as when information leaked out to the police because of spies or betrayals. Here is

Bijay again, this time as a theatre actor and director, some years after his experience
as a cultural worker. In 1987 he staged 'The Court of the Leeches' (*Jukako Adalat*) a
revolutionary drama of his own creation. They received the permission to stage the
play because they had given the censors a simple, innocuous text while aiming to
perform a different one. But the day before the debut, while they were rehearsing, a
person from his group informed the police about the two scripts. The police arrived
and arrested all the actors. During the police interrogation, Bijay repeatedly denied
the existence of a second script. In fact, the second script was only improvised, not
written. Bijay remained in jail for 11 days. Had the second script been written, he
would have probably been killed. The political climate was chaotic, populated by
the double-faced individuals described in '"I" means "We"' (*Ma Bhaneko Hami*),
by open secrets and double standards. Yet, such masquerade politics made actors
co-exist with risk. If one person 'betrayed' the group, the whole mission would be
jeopardized. The divide between private and public space was fluctuating, unstable
and governed by moral and practical rules.

Artists in the 1990 revolution

The role of intellectuals in Nepal's public life changed throughout the decades
that led to the 1990 revolution. In 1970, their role was dismissed and they were
considered as 'a band of economically castrated and socially limping angels beating
the drums of their respective fads' (Malla in Hutt, 1993, 82). During the Panchayat
years academics' compromise with the regime is evident in the political distribution
of memberships in the Academy, defined by critics as 'a graveyard of artists' (Hutt,
1993, 88) and in the phony public tributes they were obligated to pay to a system
they did not believe in (Ibid.).[62]

Literary and social movements with political purposes, however, were launched
at different times. Poets from *Aswikrit Jamat* (Rejected Generation) in the late
60s renewed literature in both content and tone, abandoning romanticism and
mythology for productions based on 'social realism' expressed in informal language
(Hutt, 1993, 85). During the Boot Polish Demonstrations (1974) organized in
reaction to an increase of censorship and authoritarianism after the government *Gaon
Pharka Rashtriya Abhiyan* (Back to the Village National Campaign), intellectuals
cleaned the shoes of passers-by for a week in protest (Ibid.). Finally, in 1979, *Sadak
Kavita Kranti* (Street Poetry Revolution) added to the protests of dissatisfaction
and anger that led king Birendra to declare the referendum. In the most intense
moment, more than 200 poets recited poems in the streets of Kathmandu seeking
the abolition of the Panchayat system (Ibid.). Hutt points out that from 1979 to

1990 poetry became more open and defiant, and as a result some poets, writers and editors were fined and arrested (Ibid. 87), just like the actors mentioned above. A parallel with poetry is useful at this point, though what can be said for poetry does not totally apply to the theatre because of the different nature of theatrical language. Hutt explains that censorship's oppression has probably been somehow overstated by the post-revolution rhetoric because except for some particularly harsh periods, in the late 1960s and late 1980s, critique was accepted if phrased through the acknowledged codes (1993, 95). In contrast to poets, theatre artists often exposed the contradictions of the allegories through body language thus making their threat more concrete. Improvisation and memorization of scripts worked to their favour as evidence of their opposition was not available, thus making theatre a more flexible tool of dissent.

The gap between the educated elite of Kathmandu and the rest of the country was deep (Hutt, 1993). Yet, after the 1980 referendum[63] and by 1990, demonstrations in Kathmandu were followed by protests in other parts of the country in a unified manner: 'Within the space of ten years, the gulf between the private and public, real and pretended, conscience and necessity yawned ever wider, and at last the structure cracked and crumbled' (Hutt, 1993, 84).

What about the role of intellectuals in the 1990 revolution and of theatre artists in particular? Theatre artists participated in what were known as 'lightening demonstrations' in which 'theatre troupes gathered audience quickly, theatrically informed them of their denied rights, and parted just as quickly before the authorities were aware of the event or could arrest them' (Davis, 2009, 106). Ashesh Malla is keen to stress the active role played by Sarwanam and the link between artists and politicians. He remembers meeting artists and Girija Prasad Koirala in his flat. The political leaders warned the artists that politicians would probably be jailed in the imminent revolution, so artists should 'do something'; and they published a book of poems.[64] Sunil, Nisha, and other artists from Aarohan participated at the sit-in with writers and artists outside Trichanda College in the heart of Kathmandu on 16 March 1990. They sat down with black scarves tied around their mouth to protest against lack of freedom of expression. 158 were arrested but most were released on the same day (Hoftun, Raeper and Whelpton, 1999, 126 ; Ogura, 2001, 78–81). In fact, 'even a token action by people of standing could provide much better publicity than a demonstration' (Ibid., 81). The network of artists joining other professional groups in demonstrations organized by civil society would play a crucial role in the 2006 movement, as the next chapter will illustrate. However, such connections can be traced back to the 1980s and were already at work in 1990.

According to Hutt, 'Kathmandu writers were not at the forefront of the democratic movement' (1993, 91), though afterwards there were arguments about those who were active and those who were not (Ibid.). Most revolutionary and pro-democracy literature appeared after 1990 although certainly some joined the protests and paraded in the capital (Ibid.). There are two important differentiations to make at this point. First, theatre artists did not enjoy the same status as poets or writers, because of the written language bias that positioned performance artists on a lower level despite their popularity (Chapter 5).

As Manjul explained, composing song lyrics and writing poems was different although the first managed to reach a wide audience. Sunil's narrative of his personal struggle for recognition is also emblematic of such hierarchies (Chapter 7), even though doing political theatre was deemed 'honour-giving' in 2006 as it was in the 1980s. Second, 'independent theatre' as we have it now was an emergent genre. Mainstream theatre was mainly linked to the Nepal Academy and the National Theatre and thus to the establishment. As a consequence, it is interesting to note that theatre artists who were active during the 1990 movement – and whose contribution is not always recognized – constitute the embryo of what is now independent Nepali theatre.

A further point is worth mentioning in this regard. Many of the actors who formed dissident theatre groups in Kathmandu were originally already active in theatre in their own home place before arriving in the capital. For example, Ashesh Malla is from Dhankuta (eastern hills) and Sunil Pokharel from Biratnagar (southeast). Aarohan Theatre itself was first established in Biratnagar where a branch still exists. They did not 'discover' theatre in the capital. Rather, they brought with them to the capital their 'local' theatrical experience. What I want to suggest is that the Kathmandu-centred research and media coverage risk ignoring the intellectual liveliness of rural and remote areas, freezing them into stereotyped simplification which have served both political and developmental representations. Secondly, the availability of higher education infrastructure and the spatial power determines Kathmandu's centrality in which theatre could develop. Thirdly, Kathmandu was and is still the place to be to be 'seen', to be recognized and to make pressure. Representations of Nepali theatre therefore have to take into account space to avoid misinterpreting the causes for the effects. The fact that modern Nepali theatre is mostly concentrated in Kathmandu therefore needs to be seen historically and spatially. Fourthly, the concept of 'intellectual', as it is commonly used in Nepal, requires critical assessment. The adjective 'intellectual' is often attributed to people or works of art associated with written culture, that is writers, academics, and book-based drama. How does the category overlap with that of élite? For example, written culture is given more consideration than improvised drama (Chapter 1). A hierarchy is at work and it strategically positions people and artistic products. Cultural workers, for example, would not find a place among intellectuals, but yet they created and used art for political change for decades. As 'symbolic creators' they indeed need to be included in this category.[65] Simultaneously, however, the category of artist works as a recognized shared identifier across political party and social strata.

Conclusion

Theatre as cultural performance is deeply embedded in the wider political and social context, not only for themes and ethos but also for presentation, form and language. Nepali theatre in the 1980s had to undergo the restrictions imposed by the Panchayat system. But independent artists found in theatre a temporary space for social sharing, a possibility of self-expression and critique that could challenge the authority because of its masked and cunning nature. Davis (2009) in fact describes the 1980s as the 'decade of dreams' in Nepali theatre. Analysis reveals strong links between artists, activists, and politicians thus suggesting that cultural performance as a tool for consciousness raising, popularization of ideas, propaganda and social critique was deeply embedded in the Nepali political culture.

Performance was used both by political parties and by activists and citizens to create alternative spaces of community and resistance. However, artists did not accept a political use of art as value free and the nature of artists' independence from party politics was and still is an open and debated controversy. Political engagement was often motivated by personal experience, but then, the actual protest performances affected the personal lives of the artists involved.

A double movement and exchange, from the centre to the periphery emerges: cultural workers, often from urban areas, travelled through rural and remote corners, and thus discovered their own country and people. Artists from different parts of Nepal met in the capital and from the centre started a political street theatre movement. The 'spatial' importance of the capital has been highlighted. Before 1990 street theatre was allegorical, just like Nepali literature in general.[66] Similarly, cultural workers used to mask their performances to protect themselves. Cultural performances were obliged to follow the 'conditions of listening' of the surrounding 'counterfeit' world (Burghart, 1993, 1996). Breaches like going out of role, breaking the fiction, speaking forbidden dramatic dialogues were often punished. But the success of a play in overcoming the authority's surveillance depended not only on following the implicit rules of the public space. It was also linked to personal relations as in the case of spying narrated by Bijay.

The question that I raised at the beginning, concerning the 'lack' of reaction after Emergency 2005, now finds an answer. Emergency 2005 not only imposed restrictions, it also brought back the memories and experiences narrated in this chapter, as well as the practices of the 'counterfeit' world, as Sunil Pokharel explains:

> We came through the Panchayat regime. We come from that time. We knew that when something changes abruptly, [we have to] wait a few months at least. Because, if you see, when the king took over power, every activity stopped, but we didn't stop our performances. Even that time there was a rule, more than five people cannot gather. We said 'no, let's do it inside, because it's safer'. Because, you see, in a dictatorship, you try a little, and then see what is the reaction. You go for a little more and then see. It's how you create the space. If you see the newspapers at that time, it's exactly what they did: they waited, started to write a little, then wait and went a little further. That's how things go. Then, also, the huge pressure was to save Gurukul. It was part of a strategy too. Because lots of people needed a space where they could meet, they could talk.[...] So, everybody needed a space. To safeguard the space we needed to do that. Afterwards we used another strategy. When we went to the streets there was a plan behind. If they would stop us, then perhaps someone else outside Gurukul would start something else and we would be behind.[67]

'Non-reaction' was therefore not synonymous with passivity but indicative of practical strategic knowledge. Sunil's analysis can be read together with the theoretical issues raised in the beginning of this chapter. The first action that he deemed necessary was safeguarding an internal but shared place. Only afterwards would it have been possible to move to the public domain and start appropriating the 'dominated' space (Lefebvre, 1991, 164–68). The social space is governed by rules, but the application of such rules depends very much on who a person is, according to role and status. By allowing ambiguities, tricks, tactical transgressions and switching into dramatic 'roles' theatre worked as a kind of bridge between spaces: a practiced 'metaxic' space. Artists became symbolic space-brokers to regain plurality, temporarily halting domination. Theatre, therefore, provides a spatial 'diversion' (détournement) (Lefebvre, 1991, 167), facilitating the production of a new space of political criticism. The next chapter will detail how this occurred in 2005–06.

Endnotes

1   *Prajatantra* is a word for democracy that can be translated as 'rule by subjects'. This term is used to indicate parliamentary democracy with a constitutional monarch as it existed in

Nepal during the 1990s. During 2005 and 2006, the popular movement demanded *loktantra* that is 'rule by the people', thus excluding the king from the political system. The discourse would afterwards shift to *ganatantra* that is republic.

2   Nepal achieved multi-party democracy in 1990 after 28 years of partyless Panchayat system (Whelpton, 2005; Hutt, 1993; Adams, 1998). In 1996, the Communist Party of Nepal (CPN) (Maoist) declared People's War against the state that ended in 2006. For more on the conflict and the transitional period see Thapa and Sijapati, 2003; Hutt, 2004; Thapa, 2003; Dixit and Ramachandaran, 2002; Karki and Bhattarai, 2003; Centre for Investigative Journalism, 2004: Seddon and Karki, 2003: Lawoti and Pahadi, 2010; Hachhethu and Gellner, 2010; Adhikari, 2014; Jha, 2014.

3   Pettigrew (2013) explains how silence became a survival strategy for villagers living in conflict ridden areas during the People's War. When having to share information in public, they would use coded language for fear of spies.

4   The Panchayat system was intended to be a form of 'guided democracy' as Mahendra believed the country was not ready for a multi-party system. The base consisted of over 3,000 villages, electing a village/town executive council or panchayat. Each would elect a district representative. The district assembly would elect a district panchayat. District panchayats would form a zonal assembly from which the members of the Rastriya (national) Panchayat were elected (for more information see Hoftun, Raeper and Whelpton, 1999, 76–78). The aim was to grant some kind of popular representation while at the same time ensuring that executive power remained in the hands of the king (Ibid.).

5   During the years of Panchayat democracy, the Nepali term corresponding to the European word 'public' was *sarkari*, indicating 'something pertaining to the state' (Burghart, 1996, 302). In Chapters 3 and 4, I will discuss possibilities/limitations presented by theatre in opening up conflicts due to its public nature and the fear of an unregulated public associated with it.

6   Even in the 1979–80 open protests would take up a performative turn, i.e., the street poetry revolution (Hutt, 1993).

7   The five (later six) social classes recognized and financially supported by the Panchayat system were women, peasants, workers, students and ex-servicemen (Burghart, 1996, 304).

8   Drawing from Aristotelian distinction between the *oikos* (the private realm of the household) from the *polis* (the public realm of the political community).

9   See Chapter 4, sections related to the royal speeches during April Movement 2006 and the gap between the international community's enthusiasm due to its inability to grasp the real meaning of the King's words as against the population's and activists' disappointment.

10 As with the teachers' token protests described by Burghart (1996, 312).

11 He also founded *Gorkhapatra*, the first daily newspaper.

12 Praja Parishad was an underground anti-Rana and pro-democracy political party established in Kathmandu in 1935.

13 The main junctions in the old part of Kathmandu.

14 Another martyr from the Praja Parishad.

15 More on Rimal in Hutt, 1991.

16 Interviewed in November 2006.

17   For how the state used music and the radio for its nationalist project see Grandin (2005, 2011) and Stirr (2012).

18   Political parties that decided not to stay underground like the Congress, could meet and debate but 'under the pretence that they were not actually political parties' (Whelpton, 2005, 111).

19   40 years later personal communication at local level still has a crucial importance in Nepal. Sudhindra Sharma and Pawan Kumar Sen (Interdisciplinary Analysts or IDA) carried out an opinion poll between December 2006 and January 2007, sampled across regional and caste/ethnicity, gender, religion, and age differences, 'to document the level of knowledge among the people at large on the processes and contents of constituent assembly.' Here are the answers to the question 'Where do you get useful information about elections?' 38 per cent media, 22 per cent local party cadres, 18 per cent local informed individuals, 10 per cent family members, 7 per cent don't know/cannot say, and 4 per cent election commission (www.nepalresearch.con visited on 8 May 2007).

20   Gorkha Parishad and Nepali Congress were reported to have 800,000 (in 1953) and 600,000 (in 1956) activists respectively out of a population of 9 million (Ibid.). The Communist Party, instead, was estimated as having about 5,000 members in the 50s. Both the Congress and the Communist parties, however, had effective nationwide networks through both political activism and student unions. Whelpton deems the figures inflated and while he considers Gorkha Parishad's figure 'merely fanciful', the Congress' was the result of a recruiting policy allowing anybody to remain member after paying NR 1 once. The Communist party worked through a cadre system whose membership was based on strict selection (Hoftun, Reaper and Whelpton, 1999, 58). However, there were many sympathizers belonging to associated fronts and bodies that played an important role while the party was underground. One of the most important associations, the Akhil Nepal Kisan Sangh (All Nepal Peasants' Union) claimed 143,000 members in 1954 (Gupta in Ibid.)

21   See Grandin (2005) for how Parents' Day programmes could becomes spaces for cultural activism.

22   Saraswati is the goddess of arts and learning.

23   For example the Tharu's stick dance (*lathi nach*) performed in the lodges of Chitwan or the Gathu dance in the Lakeside of Pokhara's hotels.

24   During the period of my fieldwork many actors would define themselves as 'theatre workers' rather than theatre artists.

25   Hutt (1997, 18) points out that while the poems Shrestha wrote in the 1940s were clearly political, his later production was also seen in political terms. For example, his most famous poem 'Mero pyaro Okhaldhunga' (My beloved Okhaldunga) nostalgically describes the life of a child in East Nepal praising the village life. Hutt remarks that '[i]nevitably, it came to be regarded as a political statement, although it could equally be argued that it means no more than what it says' (Ibid.).

26   A group of student activists from Trichanda College in Kathmandu started a revolution modeled on the Naxalite line of 'elimination of class enemies' and executed some landowners in Jhapa district (South East Nepal). The group included Radha Krishna, Chandra Prakash Mainali, Mohan Chandra Adhikari and Khadga Prasad Oli (Hoftun, Raeper and Whelpton, 1999, 83–84). Some group members were arrested and shot 'while attempting to escape' (Ibid. 84).

27 'Rise, rise from the village' (*Gaungaunbata Utha*) sang by Ramesh and Rayan has become an icon of people's power, more in Chapter 3.

28 *Bijay* means 'victory' and *Bisfot* means 'blast' – a revolutionary pseudonym still used by this artist in his daily life.

29 Interviewed in September 2005.

30 Typical Nepali drum used in folk music.

31 This power imbalance between artists coming from urban areas going to 'educate' rural audiences through cultural work is reproduced in many plays for development projects.

32 For political party rhetoric in the 1991 campaign see Hoftun, Raeper and Whelpton (1999, 176–78).

33 Describing the work of the Kirtipur circle of cultural activists, Grandin (2017) explains that the basic stance that summed up their activities was *janapakshya*, 'on the side of the people'. See Grandin (2017) for more on how the activists form connections and mobilize and on how Rayan developed the work of Indreni Samskritik Samaj (ISAS) in Kirtipur.

34 Interviewed in October 2006.

35 Theatre workers felt they had to embrace literature and foreign playwrights to gain prestige (see Chapter 1).

36 For background info on CPN and its splinter groups in late 1960s see Seddon and Karki (2003).

37 Interviewed in November 2006.

38 Interviewed in October 2006.

39 Interviewed in November 2006.

40 The Panchayat state also made strenuous efforts to co-opt artists, with considerable success, and much of the literature it sponsored was also revolutionary in tone, though this was aimed against common enemies such as illiteracy and poverty. The Royal Nepal Academy is the prime example. Poets such as Rimal and Manjul took part and even won prizes in its annual competitions (Hutt, personal communication).

41 The same criteria are used to differentiate 'NGO theatre' from theatre for social change. See Chapter 3.

42 In the next chapter, I will explain how political critique was brought up through Deusi programmes in 2005.

43 The Gaine's, as well as ethnic communities' music, can be very political.

44 The two Congress activists were hung in February 1979 (the death sentence was passed in 1977). They had been captured in 1974: one was 'the leader of a group of armed infiltrators' arrested in Okaldhunga while the other had been involved in an attempt to assassinate the king (Hoftun, Raeper and Whelpton, 1999, 87). In April of the same year, students demonstrated in front of the Pakistani Embassy to protest against the hanging of former president Zulfikar Ali Bhutto with the activists' hanging in mind. Students clashed with the police and the incident triggered off other strikes (Ibid., 88). Tribhuvan University was closed and police entered a student hostel in Amrit Science Campus and violently beat students. Student complaints, general dissatisfaction, and protests in other districts led King

Birendra to consider the students' requests. Further disturbances led the King to announce a referendum to choose between the Panchayat System and multi-party system in May 1979 (Ibid., 89).

45   Ashesh Malla had written his first drama in 2063 BS [1975-76], 'The Village Covered by Fog' (*Tuwalole Dhakeko Basti*). The play was performed in Dhankuta for a week and then travelled in different districts in the East (Dharan, Biratnagar, Janakpur and Birganj) before being performed at the Academy in Kathmandu for a month. Ashesh Malla said that while other actors returned to Dhankuta, he remained in Kathmandu and started a Master of Arts (MA) at Tribhuvan University (TU) in Kirtipur.

46   Interviewed in November 2006.

47   Performing in theatre was not considered as a good activity for women (Chapter 5). Ashesh Malla explains that in most of his early plays there were no women roles because of scarcity of female actors (Interview, November 2006).

48   Spring was a metaphor for democracy.

49   The *sutradhar* is a facilitator, connecting the actors to the audience and vice versa, or commenting like a chorus the unfolding of events. Many street plays present the role of the facilitator who gives explanations or question the audience.

50   Interviewed in November 2006.

51   Poets had travelled outside of the capital to encourage their peers also in the *Sadak Kavita Kranti* (Street Poetry Revolution) of 1979 (Hutt, 1993). It will be a recurrent modality; see Chapter 3.

52   Interviewed in November 2006.

53   More on Aarohan Theatre Group development as an organization in Chapter 7.

54   The Zonal Administration Office – Zonal Commissioner (*anchaladhish*) was part of the Panchayat structure and was dismissed after 1990.

55   Interviewed in March 2005.

56   The Spanish radical popular theatre group Els Joglars practiced mime to convey its political critique to Franco's regime. The security forces did not know how to handle it as this form of theatre was new in Spain (van Erven, 1988,159).

57   Ibid.

58   In British India, censorship was instead often overcome through a recuperation of historical and mythological themes perceived by the censors as less controversial (Bhatia, 2004). Even Ashesh Malla wrote many plays based on mythological stories, like the *Mahabharata*.

59   Ibid.

60   Interviewed in November 2007.

61   English translation of the original play titled 'Morts sans Sepulture' (1946).

62   Some of them did believe in it, or chose to pretend to believe in it for personal gain (Hutt, personal communication).

63   Urban centres and the Tarai area voted for multi-party system while the rural hilly regions supported the Panchayat (Hutt, Ibid.).

64 Interviewed in November 2006.

65 An organic intellectual in Gramsci's terms (2005).

66 After 1990 stage theatre entered a period of crisis – poets felt a similar experience, see Hutt 1993:95 – some street theatre became 'NGO theatre', cultural workers turned to political propaganda. Once the filters of the Panchayat system were removed, art went through a process of polarization. The symbols left space to outspoken language (Chapter 4).

67 Interviewed in November 2007.

3

The Streets Become the Stage

Performance, protest and theatre in a time of political crisis[1]

> Performance as an artistic 'genre' is in a constant state of crisis, and is
> therefore an ideal medium for articulating a time of permanent crisis
> such as ours.
>
> (Guillelmo Gomez-Pena cited in Delgado and Svich, 2002, 2)

Theatre all over the world seems indissolubly tied to crisis (Delgado and Svich, 2002). Sometimes it is perceived as conventional, repetitive, and marginal yet it is often thriving and dynamic in critical times (Brook, 1968; Klaic, 2002; Obeyesekere, 1999; Van Erven, 1988, 1992). Carmody asserts that

> dramatic crisis has become one of the fundamental structures of our
> [theatre people's] imaginations, one of the intellectual and emotional
> technologies that allow us to perceive and act on reality', and claims
> that 'to move beyond crisis is to move outside history, to exit from the
> stage' (2002, 24).

But conflict is also the essence of theatre. One of the reasons often given by my research participants for a play being bad was that 'there is no conflict'. 'Where there is conflict there is something to show, there is something to say' explains Rajkumar,[2] 'and if there is something to say, that place is theatre'. Theatre and crisis relate in multi-faceted ways, in particular in the streets. And the streets have a distinctive connotation in Nepal. Subedi explains that 'Nepali dramaturgy developed out of street', as '[s]treet represented a space where both men and god walked together' (2006, 45). The streets hosted festivals and dance dramas were humans personified divine characters; also, it is in the streets that 'gods travelled in palanquins', kings journeyed on chariots, the first cars looked like 'alien machines' to people, or dictators projected their power[3] (Ibid.), as we will see.

Table 3.1: From metaphor to representation. Although these different modes often overlap and co-exist they are presented here in a linear way for analytical purposes.

1	2	3	4	5
Theatre language used as metaphor for life and political life	Theatricality of politics: the 'theatre state',	Theatricality of politics: Theatrical/ Performative devices used by demonstrators during street protests, direct action[4]	Political struggle represented and enacted in the streets through theatre	Political struggle represented on stage through theatre

Source: Created by the author from this book's material.

First, theatre language is often employed metaphorically to convey paradoxical or intense moments of social life (Turner, 1974, 23).[5] Inconsistencies in political life are often described as 'theatre of the absurd'. Nepal's civil war – like all wars – was depicted as a 'tragedy'. Many journalists labeled the municipal elections that King Gyanendra ordered in February 2006 a 'farce' because in a conflictual environment no free and fair election could take place, despite the claims of royal propaganda.

Secondly, ruling élites use rituals like processions, official ceremonies, formalities, images and stories to give their actions an aura of charisma and link them with the symbols and values that a particular society considers sacred (Geertz, 1988; Cannadine and Price, 1992; Kertzer, 1988). Geertz remarks that 'the gravity of high politics and the solemnity of high religious cults originate from similar impulses' (Ibid., 155–56). The connection between the governing élites and the system of symbolic forms that express, justify and legitimize their existence and actions is described by Geertz as 'theatre state' (Ibid., 157). According to Geertz,[6] kingship is constructed through symbolic domination. For example, chiefs are turned into '*rajahs*' by the aesthetics of their role (Ibid.). While pluralistic systems allow for competitive rituals and public performances, one-party states depend on the monopoly of all political performance to maintain their power, and are strongly dependent on such public rites (Geertz, Ibid.).[7] In the first chapter I described how the Shah political power was reinforced through rituals and performance. King Gyanendra used slogans, radio advertisements, billboards and parades to display his power, especially after 1 February 2005.

Thirdly, sometimes dramatic social or political events colour the streets with highly aestheticized and ritualistic performative protests, actions and parades, outdoing both the theatrical metaphor and organized forms of streets drama

(Tilly, 2008; Wasserstrom, 1991; Cohen-Cruz, 1998; Kertzer, 1988). In 2006, pro-democracy and anti-monarchy movements employed songs, props, slogans, pictures and rituals to contrast and symbolically demolish the representations of the king's regime. The theatricality of state power was resisted and contested theatrically by the people's movement for democracy. Political struggle was not only fought in the streets through physical and often violent means. It was also a struggle over meanings and symbols, an ideological struggle that became more subtle but also more powerful because of the repressive system. Street protests fed theatre artists images, ideas and everyday life situations. Theatrical performances developed them up and distorted their reflection spurring street audiences to contemplate different perspectives and 'act' in real life.

Fourthly, theatre can enter the streets with political intentions. Political theatre, in fact, has been widely used around the world during protests with a subversive and critical function to challenge authoritarian regimes (van Erven, 1988, 64; Bell, 1999, 271). During pro-democracy meetings that preceded, accompanied and followed Jana Andolan 2006, a group of artists called Loktantrik Shrastaharuko Samuha (Democratic Writers' Association) organized various cultural programmes with music and poems in different parts of Nepal and many of them were arrested. Several theatre groups performed during the mass meetings organized by the Citizen's Movement for Democracy and Peace, and CPN (Maoist) widely employed theatre and cultural performance for mobilization.

Finally, during a period of conflict, theatre artists engage with reality by portraying the crisis on the stage. Nepali theatre artists have produced different plays tackling the war between the Maoists and the state, in particular towards the end of the conflict. 'Who is Declaring War Again?' (Ko Gardaicha Pheri Yuddha ko Ghosana) and 'Death Festival' (Mrityu Utsav) written and directed by Ashesh Malla in 2001 and 2003 respectively,[8] 'Fire in the Monastery' (Agniko Katha) and 'Journey into Thamel' (Thamelko Yaatraa), both written by Abhi Subedi in 2003 and produced in 2004, 'Khuma',[9] directed by Anup Baral (2004), 'Bari Lai Lai'[10] directed by Birendra Hamal (2005), 'Dreams of Mayadevi' (Mayadevika Sapana) written by Abhi Subedi and directed by Nisha and Sunil Pokharel (2006) are some examples. Artists did not always feel safe to engage with the conflict publicly. Despite not being fond of political theatre, Anup Baral felt that the 'bitter times' his country was facing could not be ignored. 'Khuma' ran for 15 days in Kathmandu. The director was threatened from both sides: the Maoists did not like being portrayed as criminals whilst state representatives invited him to avoid staging similar issues in the future. However, the civil war has since become a recurrent theme. It was present in different forms in several productions, especially in 2007, such as Nyayapremi (Nepali adaptation of 'Les Justes', by Camus) directed by Sunil Pokharel and 'Talak Jung vs. Tulke' (an adaptation from Lu Xun's 'True Story of AH-Q') directed by Anup Baral.

During my fieldwork, I often thought that I went to Nepal to research theatre and, in one way or another, it seemed to always end in politics. It is now time to explore this connection further. Theatre language as a metaphor for political struggle (no. 1) and theatrical performance as a stage representation of political struggle (no. 5) will not be analysed in this chapter. Rather, I will focus instead on the three middle components of the table above.

The performance of autocracy

> Beloved countrymen, The Kingdom of Nepal was built on the foundations of the unification process initiated by King Prithvi Narayan Shah the Great. It is well known that to reign in accordance with the people's aspirations, our fore fathers initiated revolutionary measures of historic importance, ensuring a bright future of the nation and her people. History is witness to the fact that both the Nepalese people and the King have, in unison, played decisive roles in each and every period of the Kingdom's process of unification, democratization and modernization.
>
> (From His Majesty King Gyanendra Bir Bikram Shah Dev's proclamation to the nation, 1 February 2005)

Until May 2008, Nepal was the only Hindu kingdom in the world. However, the way in which religion and culture supported the Himalayan monarchy changed remarkably over the centuries. In the past, various religious rituals, festivals and cultural practices such as Indra Jatra celebrated and legitimized the king's political power (Burghart, 1987; Krauskopff and Lecomte-Tilouine, 1996; Chapter 1) ; but by the 1980s, the king had lost his religious and divine authority. Burghart (1987, 269) comments that 'the ritual symbolism of the auspicious body of the king and the identity of king and realm still persist in native belief, but have lost their power to influence the believers. The pomp goes on, but there was a time when the pomp was also powerful'. According to Burghart, despite retaining a 'lordly' halo the ritual forms of political practice had lost their meaning and what emerged was 'the counterfeit reality' that I discussed in Chapter 2. In addition, Lakier remarks that while losing his ritual power, the king gained a 'nationalist stature that carried its own quasi-religious grandeur' (2005, 149). In other words, religious rhetoric that legitimized the king's rule had progressively been replaced by nationalist rhetoric channeled via similar practices. The pomp was still effective. Ritual transformed for new purposes (see Krauskopff and Lecomte-Tilouine, 1996; Toffin, 2010).

The objective of this chapter is twofold. First, by focusing on the performative[11] side of the 2005 royal coup I intend to highlight the way in which the state built up a theatrical apparatus, the 'illusion' of its power. Through this, I do not, by any means assume that the core of the king's rule was performance; rather, I intend to provide a close-up on the performative aspects of autocracy to understand another facet of how power was exercised. The section will show how the king resurrected the spirit and practices of the Panchayat period and used the same rhetoric to legitimize his rule (Borgstrom, 1980, 1982; Chapter 2). Second, I will explore the performative side of the 2006 popular movement as a way of understanding how performance supports – not replaces – political struggle. The first part of this chapter will describe how ideological domination took spatial form, how the king constructed the set to 'direct' the show of his power in Kathmandu, and how, by creating a special physical space through rallies, billboards, public processions and ceremonies, he rhetorically echoed powerful tropes of the Panchayat time such as the ideas of national and social unity, development and public order. Even state occasions were co-opted in favour of the monarchy. Controlling both the public space and people's imagination seemed to be one of the king's priorities. In fact, success in governing – as well as in fields such as managing development projects – depends on the control of interpretations (Mosse, 2005a, 8).

Silencing

Nepal was informed of the king's take-over of state power through an address to the nation aired on TV and radio on 1 February 2005, and printed in the newspapers the following day. By removing the rights to freedom of information, movement and gathering (Chapter 2), King Gyanendra's take over precluded the possibility of dissent and created a *tabula rasa*, a clear space upon which to show and exercise absolute domination. His version of reality excluded all other versions (Lukes, 2005, 7). In fact, the 1990 Constitution guaranteed freedom of expression to Nepali media which since then had grown massively (Onta, 2002; Bhattarai, 2005; Hutt, 2006). The space opened for public debate by the advent of democracy in 1990 was thus totally closed. No demonstration of dissent was allowed in the streets. Although some theatre groups managed to perform, street performances were banned (see next section). The citizens had no choice but to become mute spectators of the king's 'show'.

From 1 February 2005, censorship was overt.[12] The Army entered television and newspaper headquarters and stayed for a week to monitor and censor the news from the editorial offices.[13] By physically occupying the space, the security forces controlled the nation's access to information. A government edict, printed in the state run newspaper *Gorkhapatra* on 4 February 2005, stated that any form of media publishing reports, which criticized 'the spirit of the royal proclamation' or supported the 'terrorists' would be condemned.[14] In a Ministry of Information and Communication (MOIC) notice following the 1 February directives, the royal government announced that all radio stations were obliged to broadcast only 'purely entertainment programmes' and not 'any news, information, write-ups, opinions and expressions'.[15] It also warned of penalties against the violators of the notice.[16] The line beyond which items were considered news and current affairs programming became blurred and very subjective. Security forces were sensitive even about the kind of music that was broadcast. Nepali folk songs on social issues were usually banned, on the grounds that 'patriotic' songs would raise the Maoist morale (*Nepali Times* #238). A journalist reported that his 'station used to play Nepali and foreign (Hindi) songs in an approximately 80:20 ratio. After the restrictions, the proportion changed in favour of foreign, mainly Hindi, music.'[17] Responsibility for distinguishing what was 'news' and what was 'entertainment' was manipulated and used in instrumental ways. One broadcaster complained that he was not allowed to talk, 'even if it was on ways to grow cauliflowers or getting rid of pests in the field' (*Nepali Times*, ibid). An example of the defence of official narratives and the negation of events is worth mentioning. In July 2005, the Information Minister told the British Broadcasting Corporation (BBC) that FM radio stations all over the world only broadcast music, not news (*Nepali Times* #258). In the meantime, state television and radio aired songs and music identified with the Panchayat period (Shah, 2008, 14).

But King Gyanendra's speeches to the nation are probably the most striking examples of one-way, top-down communication. The king strongly adhered to his 'version' of reality in which he had absolute power and control of his country up to the very climax of the People's Movement in April 2006. In the speech to the nation delivered on 1 February 2006, the anniversary of his assumption of power, the king justified his action despite the previous month's heavy street contestations and held administrative elections ignoring the opposition carried out by the main political parties. In the middle of general strikes and street repression, on 14 April 2006, King Gyanendra talked to the nation. It was the beginning of the Nepali New Year. He called on all political parties to enter a dialogue so that multi-party democracy could be initiated. He didn't mention the massive opposition he was facing or people's demands. Pressed by the international community and in danger of losing his throne, the king delivered another speech on 21 April. While returning 'executive power' to the people and asking SPA (Seven Party Alliance) to name a prime minister, he once again ignored the core reasons of the protest, as well as the demonstrations themselves.

In was only in his last speech, on 24 April that King Gyanendra restored the parliament that he had sacked in 2002. He publicly expressed his condolences 'to those who lost their lives in the People's Movement'. For the first time the king acknowledged the existence of an opposition to his government. By doing so, he released part of his 'royal power' as he had to listen, and then admit the lack of unity within the body politic. This point is particularly important. According to the Hindu conception of an organic universe, the king is ritually at the highest rank in the terrestrial realm (Burghart, 1987; see Chapter 2). As the mind, he governs and takes care of the rest of the body's organs (Ibid.). As Burghart points out, in hierarchical societies equality is not given, 'only the mind is invested with intentionality, and hence with desires, purpose, and authoritative speech' (1996, 304). The king exercised his power by ignoring 'unwanted' bits of reality. By listening, the king had to acknowledge the people's agency in dissenting, and that their desires and intentionality differed from his. The meaning of the Emergency 2005 may be taken beyond the practical and obvious readings. By silencing a whole country through censorship and the curtailment of liberties, the king removed the possibility of agency beyond his own and reinstated the hierarchical principles that governed the body politic of the Panchayat system where he was the all-encompassing divine lord.

The Shah 'theatre state'

Having cleared the space of any possible expression of dissent, the royal government set off to construct and disseminate a narrative centred on the role of king, on his benevolence and on his historical affection for his country. Soon after 1 February rhythmical slogans echoed on the hill of Gurukul. People walking towards Maiti Devi Chowk chanted *Hamro Raja Hamro Desh, Pran Bhanda Pyaro chha* (Our King, Our Country, Dearer Than Our Lives). An artist explained that these were old slogans from the Panchayat period. Despite the ban on public gatherings, during the days immediately after the declaration of the Emergency, small carousels of people holding Nepali flags and singing pro-monarchy slogans could be seen walking around Kathmandu to 'show' that the king, backed by his people, was in control of the country. The process of 'creating' state power had started. Participating in processions, travelling around the country, taking part in parties or public ceremonies were ways by which the king tried to reaffirm his power.

It was usual practice for both royalists and other parties in Nepal to go to the villages around Kathmandu Valley and 'collect' people and transport them to the capital to support demonstrations. Sometimes they received a few rupees in exchange, sometimes only tea and biscuits. Propaganda and counter-propaganda struggles had a long history. For example, in January 1990, the Nepali Congress called people to join a movement against the Panchayat system that was due to start on 18 February (Hachhethu, 1990, 178). His Majesty Government (HMG) organized a counter-propaganda war, arranging *pancha* rallies in different parts of the country (Ibid.). The multi-party system was defamed as an 'alien' idea, and popular demonstrations were labeled 'as anti-social, anti-national, anti-constitutional and destructive/subversive/hooliganism' (Ibid.).

The royal government also made use of 'props' to create a benign monarchical environment. The main junctions of Kathmandu were decorated with huge hand-painted metal billboards[18] publicly declaring the king's commitment towards the welfare of his country. They were signed by HMG's Department of Information and used quotations from members of the royal family or national poets as if to find in history the legitimization for his action. All of them were sealed with an oval containing an emblem of either the royal crown or the flag of Nepal.

Figure 3.1: One of the king's hoardings

Through the billboards, the king revealed the different shades of his 'lordship' (Fig. 3.1, photo by the author). For example, his role as benevolent monarch, the 'all providing universal man' (Burghart, 1987, 242–43) who fulfills his sacred duty of providing for the welfare of his subjects, is expressed in the following:

we have no interest other than restoration of sustainable peace and
the exercise of meaningful democracy
(Opposite the west entrance to the Royal Palace along Kantipath)

> if violence is done against the country and the citizens, the citizens
> will not tolerate it and the rules will not allow it
>
> (Ratna Park Junction, towards Bagbazar)

In the second slogan the king claims not only his monopoly in the use of force, but also the state 'monopoly on public service' (Burghart, 1996, 303; 1993, 8). Other billboards denounced selfishness and corruption:

> to fulfill the personal or party selfishness is not only a crime but also
> a great sin
>
> (Exhibition Road Junction)

Targetting 'personal or party selfishness' clearly aimed at reinstating the king as the paladin of the public good. During the Panchayat time the public domain was represented by the king and his will was to represent the common good of the indivisible body politic (Burghart, 1996, 303). The political parties were identified with the private sphere and characterized by the self-interest of the leaders or the collective self-interest of their followers (Ibid.). The privileged connection between the Shah family and Nepali people, used also as a justification for the state of emergency, reappears and another relic of the Panchayat rhetoric, 'development', emerges as a priority in the king's agenda. Most of these banners were in Nepali language:

> the Nepali king's crown is for the citizens, the Nepali citizens are for the
> king's crown, the king and the citizens are both for Nepal and Nepali
>
> (Thamel Junction)

> unity, honesty and country development is and should be our only
> target
>
> (Thamel Chowk)

A few, along tourist routes (Thamel Junction, near the Royal Palace and in New Baneshwor Junction, near Birendra International Conference Hall, as well as in airport area), were written in English and dealt with the monarchy's dedication to peace, multi-party democracy and human rights. The billboards seemed to be a display of power for the consumption of the urban literate middle class and probably had the function of publicly reassuring the king and justifying the role of the monarchy.[19] However, many of the people I talked to did not give much importance to these messages and were actually surprised about my interest. In some places the royal banners hung alone. Placed among other commercial ads of beer, food and urban commodities, others were perfectly mingled with the urban landscape.

State occasions such as Democracy Day on 18 February 2005 or Unity Day, celebrated on 17 January 2006, were co-opted by the royal government to publicly link the interests of the king to those of the country and its citizens. Similarly, the birthdays of the royal family were publicly celebrated through an ample display of banners, billboards, and images.[20] For example, for Prince Paras' birthday, in December 2005, dancers from different ethnic groups wearing traditional costumes opened the celebratory parade heading towards Durbar Marg. At the back, a billboard with the image of the prince was carried on a wagon. It was placed at the end of Durbar Marg, blessed with flower garlands and a lamp. Paradoxically, the small posters which hung around the chok as if on a clothes line reminded me of the ads that adorn many tiny bazaar shops in the outskirts of the capital. The amalgam of political power and religious symbolism conveyed through a traditional and commercial-like manner created an uncomfortable juxtaposition. The parade took place in almost empty roads. The traffic was blocked and indifferent passers-by would stop for a few minutes, and then walk away.

Private business people and religious institutions publicly displayed their loyalty to the royal family. Birthday posters showing wishes for the prince were pasted all over the city, on walls lining the roads, on light poles, on construction sites, and over the posters of the Nepali hit film of the moment, 'You are Mine' (*Timi Meri Hau*). One of them read (Fig. 3.2, photo by the author):

Figure 3.2: Pamphlets celebrating the prince's birthday are stuck over commercial movie posters

On the eve of His Royal Highness Crown Prince Paras Bikram Bir Shah Dev's auspicious birthday, the holy establishment of Tirupati

Balaji Temple in Nepal Prays for the glory of the Royal Family of
Nepal, the welfare of the Nepalese society, eternal peace, good
governance, Constitutional Monarchy and multiparty democracy.[21]

Thamel Tourism Development Board took advantage of the situation and placed
the birthday wishes for the prince and New Year wishes in the same plastic gate –
sponsored by Pepsi – placed at the entrance of the tourist area reading:

We extend our best wishes for Long Life of our beloved Crown
Prince on the occasion of his Royal Highness 35th Birth Day' and
'May peace prevail from the beginning of the Happy New Year 2006'
[in English and Nepali].

The discourse the king's government conveyed was that the monarchy was the
benevolent and the god-like protector of all the people of Nepal.[22] What could be
seen displayed on the Kathmandu walls seemed to be a superficial, public lip service
paid to the king. The popular movement that led to the April 2006 Jana Andolan
showed that there was no strong support for the monarchy.

11 January marked the birthday of King Prithvi Narayan Shah, the founding father
of modern Nepal and ancestor of the Shah dynasty. It used to be celebrated as Unity
Day.[23] In January 2006, the weeklong celebrations culminated in a cultural programme
at what was the Royal Nepal Academy. The rhetoric of the national state was fully at
work. A big picture – about 3x2 metres – of a triumphant Prithvi Narayan honoured
with a *mala* of colourful flowers was standing on the right side of the stage. Nearby, the
photos of King Gyanendra and his wife were similarly worshipped with flowers and
a camphor flame. Representatives of the government and the chair of the Academy
opened the programme, which presented the classical drama *Kiratarjuniya*, written by
Vatsraj Amatya and directed by Shakuntala Sharma, as well as national songs performed
by senior artists. The drama was introduced in the leaflet as a story evoking feelings
of good governance, union, and protection through religion. The event culminated
with an actor impersonating the king entering the stage among swirling dancers. After
reaching the front of the stage, the king delivered a speech. In the background, men
and women dressed with traditional ethnic costumes climbed the platform, waving
Nepali flags. The scene ended in a still picture of national diversity, unity and glory.[24]
The government cancelled Unity Day in 2007, in the same way as it had cancelled the
public celebration of royal birthdays in the previous months; a group of demonstrators
damaged the statue of Prithvi Narayan in front of Singh Durbar. The representation
of Nepal's unity performed at the Academy in 2006 had already disappeared. The
country was going through a reassessment of past symbols. References to the royal
past were gradually being removed from the institutions and their productions. Even
the performative illusion of national unity within diversity thus had a short life.

Silencing the nation was part of the king's role as lord. The rest of his role was conveyed through slogans, rallies, billboards, ceremonies, and tours around the country. The messages aimed at fully restoring the Hindu lordship through a nationalist rhetoric that recalled the Panchayat time. However, was the pomp enough to bring back power? Burghart suggested this disjuncture between form and content was already evident in the 1980s. And in fact, in 2005 opposition grew very quickly, first in the private space, and then in the public, as we shall see in the next sections.

The performance of dissent

Despite repression preventing an open challenge to the royal regime, information circulated underground through non-official and non-traditional channels. In the months that followed the 1 February coup, blogs linked with providers outside Nepal spread widely (Sharrock, 2007). Some websites were blocked, discussion forums were closed, and emails were said to be under surveillance. Although in July 2005 27 websites were banned, most of them continued to upload news received via email from activists in loco through proxy web services.[25] The cyberspace – in the private realm – emerged as an alternative 'public space' to counter the ban on both the physical and the symbolic space.

Similarly, a looser form of self-censorship marked the boundary between what could be 'read' or 'watched', and what could not. An example from my personal experience may be useful to shed light on how personal trust could allow for the trespassing of these boundaries. Manjushree Thapa's 'Forget Kathmandu. An Elegy for Democracy' (2005), a book about Nepali history, quite popular in Nepal before the Emergency, was 'banned'[26] after the king's coup. A few weeks later, I was glancing through books about Nepal in a big bookstore. The bookseller knew me. Before paying, he proudly picked up the book for me. It was hidden in a newspaper wrapping under a huge pile of other books. The same day I told a person who was looking for the same book where to find it. When he went to the bookshop, the seller told him he did not have any copies.

Political parties in the government had been agitating since October 2002, after the king dismissed Deuba's government on charges of incompetence and appointed a new cabinet composed of old loyalists (Shah, 2008, 13; Adhikari, 2014). Because of internal differences, power politics and corruption, political parties had lost credibility and had not been able to attract support from the citizens, even when they joined the SPA[27] soon after the royal take-over. Before 2005, both the political parties and the king were, with shifting positions, trying to fight the Maoist movement. Some sections of the population hoped that the king could tackle the national crisis and lead the country out of the standstill. However, as months passed, it became clear that the royal government was stumbling: security had not improved, the Maoists were perceived as expanding as a military and a political organization, the government seemed to focus on secondary issues such as corruption control, civil service reform and school textbook redesign (Shah, 2008, 14). Ultimately, the attempt to hold municipal elections in February 2006 while the country was enmeshed in a civil war questioned the royal government's legitimacy and competence. As months passed, the political scenario changed: in September 2005 the Maoist announced a three month unilateral ceasefire and in a major political shift, on 22 November 2005, SPA signed a 12-point accord with the Maoists in New Delhi to end what they called 'autocratic monarchy' and elect a Constituent Assembly. Burying their profound differences, the political parties' agenda converged with the Maoists' against the common enemy: the king.

During the summer of 2005, a civil society group[28] organized around Devendra Raj Panday[29] including journalists, academics, lawyers, writers and other professionals, unified as the Citizens' Movement for Democracy and Peace/CMDP (*Shanti ra Loktantrakalagi Nagarik Andolan*) started organizing public meetings (*dharna, janasabha*) in different areas of the capital.[30] Heralding a radical agenda, they encouraged people to resist state repression and to demand the restoration of democracy and peace in the country (Heaton Shrestha and Adhikari, 2010; Gautam, 2007; Dahal, 2001; Bhatta, 2007; Shah, 2008). Defining civil society is difficult because of the different forms and functions it can take cross-culturally. The term is particularly fuzzy as it incorporates 'flexible portfolios of development, welfare services, advocacy, and political activism' (Shah, 2008, 2). Shah explains how Nepali civil society, unlike its European counterpart, is not separate from the political realm but 'intrinsically linked to the political process and its contestation over power and resources' (Ibid.). Including professionals,[31] because of their 'high concentration of wealth, scientific knowledge and social capital', civil society in Nepal accrues a great deals of symbolic power which 'accords a relatively small, self-selected group the ability to enjoy a disproportionate voice in setting the tone and tenor of public discourse' (Shah, 2008, 11). This claim to knowledge becomes indirectly a claim to power as unlike political parties fighting for power and factional interests, civil society portrays itself as selfless and impartial, 'motivated solely by enlightened collective good' (Shah, 2008, 12), and composed of 'enlightened people' (Hachhethu cited in Heaton Shrestha and Adhikari, 2010). Bracketing distinctions of class, caste, race, gender, and ideology, civil society emerged as a 'rational, nonpartisan, and universal authority with privileged access to the public domain' (Shah, 2008, 12). Scholars point out that, civil society in Nepal is essentially elitist and exclusive, 'dominated by high caste middle class professionals based in the capital' (Heaton Shrestha and Adhikari, 2010; Shah, 2008, 35).[32] The CMDP constructed itself as morally powerful by defining itself as guarantor of 'purity' in contrast to 'dirty politics' or 'NGO business' (Heaton Shrestha and Adhikari, 2010, 306) and created and sustained public mass meetings as an 'apolitical space' (Ibid.). Apoliticality allowed the movement to exercise a 'softer' form of power and respond to a politically repressive environment.[33] However, CMDP public meetings followed the same format not only in Kathmandu but also in Dharan, Biratnagar, Pokhara, Narayangardh, Nepalganj, and in smaller cities (Heaton Shrestha and Adhikari, 2010) thus creating strong ideological and affective connections between the capital and the rest of the country.

In a public meeting held in Naya Baneshwor on 5 August 2005, leaders of the major political parties were invited as guests to listen to CMDP leaders' requests. The major discourse focused on the need to 'complete' the 1990 Constitution in order to avoid any possibility of the palace seizing power undemocratically. Inviting political party leaders as auditors implied the existence of different views between political parties and civil society. Because of the 'conditions of listening' (Burghart, 1993; cf. Chapter 2), politicians, as 'smaller lords', were usually able to exercise 'non-listening' as a strategy to assert their superiority. Within this context, however, the typical hierarchy was reversed, as CMDP representatives were determined to be heard. CMDP leaders spoke after symbolically silencing the political authorities, who had, de facto, been silenced by the king. For the first time after 1 February, the speakers on the stage and people in the streets did not openly talk of *prajatantra* (democracy linked to the king), but of *loktantra* (people's democracy) and of *ganatantra* (republic), words that continued to be used in the street protests.[34]

The meeting also marked the beginning of organized political mobilization and a public, collective form of resistance through mass meetings where the speeches of members of civil society were alternated by cultural programmes. A member of the CMDP who organized the programmes explained that inviting artists was a strategic move to overcome the restrictions imposed by the government on political demonstrations, to attract a wider range of participants and decrease fear.[35] He explains that unlike political parties that usually employed cultural programmes for campaigning, the CMDP increasingly used cultural events to turn the movement into a celebration. 'What we think is that people are highly aware of what they want', he adds, 'so we don't need to campaign, the *bhasan* (speech) thing. We need something else, so we can show people's strength in favour of republic and of other political demands.'[36]

Art-activists (*kalakarmiharu*) joined in big numbers and pro-democracy artistic performance flourished (Fig. 3.3, photo by the author). At the forefront

Figure 3.3: Cultural programme during a CMDP meeting in Ratna Park, August 2006

janagayak (people's singers) Ramesh Shrestha and Rayan brought back songs from the progressive tradition (Grandin, 1994; Shrestha, 2006; Ghimire, 2005). Often sang at the end of the programmes by artists and audience alike, they became symbols of the movement. But other presences recurred month after month in the public meetings, adding variety to the performances and strengthening the emotional connection among demonstrators: Nandakrishna Joshi's *deuda*,[37] Badri Pangeni's *lok dohori*[38] (Shrestha, 2006) or the pungent lyrics that Rubin Gandharva accompanied with his *sarangi* (Giri, 2005). Similarly, often referred to as *andolan kabi* (protest poet) Arjun Parajuli (Ghimire 2005) ignited the audience with his sharp critique of the political system that he updated meeting after meeting through a process of poetic documentation. Aarohan Theatre's *loktantrik natak*, as well as the performances of Sarwanam and other theatre groups, have to be understood within this organized context of shared images and language that brought together artists and professionals who belonged to the same social networks since the 1980s. Before analysing two of Aarohan Theatre's *loktantrik natak* performances, one staged in January 2006 and the second in August 2006, it is worth focusing on the repertoire of protest that characterized the April 2006 movement. In this way it will be possible to understand Aarohan Theatre Group's critique at different levels of political control as well as how the images, songs and narrative of the performances relate to the political events and street protests of the time.

Jana Andolan II contentious performances

Only in April 2006, when opposition became widespread and turned into a popular mass movement was dissent expressed in more colourful and performative ways. The SPA announced a four-day strike in the Kathmandu Valley from 6–10 April that would be prolonged to 19 days and turned into a second Jana Andolan (People's Movement) that shook the 237-year-old monarchy at its basis. A curfew was imposed on 8 April in the Kathmandu Valley to prevent the SPA from celebrating the anniversary of the successful 1990 Jana Andolan. Curfews were re-imposed on 9, 10 and 11 April but they were widely defied. In the meantime, the Maoist restated their support for the strikes and by the third day of protest, doctors, lawyers and other professionals joined in (Aryal and Poudel, 2006; Raj, 2006, 31; Adhikari, 2014; Routledge, 2010). The SPA slowly brought life to a standstill by ordering private banks to close, businesses not to pay taxes or other charges like electricity, telephone, and water (Raj, 2006, 32); government workers started to support the protest and industries owned by the royal family were boycotted (Ibid.). There were clashes and human right organizations denounced the government's excessive use of force against demonstrators. Already isolated by members of the international community, condemned by donor countries, pressed by the media and by the massive internal opposition, the king issued a public address accepting the SPA demands on 25 April. A coalition government established soon after stripped the monarchy of all its constitutional, ceremonial and customary authority. Moreover, the country was turned into a secular state.

Let us return to the street protests. Slogans, symbols, and 'props' used in street rallies became explicit both in the capital and in the rural areas. Working tools, sticks, torches, green branches, conch shells, puppets, flames and photos transformed the street into a vibrant and radical stage. The SPA organized general strikes and the CMDP planned public mass meetings. The king's state answered with a new wave of arrests – of politicians, civil society leaders, activists – and curfews. Like in the 1990 movement (FOPHUR, 1990, 123), protests were often carried out by professional groups organizing in separate venues, as if society wanted to display itself in an ordered way. The security forces repressed dissenters during the April demonstrations, every day a new category was targeted: lawyers, doctors, teachers, journalists, artists. However, the last days of the People's Movement[39] seemed to be characterized by a unity that was noticed by enthusiastic commentators:

> The up swelling of street power has given the citizens of Nepal–
> totalling 26 million and not at all a small country–a newfound unity
> and national self-confidence. For a people that has been historically
> divided by ethnicity, caste, faith and geography, the entire population

came together to fight for pluralism. This has provided the energy for reinstating a Parliament disbanded four years ago and emplacing an interim government that, having sidelined Gyanendra, is now all set to bring the Maoists in from the cold and re-engage in the task of nation-building.[40]

A *communitas* was being created. *Communitas*, as Turner suggested, describes those moments in which the audience or the participants of a theatrical event or a ritual feel themselves as part of the whole in an organic and almost spiritual way (Turner, 1982; Dolan, 2005, 11). The spectators' individuality dissolves as they become attuned to those around them. The audience is submerged in a cohesive, fleeting feeling of belonging, of affinity to the group – in this case the common enemy to unite around was the king. Bridging past and present, hopes and histories, familiarity and newness, cultural performances can create and strengthen the sense of community and belonging as suggested by Turner. Turner (1982, 48) also describes *communitas* as the experience of ritual camaraderie, when in a liminal, anti-structure state, people are freed from everyday life roles and all personal and social differences are erased – unlike in the first days when people would join the movement by professions - a moment when people are uplifted, very close to many descriptions of the April Movement.

Protests are characterized by historically and culturally specific ways of 'staging' dissent acquired through previous practice (Tilly, 2008). Like acting, protesting is a form of behaviour that is learned through observing and participating in various social activities. As in theatrical performances, the people involved improvise and innovate out of a common set of familiar 'scripts' or 'repertoire' that constitute systems of collective representations. Schechner brings into play two concepts from theatre that can also be useful to understand such protest: 'rehearsals' and 'preparations' (1993, 54). While the former sets an 'exact sequence of events', the latter makes members of a group ready to 'do something appropriate' at a given moment. In fact, demonstrators employ past successful scripts and spontaneously improvise out of a common set of experiences. Demonstrations thus become cultural laboratories in which to experiment and rehearse new ways of being and prepare for actualizing them. Protests, a heightened behaviour to increase visibility often take up the forms of performative actions in which the protestors in the street, at the climax of their protest, enact in different ways the world in which they would like to live and anticipate the movement's success.

What follows is an outline of the dramaturgy of protest that emerges from the analysis of secondary sources integrated with interviews. News websites[41] reported the slogans that were sung in the streets. Other than the common *loktantra jindabad* 'long live people's democracy', *nirankustantra murdabad, rajtantra murdabad,* 'down with autocracy and monarchy', others slogans focused on the king and his close collaborators. For example *Gyané chor, desh chhod* 'Gyané[42] thief, leave the country', 'burn the crown', 'Hang king Gyanendra', and 'Hang Thapa' which referred to the Minister of Internal Affairs who was considered responsible for the violent street repression. The prince was targeted through *Paras gunda, rukhma jhunda,* 'Hang Paras, the thug, on a tree'. Other question/response choirs invited all the Nepali citizens to join into one voice:

> *Nepali jantale ke bhanchha?* What do Nepali people say/order?
> *Ganatantra lyau bhanchha.* Let's bring in republic

Others, instead, personified Arya ghat in Pasupatinath calling the king and his son to their last rites:

> *Arya ghatle ke bhanchha?* Who does Arya ghat call?
> *Gyan Paraslai bhanchha.* It calls Gyan and Paras.
> Or
> *Ja ja Paras katro kin.* Go go Paras buy a *katro* (shroud).
> *Tero bauko ayo din.* Your [low form] father's day has come.

Others reclaimed the people's agency in governing the country

> *Shreepanch hami jalaunchaun.* We will burn the crown.
> *Desh hami chalanchhaun.* We drive our country.

Slogans also found technological ways to travel. The following SMS was being circulated throughout Nepal in reaction to the curfew: *Yadi tapaiko mutuma Nepali Ragat bageko chha bhane Swatantra Nepal ko Nirman garna Baishak 7 gate sadak ma utrunus!! thulo sworma bhannus, 'Loktantra Jindabaad'.*

> If you have Nepali blood flowing in your veins, come to the street on 20 April to establish an independent Nepal and say 'Long live people's democracy'. IF you cannot come to the street AND NOT IN KTM, just say, 'LOKTANTRA JINDABAAD', wherever you are. And, pass on....[43]

The impact of these slogans on the everyday lives of Nepali citizens is not easy to assess, but certainly continued beyond the liminal time of the protests. Travelling in west Nepal in May 2006, Amit Sengupta (2006) tells of children playing with the demonstration slogans, shouting *'Loktantric Ganatantra',* democracy, democracy, republic, republic, like a childhood chant of magical freedom'.

Under 'ordinary circumstances', the king has the authoritative role to utter declarations that can change the social world. The protestors reversed his role by temporarily and imaginatively taking up the authority to proclaim alternative forms of government.[44] Protestors declared many areas 'free zones'. For example, despite the restrictive orders imposed by the government, on 6 April demonstrators gathered in Chyasal, Patan, chased away the security forces and released the arrested leaders of political parties declaring *Chyasal mukta kshetra*, a 'liberated zone'. Similarly, Chitwan district (South Nepal) was declared a 'republic region' on 8 April.[45]

Renaming' was also employed as a means to erase the monarchical past and establish a new secular reality. 'His Majesty's Government' was replaced with 'Nepal Government' well before the declaration of the House of Representatives on 18 May 2005.[46] Groups of protestors altered the signboards of the local offices. The symbolic redesign of the landscape included also the renaming of streets and roads. For example, 'Mahendra Multiple Campus' in Gorahi, Dang District, was declared 'Republican Multiple Campus'.[47] Bhorletar Chowk, the main crossroad of Damauli, was renamed 'Republican Chowk' while 'Clean Road Chowk' became 'Democracy Chowk',[48] thus sweeping away at once both royal – as in the government offices and campuses – and developmental histories. Student organizations affiliated to the SPA changed the signboards of many campuses. The whole Shah family was the target of a symbolic historical erasure. Particularly significant spaces in the capital were renamed. Kalanki chowk, an area in the western part of the capital in which violent clashes between protestors and security forces led to the killing of some demonstrators, was renamed Loktantra chowk, 'democracy junction'.[49] One of my interlocutors told me that in everyday conversations in 2006, students still referred to a chowk inside Tribhuvan University as Loktantra chowk, as it was renamed thus during the movement. Soon after the House of Parliament declaration, employees of many government or semi-government agencies were reported as painting or printing new signs for the boards of their offices, anticipating the official restructuring.

Political slogans and renaming do not fit easily into Austin's category of 'speech act'. Both Austin and Searle used the term 'speech act' to describe performative utterances in which 'to say something is to do something'. They both distinguished 'normal real world talk' from 'parasitic forms of discourse' such as poetry, fiction, or theatre in which the words don't actualize the action. However, performance theories and practices have revealed the collapsing of differences between 'fiction' and 'real', and thus question Austin and Searle's theories on the account that they don't recognize that art can be a model for, rather than a mirror of life (Schechner, 2002,110–12). Political slogans fall into a different category from the dialogue spoken by an actor onstage. Because of a symbolic enactment of the action, the context of performance and the way in which they affect the environment, political slogans may become a model for what they 'perform', and are perceived by the opponents as a serious and real threat. As elements of the political landscape, place names express both the ideological themes of the state and the political processes that states are involved in (Yong, 2007). Place names are 'active', 'context-generating as well as context-reflecting' (Ibid.). 'Renaming' is an action, an act of creation, the exercise of agency and a claim of authority. Like singing slogans, renaming is a speech act that symbolically accomplishes the action performed in a real way. While slogans represent a powerful, and yet transient, political threat, renaming represents a more permanent challenge. The signs of this symbolic battle outlived the people's movement. Silent witnesses on the walls of Kathmandu, the new names adjacent to the cancelled-out old ones, remained for many months after April 2006.

Burning was a common street protest action. It was often carried out together with road blockades and stone and brick throwing. Burning the tyres of government vehicles and offices characterizes many agitations in Nepal, from student rallies to the protests carried out by some Hindu organizations[50] against declaring Nepal a secular state.[51] Royal authority was also debased through the act of burning. The photos of the king and queen of Nepal adorned most Nepali houses and were compulsory in all government offices. Traditionally, the royal couple was not supposed to be depicted in cartoons. Yet, during the April Movement, not only symbols of the state were ignited, but also effigies, posters, photos and images of the royal family.[52] They were first displaced from their place of authority and veneration inside offices and hospitals, and then set on bonfires in the streets. Fire is a particularly loaded symbol. Destruction by fire recalls death and purification.

Black outs and *mashal julus* (torch rallies) were organized by the SPA in Kathmandu against the mass arrests, the repression of demonstrations, and against the royal proclamation. The valley observed a black out from 8:15 to 8:30 p.m. amid the singing and clapping echoing in the city. Symbolism connected to light/darkness is rich and widens the significance of both black outs and julus. Burghart (1996, 312) reports that in 1985 teachers organized a protest lantern rally in broad daylight to publicly state that 'the kingdom had become so dark from injustice that honest men now found themselves obliged to guide themselves by lantern-light even in the light of day'. The connotation of the light of fire therefore works at different levels. Flames can bring destruction and death, but after that they can bring justice.

During street rallies, some traditional rituals were adapted to the situation, transformed, and their religious meaning was reversed. Staging the funeral of the monarchy while the king was alive recurred in different forms as if to eliminate the whole genealogy, a de-Shahization of Nepal. Puppets of the king were taken to Pashupatinath, conch shells were blown and green branches waved during rallies. In Bhadrapur, headquarter of Jhapa district, the 'corpse' of autocracy was prepared and taken out in a 'Shroud March': after setting out from Chandragadhi and circumnavigating the bazaar, the Shroud March reached Sagarmatha Chowk where last rites were performed for the corpse of autocracy. In the Shroud March, just like in a real funeral procession, the corpse was bound with freshly cut bamboo and conches were sounded while at the same time slogans against autocracy and for full democracy were chanted.'[53] It is tempting, at this point, to elaborate a bit on these puppets in Taussig (1993)'s manner. Taussig equates the power of mimesis to sympathetic magic where the copy acquires the power of the original, the representation the power of the represented. Therefore, by making puppets of the king, protestors got the power to symbolically disempower him.

The statues of the Shah kings became the targets of the crowd's anger in different places. For example, in Mahendranagar pro-democracy activists toppled the statue of Mahendra and removed the royal sceptre, glasses, and crown.[54] In the Mahendranagar bazaar, students paraded the photos of King Gyanendra and Queen Komal garlanded with a necklace of shoes:

> Despite the efforts by the police to snatch the photos away, the students put up fierce resistance and completed their circuit through the bazaar. As they processed through the bazaar residents standing on the sidelines clapped and offered flower necklaces (mala) to the protestors, in welcome and as an expression of their solidarity. Among those welcoming the spectacle were government office workers. After the procession the royal couple's photos were smeared with soot, draped with sandal and set on fire.[55]

In such a way, protestors adopted, adapted and then subverted a deeply humiliating punishment traditional in the villages. When someone has done something that the community condemns as absolutely despicable the person is decorated with a shoe mala, the face smeared with black soot (kalo moso) and often banished forever from the community. Parading throughout the public places of the city is a cultural device that deepens dishonour and damages people's reputation. This time, it was the king's turn. Such mocking displays contrast with the royal tours of the Emergency period.

On one occasion, a photo of King Gyanendra was tied on the head of a donkey and paraded in a donkey rally. According to some of my interlocutors, donkeys are commonly seen as animals that do not use their intellect, that do not have their own volition and operate through vested interests. The political reversal is striking. In the Hindu polity the king was supposed to embody the intentionality of the nation (Burghart, 1996, 304). On another occasion, demonstrators made a very simple effigy of the king, a plastic balloon as head, sticks for the arms, dressed with rags and a few shoes on his neck. The divine king was 'constructed' as a poor man. His role was desecrated. Images of animals were recurrent: the dog, a 'low' and 'mean' animal was given respect and honour like a king through the *Abhinandan* (Felicitations), a formula that is employed when addressing respectful people. The king was thus equaled to a dog. Both in Kathmandu and in the rest of the country journalists reported mass rallies in which protestors chanted slogans while 'playing' household utensils and tools.[56] Moreover, very often during demonstrations or work, people wore black bands on their arms to symbolize the repression they were resisting.

Flags are another important element in the mass movement. Most of the photos and reports described people waving party flags, either the red and white-starred flag of the Nepali Congress or the hammer and sickle flag of the Communist parties. There were no national Nepali flags, which had previously been flown in national celebrations or royalist rallies. This suggests that in that context, most of the people identified with political parties rather than with a 'national' identity or saw correctly that the king had arrogated national identity to himself.

From the analysis of the dramaturgy of protest, two overarching symbolic and opposite themes emerge, life and death, as if to mark the end of an era and the birth of a new one. During the movement, innovation and tradition went hand in hand with the colourful, bizarre and spontaneous performances described earlier. Street protests can thus be conceptualized as events that create the lived-in-world (Handelman, 1990). Their design aims at bringing about change but the cultural means through which it is advocated is embedded in local practices. The cultural repertoire that delegitimized the king's power paradoxically belongs to the same well-known rites of Hindu Nepal. Yet, symbols and rituals were appropriated and then employed through reversal. Power was dissolved through reversing the rituals that legitimized it. The commonly accepted codes and rituals that legitimized the 'theatre-state' served to dismantle it and once again revealed its fictionality. Not only was the pomp not powerful anymore, it became ridiculous because it was no more contained within a structure of order/authority.

The correlation between the dramaturgy of protest performed in Jana Andolan 1990 and 2006 are surprising, as well as the government's reaction. Propaganda war, detention of party activists and common citizens, governmental repression which aroused international indignation and concern, unemployed youths and campus students at the forefront of the rallies, professional groups actively involved in the movement, citizens marching on the streets brandishing kitchen utensils and agricultural tools, civil servants supporting the protests, are all common to both movements (Hachhethu, 1990). In 1990 the palace failed to acknowledge the existence of an opposition until finally King Birendra deleted 'partylessness' from the

Constitution and lifted the ban on political parties (Ibid., 183). The 1990 Movement was also strongly anti-royalist: 'the king's active patronage of the PS (Panchayat System) had become a focal point of public criticism throughout the movement. In every corner of the city, there were cartoons and wall paintings showing popular resentment against the palace' (Ibid., 181). Not only did symbols and tactics reveal continuity with a past tradition. Earlier protests also lent legitimacy to the newer movement.

Although 'end', 'destruction', and 'death' were recurrent symbols in the streets, the reported atmosphere was not gloomy. It was an end that brought the excitement of a new beginning. Some of my interlocutors wrote emails saying that despite the danger and violence, the environment at the mass rallies was cheerful, especially at the last ones. People in the streets were cheering. Street protests were characterized by a festive, carnivalesque and joyful mood, danger, fear and death co-existed in a creative tension. Demonstrations were full of excitement for the unknown that opened the space for improvisation. Such excitement 'is rooted in the tension between known patterns of action, stunning instantaneous surprises, and a passionately desired yet uncertain outcomes' (Schechner, 1993, 71). Such enthusiasm, however, is also strongly linked to the real possibilities of change, not just to dreams and imagination. The symbolic actions of renaming, or enacting the death of oppressors, represented a physical materialization of a desire. Though the object was shifted because of obvious reasons, through their theatrical dimension the actions performed were real. As a result, participation gave protestors power, the assertion of agency itself was a reason for acting, a 'constitutive and expressive reason' (Wood, 2001).

Let us move now from the 'theatre of protest' to the 'theatre for protest' on the makeshift street stages. The next sections outline how the political turmoil affected both theatrical stage production and the performance of development theatre. I will then depict how theatrical street plays added to the creativity expressed in the street protests. Actors' experiences and motivation will subsequently substantiate my ethnographic account of how the theatre world incited Kathmandu citizens into real political action.

The space of resistance: Closed streets and an open stage

The royal coup deeply impacted on the work of Aarohan Theatre. *Kachahari* theatre could not be performed in the streets anymore because the state of emergency laws banned public meetings of more than five people. Yet, inconsistencies in those regulations quickly emerged. It soon became evident that the distance between the ordinances in theory and their actual implementation in practice, or the police's control over them, was rather loose. From 3 February 2005 Gurukul had planned to stage three plays: 'Dreams of Peach Blossom'[57] (3–5 February), 'Fire in the Monastery' (9–12 February), both written by Abhi Subedi and directed by Sunil Pokharel, and an adaptation of Ibsen's 'A Doll's House' (6–8 February), also directed by Sunil Pokharel. The schedule was meant to mark the beginning of a new strategy aimed at staging daily performances to create a regular theatre audience in Kathmandu.

Despite the Emergency and the strike that paralyzed the capital, the rehearsals at Sama Theatre continued. Resistance in Gurukul took an immediate, though 'invisible' shape: Sunil decided that the group would carry on with everyday activities and performances 'as if nothing had happened', despite the bans. They would stop the plays only if soldiers had entered the compound to prohibit them. They did not come. During the first performance the artists were tense because of the unpredictable government reaction to the breach of the ban on assembly. However, it soon became clear that there would be no interruption. In the months that followed, Gurukul became a strong reference point for Nepali theatre. It was the only place where performances were running on an almost daily basis. However, the current political situation of the country was totally absent from the content of the performances staged. In a strategic self-censoring Aarohan Theatre group decided to keep a low political profile, and thus retained their power. The director explained that his main objective was to keep Gurukul open throughout the government prohibitions, so that it could become a safe meeting place in case opposition groups needed to gather. Throughout 2005, the group never performed radical dramas directly challenging the regime. At the same time, the king's government never interfered with the shows. Sunil was conscious of the danger of defying the Emergency laws[58] but it seemed a reasonable risk. The group's strategy to cope with the Emergency restrictions therefore aimed at maintaining a 'public space' inside Gurukul while providing distancing, harmless entertainment that was far from the pressing political reality and would not directly question the authorities. Artists were asked not to comment in public about the political situation. The compound was deliberately created and sustained as apolitical, 'fictional space' required by the state of emergency laws. In the editorial of the group bi-monthly magazine *Nepathya*, the director replaced his usual article with a reversed mask and the following caption (Fig. 3.4, reproduced with permission): 'The country is in emergency. This time the *sutradhar* self-censored himself, the space is empty. In this empty space you can write your own thoughts'.

The Emergency period saw a rebirth of independent stage theatre despite

मुलुकमा संकटकाल लागेको छ । यो पटक सुत्रधारले आफूले आफैलाई सेन्सर गन्यो ।
ठाउँ खाली छ. आफ्ना विचारहरु यस खाली ठाउँमा
लेख्न सक्नु हुन्छ ।

Figure 3.4: Editorial in Aarohan's magazine *Nepathya*, February 2005

the repression carried out across other media. Prevented by the censors from commenting on any political or news-related issues, the media extensively covered theatrical performances. Newspaper articles about the three different plays that were scheduled for February 2005 were published daily. The plays were featured during television news broadcasts. Artists would gather early in the morning under the thatched gazebo in the compound, shivering with the cold, sipping a cup of milk tea while the haze hugged the valley. They checked and commented on newspaper reviews and photos. Meanwhile, the audience numbers increased day after day.

Soon after the three plays, the rehearsals for 'Ask the Yogi about his Caste' (*Jat Sodhnu Jogiko*) started. The play, performed by Aarohan and directed by Anup Baral became a smash hit. The comedy was adapted from a play written by the Marathi playwright Vijay Tendulkar. After 'Ask the Yogi about his Caste' – performed from March to May 2005 almost without interruption – was the turn of 'Bhairav the Tiger' (*Bag Bhairav*), a play written by Satya Mohan Joshi in July and August. Next to be performed was 'Tara Baji Lai Lai', an improvisation-based play directed by the Norwegian Morten Krogh, part of a project funded by the National Theatre of Norway, centred upon images of childhood. In December 2005 'Bari Lai Lai', directed by Birendra Hamal, ran for a week. Since the play was about women's suffering during the armed conflict, the political context clearly re-entered the stage for the first time since 1 February 2005.

Contradictions in the application of the Emergency laws paradoxically also affected government institutions. In mid-April 2005, that is during the Emergency and despite prohibitions on mass gatherings, the Royal Nepal Academy ran the National Theatre Festival. It was a great success. After years of crisis it attracted huge audiences. At a rate of three performances each afternoon, theatre groups from different parts of the country performed their unique visions of Nepal and of its theatre. The atmosphere became tense with anticipation when, despite the Royal Nepal Academy being a government run body, a group staged a very realistic play in which two brothers, one belonging to RNA (Royal Nepal Army) and the other to PLA (Maoist People's Liberation Army), met in their natal home. After some moments of fear, instead of killing one another, they hugged. The auditorium, usually noisy and full of chattering during the performances, became silent at the portrayal of a real life dilemma.

Other theatre groups reacted to the state of Emergency in different ways. In contrast to Aarohan, who continued to perform despite the King's ban, Sarwanam Theatre Group protested the restrictions by cancelling their annual April commemorative performance, which celebrated the group's establishment. However, in December 2005, they engaged in a nation-wide tour that re-enacted resistance through the performance of a play first staged 25 years before, when the country faced similar oppression and lack of freedom. History was repeating itself and the staging of 'We are Looking for Spring' (*Hami Basant Khoji Rahechhau*) bore witness and explicitly emphasized this. Ashesh Malla selected actors below 25 years of age to testify that Nepali youth were facing the same problems as their fathers. If for young people the play reflected the country's contemporary struggle, for older members of the audience the play was particularly effective in reviving past sentiments.

Well before August when the CMDP started its mass meetings, resistance to autocracy in 2005 had linked to its historical roots. Before focusing on *loktantrik natak* performed during the CMDP public meetings, I want to focus on three instances in which Gurukul defied autocracy in their in 'private' space.

May 2005 – Ramesh in concert

In early May 2005, Gurukul invited Ramesh to perform, his first public appearance after many years. Ramesh (Chapter 2), sang his people's songs that invited everybody to go into the streets and protest for freedom. Both concerts, performed on two consecutive days, attracted a full house and ran smoothly, despite the recent end of Emergency rules and the songs' revolutionary content. Most of the people in the audience knew the lyrics by heart and danced in excitement at the popular tunes. Reminiscences of the people's movement in 1990 were brought back through singing the same songs, an anticipation of the cultural programmes organized by the CMPD that will be discussed in the next section. What was being created were new moral spaces made of sounds, symbols and slogans that were starting to challenge the government's domination and to link past memories with present hopes and struggle. 'Rise, Rise from the Village' (*Gaun Gaun Bata Utha*)[59] written by Shyam Tamot of Bhojpur in 1978 and sang by Ramesh and Rayan became one of the symbols and the musical icons of the popular movement for democracy in the months that followed. The song encouraged people to rise with whatever they had, working tools, pens, songs and music, or simply their voices if they had nothing in order 'to change the face of this country'. The king's pomp and his attempt to resurrect the Panchayat spirit were countered by performing old songs of resistance during CDMP political mass meetings. The resurrection of those songs invoked the pleasure of familiarity but also anger, because little had changed. As Diamond (1996) suggests, performance can bridge and merge the past and the present, memory and consciousness. Diamond (Ibid., 2) highlights the 're' discourse present in performance: *re*-embody, *re*-inscribe, *re*-configure, *re*-signify. While acknowledging the pre-existing discourse and the pleasure of repetition, possibilities are available for the new to materialize (Ibid.), in a multiplicity of visions. Well before the beginning of the public democratic movement led by the CMDP, progressive songs had already started spurring the audience's imagination in these two dates in Gurukul.

August 2005 – Shrawan Mukarung poetry reading

Shrawan Mukarung emerged as another strong voice during the 2006 CMDP cultural programmes. His poem 'Bise Nagarchi's Account' (*Bise Nargachi ko*

Bayan) powerfully explained the long-seated reasons for the country's dissent against the monarchy and social exclusion (Shrestha, 2006). In August 2005 Gurukul organized a reading of his poems and the Sama Theatre hall was packed, just like it was for Ramesh's concerts. Here are the first two stanzas:

> Master!
> Here in this Gorkha kingdom
> After 250 years I've gone mad!
> My head is spinning,
> The ground is the sky,
> The sky is the earth,
> And as my eyes are dazzled
> I see you with ten heads.
> Oh, where are my feet?
> Where is Bise Nagarchi?
> Master! I've gone mad!
>
> I should serve Maharaj,
> To protect history
> I should touch the feet of the Gorkhali,
> Remain true to my salt;
> After 250 years what has happened to me?
> This Bise is in a bad way Master!
> I've gone mad.
> (Translated by Michael Hutt)

The success surprised everyone and is described as such by Kunda Dixit (2005):

> Something unheard of had happened–people paid to listen to poetry and Mukarung made nearly Rs 40,000. Not only is it rare for Nepalis to buy tickets for a poetry recital but the audience clamoured for Mukarung to recite Bise Nagarchi ko Bayan over and over again.

November 2005 – Arjun Parajuli and Sisnupani Parivar programme

Instead of re-evocation, a process of appropriation, reworking and transformation of traditional cultural performances was at work during the Deusi-Bhailo programme performed by Sisnupani Parivar and led by the poet Arjun Parajuli in

Gurukul during Tihar in November 2005.[60] Singing carols during Tihar, especially during the third day of Laxmi Puja, is a well-established practice. While *bhailo* is traditionally sung by women during 'Laxmi Puja' (Gai Tihar or Diwali), *deusi* is sung by men on 'Goru Tihar' (the day after Diwali) and *bhai tika*.[61] Gathering according to interest or ethnic group, or for particular charity purposes, people travel by foot or bus around the city. Going from house to house, mainly to friends' places, where they sing, play the *madal* (drum) and dance. In exchange for their blessing and entertainment, singers and dancers get food, *mithai* (sweets), *roti* (bread), fruit and money. While creativity may run free, some songs are typical and recurrent, like *deusire*. The lyrics below are an example of a standard version. The lead singer starts the song. The chorus replies after each line:

Lead Singer	Chorus
Bhana Mera Bhai ho	*Deusire*
Say it my brothers	*Deusire*
Swar Milai Bhana	*Deusire*
Say it in tune	*Deusire*
Rato Mato	*Deusire*
Red trail	*Deusire*
Chiplo Bato	*Deusire*
Slippery trail	*Deusire*
Laddai Paddai	*Deusire*
Slipping and Sliding	*Deusire*
Aeka Hami	*Deusire*
Finally we made it to your home!	*Deusire*
Yo Gharma Laxmi	*Deusire*
In this home Goddess Laxmi	*Deusire*
Sadhai Aun	*Deusire*
Always come	*Deusire*
Hamilai Dinus	*Deusire*
Give us [money or food]	*Deusire*
Bida Garnus	*Deusire*
Say good bye to us	*Deusire*

The Deusi-Bhailo programme in Gurukul opened with groups of children wearing traditional costumes, singing songs and performing folk dances. It moved towards political critique only when the Sisnupani Parivar entered the open-air stage. Some Gurukul actors placed themselves at the back of the choir, not to miss the opportunity to sing. Performed in the Gurukul yard in the late afternoon, the atmosphere was festive and cheerful. Before the beginning of the singing, a *diyo* (oil lamp) was lit near some offers of food and flowers. The audience sat on carpets and chairs in front of the artists. The name 'Gurukul', flashing in big blue neon tube lights, gave a surreal touch to an otherwise extremely intimate, simple and familiar environment. Arjun Parajuli took the traditional song and re-inscribed it with contemporary images. Using metaphors the audience was familiar with, the contemporary lyrics were bitter yet hilarious. Below are the opening lines from a performance that lasted more than an hour, a poignant poetic rendition of a complex political and social situation. Once again, the lead singer introduces the line and the chorus replies:

Lead Singer	Chorus
Bhana mera bhai	*Loktantra*
Say it, brothers!	*Democracy*
Bhana mera bahini	*Loktantra*
Say it, sisters!	*Democracy*
Jodle bhana	*Loktantra*
Speak loud	*Democracy*
Bandukle sunun	*Loktantra*
May the guns listen	*Democracy*
Golile sunun	*Loktantra*
May the bullets listen	*Democracy*
Goli haanne	*Loktantra*
To shoot	*Democracy*
Tolile[62] sunun	*Loktantra*
May the groups listen	*Democracy*

Hami tyassai aenaun sisnupanile ahrayo
We have not just come here casually, Sisnupani ordered us
Deusi aja, hijai rati topi harayo
Today [we sing] Deusi, yesterday night the cap was stolen/lost

Hijo madhyeratama sarkaar savaar bhaechha
Yesterday at midnight the government knight came
Kinabhanda hamro topi lutna rahechha
Why? To steal our caps!

Daura surwal lutnalai bholi rati aune re
People say he will come tomorrow night to steal our daura suruaal
Sabai daura surwal sarkar eklai laune re
People say that only the king will wear daura suruaal

Jaska luga jati chhan laau ajai thapera
All the dresses you may have, wear them all today
Bholidekhi hidnuparchha hatle chhopera
From tomorrow you will have to walk covering yourself with your
hands

Pohor pohor hamile Deusi gungunayaun
Last year we sang Deusi
Ahile Deusi khelenau samchaar sunayaun
This time we did not play Deusi, we read out the news [instead]

Given the political moment, the text is intriguing. Although the Emergency had
formally ended in April, in early November 2005, the king's cabinet was still ruling.
The People's War was not over. In the adapted version, the song calls for brothers and
sisters to sing loud so that the 'gun' and 'bullet', as metaphors for the revolutionaries
in the jungle, may hear their call and fire. The traditional refrain '*deusire*', is replaced
with the word 'democracy', chanted as if a magical invocation. The second part,
instead, depicts the citizens stripped naked by the king.

The revival of people's songs sang by Ramesh, brought the past into the present,
and brought the village into the city. Yet, the experience of the performers for both
artists and spectators was permeated with new contemporary overtones. Similarly,
in the *Deusi* song, past traditions, associated with the monarchy, with religion, with
the memories of childhood and families were the basis upon which 'the news' was
transferred. The audience expressed its involvement by clapping rhythmically,
and laughing about the innuendos. Some men took centre stage and engaged in
spontaneous dance.

The performance triggered a chain effect. The day after the programme Aarohan
artists organized a *Deusi* tour around friends' houses in Kathmandu. Travelling in
a rented bus, we sang political songs mixed with traditional songs, similar to those
performed by the Sisnupani Parivar. The programme spread beyond Gurukul. The
public space was banned. But from a private position, through the transformation

allowed by the aesthetic space, artists recreated a temporary public space of agency, in the manner outlined by Arendt (Chapter 2). And these spaces multiplied themselves.

Despite the Emergency prohibitions, the theatre in Kathmandu flourished. Through a careful balance of defiance and self-censorship, the aesthetic and heterotopic space of the theatre was protected. Mainstream theatrical activities found great popular appreciation, probably fulfilling the citizens' need for breaking away from the hardships of daily life. But it was not simply the imagination of a democratic country, the theatre as a physical space played an important role in the development of the resistance and opposition movement in Nepal, as will become more apparent in the next section.

The space of action: *Loktantrik natak*, or theatre for democracy

As the organized resistance entered the streets, Aarohan's active involvement gradually shifted outside Gurukul. Between 2005 and 2006 Aarohan participated at various CMDP mass meetings, staging plays that they called *loktantrik natak*, simple sketches performed in the realistic and minimalist street theatre style but produced without receiving any contribution from donor agencies.[63] Artists participated out of personal choice, as their individual contribution as citizens to the popular movement.[64] The framework provided by CMDP allowed for a different level of audience engagement. I will now focus on two *loktantrik natak* performances, presented at different stages of political domination – January and August 2006 – to see how the artists' tactics of engaging the political crisis changed. In between, there came a specific moment when the political space of the popular movement merged into the theatrical space of Gurukul.

New Baneshwor – January 2006

Tension characterized the pro-democracy meeting in New Baneshwor on 29 January 2006. CMDP members prepared the stage for the speakers on a lorry. The organizers had to negotiate permission from the police patrolling the area. Aarohan actors were very worried because the previous days a group of artists had been arrested after street poetry readings. The simple, squared performance area in front of the lorry was marked by ropes, around which the audience sat and stood. The artists chose to perform an allegory because of the high risk of being arrested (Figs 3.5-3.10, photos by an unknown audience member with the author's camera).

> Sunil sets off by explaining to the audience that the poem he was going to read and the story the actors were going to present was not about Nepal. It was about Germany during Nazi rule. His words starkly contrast with the scene that was being developed by the actors inside

Figure 3.5: Sunil on the microphone recounts the tale while the artists perform the actions

Figure 3.6: Om Prakash sets the ropes delimiting the space where the citizens are obliged to move

Figure 3.7: Bhola, other citizens and the author still searching for a way out

Figure 3.8: Kamal manages to free himself while Rajan juggles between co-actors, speakers and photographers

Figure 3.9: Pashupati and Mahesh exult. Performers and spectators mix

Figure 3.10: Samuna and Nisha also enjoy the newly conquered freedom

the square. Actors shape a map of Nepal on the street with two ropes, and then, around the map, they embody different sketches of everyday life in Nepal: kids playing with pebbles, women engaged in house chores, men in the fields or talking, people squatting and watching. The images remain frozen for the whole duration of the poem.

When the recitation ends, two Nazi soldiers enter to the sound of machine-gun. Wearing black leather jackets, the two actors mime the shooting with empty hands and push all the people inside the map, violently throwing one over the other. The soldiers pick up the ends of the ropes that mark the map. They then form a corridor with the ropes, from where all the actors emerge wearing black bands (*kalopatti*)[65] on their eyes, and stumbling in the darkness. People inside the corridor/ropes move slowly, trying to figure out what is going on, groping in the air with raised hands. The two soldiers dressed in black can thus govern the corridor of dictatorship. The people inside are powerless. Then, one person among the blindfolded manages to find a way out and starts walking, hesitantly, soon to be pushed back inside by a few rounds of machine-gun. People continue to falter and search in the dark. Another person moves out, and then one more. But again, they are frightened back in by the sound of the machine-gun. Tension increases. This time, however, those who survive the previous exit begin whispering to others. The whisper forms a chain and spreads. The corridor becomes animated. People spread their voice in different directions. Suddenly, lifting the blindfolds, they burst free, forcing the ropes open, and regain liberty.

The allegory was clear. By displacing the story geographically and historically, the actors never mentioned the king or Nepal by words. The black bands signaled the darkness produced by the autocracy, obliging people to stay within 'the lines' guided by one person. The connection between Hitler and the king was straightforward. However, even the people who did not know about Germany could clearly understand what actors meant and what they encouraged the audience to do. The aesthetic space multiplied the image of reality that the actors wanted to reflect, allowing the audience to imbue with personal significance the suggestions acted in the street. Allegory is a rhetorical device often employed to defy censorship.

Gurukul – April 2006

During the April 2006 Jana Andolan II, the group decided to stop regular stage performances and moved into the streets. The actors' double role as artist and citizen fused. The street protests called for a more active involvement. The networks that linked engaged artists and intellectuals since the 1980s re-emerged and were renewed.

Gurukul hosted the annual celebration organized by Srijana Chaitra 3, a group founded to remember 3 Chaitra 2046 (16 March 1990), the day on which artists jointly tied a black band (*kalopatti*) against the Panchayat rule at Saraswati Hall in Trichanda College and were arrested (Ghimire, 2006; Chapter 2, p.57): signing a press release 35 organizations including 91 artists – from literature to theatre and cinema – gathered to express solidarity to the movement (Ibid.). Two days later, the meeting was repeated. Basanta recalls that around 350–400 people – poets, artists, journalists, film producers and actors – attended the gathering to put pressure upon political parties and civil society, and to publicly condemn the repression in the streets. 12 April 2006 turned into another 'black day' for the movement. The senior Newar intellectual and academician[66] Satya Mohan Joshi chaired the meeting. A poem recitation followed 'The Funeral Rites of the Panchayat' (*Panchayat ko Shraddha*), a 1991 hit by Hari Bansha Acharya and Madan Krishna Shrestha staged at Sama Theatre. Yet, when the whole group moved into the street towards Purano Baneshwor Chowk to recite poems outside the compound, the police attacked the demonstrators, beating and arresting many artists (Ghimire, 2006; Anushil, 2006). They hunted artists even when inside the Gurukul compound, where some tried to find protection, firing bullets in the air, and arresting 10 of them. An artist remembers fearing for the closure of Gurukul, the desire for freedom, the wish to go into the streets, the concern for the future of the People's Movement, and for the destiny of Aarohan Theatre itself. The artists who had lived in Gurukul temporarily moved to other houses for fear of government retaliation at night. Police surrounded Gurukul for three days, and stationed themselves inside. The artists temporarily abandoned their 'membership' participation in street protests but continued, divided through their residential locations, as individuals, as citizens rather than artists. The People's Movement ended with the restoration of the Parliament on 18 May, depriving the king of many of his powers and leading to the beginning of the peace process that would end the 10-year internal war and brought the Maoist revolutionaries into mainstream politics.

Loktantrik natak – August 2006

In August 2006 CMDP organized a meeting around the *dabali* of Durbar Square to press for the completion of the peace process. As usual, it also involved cultural performances such as songs, poems and drama. The view from the *dabali* was spectacular. A huge mass of people sitting on the big steps of the Durbar, the square was packed, all eyes focused on the open stage. Since the political space had opened after April's movement, the play performed by Aarohan dramatized and referred to the political development in a much more detailed and specific manner. All the key political actors were represented: the king, the political leaders, civil society, the UN. The characters in the play became individually characterized and immediately recognized by the audience (Figs 3.11–3.16).

Figure 3.11: The audience around the *dabali*

Figure 3.12: The king addressing the crowd

Figure 3.13: The common citizen listens to the UML leader

Figure 3.14: The common citizen interacts with the Maoist leaders

Figure 3.15: People get tangled in the complexity of the political scenario

Figure 3.16: Rehearsing the continuation of the play in Gurukul

Note: 3.11–3.15 Screenshots from video, courtesy of Gurukul; 3.16 photo by the author.

SCENE ONE

The play opens with a still image of an actor pointing his index finger towards the sky. At the sound of cymbals, a voice from the backstage recalls key dates in the history of Nepal: posing as a statue the 'king' greets the audience and smiles, until the start of the People's Movement, when actors who were kneeling around the statue, raise themselves, and cover the statue with a black cloth, bringing it down. They start shouting slogans and the atmosphere of the protest was recreated: 'Ganatantra – Jindabad', 'Loktantra – Jindabad'. The play proceeds apace. The black cloth becomes a sheet, and is held across the opened arms of a common citizen (Ram Hari), as if for begging. Malai chahiyo (I need it) he shouts repeatedly, while walking around the platform asking for democracy. 'Nepali Kangress, malai chahiyo' (Nepali Congress, I need it), he cries to another actor wearing a topi (Nepali hat). The NC [Nepali Congress] leader (Suresh) puts some money on the black sheet. 'I don't need money, I need loktantrik ganatantra' the common citizen replies. The NC leader sends him away to look for it somewhere else, explaining they are 'subject to international pressure' and there is 'a long waiting period ahead', through an unmistakably NC rhetoric. Whirling, the citizen, approaches the UML [Communist Party of Nepal (Unified Marxist-Leninist)] representative (Yubaraj) with the same question. 'Loktantrik ganatantra bhanera bhanda kheri...' (What I mean by republican democracy is....) [just rambling, no meaning in the sentence] answers the UML leader. The monologue, overstated through concerned gesticulation, does not reach any point, and the citizen is sent away again. 'Hajur, malai chahiyo' (Sir, I need it) repeats the citizen, spinning on the dabali to the next corner, where a couple composed of a tall and a short man (Saraswati and Bhola) is standing. The tall fellow wears a cap and stands to the back, while the short one does all the talking. 'Tapailai ke chahiyo? (what do you need?), begins the Maoist leader in the typical straightforward manner. 'We first need to find an agreement about arms management', he continues, reassuring the citizen, 'Your things and our things are the same. I'm also committed to loktantrik ganatantra'. 'Malai chahiyo', the citizen repeats. 'Malai loktantrik ganatantra chahiyo' he continues, moving towards the representative of civil society (Sarita) who replies that they want the same thing too, but the government is slow, the issue is complex, and they are suffering like him. Then the 'citizen' moves towards the front and addresses the real audience directly with the same, recurrent question, 'Malai chahiyo, malai dinus' [I need it – republican democracy, give it to me]

SCENE TWO

The scene shows a comic recruitment of vigilantes. The king's officer (Rajan), who wears a joker's hat, explains the job to the recruits: basically, saving Vishnu *bhagwan* - God Vishnu - the king, circulating propaganda, beating and arresting people, all for a wage of NRs 14,000 a month. He adds that 25,000 *sadhus* (ascetics) are coming from India because 'Nepal is a Hindu country and they have to take care of *bhagwan* Vishnu'. The candidates, grinning as they accept the offer (Pashupati and Bikram), show off their beating skills. They are ritually, and mockingly, invested with power through the placement of a cymbal over their heads. The recruiter tunes up a Hindu religious hymn, *Raghupati raja rajaram* and the vigilantes start rapping a reply on the same tune, but with different words....*paisa lina darbar jaun* (Let's go to the palace to take the money), one of them waving a stick in the air.

Actors embodying citizens' emotions enter one after the other, lamenting that the people's movement is over but that nothing had changed. They express disillusionment over the politicians' idle chatter. In fact, in reality, the process of arms management is not proceeding, there is no security, some people are still collecting forced donations, the army is still singing songs for the king, there is no interim constitution, etc. Back on stage, the citizens hold hands and try to find a solution but the more they move, the more entangled they become. Meanwhile the vigilantes enter, singing their songs, and like puppets try to break through the group of citizens. Then the song stops. What remains is a rhythmic, and ridiculing 'hee, hee, hee, hee'. Pretending to be citizens, the vigilantes enter the group and break the, however confused, unity.

SCENE THREE

TV news anchored by a comic presenter (Kamal). First, he introduces the American ambassador (the author), who peremptorily affirms that the US government would never accept a government that includes the Maoists, unless the rebels renounce their weapons. Sitting in the centre of the *dabali*, the TV audience mime that they could not understand English. Then the NC representative arrives, and referring to their long history, states that they need to maintain a ceremonial king. People spit. Grounding their commitment on the fact that they have 'stomachs' just like the audience, the Maoists

reaffirm their stance towards *loktantrik ganatantra* and explain
that collecting money was necessary to feed their soldiers. The
UML leader rambles, rambles and rambles... they are ready. What
they are ready for... is just not clear from the speech. An airplane
suddenly arrives. A UN representative (the author) steps out with an
interpreter (Saugat). They admire the landscape and smile like idiots
to the photographer. They undertake a hopeless tour of the parties in
order to understand the political situation. The sleeping NC leader
is waken up, whereby he repeats the same story as the TV interview
before. At the beginning, the interpreter translates a few words, but
in a short time the dialogue turns into a mocking gibberish dance, as
each leader dismisses responsibility and send the pair to talk to the
next party. Finally, the UN representative and her translator, shocked
and confused, board the plane and take off.

SCENE FOUR

The civil society leader (Sarita) reminds the real audience about their
suffering during the movement, and asks them not to close their
mouths, eyes, and ears. Actors were not dancing, she says, and warns:
khabardar (watch out).

Loktantrik natak grew spontaneously in response to the political situation.
Originating within the political street theatre tradition of the 1980s, *loktantrik
natak* presents both similarities to that form as well as innovations. The plays
were constructed collectively through improvisation and never fixed in a written
script. During the rehearsals, artists would vary phrases and gestures from a basic,
agreed *canovaccio*,[67] to further explore the situations represented. Variations would
be introduced even during the performances themselves, to suit the changing
perceptions of the context, as I will detail next. Therefore, the production process
would only end with the performance itself. The form of the second play described in
this chapter seems to have been influenced by Boal's forum theatre, and the *kachahari
natak* that the group performed for development agencies. In fact, the play does not
present a clearly defined message but ends with a warning to the audience, to watch
out for what politicians do, and engage actively. It was a call to participation, aimed
at turning spectators into what Boal calls 'spect-actors' or simply into social actors,
after having being silenced and dehumanized by the king's action. Both plays were
staged in the realistic and minimalist style of the street theatre, but were profoundly
different in format.

Although the performance space was well-defined in both dramas, the artists chose to perform with their own everyday clothes, without using any theatrical costumes. The props were reduced to the minimum so that the few elements present on the stage acquired symbolic connotations (e.g., the rope and the leather jackets of the Nazi soldiers in the first skit, the black cloth, the *topi* (Nepali hat) and the vigilantes' stick in the second). In the second performance, the political critique became overt and situation-specific. Despite internal contradictions, in reality both the government and Communist Party of Nepal (Maoist) had sought UN intervention in the peace process by similar but independent letters. Satire could easily develop.Political leaders were caricatured. Actors used body language and rhetorical linguistic mannerism to characterize the different roles. For example, the king's celebratory and reassuring gestures became a mask of fear just before the crowd subsumed him. The NC leader wore just a *topi* (Nepali hat), but his rhetorical reference to the history and battles of his party, pointing his finger towards the sky, left no doubts about his identity. When the UN mission knocked at his door suddenly, waking him up, the figure of G. P. Koirala emerged clearly. In fact, because of his old age and sickness, at that time he was spending more time in bed than at the parliament. The Maoist duo was represented through dark glasses and simple, resolute speaking mannerisms. Similarly, the UML rhetoric was unmistakable to the spectators. And, as soon as the audience recognized the characters portrayed, they burst into laughter and clapped.

But laughter brought also the realization of the drama of power: Aarohan's second play conjured up the politicians' '*natak*' (theatre), the gap between their words and action that led to a lack of 'real' change. Without ever mentioning the names of the leaders or the parties or openly criticizing their failed promises, the actors fleshed them out through actions and rhetoric in such a precise way that the drama of power became apparent. Rather than stating, actors evoked what was behind the public appearance, leaving no easy solution for the audience, except for the warning of being alert and 'active'.

Aarohan's plays were the product of the collective work of the actors and were built through meetings and rehearsals carried out beyond their daily work schedules. Such performances were the result of the actors' 'feel for the game' (Bourdieu, 1990, 66), of their attempts to see and express the gaps and ironies of everyday life, without any interest-group specific design over the audience. On the one hand, actors deliberately manipulated cultural elements such as the Hindu hymn '*Raghupati Raja*', which were promptly recognized by the audience. By changing its words, the artists reversed its meaning. Rather than praising the king, the hymn turned into an open critique. The performance was relational as it triggered a process of co-creation with the audience that could take unpredictable forms. For example, in the second sketch, I played the

UN official with Saugat who played the interpreter. During the construction of the play, I followed Saugat's lead in caricaturizing the UN mission, admiring the wonderful landscape, and posing for the photographer, thus emphasizing the touristic aspects of the visit. Through rhythmic sounds and dance-like movements, Rajan, playing a photographer, led the UN officials to meet the first politician at the corner of the stage. Throughout the tour of the politicians, Saugat and I maintained the mocking rhythm improvised by Rajan who ended up characterizing the UN officers. A few weeks after the play, in an area near Thamel, an adolescent girl selling Tibetan bags called me. She remembered I had acted in Durbar Square. When I asked her what she liked in the play, she mentioned two moments: first, the vigilante recruitment which she mimed by punching into the air, and also the foreigners' scene. She thus showed me how *bideshi* (foreigners) walk and mimed the hip movement. It was only then that I realized that what we started as a caricature, without deliberately searching for 'foreign' elements, was later recognized by the girl as 'foreigner'. During the rehearsals, in fact, we had never discussed how foreigners walk. The movement just came up 'naturally', following the rhythm. The girl in the audience filled the movements with her own experience, multiplying the original meaning. This is an apparently trivial example. However, it shows how the multi-vocality of performance could facilitate communication with the public and potential engagement.

Doing theatre from the heart

Performing during public meetings organized by civil society or artists' groups was dangerous both during the summer of 2005 and after the People's Movement. In this section, I will introduce the life experiences of Kamal, Rajan and Bhola to understand how some artists interpreted the connection between theatre and politics, what motivated them to actively participate and take personal risks. Kamal explains that

> theatre and politics go together. Theatre affects politics. Politics affects theatre. Sometimes whatever is performed in theatre helps to highlight politics... In drama there is also politics, if there is no politics there is no drama. That's why they are synonyms. Without drama there is no politics, without politics there is no drama.[68]

Yet, on a practical level, drama seems to outdo the dualism between appearance and reality. In fact, theatre has real and deeply felt emotional and affective power. Kamal, for example, tells that at the beginning of his career he thought that drama could not make any difference in society. Yet, after performing many shows in different locations such as schools, villages, and streets, he realized that when people see a drama they become highly emotional, they cannot keep quiet: 'They want to speak', he remarks, 'and whatever they speak, they speak from their heart after watching drama'. It's very important to reflect on the emotional and affective involvement that theatre very often triggers. Kamal continues explaining that when they perform in the streets, the audience sides with the oppressed and attacks the oppressor. At times, people really believe that the actor is the oppressor and beat him up. This is the reason why he thinks that theatre works. Seen from a different point of view, such cases of intense emotional involvement are often 'rationalized'. An audience that is 'over-affected' by the performance is regarded as simple, naïve, or labeled as an 'illiterate from the villages'.

Emotions, subdued to rationality, should allow the spectator to get involved, but not too much, maintaining a safe distance from the performance. Both social and political science had trouble incorporating emotions in the analysis of politics and social protest (Goodwin, Jasper and Polletta, 2001). Emotions are recurrent in artists' narratives as they are in Maoist artists' and indeed seem to have transformative power. For Kamal it is this emotional and affective power that explains the success of political theatre, not theatre in support of politics but theatre that exposes the dark sides of politics, as he is keen to clarify. For Kamal, theatrical performances help the spectators reach deep inside their 'hearts' and get involved through singing and clapping. 'Like when we performed the play in Baneshwor', he continues,

or in front of Singha Durbar, or when we take up political issues, whenever the issue comes into the play, the audience starts hooting, clapping and chanting slogans. It touches the people's heart and they see in the play what they were suffering. That's why drama gives them a kind of power. Because of that power, they are able to hold their hands up and chant slogans. In that way drama really works for political issues.

Kamal also supported his understanding by adding that when they represented demonstrations and showed the oppression carried out by police on the stage, he noticed that the real policemen standing near the stage were feeling very uncomfortable. Their power was being questioned. Bhola draws feelings into the discussion as well. He characterizes the political drama they performed for democracy as 'drama from our heart', as it had the objective of making people aware and bringing out their inner voice, in a kind of heart-to-heart communication. And 'when people are aware, anything can happen', adds Kamal:

That's why to make people active, theatre works as fire, to activate them. That's why we started to do political theatre.... to activate the people, not to let them remain passive, in silence. We are making pressure from below to tell them not to stay in silence. Theatre can only make pressure. Theatre doesn't change anything, theatre makes pressure so people change from below. Earlier we gave pressure but nothing happened. Now people know that if they do, then anything can happen. If we keep pressuring them, they will not keep quiet and politicians will be afraid that if people raise their voices, they will not be there again. Where will we go?[69]

Theatrical experience not only elicits emotions that are real and intense. The outcomes of actions 'fictitiously' performed on stage are also real, deeply felt, fearsome and feared. Actors themselves were afraid of possible attacks by *mandales* (hooligans that backed the king). While leading the audience into a world of imagination, actors are strongly grounded on reality. Personal experiences, in fact, determined the ways in which actors engaged in political performances. Kamal, Bhola and Rajan, for example, were into student politics before joining Aarohan, or had relatives who were politicians in their villages. Such experience allowed them to have an informed understanding of the political situation and a keen interest that allowed them to draft street dramas. However, they were also well aware of the implications hidden in any public political performance. The last play that I described is emblematic in this sense. At the last rehearsal inside the hall in Gurukul, just before moving to Basantapur Square, comic elements were dominant. Kamal is the main character actor in the group and his caricatures of both the vigilante recruiter and the TV announcer were precise and exhilarating. Yet, on the stage in Durbar Square, in a domino-like effect, all the actors reduced both the number of lines and the broad gestures rehearsed earlier. For some actors this was a conscious decision. For me, playing both the American ambassador and one of the UN officers, it was an unexpected and startling surprise, as my dialogue was supposed to come soon after Kamal's. Yet, when he cut his harshest parody short, I was startled, and reduced my dialogue as well. Somehow the others did the same. Later on, Kamal explained that what I had sensed as an unexplainable mistake was in fact intentional. He was scared of being beaten by the king's people and told about his previous experiences. He had been beaten because of his active involvement in politics:

> I felt afraid. Politics is really a big issue and in this big issue we feel afraid, maybe somebody hit us. Like last time we did [the play], we used the word 'vigilante', I thought that I shouldn't say and do more than that. Maybe outside the play somebody [may] beat me. I feared this. We are talking to do this drama in our *kachahari*, and yesterday I said to my friends 'let's put a small part, not big, because we have to do it in many places'. I feared that going to many places there may be many reactionaries, from the king's people. Any time we could be attacked. Because we did our social drama on their issue when they

hear the word 'hee, hee, hee hee' they understand that we are against them. That's why they can beat us any time, or they can do anything. That's why I wanted to make that part small. This fear is always there.[70]

I could see once again the limitations of doing participant observation, the difference between 'I' and 'them'. I was acting, fully 'participating' in anthropological terms. I was even 'over-participating', totally taken over by my role, concentrating on the performance, thrilled by the thousands of people sitting on the stairs of the temples in Durbar Square, excited by the topic that we were challenging through the play. Conversely, Kamal and other actors were conscious of the dangers that I could not see. Our perceptions of danger were different, just like the potential of real danger because my identity of a 'real' foreigner granted me more security. Nonetheless, the audience and the CMDP organizers enjoyed the play thoroughly, nobody realized what was lost or why. Paradoxically, only by 'participating', could I realize the limits of my 'participation'. At the same time, my 'shallow participation' enhanced my understanding of how artists modified their performances of the spot in tune with the shifts occurring around them.

Personal experience in fact provided ground for interest in political drama. Kamal explains that both his father and his uncle were politicians in his village. Through personal experience he also learnt the tricks of playing the roles of the political leaders, with maximum detail:

> Since I was a child I went to demonstrations, public assemblies, rallies and from them I had something in my mind about politics. When I finished school and started college, I did politics in college. I engaged in student union elections. In Baneshwor Campus, I won also, and I worked in the unions for 2 years. Then I came to the theatre and left politics. Otherwise, I used to do politics. That's why I have knowledge of politics that I use in drama in different places, how they speak, how they walk. I also experienced, while doing politics, how the problems come to you. I experienced a little. That's why I also enjoy working [in theatre] about politics. When I worked in the union, I saved myself many times by running. Otherwise, I would have been beaten. What happened [once] was I won in the union [elections]. My friends insisted in celebrating the victory with beer but when I declined they ran after me with knives. I kept running till I reached Maiti Devi. For 3 months I didn't go to college. There was another friend, who won the elections. We were in the union office. Other people broke my friend's nose. That's why I like doing political drama.[71]

Bhola started performing in political plays in his village. He remembers that before 1990 there were more plays for democracy than for entertainment. Many groups organized cultural programmes including songs, dance, and drama, which he loved. If for many artists getting involved in political theatre was just continuing a personal process initiated well before, for others it was the result of the new enthusiasm for politics that grew after Emergency 2005. Female artists in Gurukul, except for Nisha who was with Sunil at Trichanda College in 1990, played roles in political theatre for the first time in 2005 and got immediately caught up. While remembering the demonstrations, Pashupati admits that she sometimes asked herself if what they had lived in those days really happened considering it was so unbelievable. Aarohan's director allowed total freedom to the actors. Their participation in political theatre was their own personal choice that artists handled differently. Many artists talked about social responsibility, like Bhola who explains 'we are also people of this country, we have also responsibility towards our nation, because of that responsibility we do it. We do drama from our heart, doing political theatre is our responsibility'.[72]

If taking part in a big mass event is energizing, playing for thousands of people sharing the same cause is an extraordinary event for actors embodying the double identity of social and dramatic actors within the doubly heightened situation of a dramatic performance within a protest programme. The fear mentioned by Kamal co-existed with its opposite, that is, the pride expressed by Rajan, in a kaleidoscope of emotions. Yet, Aarohan's performances questioned first and foremost the actors themselves, who composed the performances and acted. Rajan feels the urgency of self-questioning and reflection that links the personal to the political, social and professional, the need to fill the gap created by the desire dramatized on stage:

> If I'm going to demonstrate against the government for democracy, we should be in a democracy first and after that we could go there. Sometimes there could be personal problems and maybe another society blocks the people from going forwards. We need to fight it, on both sides, personal and in society.[73]

What Rajan advocates is a collapsing of what is publicly projected on the stage and everyday life practices offstage, a correlation between inner and outer coherence. Even Bhola highlights the importance of initiating change within oneself in order to transform the outer social reality and thus prevent dramas from being just idle chatter:

> Now we can't do theatre to change the prime minister. It's not in our hands. But the situation is like this, so, we can say what is our role. If I

change myself then only I can change you. If I don't change myself, I cannot tell you to change yourself. We are doing to know what is the role of the people.[74]

But what is really in our hands? Is the personal really an easier starting point than the social or the political? Certainly, actors' reflexivity upon the country's political situation triggered personal reflections about their own lives, their group, freedom, and democracy.

Conclusion

After contextualizing *loktantrik natak* and drawing the connection between Aarohan Theatre and civil society, this chapter described how theatrical performances were not extemporaneous endeavors but rather grounded on a pre-existing social movement and networks. The theatre's link to crisis and politics has been reasserted in Nepal by the recent turmoil and by actors' narratives. Symbolic action acquired central importance in negotiating power during political contestation.

The performance of kingship and the performance of dissent refer to a specific mode of communication already mentioned in Chapter 2. Burghart (1993, 1996) pointed out that in hierarchical societies, and I would add in 'hierarchical communication', the role of the speaker and that of the listener reproduce social hierarchy and are not based on equality. What characterizes the voice of authority is that their role permits them 'not to listen' to a speaker who is lower down in the hierarchy, and thus the speaker has no 'moral' authority to be heard. In the examples analysed in this chapter, the king prevented the people from gaining voice both by not listening and by silencing them. Acts of street protest can be framed as extreme responses to the experiences of 'not being listened to'. More than a culture of silence, what emerges is a culture of silencing across time, caste (see 'Bise Nargachi's Account') and class. The appearance of performative means of protest, 'heightened behaviour'/'twice behaved behaviour' (Chapter 1) is linked to the lack of other possibilities of being heard, a behaviour that is itself reproduced hierarchically. The theatricality of dissent contributed to creating a moral space for being heard, to transform the collective representations and motivate the social movement. The street was turned into an aesthetic space, through the focus of attention. And thus protestors could exercise agency by performing alternative representations of reality (Chapter 2). The streets became a temporary heterotopic space of transformation where hierarchies were reversed, and demonstrators claimed the moral authority to speak and be listened to.

The theatrical metaphor is employed to describe the misaligned, the unexpected, the paradoxical, the mismatch between appearance and 'reality'. Theatrical performances 'acted' out similar paradoxical situations. Symbolic inversions, irony, parody and paradox characterize radical popular theatre. They test and undermine the limits of dominant discourses of power, and challenge human understanding by crossing the boundaries of different categories. Political theatre during the 2005–06 movement exposed the gaps, the invisible mechanisms that 'do' power. The 'nothing' of symbolic inversions and irony itself strikingly recalls the 'double negative' that characterizes dramatic roles (Schechner, 1985, 123) and that allows for the creation of an aesthetic space. Contradictions and incongruous juxtapositions encouraged spectators to explore alternative viewpoints and incorporate new roles and ideas.

Endnotes

1   Part of this chapter appears in Monica Mottin, 'Protest, Space and Creativity: Theatre as a Site for the Affective Construction of Democracy in Nepal', in *Political Change and Public Culture in Post 1990 Nepal*, edited by Michael Hutt and Pratyush Onta, New Delhi: Cambridge University Press, reproduced with permission.

2   Interviewed in January 2006.

3   For more on the heritage of street and travel in Nepali theatre see Subedi (2006). For how the street could be politically closed by strikes see Lakier, 2007; Snellinger, 2007.

4   See Boal, 2006, 16.

5   In English the verb 'to stage' is used both to refer to a theatrical performance and to the staging of a rally. Political stakeholders are commonly termed 'political actors'. The 'theatrical' metaphor is commonly employed also in Nepali language.

6   In 'Negara' (1980) Geertz reconstructs the way the Indonesian state was governed by rituals and symbols and explains how power was exercised through spectacle rather than force.

7   The theatricality of the state has been the subject of anthropological study (Geertz, 1980, 1988; Fuller and Benei, 2001; Gellner, 1999).

8   See Davis (2010) for an analysis of the plays.

9   *Khuma* is the name of the lead character, a Magar girl caught between the two conflicting sides. The play is an adaptation from a short story written by Mahesh Vikram Shah.

10   '*Bari lai lai*' is the sound that ends the refrain of a popular women Teej song. The play represents women's point of view on the suffering caused by the war.

11   I focused on the performance of kingship, not on the rituals that sustained it.

12   Hutt (2006) explained in depth that since 2001 the press was under strong pressure. First, independent journalists were prevented from reporting about the royal massacre because of a barrier of silence imposed by the palace and also the dangers involved, and the power of the 'things that should not be said'. Second, the relationship between the Maoists, the Royal Nepalese Army, and the Press was rather complex. The situation degenerated with

the nine months of Emergency started in November 2001, forcing journalists into self-censorship. For a detailed description and analysis of the press censorship and intimidations under Gyanendra's regime and how the direct censorship of the first days was replaced by intimidations and economic and legislative measures see Bhattarai (2005).

13 More details in www.nepalpressfreedom.org.

14 See Hutt (2006) for similar directions promulgated in the Emergency 2001; see Bhattarai (2005) for more about how the media was harassed after the direct censorship of the first day was over.

15 The validity of the notice was supposed to be for six months, even though Emergency laws might have been lifted earlier. Emergencies in fact was to be renewed by the House of Representatives every three months. The Emergency declared on 1 February was actually lifted on 29 April 2005, but the struggle between the media and the royal government remained heated even in the months that followed.

16 From www.fnjnepal.org.

17 INSN Media Update 23 March 2005.

18 I photographed 90 billboards only in the central area of Kathmandu, but there were more that I did not manage to document. According to a website United We Blog (accessed on 27 May 2006) in May 2005 the Department of Information had 149 hoarding boards hung in the capital, which cost the state NR 1.5 million; 50 were demolished during the April 2006 street protests. For an analysis of the impact of blogging and the internet during 2005–06 see Sharrock (2007).

19 For an in-depth analysis of the royal billboards see Baltutis (2011).

20 Royal birthdays were important for the legitimization of power. In 1987, party members elected in the local elections were removed from their place by the government because of their refusal to participate in public processions on the king's birthday (Burghart, 1996, 306; Chapter 2).

21 The English translation and the capital letters come from the poster. While 'constitutional monarchy' is capitalized, 'multi-party democracy' is not

22 Praises were published on newspapers even on the days following Prachanda's election as Prime Minister in August 2008. It would be interesting to see if the businessmen who sponsored them were the same who sponsored the wishes on the royals' birthdays.

23 Prithvi Narayan Shah 'unified' Nepal and is praised by nationalist rhetoric as the first ruler who acknowledged the idea of unity within cultural diversity. This interpretation is rejected by Gellner (1997, 24).

24 It is interesting to notice similar aesthetics at work in some Maoist programmes with totally different content but also aiming at recreating a living picture, a colourful 'tranche-de-vie' on the stage.

25 Together with Maoist websites, both insn.org (a website ran by Nepali and international activists aiming to develop dialogue on human rights and democratic peace) and samudaya. org (a website run by Nepali diaspora in the US initially focusing on art and literature) were blocked in Nepal by an order from the Ministry of Communication and Information of Gyanendra's government on the grounds that they encouraged Maoist activities in Nepal. Both sites, however, did not advocate for either of the parties. Nepalipost.com, run by

independent journalists was blocked before that date. A Media Monitoring Group point out that despite wide censorship a blog run by high caste Kathmandu-based elite – unitedweblog – was never blocked. Several proxy web services were also banned.

26 Tulsi Ghimire's film *Balidan* (Sacrifice) was also banned and similar practices were at work in a shop selling the film VCDs that I contacted.

27 The parties that signed the agreement were Nepali Congress, Nepali Congress (Democratic), Nepal Sadbhavana Party (Anandi Devi group), CPN-UML (United Marxist Leninist), Samyukta Jana Morcha (United People's Front), Nepal Peasant's and Worker's Party, and United Left Front.

28 Other groups identified with the term 'civil society' organized public events, such as PAPAD (Professionals' Association for Peace and Democracy), Human Rights and Peace Society; see Shah (2008, 24–28) for more. For the purpose of this chapter as I will only focus on CMDP as the group I was associated to participated at their events. Besides, other professional organizations like the Nepal Medical Association, Nepal Bar Association, etc., were very active in mobilizing the citizens.

29 Other renowned members of CMDP were human right activist Krishna Pahadi, painter Kiran Manandhar, literary figure Khagendra Sangroula, and Shyam Shrestha.

30 The group organized similar meetings also in all the districts of the country.

31 See next section for a description of how professional categories participated in the protests in group, reasserting their categories as well as raising political claims.

32 Aarohan Theatre Group is often defined as an elite group, although many group members would not accept such definition. See Chapter 4 for a discussion about the group organization and the social status of theatre artists in Nepal.

33 See section three of this chapter about how Aarohan Theatre Group created and sustained Gurukul as an 'apolitical space' since 1 February, 2005.

34 The word *prajatantra* comes from *praja* which means 'subject' and activists felt this word was relevant only if Nepal were to remain a kingdom (Raj, 2006, 9). In contrast, the preferred word *loktantra* comes from *lok*, which means people and is also the word used for democracy in India (Ibid.). A slogan during Jana Andolan said '*Praja hoina nagarik banaun*' meaning 'let's be citizens and not subjects' (Rai, 2006, 9). In contrast, the Maoists would talk of *janatantra* meaning 'people's republic' (Ibid.).

35 Interviewed in November 2006.

36 Ibid.

37 A form of folk music from western Nepal, see Stirr (2012)

38 Nepali folk songs consisting of two groups debating in a quick musical conversation, see Stirr (2008) for an in-depth analysis of *lok dohori*.

39 Despite the curfew, on 20 April around 200,000 people entered the streets and many tried to enter the city in Gongabu, Balaju and Kalanki where clashes with the police led to the death of three people and injured more than 100 (Raj, 2006,33). It is estimated that more than one million people participated in the movement and at the end of the 19 days, 18 people lost their lives and more than 5000 were injured (Shah, 2008, 16).

40 Kanak Mani Dixit, THTonline, accessed on 8 May 2006.

41 In this section I have collected data from websites like nepalnews, kantipuronline, the himalayantimes online, and independent blogs between April and May 2006.

42 'Gyané' is the short name employed by protestors to contemptuously address King Gyanendra.

43 The translation comes from an email received by the author.

44 During the months before the April Movement civil society groups staged mock parliaments in the streets though I have never personally seen any.

45 From nepalnews, various dates in April–May 2006.

46 On 18 May, the House of Parliament unanimously passed a proposal in which royal power was drastically curtailed, executive power was handled over to council of ministers, 'HMG (His Majesty's Government of) Nepal' was changed into 'Government of Nepal', RNA (Royal Nepal Army) turned into 'Nepali Army'.

47 INSN reports.

48 From nepalnews, various dates in April–May 2006.

49 From www.nepalnews.com, 21 April.

50 THT, 24 May 2006.

51 Ibid., 18 May 2006.

52 Photos of the royal family were also burned in the streets during the 1990 Movement (FOPHUR, 1990, 59).

53 INSN report 8 April 2006.

54 In a statement reported by Workers World (14 April 2006), Prachanda and Bhattarai were reported having ordered the PLA to destroy of all royal statues and signs referring to HMG.

55 INSN report, 11th April 2006.

56 Citizens protested with their working tools and joined in professional groups even during Jana Andolan 1990 (Hachhethu, 1990, 177).

57 For an analysis see Davis (2003).

58 Cf. with the apoliticality produced by the CMDP meetings pointed out by Heaton Shrestha and Adhikari (2010) and intended as a space exempt from the divisiveness and pursuit of power that characterizes politics.

59 See Grandin (1994) for an analysis of this song and more about progressive music.

60 Arjun Parajuli, named the *andolan kabi* (protest poet) was another acclaimed guest of the CMDP meetings.

61 Maoist Cultural groups would also organize Deusi programmes after the end of the conflict.

62 The word *toli* is used to indicate a group of students, a batch, a sport team or a group of soldiers and a political team.

63 This is an important remark as in Nepal most street theatre is perceived as being tied to the development industry, see Mottin (2007).

64 The second play that I will describe was occasionally performed in the streets of Kathmandu by Aarohan as a forum theatre play by artists out of their own will. Yet, in the unframed space of the streets, the play was often confused by the audience with a development street play and in some occasions the spectators asked the artists who paid them.

65 A citation of one of the symbols of protest used by the artists in the 1990 Movement that I mentioned earlier.

66 Satya Mohan Joshi was often described as a 'culture expert' as he was considered the bearer of traditional knowledge about folk dance, music and festivals.

67 A *canovaccio* indicates a rough plot outline used by *Commedia dell'Arte* players. It consisted of a list of acts, scenes and characters. The details were left to the actors' improvisation skills. Aarohan outlined scenes in a more detailed way but actors were nonetheless free to vary dialogues and gestures if they found more effective ones.

68 Interviewed in October 2006.

69 Ibid.

70 Ibid.

71 Ibid.

72 Interviewed in September 2006.

73 Interviewed in August 2006.

74 Interviewed in September 2006.

4

Kachahari Natak
Fragments of an aesthetics of theatre for social change

The intersections of power, politics and theatre have been the focus of the previous chapters. Political power creates powerful but 'real' illusions to sustain itself. Theatre and the 'theatrical mode' may undo the inconsistencies of political power and challenge it by revealing its gaps. But the reverse is also true. Theatre and cultural performances can objectify identity claims and strengthen ideological belongings. As a result, stage representations appear as thick, contested, and simultaneously grounded illusions/allusions, far closer to 'reality' than the strategic performances of everyday life and politics. Because of the intentionality of its production, the world of 'make-believe' takes up tangible material forms. But it is the declared and assumed theatricality and illusion of the performance that creates a space for the 'rehearsal' of unpleasant or unwanted social truths. They can, if necessary, be dismissed as 'theatre'. Through playfulness and irony theatre destabilizes fixed notions of 'truth', and calls up every spectator to identify what is 'real' and what is not. While engaging the personal, *loktantrik natak* challenges power at macro-level; in contrast, *kachahari natak* focuses on micro-level power dynamics. This chapter focuses on how street theatre, namely *kachahari natak*, represents and questions social issues within the context of planned development projects. In particular, the practices of doing *kachahari natak* in Kathmandu will be unpacked. After exploring how Boal's format of forum theatre was adapted into the Nepali form of *kachahari natak*, the process of its standardization/mechanization as another form of development drama will be detailed. What emerges is that creativity needs to be 'regulated' to fit both planned and organizational development, the 'special' of theatre is moulded into the 'ordinary' of manageable, daily working practices (Chapter 7). But first, I will focus on the moment when the political street theatre described in Chapter 2 entered the world of international development after 1990. In particular, I will draw from actors' narratives to describe Aarohan's urge to get involved in theatre for development.

Theatre in development: A background

In contrast to many African countries, where theatre for development originated from the drama departments of universities (Harding, 1999; Mda, 1993), in Nepal it developed directly from artistic proscenium theatre and the political street theatre of the 1980s. The exploration of how this happened takes an actors' perspective. It is based on interviews and informal conversations rather than the analysis of past development project papers. My position – an outsider, not 'internal' NGO staff – did not allow me to have access to full project documentation. My requests to various theatre groups for access to past project reports, in order to understand possible shifts in discourse, changes in policy or financial support, were partly dismissed with the justification that such documentation was not available anymore. However, while that would have helped present a larger picture, my purpose now is to interrogate theatre internally by analysing the theatrical voice as it is espoused by the actors themselves. The financial side of project work emerged as a sensitive issue and could not be accessed.

In the late 1980s, sporadic projects using theatre to disseminate information about health issues were first introduced in Nepal. However, it was only after the emergence of multi-party democracy in 1990, when the ban on the right to organize was lifted, and when the number of INGOs-NGOs increased exponentially (Heaton Shrestha, 2001, 69), that theatre began to be more extensively included in development projects. Before Nepal was 'opened' to the world in 1950, travel narratives had stereotypically represented Nepal as a Shangri-la that existed outside of time. After it was 'opened' to the 'world', it was, again stereotypically, portrayed as being remote, isolated and, thus, in need of development (Pigg 1992, 1993). As Pigg (1992) observes, 'development' was a powerful concept employed by the government and defined the positive pole in a series of dichotomies that moulded society and identities: *bikasit* (developed) vs. *abikasit* (backward), modern vs. traditional, foreign vs. local, city vs. village, developer vs. under-developed, wealthy vs. poor (Ibid.). Most rural Nepalis were homogeneously conceptualized as illiterate, simple, and under-developed. As a result, theatre soon became a privileged tool for development communication (Mda, 1993).[1] This link between a paternalistic development establishment imbued with a dichotomous modernity-tradition cosmology applied to a 'civilizing' purpose and theatre as one of its amplifying instrumentalities had somewhat infectious negative consequences. While themselves being on the 'developed' side and mediating development to rural audiences, in their reflections on Nepali theatre, some artists tend to see themselves and Nepali theatre itself as being under-developed and in need of help and assistance.

Artists and development specialists alike talk in passionate terms about the beginning of applied theatre in Nepal. At that time, theatre groups were not permanent organizations with full-time 'professional' actors. Artists were engaged in other jobs for a living and met when they could for rehearsals. Sunil recalls that soon after 1990, artists from his group got together for a project and set off on a tour to different districts, performing a play on community development. They travelled with a small light, a generator, some costumes and a few props. The group performed skits exploring the concept of 'development' itself. These plays sought to communicate the idea that development is a mentality and should not be associated with physical infrastructure but with a change in people's attitude. This was the early purpose of development theatre, to propagate and disseminate 'development ideologies'.

The establishment of multi-party democracy in 1990 represented a big challenge for Nepali theatre workers. Many theatre groups formed during the Panchayat time had a strong political, anti-establishment and pro-democracy identity. Artists argue that once the objective of democracy was fulfilled, Nepali theatre entered a period of crisis. Such crises of theatre following the overthrow of authoritarian regime have occurred in other countries. For example, Romanian actor and director, Ion Caramitru argued that during the Communist Era, theatre was a stronghold of moral and artistic resistance. After the collapse of Ceausescu regime in 1989, theatre lost its audience and actors had to work hard to rebuild the whole structure with the help of philosophers and artists who returned to Romania after years of exile (Caramitru, 1996, 58–66). The crisis, however, lasted only a couple of years, much less than Nepal's theatrical crisis, as perceived by the actors I interviewed.

Artists' opinions about the perceived decline of theatre in the country after 1990 vary. Some believe the introduction of new electronic media such as television and cinema shifted a large part of the audience away from the theatre halls. Anil explains that TV was more easily accessible to viewers than theatre. Audiences can watch tele-serials and films at home without having to travel. Watching television – as well as acting in tele serials – was also a source of social status and its popularity spread rapidly (see Liechty, 2003). The new media lured some theatre artists as well. As a result, the decline in theatre practice is also, partly explained in terms of a decrease in the availability of artistic personnel. New media provided glamour. Easy popularity and recognition attracted actors. In contrast, drama was still stigmatized and considered the preserve of 'people who don't have work' (Chapter 1 and 7). Inevitably, the 'lower' status assigned to theatre artists in comparison to film or TV actors, played a part in the decreased interest in theatre as a profession. Other artists, however, believe that the audience alone cannot solely be blamed for the decline of theatre. Instead, they attribute waning audience interest to a decline in the quality of the stage drama on offer. For others, the decline of theatre needs to be understood primarily as a consequence of the lack of government policies.

Sunil locates the reasons for theatre's decline elsewhere. Having developed a theatrical language around the limitations imposed by the lack of freedom of expression, it took theatre groups almost a decade to develop a new language after the enemy was not there anymore. He talks about a deep aesthetic and identity crisis that affected the whole political theatre movement once the goal of political struggle for democracy was seemingly achieved, a crisis that coincided with the expansion of NGOs and INGOs soon after 1990:

> [street theatre before 1990] was totally political. It was performed because of the spirit and the political thought. We were not asking for any money from anyone. It was totally our commitment, the theatre of people's commitment towards democracy. Then when the NGOs entered the scenario, after '90, street theatre of Nepal, all the street theatre movement went to the NGOs hands and it lost the spirit, and it was totally [reduced to] the money-making of propaganda theatre, it was also propaganda theatre at the beginning but with a different spirit.[2]

Donor involvement in theatre is still a sensitive issue. Most theatre groups rely on project work for their survival. At the same time, as Abbing (2002) notes with regard to western art, the marriage between art and economics is a terribly uncomfortable one. Sunil explains that

> afterwards it was an easy money making thing too. There was a lot of street theatre, and we forgot the aesthetic of theatre. Somehow it was more speech and speech and speech and theatre people lost their…, in a way not ethics, but way. In a way the funder, who gives the money, decided the content. They gave you the message and you just need to deliver it[3]

For some time, Sunil feels, theatre groups lost their 'agency', becoming somehow the means by which other people's messages were communicated. Sunil suggests that artists lost the theatrical language, the aesthetics of the theatre and so at one stage when people heard about street theatre, they thought OK, it's something about the toilet [or some other development issue] or something we don't need to see'.

Many theatre groups grew in association with development campaigns, usually starting from Kathmandu and moving out to the periphery. Artists' tales of those adventurous trips are fascinating. Because in rural areas the possibilities of entertainment were limited, in these artists' representations the troupes were always welcomed with great enthusiasm, in a way that resembles the cultural workers' tales; gathering an audience was easy. In fact, like political cultural programmes, theatre had the double function of delivering the 'development message'[4] and entertaining the spectators. The working schedules were tight. For example, Aruna performed in street plays in East Nepal for two years in the mid-1990s. Her team was composed of 10 artists, playing between 60–90 performances a month, 2–3 per day. They walked from village to village on foot and earned an average of NR 150 per show.[5]

The late 1990s, however, were also years of methodological experimentation. Theatre groups tried out different dramatic techniques to merge commitment to the art and cause, with financial survival. For example, Aarohan Theatre replaced long tours across faraway districts with theatre training courses for local partner groups. This was advantageous because local groups had a deeper awareness of the local socio-political situation as well as the ability to use specific idioms, manners and language. Plays were, thus, more topical, costs were reduced, and resources were managed at a community level. Nonetheless,[6] according to many artists, the aesthetic quality of street dramas decreased, and was often replaced by long morality tales and speeches.

Artists' representations of the relationship and impact of donors funding on Nepali theatre are varied and contrasting. At one extreme, some would refer to NGO finance as a 'sweet poison';[7] at the other as a *badhyata*, or compulsion. The relationship with donors and foreign funding is certainly a heartfelt theme that triggers heated debates. 'NGO theatre' has become a genre in itself in Nepal, as well as a source of contention. Nobody wants to be labeled as a group doing 'NGO theatre', alternatively known as *bikase natak/bikase kam* (development theatre/ work), propaganda *natak* or *pracharbadi natak* (advertisement theatre) (Ghimire, 2007). Yet, most of the theatre groups that I encountered in Nepal depended upon foreign funding for survival. The stigma went beyond the wider crisis that affected the development industry (Heaton Shrestha, 2001, 18; Dixit, 1997; De Chenes, 1996). Street theatre, in fact, was considered a 'low' form of drama by some intellectual when I started my fieldwork. There seemed to be a hierarchy of artistic genres defined through form (oral vs. text-based performance), location (street vs. proscenium stage), and audience (casual and non-paying vs. paying). For example, text-based theatre and literature were considered 'superior' to oral, improvisation-based, or street–performed ones. Even acting in cinema and TV shows was regarded as more prestigious than theatre because these professions offered more lucrative income. The definition seems to indicate a high-caste cultural hegemony, since most oral performances traditionally were the realm of lower-castes and classes (Chapter 7). Financial remuneration and fame also played important roles in defining the status of dramatic genres.

Although it is not possible to generalize across theatre groups or the ways in which donors fund theatre projects, in the late 1990s some artists started to consciously struggle to differentiate 'street theatre' or development theatre from 'NGO theatre'. Aarohan's turn towards *kachahari natak* constitutes one of those attempts.

Kachahari natak

An open ground near the Ring Road, in Kathmandu. Actors sing folk songs to gather an audience (Fig. 4.1, photo by the author):

Figure 4.1: Crowd gathered around a *kachahari* performance in Balaju Market, Kathmandu

Lured by the rhythm of the *madal* (drum),[8] passers-by stop. The familiarity of the songs creates a friendly and joyful atmosphere. Actors and audience connect. An aesthetic space is being conjured up. Children find place in the inner part of the circle that spontaneously forms around the performance area, a diameter of about 6–8 metres. Some spectators sing along with the actors, others smile and move on. From time to time, someone is totally taken over by the mood of the songs and improvises folk dance moves. More and more people find a place around the circle that will host the play. By the end of the second song, a crowd has formed and is ready to watch the show. The *sutradhar* (facilitator/narrator)[9] introduces the theatre group and explains the 'rules' of *kachahari natak*.[10] Then all the actors gather at the centre of the space. Bent forward, arms on the shoulders of their companions, the actors form a close circle to amplify the sound of their opening song that introduces Devi's story:

Aama malai pathaauna padhnalai
Na roka hai agaadi badhnalai

Mother send me to study
Don't stop me from going ahead

An ordinary family lives in a remote rural area. Devi studies in class 3. Her father's call interrupts her game in the courtyard. He is ready to leave for the capital. Because of the civil war,[11] life in the country is hard and schools are frequently closed. Through the help of a relative, a broker, Devi's father brings the girl to the house of a rich family in Kathmandu. She is expected to help with the family chores and continue her studies in her free time. The father will work in a brick factory nearby. They travel to Kathmandu by bus and Devi settles with the new family. Despite the promises, Devi is given too much work and never has the opportunity to go to school. Physical and psychological violence are also part of her daily regimen. Day after day Devi becomes bitter and sad as she sees the landlord's son going to school. One day she finds the courage to ask the landlady permission to go to school. The lady denies, and continues oppressing her. The play is stopped and the *sutradhar* asks the audience: 'In this situation, what can the little girl do?'

This tableau portrays the beginning of the hundreds of street plays – *kachahari natak* – performed by Aarohan Theatre around Kathmandu during the period of my fieldwork. Aarohan Theatre turned to *kachahari natak* to increase audience participation and in the attempt to move away from what they perceived as top-down forms of street theatre. *Kachahari natak* was systematically introduced into Aarohan's activities with the establishment of Gurukul, thus marking an important turning point in their street theatre practice. The practical experience of Aarohan's senior actors in the 1990s made them realize that travelling out of the capital to perform street theatre was not a beneficial methodology because of the problematic relationship between city-based artists and local communities. The topicality of the content, audience participation, and the local 'flavour' of the performance and language were key elements in determining whether or not a play was successful. Basanta explains how sometimes the solutions to problems suggested by street plays needed to be 'tuned' to the location. He gives an example of a development issue, 'sanitation', discussed through a street play showing the necessity of boiling water. But 'what if a community is so poor as not to have the kerosene to boil water? Why not think about cleaning the water canal instead?' remarks Basanta, pointing at the mismatch between lived reality and its standardized representation offered by street plays. Aarohan Theatre dealt with these problems by changing its strategy. First, it started training local groups instead of performing out of the Kathmandu Valley. Secondly, it experimented with a more participatory theatre methodology, that is, forum theatre. The next subsection will show how the global methodology of the theatre of the oppressed (Schutzman and Cohen-Cruz, 2006; Cohen-Cruz and Schutzman, 1994) was locally adopted and then adapted into *kachahari natak*. The continuities with the 'original' form as well as the variations introduced in the Nepali context will be considered.

Nepalizing forum theatre

Sunil recollects the first[12] forum theatre workshop in Nepal[13] as a tale of risk and courage (Pokharel, 2004, 8). In 2001, a Danish NGO, MS Nepal contacted Sunil to discuss theatre. That particular year's slogan for MS Nepal's head-office was 'Peace, conflict resolution and reconciliation'; the Nepali office wanted to organize a project on this theme.[14] Sunil met Tim Whyte, a Danish adviser in Dang, who asked Sunil for help in preparing some 'theatre for conflict resolution' activities. Because he thought street theatre had been overused in Nepal, Tim Whyte suggested that Sunil employ forum theatre instead. They planned a 10-day workshop in Banepa (Kavre) to train five partner groups that would perform in their own areas. A few days before the workshop, Sunil met Tim, assuming he would know how to perform forum theatre since he had suggested it. Sunil, in fact, had heard of it but was not familiar with the methodology. But Tim had no knowledge of forum theatre and assumed that Sunil, as a theatre person, knew about it. The beginning of the workshop was approaching but no manual about forum theatre was available in Kathmandu. A friend of Sunil's found a two-page article written in English. Therefore, the first workshop on forum theatre he conducted was based on improvisation out of those two pages, but the form seemed to work well anyway. During the workshop Sushil Chaudhari, an actor from Bardhiya, suggested giving the technique a Nepali name: *kachahari* (Ibid.). In Nepali *kachahari* indicates a traditional court where village leaders gathered to hear and resolve conflicts in their own community (Upreti, 2008).

But the adoption of a Nepali name introduced a particular mode of conflict resolution. I understood the specific connotation of a '*kachahari* solution' only when

I came across a real life example. In 2005 I was in a village near Biratnagar, as a guest of relatives of Aruna and Mani. Mani told me that his uncle's cow had been stolen. Therefore a group of villagers were going to hold a *kachahari*. Mani explained that they were almost sure about the identity of the thief but if they had gone to the police, the man would have simply been arrested and released after few days. The villagers were not interested in punishing that man. What they wanted was to have the cow returned. The solution sought by the *kachahari* meeting was therefore a very 'practical' one, focusing more on serving the interest of the 'oppressed' rather than punishing the 'oppressor', through using the community's capabilities and knowledge. *Kachahari* meetings are still held in rural areas of Nepal. Even though in the capital many people may not have had real-life experience of a village *kachahari*, according to the artists most understand what it is about. *Kachahari* is conceived as a 'traditional, national institution',[15] neither caste nor region specific. 'It is our long tradition in Nepal', explains Rajkumar.

Anil visualizes the difference between street theatre and *kachahari natak* through a powerful metaphor. He recounts that when the actors perform street plays, they 'go with a head full of things and come back empty'. They discharge their knowledge to the audience. The image suggests a one-way flow, a monological form of communication (Freire, 2004; Boal, 1998). Conversely, when they perform *kachahari* theatre, they 'go with an empty head and come back full'.[16] This statement highlights two key moments in the process of performing a *kachahari* play: the lack of preconceptions preceding the construction of a performance and the quality of information produced by the performance itself.[17] The flow of information is the very opposite of that which occurs in street plays. In the case of *kachahari*, information is not 'delivered' by the specialists but 'comes out' from the audience.[18] What emerges from confronting the two forms is a different theory of mind. Street theatre is backed by the assumption that the audience lacks knowledge and needs to be fed with information from 'outside'. Street theatre as a form of 'Behaviour Change Communication' is thus legitimized and the practice fits well into the ideology of development that reads reality in terms of lack. In contrast, *kachahari* theatre is based on the assumption that the audience may have ideas on how to solve their problems. Theatre is used to facilitate the dialogue within the audience and as a form of rehearsal and reflection on different possible solutions.

To sum up, while the Theatre of the Oppressed has now become a global technique of staging power relations, in Nepal it has found a particular local character, which is not defined through the revival or the adaptation of pre-existing traditional artistic performances. What is referred to and reinvented is a pre-existing form of local government practice, of problem resolution. However, what is easily framed by theatre specialists is not so obvious to non-specialists. Theatre artists who are not familiar with the origin of the Theatre of the Oppressed perceive *kachahari* as a 'foreign form' (see Chapter 1). One artist once explained to me that it came from India, which is usually considered the main source of new theatrical practices entering Nepal. The audience recognizes the word in its original meaning, although many spectators do not practically distinguish *kachahari* from other forms of street theatre.[19] However, such a pan-Nepal view of the *kachahari* meetings portrayed by Rajkumar cannot be accepted at face value either. Upreti (2008, 152) locates *kachahari* meetings in the hills. Moreover, *kachahari* meetings may have inbuilt a power imbalance as only the village leaders took part in the meetings. As an arena for display and context of power, they may not be neutral arenas for debate in the Habermasian sense. How the 'rules' of the public space that govern the *kachahari* meetings translate into the aesthetic space of *kachahari natak* will be discussed in the case-studies outlined next.

Mainstreaming *kachahari natak*

Conflict constitutes the heart of theatre (Boal, 1998; Chapter 3). Conflict is also the starting point of *kachahari natak*. Establishing how to frame a conflict and, in particular, what kinds of conflicts to dramatize was a crucial issue, especially in a conflict-ridden country. Aarohan Theatre tried to use theatre in conflict transformation after a series of workshops organized by MS Nepal. A publication from a workshop that brought together four South Asian theatre groups in Kathmandu (2003), to discuss theatre for social change, highlights that 'one of the ways to give room for positive conflict transformation is through theatre because it allows for conflicts to be analysed and explored on a 'neutral' ground, namely on stage' (MS Nepal, 2003, 13). Through theatre, the booklet continues, conflicting parties can see their situations from different points of view and try various solutions, 'without necessarily having to agree with them or accommodate any consequences afterwards' (Ibid.). But can the street 'stage', as a public space, really be neutral? Is the performance space exempt from the rules of the public space? Under which circumstances can it be so? In fact, public events often been understood as part of the process of ramification through which conflicts escalate (see Chapter 5; Breed, 2009).[20]

This section explores the assumed 'neutrality' of the stage and suggests it may itself be a construction more useful to development agencies than to the audience and theatre practitioners. The second question presents another tension: is the audience really exempt from any consequence when the performance is over? This statement is based on the assumption that the aesthetic space created by the performance is totally detached from the everyday space of social interaction and that the boundaries between the two are clear-cut. The aesthetic space would thus become conceived as an apolitical space. Thirdly, community involvement and the possibility of personal action in similar real-life situations are considered essential to participatory theatre (Chapter 6). In short, the assumed neutrality of the aesthetic space, boundaries between life and theatre, ideas of 'community', and 'participation' are critical concerns which will be analysed and discussed in the next sections.

A standard model to analyse conflict put forward in the workshop booklet, and used by theatre groups, suggests focusing on three concentric circles:

Table 4.1: Conflict-analysis model

	3	2	1
	Personal sphere	**Local sphere**	**Outer sphere**
Example	Impact of the People's War on the personal lives of the people living in conflict areas	Impact of the People's War at village level	The People's War at political level (government-leaders)

Source: Diagram by the author examplifying the model

The innermost circle represents the personal sphere closest to the individual. The level two circle, represents the local sphere, near the individual. There, the conflict is visible and approachable, although the underlying driving forces and structures may be hidden. The first level stands for the outer sphere, 'faceless, social, political, economic or cultural' issues people usually don't have direct access to'. The material suggested translating level-three conflicts into level-one or two in order to address them through a *kachahari* play (MS Nepal 2003, 13).

In 2004, Aarohan artists had already excluded level-one conflicts from forum theatre. They were considered out of reach in theatrical terms. Although actors could explore the roots of those problems, they felt unable to address people in power. Therefore, they were not able to look for real-life solutions or transformations. For example, the ideology of caste was considered a problem at level one. But the everyday forms of caste discrimination were regarded as a level-two or three conflict and could thus be portrayed by a *kachahari* play. In contrast, the insurgency was at that time considered level-one as well, but war-related conflicts that impacted the daily life of villagers were deemed out of *kachahari*'s reach. This inconsistency questioned the assumed neutrality of the *kachahari* aesthetic space.

The following case study shows why the issue of the insurgency, and, therefore, staging conflict, was dropped. During the last days of a training workshop that ran in Gurukul in December 2004, a group of artists devised a skit based on a story of double allegiance experienced in many Nepali villages to experiment the possibility of staging a full play based on a real story narrated by one of the artists. The frame ran as follows. Some Maoist activists threaten a schoolteacher with requests of donations. The teacher is afraid, and is also worried for his son. Discussions about how to behave with the rebels involve family and neighbours. One night the Maoists arrive and ask for shelter and food for 15 guerrillas. The family says they have no vegetables and no money. Moreover, they are afraid that if the army comes they might be caught in the crossfire or be accused of supporting the rebels. The frame[21] was stopped. The question raised by the *sutradhar* was challenging: if the man helps the Maoists the military may come and arrest his family members. If he doesn't, the Maoists may take revenge afterwards. The actors' discussions and rehearsals revealed that the plot was problematic, as it was not possible to determine who were the respective oppressor and oppressed. They abandoned the attempt to devise the play. The problem was considered beyond the possibilities of theatrical intervention. As a result, war-related topics were considered unsuitable for *kachahari* in Nepal at that time. Indeed, this situation did occur. Pettigrew's ethnography shows that villagers had no choice: they had to house and feed the Maoists despite the risks (2013).

The rehearsal revealed that the criteria agreed upon by the group were not necessarily in accordance with their real-life experience. It seemed not a matter of proximity to the problem or of centrality in the community that made the difference, as the previous model suggested; rather, the opposite was true. The insurgency, a level-one political problem had very practical consequences for people's lives, even at the 'personal level' (level-three). But this is exactly what prevented its fictional representation through theatre. What was significant was that 'public exposure' turned the personal political. Actors' discussions showed that certain situations carry their consequences well beyond the aesthetic space; the audience infers meaning from the putatively 'fictional' roles taken up by the actors/spect-actors. Yet, the level of exposure varied in context and time. Living inside the conflict areas exposed actors of partner groups[22] much more than those based in Kathmandu. The aesthetic space is indeed a political space; the distinction disappears, as the political performances and actors' fears of questioning power too openly described in Chapter 3 also show. The aesthetic space does not exist separate from its everyday fluid social space. It is this timely connection that makes representation in general and theatre in particular such a powerful and controversial political tool. The next section will illustrate how *kachahari natak* was adapted to the particular conditions created by the declaration of the state of emergency in 2005 and how this format was then reproduced in Kathmandu even after its end.

Searching for a format: An 'urban forum'

Street theatre is frequently associated with rural areas, because it is conceived as a way to facilitate communication with illiterate groups. Why, then, perform street theatre in urban Kathmandu particularly where other media are available? Aarohan Theatre decided to train local groups for street performances in their own areas and to directly perform only in the capital. Rajkumar believes that *kachahari* should not only be performed in the villages. He regards *kachahari* as a way through which artists can fulfill their commitment towards their society. '*Kachahari* is our way to change society' he says.[23] Aarohan's exploration of a suitable forum format coincided with its adaptation to an urban environment. I will now outline the dramaturgical development of the form and subsequently the aesthetics of forum theatre in Kathmandu.

Boal's 'original' form of forum theatre (Boal, 1979) recommends the performance of the whole script once. Subsequently, during a second performance, the audience can stop the play when oppression is perceived, so that the spect-actors can modify the course of action and try out ways of overcoming it (Ibid.). Forum theatre, however, has been adapted and modified in different ways (Cohen-Cruz and Schutzman, 1994; Schutzman and Cohen-Cruz, 2006). Boal himself warns against dogmatic interpretations of his techniques and suggests actors follow the people's desires: 'TO [Theatre of the Oppressed] is not a Bible, nor a recipe book: it is a method to be used by people, and the people are more important than the method' (1998, 120). Aarohan had adopted a classification distinguishing between Forum A and B. In the first form, it is the *sutradhar*[24] who stops the play at the end of the frame. In the second, the play is stopped by the audience at any time (closer to simultaneous dramaturgy). In neither, however, was the frame replayed a second time as in the original Boalian version. During the period of my fieldwork, Aarohan always performed Forum A. The actors play the frame, stopping at a critical point. Then the *sutradhar* asks the audience for suggestions about how to move out of the challenging situation. It is not the audience that decides at which point to change the characters' action, rather the *sutradhar*. Therefore, the audience can only change the course of events from the crisis point chosen by the actors. The audience's range of choice is thus restricted in comparison to the original form. Afterwards, as in Boal's model, the actors/spect-actors perform the suggestions. Finally, the *sutradhar* inquires about the feasibility of the suggestions offered, that is, whether they can be actually practiced in real life.

A further issue worth considering is the construction of the *kachahari* frame. Aarohan's practice changed throughout the period of my research. For the first two months (November and December 2004), the group arranged workshops with representatives of the target community. Artists and community members discussed their problems to find a critical issue, which could then be worked through with *kachahari*. Artists would devise and rehearse a storyline with community members that would then act the frame with Aarohan actors. The performance would then involve the whole community. From January 2005, the group decided to prepare a standard play in advance and then perform it repeatedly in different locations. This shift in production mode recalls a much-debated problem in Theatre for Development and draws attention to the difference between process-oriented theatre and product-oriented theatre (Epskamp, 2006). The first is workshop-based: a specific, localized community is identified and through participatory methodologies actors and community representatives construct a performance. It is considered a 'people-centred/learner-centred' form of theatre exploring solutions to specific problems identified by community members and then raising grassroot's awareness (Ibid., 44). Epskamp includes both forum theatre and community theatre within this category. Theatre as a 'product' is instead considered 'message-centred and sender-oriented' (Ibid.), focusing on behavioural change through persuasive communication. Street theatre, propaganda theatre and agit-prop usually fall into this category. The degree of community involvement is different, as I will detail later.

Greater community involvement also means that actors need to devote more time to work with communities. The number of *kachahari* plays performed by Aarohan increased from 3–7 a month in Nov-Dec 2004, to 14–15 a month from January 2005, with the introduction of a new partnership. In January 2005, many artists travelled to India for a theatre festival. When they returned, they had to perform all 15 performances within 10 days which meant performing twice a day. The group was funded to perform a fixed number of *kachahari* plays per month but had the freedom of choosing the topic with local communities. This hectic schedule produced a change in the previous *kachahari* practice. Artists chose to present a previously performed *kachahari* about corruption in government offices. The plays were performed in the streets. As a result, *kachahari* theatre lost the connection with the specificity of a community. What I argue is that contextual circumstances and financial pressures affected the methodology adopted by the group. Except for technical differences – that is, the audience's participation in the forum – the new version of *kachahari natak* became similar to mainstream street theatre. With the exception of a performance during the opening of a photo exhibition, for the three months of the state of emergency (February–April 2005), no *kachahari* was performed because of government restrictions. The end of the state of emergency and the gradual opening of the streets marked a shift to a further phase in the development of *kachahari natak*: in May 2005 artists inaugurated Devi's story on child labour, performing mostly in schools. They would continue to stage the same play for more than a year and a half.[25]

Let me now analyse the generation of issue-based *kachahari* ('child labour') and workshop-based *kachahari* frames ('construction workers' rights') as a comparative case-study on the production process of a *kachahari natak*. Aarohan Theatre is the only group that I met in Nepal that negotiated a particular form of partnership with funding agencies. Unlike others that received performance topics from funding agencies, *kachahari* theatre was part of a project aimed at strengthening local democracy and developing artistic practices. These partnerships therefore placed Aarohan in a privileged position in comparison to most theatre groups working in Kathmandu as they had neither thematic nor aesthetic pressures from the donors. The analysis of the standardization of the form shows that in my year and a half of observation contextual pressures emerged: the content presented to different schools remained the same and was not chosen by the community, but rather was imported 'from outside', like in top-down development theatre. Despite this crucial variation in the theatrical methodology, the genre continued to be called *kachahari* and be linked to forum theatre. Comparison with cross-cultural examples of forum theatre will be explored at the end.

Issue-based *kachahari*: 'Child labour'

The topic: Devising the frame

Aarohan's artists practice the same form of collective creation in producing both *kachahari* frames and political plays, although the process is situation specific. Collective creation is a methodology used by many alternative theatre groups who challenge the two-step traditional process, which separates the specialized tasks of scriptwriting by a playwright and the staging of the play (Shank 2002, 122). Collective creation, though irreducible to a single formula, is characterized by carefully researched themes determined by audience context, lengthy creative processes through improvisation, and 'simple and flexible production techniques suitable for both indoor and outdoor venues' (Zavala, 1980, in Van Erven, 2001, 138). According to theatre theorists and practitioners Garcia and Buenaventura (Ibid.) collective creation goes beyond methodology and requires a particular kind of actor, 'a self-conscious socially responsible co-owner of the means of creative production' (Ibid.). For example, in Colombia a typical process of collective creation can be divided into three stages:

1. structural analysis of the stories collected in the field or through research, singling out conflict, characters' forces and motivations;

2. verbal and non-verbal improvisations by a group of artists to explore the conflicts while another group act as critics, evaluating the artistic effectiveness and ideological impact;

3. different subcommittees specialized in music, design, and scriptwriting
    produce the different components of the performance that are subsequently
    integrated with the director (Van Erven, 2001, 140).

The process of creating a new play in Gurukul was not as structured as in the
Columbian case. Artists usually called a meeting and discussed possible topics,
often splitting into subgroups. The following is an extract from my field notes taken
during a meeting in which a *kachahari* topic was chosen.

> 21 December 2004 - The meeting to decide the topic of the next
> *kachahari* is postponed several times. Second day of bandh, all the
> shops are closed and no public transportation is functioning. Actors
> tell me to eat quickly because the meeting is about to begin at 10am.
> It's 11 am, nothing is happening, artists are chatting in the sun, or
> reading. The meeting is postponed to 1pm. The hall is occupied by
> a dance group so rehearsal will start afterwards. The meeting starts
> at 2.30 pm. Suresh, Mani, Sarita, Bhola, Rajkumar, Aruna, Rajan,
> Kirstine,[26] and other actors. Suresh is the leader. Artists propose 6
> topics that are voted by the group:
>
> - women issues- domestic violence 1 vote
> - children rights 6 votes
> - overseas employment 4 votes
> - internal struggle 1 vote
> - corruption 1 vote
> - human rights 2 votes
>
> The topic decided by the majority vote is for the next *kachahari*
> to be children rights. The group is divided into two subgroups.
> Kirstine and I are asked to participate in the discussions. I suggest
> starting with a workshop with some child workers, to get first hand
> account of their lives to make a strong story and avoid stereotypes.
> The group accepts the idea. Kirstine suggests problematizing
> the issues, trying to explore wider connections, to avoid simply
> condemning child labour without exploring its root causes and
> complexities. The discussion falls into our daily experience. Biru
> is a teenager who works in the canteen. Yubaraj is against the fact
> that he is working in Gurukul instead of going to school and says
> that Thulo Manche,[27] another young man working in the canteen
> does not want to go to school as he does not realize the importance
> of education. Yubaraj himself pushed him to go to school, to learn
> to read and write, to play a musical instrument but he refused.

Yubaraj thus raises a question: how far can you 'push' people if they don't 'realize'? Biru and Thulo Manche have never gone to school. He shares his feelings of uneasiness about these facts. The groups join and share in the discussions. It is decided to divide the tasks. A small group will contact children's associations to check if Nepal has signed UN child rights papers, to check for the number of street children; others will go to talk to children working in hotels and in the streets. The next meeting is scheduled for the next day at 4 pm. Afterwards the group continues rehearsal of the play performed for construction workers some days before. The rehearsal continues until 7 pm. [...] The morning after Rajan, Kamal and I, go to Save the Children Nepal to ask for some data but the person we were looking for was out. At Bal Mandir, the person responsible for the office is out too.

Artists would then meet again a month later to devise the play storyline and fix some scenes. The planned research was not carried out and the story was based on actors' personal experience. The central idea would be retained in the final version, while the development of the story and the construction of the climax would change afterwards. The Emergency stopped the progress, which could be taken up again in May 2005. The story was enriched through a workshop with a partner group, the Kamlari Natak Samuha from Dang-Deukhuri (Chapter 5). In April 2005, the Kamlari Group attended a 10-day workshop in Gurukul directed by one of Gurukul's artists, Saugat. They prepared a stage production based on their *kachahari* work and their first-hand experience of exploitation while working as domestic helpers. Boal stresses the importance of accurate information regarding the conflict to be dramatized. The protagonist/oppressed in fact encounters several obstacles/ oppressors, he warns that

> this search for suitable oppressors must not be random; the group which is creating the play must have genuine knowledge of the problem and must present an organic vision of the situation in which all the elements are true. Theatricality must not sacrifice truth (1998, 62).

When the group returned to work on their child labour frame, elements from the stage production, like plot, movements and lines were introduced in the child labour *kachahari* frame performed by Aarohan in Kathmandu together with comic elements. Characters and context were fleshed out in depth. Thus, the process of play construction was discontinuous, affected by the political crisis as well as by the group artistic work and priorities. The initial play was mainly created out of the group's internal experience. However, the first hand experience of the Kamlari artists added fresh, real-life elements to both the frame and the actors' artistic skills, turning it into a very powerful and sophisticated presentation (Fig. 4.2–4.7, photos by the author).

Figure 4.2: Rajan as joker introduces the rules of *kachahari natak* to the students and performs a game requiring arms coordination

Figure 4.3: The artists gather in a circle and sing the opening song

Figure 4.4: The father performed by Suresh and daughter performed by Pashupati travel to Kathmandu, the banner symbolizes the bus

Figure 4.5: Father and daughter are greeted by the house-owner played by Saugat

Figure 4.6: The wife, played by Aruna, shows Devi the different rooms she has to clean

Figure 4.7: Devi helps the son to get ready for school but she cannot go herself

Figure 4.8: A teacher (wearing a sari) enters the forum section and tries to persuade the couple to send Devi to school

Figure 4.9: A student replaces Devi

The set: Choosing a location

The responsibility for the organization of the *kachahari* performance is a task that was shared among actors. Rajkumar, Bhola, Kamal and Suresh were in turn responsible for choosing a place and arranging the details of the performance with a contact person, such as a youth club leader or the headmaster of a school. Very often the contact was chosen through personal connections. When *kachahari* was performed in the street the general location was usually selected by the team-leader, and then the group agreed upon the specific place. Performing in the streets means engaging in a continuous negotiation of physical and symbolic spaces. Most of the time, space was negotiated with street vendors or bus park keepers who willingly agreed to temporarily clear a piece of road for the sake of the theatre. In order to gather a crowd, actors looked for a place of dense human presence. But for the success of a play, they also tried to avoid places that were too noisy. As a result, actors always had to compromise between visibility and audibility. Performing inside schools was less problematic as the group leader would arrange a time with the principal and the audience – students and teachers – was usually disciplined. During the performance of a play, the circle of the performance becomes the focus of attention of the whole area. Because of the huge crowd that usually watches the performance, street vendors selling snacks like corn, peanuts, soybeans, or even clothes were also attracted. As soon as the play finishes and the actors leave, the sellers regain their space, taxis return to their parking corner. A street performance is a fluid event, at the intersection of social, artistic, and practical concerns.

But the public space is also an administered space governed by authorities. In 2004, due to security reasons, the government established a rule that required actors performing in any public road to apply for a letter of authorization (*anumatipatra*) to the Chief District Officer (CDO). At the beginning of the month, members of the group had to request permission and then show the CDO authorization to the police who were patrolling the *chowks* (marketplace), on the day of the performance. Performances in the streets usually ran smoothly, and sometimes police stopped to watch the play themselves. The capital in the months preceding the Emergency was militarized. In January 2005, a policeman stopped a performance in the market space in the New Bus Park area. When he arrived, the large group of people following the play dispersed. Some actors remained in the circle. Others went to talk with the policeman, followed by nearly half of the audience. Although the stop created moments of tension, the problem was sorted out quickly. The place was a private area patrolled by local security. Artists had talked to the police, but did not know about the local security. The policeman wanted to stop the play. Aruna went to talk to the boss of the Bus Park Office and the problem was solved easily, facilitated by personal relations, as the boss was Aruna's *dai* (older brother), in this case a relative. Other people left the space because of the interruption, the performance was indeed affected. When the play restarted, and Rajkumar, the *sutradhar*, took up the last suggestions to continue, the environment was different, the connection with the audience was partly lost, so the *sutradhar* finished the forum quickly.

The frame performed

The frame of an issue-based *kachahari* play is a script workshopped among actors that presents a problem to the audience. Since Aarohan did not play the frame twice and the play was stopped by the *sutradhar* rather than by the audience, the frame had the function of leading the audience to the climax of a conflict. Boal suggests representing a 'Chinese crisis' (1998, 56) that is a situation in which the character is in danger but still has possibilities of finding a solution to their problems.[28] For example, forum theatre would not work in a situation in which the oppressor is pointing a gun to the oppressed and is ready to shoot (Ibid.).

The frame is the fixed part of a *kachahari* and Aarohan actors throughout the months of performance had specific roles. If necessary, actors were substituted through doubling. Despite the absence of a written script, the performance was stable, as all artists knew each other's key lines and could improvise around them when required. During the construction of *kachahari* scripts, artists never engaged with the idea of introducing isolated cultural 'items' for artistic purposes. Yet, each play is deeply embedded in 'Nepali culture'; songs, body language, posture, clothes, and language locate both actors and audience in an immediately familiar environment. For example, at the beginning of the play, Devi is in her village and recites a child's rhyme that is usually learnt at school. Swinging rhythmically, the children in the audience smiled and recognized both the lines and the movement – thus 'click *bhai halchha* (it works/it will do)' explains Pashupati. Here is a passage:

Cock-a-doodle-doo	*Kukhurika*
Eat stale rice	*Baasi bhat khaa*
Where's my stale rice?	*Khoi mero baasi bhat*
The cat ate it	*Biralole khayo*
Where's the cat?	*Khoi biralo*
It's gone to look for mice	*Musaa marna gayio*
Where's the mouse?	*Khoi muso*
It's gone inside the hole	*Dulo bhitra pasyo*
Where's the hole?	*Khoi dulo*
The cow has stepped on it	*Gaaile kulchyo*
Where's the cow?	*Khoi gaai*
The river has taken it away	*Kholaale bagayo*
Where's the river?	*Khoi khola*
It's all dried!	*Jammai suyo!*

Artists follow their 'feel for the game' (Bourdieu, 1990, 66) in constructing the situations and the characterizations, performance after performance. The use of traditional artistic forms is often recommended in development theatre performance (Epskamp, 2006, 47). Srampickal (1994) however warns against the revival of performances that existed in the past, but are no longer practiced, in the name of cultural preservation. Safdar Hashmi was critical about the use of traditional Indian performing art forms in street theatre. While admitting the importance of working with forms that the audience can be familiar with, he warned that such forms carry 'the traditional content with its superstitions, backwardness, obscurantism, and its promotion of feudal structures' (1992, 141). He also criticized the decorative use that 'bourgeois intellectuals' and western development agencies make of the 'Indianness' of traditional theatre, isolating it from the contemporary concerns of the people (Ibid., 142), and then exploiting the form (Ibid., 143). Hashmi instead praised the tradition that lives inside the artists. For example, he admitted that the songs he created for his plays were often based on folk songs that he learned as a child. Aarohan's actors, in building up both dialogues and songs, adopted the same procedure: they improvised and created out of shared cultural patterns that are also employed in the construction of political street plays (see Chapter 3).

There are several aesthetic elements that can be singled out in order to analyse a street play and how the actors establish a connection with the audience: the structure of the story, the balance between entertainment and information (use of comedy), cultural and traditional elements (songs, clothes and postures), the use of language (register, sayings). The *kachahari* performed at the Pinnacle Academy in Kalanki (Kathmandu) in July 2005 will be taken as a reference for the text and performance details.

The play is introduced by popular folk songs that are used to establish contact with the audience. The students sing along with the actors and clap. The *sutradhar* welcomes the audience and explains how *kachahari natak* works. He says the actors will perform a problem. When the play is stopped, the audience will become the directors and move the story forward. He asks them to watch quietly and attentively so that they will be able to help the actors. The atmosphere is very easy going and friendly.

Comedy is a powerful means by which to keep the audience engaged and at the same time allows the story to unfold. For example, at the beginning, Devi's painful departure from her village is accompanied by the jokes of a humorous bus conductor who is a friend of her father. He speaks in a very loud voice, wears funny hats, often back to front. Kamal, who regularly plays the conductor, is an outstanding comic actor. His miming abilities are extraordinary: great gestures with the hands, often ending in the typical Nepali upturn to indicate that there is not much else to do, and he captures the audience with a direct and inquisitive gaze. Introduced by drumming of increasing intensity to create suspense, his character arrives from the back of the stage area, from behind the audience. He speaks directly to the audience, half singing half talking, and often pausing to stare at the other characters. The audience laughs. The conductor also mispronounces words and speaks very fast, with the rising high-pitched 'ehhhhh', typical of the spoken street language.

SCENE TWO
(bus stop– trip towards Kathmandu)

BUS CONDUCTOR	enters, talks to the audience - sings –
[AUDIENCE LAUGHS]	
BUS CONDUCTOR	Namaskar
FATHER	Namaskar
BUS CONDUCTOR	Where are you going?
FATHER	To the city. These are no conditions for living in the village. All villagers have moved to the city. What shall I do living here? What will I eat?
BUS CONDUCTOR	Is that your daughter?

FATHER	Yes...
BUS CONDUCTOR	She has grown big....I've become a *khulasi* (bus conductor)
FATHER	*Khulasi?* What is a *khulasi?* I've only heard about *khalasi.*
BUS CONDUCTOR	The one who bangs the bus doors.
FATHER	That is *khalasi.*
BUS CONDUCTOR	Why are you going to Kathmandu?
FATHER	There is a family which needs some help with their household chores. They will also send her to school.
BUS CONDUCTOR	Good, good. Have you got a bus ticket?
FATHER	Yes
BUS CONDUCTOR	(He has a look at the ticket) This is the ticket of our bus.
FATHER	Yuck! (spits) There is no *aachi* (excrement)!
[AUDIENCE LAUGH]	
BUS CONDUCTOR	No, no. It's not like that. AA is for *alu* (potatoes) and CHI is for *chiura* (beaten rice). Would you like to eat BCR?
FATHER	Now, what is BCR?
BUS CONDUCTOR	B is for *bhatmas*, C is *chiura*, R is *raksi* (alcoholic drink).

[...]

The story is built up through a progression in which the girl's problems are presented alongside comical situations. The landlord's arrogance and disrespect for poor villagers is portrayed from the very beginning, when he mistakes his wife's relatives for flood refugees. Even the most dramatic moments, such as when Devi, played with great intensity by Pashupati, is severely scolded by the couple, or when the landlord and his wife engage in endless hysterical squabbles, are punctuated with comical elements that carry the audience along with the story without disguising the oppression or excusing it. The son, played by Bhola, breaks into his mother's narration a couple of times by unveiling her blatant lies, thus becoming Devi's potential ally in the forum. In fact, the audience frequently chose to replace him in order to help Devi.

SCENE EIGHT

(Family arrives – The wife rings the bell)

WIFE	Come fast, come fast! What the hell is she doing?
SON	If she has died, how could she come?
WIFE	What the hell are you doing?
DEVI	I was there.....
WIFE	If you were there, why didn't you open the door for two hours?
SON	Oh, mummy, it's not even been two minutes!

[AUDIENCE LAUGH]

WIFE	Shut up! (to her son) Where is your father? (to Devi) Did you finish your work?
DEVI	All, I washed the dishes, I washed the clothes
WIFE	Have you changed the bed cover?
DEVI	I did everything
LANDLORD	(enters complaining) They are all robbers [about the neighbours outside]
SON	Sir, who is a robber?
LANDLORD	Why are you calling me sir?
SON	My teacher's hair is like yours!

[AUDIENCE LAUGH]

LANDLORD	They have broken our car windows!
WIFE	It was your fault, so shut up! [...]

Comedy is used by actors to shed light on the inconsistencies of the wife's claims, thus exposing the oppressive situation. The climax of the play is reached when Devi asks the landlady to keep the promise made to her father and let her go to school. But the lady refuses.

Aarohan usually uses few and simple props in *kachahari*. Once aestheticized in the play, they acquire metaphorical meanings that strengthen the emotions conveyed by the actors. As Boal suggests,

> the important thing is the reality of the image, and not the exact image of reality. The important thing is to show what things are really like, as Brecht used to say, rather than merely showing what real things are like (Boal, 1998, 54).

Devi wears a school uniform while her father, often played by Rajkumar, wears a worn out *topi* (Nepali hat) – village clothes – and carries a bag, to indicate that he is going to travel. His 'village' background is also shown by deferential manners and a stooped posture while walking. His characterization is totally different from the landlord, played by Saugat, who is all the time rushing, and who wears dark sunglasses and a trendy cap in a fashionable urban style. Devi carries a black cloth that represents the carpet but it also symbolizes the oppressions she has to face. After work, she picks up the son's book to study. But the book symbolizes the education that she is excluded from. All these elements give the *kachahari* frame the immediacy and familiarity that allows the audience to identify with the characters. Aarohan artists adopt a casual style. Rather than creating an 'objectified' culture for their plays, they make use of fluid 'culture' as it is performed in everyday Kathmandu life.

Characterization

Pashupati played Devi since the beginning of the child labour *kachahari* and her experience is a fascinating example of how artists build characters by relating (*jodne*) them to their own daily and personal life experiences. Pashupati explains that this character 'happened *bhako*' (it happened) rather than being the result of a lot of 'workout'. Her experience both in stage and in street theatre led her to feel that characterization in Nepali theatre does not work through what she perceives as the western acting tradition, where it's necessary to 'workout a character, to work on a character, to look for a character'. She explains:

> I have a lot of feelings within myself, lots of experiences. You foreign actors do a lot of workout for your characters, probably you don't carry all the stuff Nepali actors do, because in order to understand a feeling you go through the story, through working out the character. But we join a lot of things from our own experience, I don't have to go very far, I can look at my life, my environment, I don't need to do a lot of workout. After linking them I can feel and there comes the character.[29]

However, she recalls that Sunil advised her to actually work on the character, on Devi's thoughts, feelings, to think about the story, her family in order to differentiate Devi from her own life. Pashupati clarifies that once in role, she forgot about all these thoughts and what emerged was her own life experience: 'A lot of Pashupati might have come out in Devi!' she laughs, aware that this can happen once, but if extended, it can turn into a limitation.

Pashupati comes from a middle class family. She did not go through Devi's hardships herself, because when she was a child she loved studying and her parents did all they could to support her. Nonetheless, she could relate to her real experience and feelings because in her native neighbourhood she witnessed the struggles of poor children. When the group started rehearsing, Pashupati was naturally selected for Devi's role because in comparison to other artists she looked very young. Besides, the group chose Devi as the character's name. Devi is also Pashupati's real name: Pashupati is the name that she used at school but all her family members call her Devi. Her Gurukul friends discovered this by chance, when someone on the phone asked about Devi and nobody knew it was her. As a result, choosing this name made it easier for Pashupati to play this role because, she explains, 'attachment *chha*' (there is attachment). When Devi is scolded – Pashupati continues – there is a sort of automatic activation of her own past experiences of being reproached, *aphai jodiera aunchha* (they join by themselves). Moreover, Pashupati lost her father, so some *kachahari* lines resonated strongly within herself to the extent that at times she struggled terribly to control her tears, especially when Devi is dropped at the landlord house and greets her father who is returning to the village saying: 'Father, from time to time come to see me'. Paradoxically, because of her real-life grief, in this case it was very hard to connect real life to the character. One day she felt that she was starting to cry, going out of role. She remembers that Aruna (who played the landlady) realized this, her quick 'hee' brought Pashupati back in role. Pashupati believes that because the characters they often play are so close to their own lives, it's very easy for actors to build them. Pashupati played the vigilantes in the *loktantrik natak* described in the previous chapter. Even in that case, it was very straightforward for her to build the character as she had seen similar characters striding the streets of Kathmandu for months during the movement.

Costumes played an important role in characterization. Pashupati explains that they chose two key elements: the uniform, not well-stitched, and simple *chappals* (flip-flops) so that the audience could understand that Devi was poor. She would also add an interesting detail to Devi's outfit: ribbons. Hair ribbons are compulsory in private schools and often girls don't like them. But in the village buying ribbons is a very big thing. School girls adore them and also wear them at home. For this reason Pashupati chose ribbons for her hair, to capture the audience 'sympathy'. Devi does not speak much because of her young age and also because, according to Pashupati's experience, children who work as house helpers don't talk much. Besides, they don't look at the interlocutor's eyes, they keep their eyes down, and reply through monosyllables, like '*la/hajur/hunchha*' (yes). The only full sentence that the character utters is '*ma pani school janchhu*' (I also go to school) at the end of the frame.

Devi's character seemed to work wonders. At times, in particular in street performances, the process of identification with the character when so far that some audience members actually thought Pashupati was a child labourer and the scene was real. Others would be suspended in a space in between and would wonder whether it was reality or theatre. In Kathmandu, many children work as house helpers, they often come from the rural areas. While the group was performing in New Baneshwor, a spectator questioned the actors. He thought that Pashupati was a real house helper who had been taken to Kathmandu and asked to perform to get 'NGO money'. The man warned the group that they should not play with the feelings of a small child and asked Pashupati if she works as a house helper for real. At that time Gurukul had just been opened, not many people knew about it and actors had a hard time to convince him it was just a play! Besides, Pashupati explains that while discussing, people often become aggressive and what was at first perceived as 'theatre' turns into reality. In Sundhara, it started raining while the group was performing. They opened umbrellas. An old man approached Pashupati. From his clothes it was clear that he had just come from a village. He asked her if she can study and gave her two rupees, saying '*mithai khau*' (Go eat some sweets). Caught by emotions, Pashupati was unable to answer, and tell him that what he saw was not reality but theatre. But she kept the two rupees as a memory. In the school environment, such overlap between reality and theatre is less probable as the play is clearly framed as theatre from the beginning. However, Pashupati recalls that once in Kopan, while she was changing her dress, a little girl gave her a toy pot and ran away without saying anything. She imagined that the little girl must have thought that Devi – as represented in the drama – cannot play, so she offered one of her own toys.

Actors and directors

When the frame finishes, the *sutradhar* invites the audience to participate in finding a solution to the problem. At first, he involves the audience collectively, re-establishing the channel of communication created at the beginning. Yubaraj was the *sutradhar* in many of the *kachahari* plays performed by Aarohan. This is an abstract from the video-recorded performance:

SUTRADHAR	You have seen all the problems here, what is happening in this drama, what do you think?
AUDIENCE	Nice, nice....
SUTRADHAR	The girl is not allowed to study, what are your feelings?
AUDIENCE	Bad
SUTRADHAR	Should this girl get to study or not?
AUDIENCE	Study, study

SUTRADHAR	Therefore, what should this girl do to study in this house?
AUDIENCE	Struggle
SUTRADHAR	How? In this situation, what should the girl do?
AUDIENCE	Should protest [SOME AUDIENCE MEMBERS LAUGH]... run away....
SUTRADHAR	Now you are the directors of the play, whatever you suggest we will do it here, as the boy suggested, we will make her run away from the house. Where to go?
AUDIENCE	To her father, her home!

The *sutradhar* establishes proximity with the audience in order to create a 'safe' environment where the audience can talk openly. In this case, the life situation of the girl is not close to the real-life experience of the students. No potential real life 'oppressor' is present in the school. Thus, creating a 'safe' environment basically involves helping the children overcome their shyness and encourage them to participate with suggestions. No power relation is challenged. The *sutradhar* facilitates the enactment of any suggestions offered by the audience, even those that are not agreed by all. For example, the first suggestions, involving fighting or escaping, are not consensual:

REHEARSAL 1

SUTRADHAR	(Devi plays the first suggestion) She picks up her clothes, runs away, where to go now? Now what to do?
DEVI	I have money but I don't have the address of my father where should I go?
SUTRADHAR	Now what should she do?
AUDIENCE	Go to the police, send her to a ladies hostel!
SUTRADHAR	How to reach the hostel? This girl is studying in class 3, can she run away from her house, what can she do?
AUDIENCE	She can't

(A teacher gives his suggestion)

SUTRADHAR	The teacher said it's not possible to run away from the house and find her father, we have to do it again. What else can she do? ...which can also be practiced in real life....

AUDIENCE	Go to CWIN
	[an NGO working with street children]
SUTRADHAR	Who will take her to CWIN?
AUDIENCE	Social workers...

[LOTS OF SUGGESTIONS SHOUTED TOGETHER]

SUTRADHAR	How can she meet them? She said neighbours can help (they rehearse) first she will try to convince the lady [neighbour]

Mohan (2004b) describes the forum plays performed by Jana Sanskriti in India as a 'project of persuasion'. Indeed, persuasion plays a central role in carrying the audience into the aesthetic space of the performance where fiction and reality blur. The frame, in fact, through a skillful alternation of comedy, familiar daily situations, gestures and phrases, prepares the ground for the forum where the relation between actors and audience becomes closer. By means of direct address, eye contact, and reassurance through smiling, the *sutradhar* and the actors persuade the spect-actors into 'believing' and make the performance space accessible, casual and informal. Yet, the *sutradhar* moves beyond the role of persuading the audience to identify with the characters on stage by actually bringing them into the imaginative space. The *sutradhar*, in fact, opens possibilities by creating voids and gaps, by asking questions to which spect-actors have to provide practical answers. By opening these gaps, the *sutradhar* acts on the audience's 'desires'. Desire is entrenched in the theatrical experience. Hastrup remarks that 'desire is born of absence; what is already possessed is no longer the object of desire' (2004a, 43); in particular, she affirms that 'players desire to become what they are not' (Ibid.). The *sutradhar* helps the audience become 'players', and helps them fill with actions and words the gaps and doubts created by his questions.

Yet, once again, 'make-believe is making, not faking, and rooting imaginative action in facts' (Ibid., 51). Only if illusion is real and grounded can the process of identification take place. Acting in a *kachahari* performance is very demanding and requires a mix of technique and profound knowledge of both the issue performed and of the socio-cultural context of the audience. Acting becomes even more challenging during the second part of a *kachahari* play, when the actors have to enact the suggestions given by the audience and improvise when the spect-actors enter the scene and take up roles. Alertness and competence are crucial. Mani is an actor who also works as a government officer. In the *kachahari* on corruption, he played the role of the officer himself. It is a role that he knows very well because of his job. He emphasizes that to play a role well, you need to 'have knowledge on what to do'. He explains how he plays the 'oppressor':

My role is very strong and quick, you need to think fast and take decisions. [...] I write many times [in role] but while writing, I always listen to the audience. My mind and my ears listen to the audience all the time. When a person comes to the stage and give[s] suggestions, I have a quick answer.[30]

There is no time for thinking in a *kachahari*; improvisations have to be fast as Mani explains, in order to be 'credible', just like in a real life situation.

The boundaries between reality and fiction are in fact very subtle. The process of identification can break at once if they are not sustained by 'credible' replies. In May 2005, Aarohan conducted a workshop in a *sukumbasi basti* (squatter slum) in the eastern part of the capital. Some residents gathered at a cultural centre for the workshop preceding the performance. What emerged as the most urgent problem was the fact that due to the heterogeneity of the inhabitants, it was very hard to organize collective activities like shifts for road cleaning. Moreover, it was also difficult to hold preparatory meeting with workshops, because despite agreeing a time, many people would not turn up and therefore no discussion could take place. Actors and participants created and rehearsed a short frame on this topic that was performed immediately after the workshop on the local green.

The *sutradhar* ended the frame at a critical point concerning the representation of an unattended meeting. He asked the audience how to solve the problem. The audience gave different suggestions that the actors performed and spect-actors even entered the circle to substitute actors. In this frame, the organizer of the meeting represented the oppressed, as his efforts were systematically boycotted by the inhabitants of the slum. A young woman from the audience replaced the organizer/oppressed and started knocking at different imagined doors to spread information about the next scheduled meeting. At a certain point, an artist playing a community member dismissed the invitation saying she was busy at work, as she was a teacher. Hearing the line, a woman standing near me in the audience sighed with surprise and incredulity. She said it could be true. This could not be their story as none of them had such a prestigious job as teaching. Her identification with the story was broken. She lost 'belief' in what was going on. The artists did not even notice her comment, they continued playing, and finished the forum. I could not find out if the woman's reaction was shared, or if it was an isolated case. But her reaction certainly showed that she was seeking some resonance with her real-life experience, that she had begun identifying with the characters, and she had been carried away by the 'magic', until the actress introduced the implausible element and disrupted her sense of imagined possibilities for her everyday reality. It was no longer 'her' life. It was 'fiction'. Unaware of the complex social structure of the *basti*, the artist introduced a notion so alien that it ceased to have any meaningful relationship with the possibilities inherent in her everyday situation and broke the exploration of real life. This example shows that acting in forum theatre is an extremely challenging activity. Over and above the necessary crafting of the imagined-reality space, it requires a heightened awareness, a particular sensibility, in order to avoid transgressing the socio-political context in which the audience live, losing their attention, and dissipating that moment when theatre helps in self-reflection, self-awareness and in the discovery and realization of possibilities inherent in every problematic situation.

The audience

The audience was not initially intended to be part of this inquiry. However, in order to determine the topicality of 'child labour' among school children,[31] a survey was carried out among 748 students from classes 5 to 10 in nine private schools. The objective of the research was explained to the headmasters. Teachers were directed as to how to conduct the questionnaire so as to maintain consistency i.e., giving students 45 minutes maximum, not helping students with the answers, etc. This was not to be intended as an evaluation of the practice but a way of understanding how *kachahari* was perceived by the students and how it related to their own lives.

The results revealed that 15 per cent of the respondents had a house-helper in their home, 81 per cent did not and 4 per cent did not answer that question. Among the 15 per cent, a great majority responded that their house-helper was not interested in studying or was over the age for school. In only two cases did the students record that they felt uncomfortable and bad after seeing the play because they were living in a similar situation. The play was much appreciated: 39 per cent liked it 'very much', 45 per cent said it was 'good', and 14 per cent found it OK, while only 2 per cent did not like it.[32] Students took the play very seriously. When they had to categorize it, 45 per cent found it 'serious', 16 per cent found it 'fun', and for 11 per cent it was like a 'game'. Extra definitions were added by the students in a blank space: for 10 per cent it provided 'education' and 13 per cent saw it as a representation of 'society'. The overall data for physical participation were rather low: 12 per cent managed to give suggestions while only 4 per cent entered the play to act during the forum part. The most frequent reasons cited for not giving suggestions or acting were lack of time and opportunity, and perceived lack of acting skills.

This data raises interesting questions. On the one hand, students recognize 'child labour' as a real social problem. On the other, it does not seem to be an issue they regard as their own. The protagonist, who is usually replaced by an audience member, is the house-worker who cannot study. Students attending private schools are more likely to have a house-helper at home rather than being house-helpers

themselves. Therefore, the students replacing the protagonist could not fully identify
or empathize with the character and circumstances of the protagonist, though they
would certainly learn from the play as their responses regarding the *kachahari's*
message suggested. Boal (2006, 126) describes three kinds of identification the
spect-actor can have with the protagonist:

1. absolute identity – when the protagonist incarnates exactly the same problem
    as the audience faces;

2. analogy – when the audience's problem is not exactly what is shown, but a
    strong analogy exists between the two; and

3. solidarity – when the audience's concerns are not identical, nor analogical,
    but a relationship of deep solidarity allows the spect-actor to offer his or her
    sensibility and knowledge to try to open up a range of possibilities, so that the
    protagonist may find solutions to his or her own problem.

A consideration from within this forum theatre experience can be drawn at this
point. Spontaneously, at times, during the performance of the play the *sutradhar*
allowed the sympathetic son of the landlord to be replaced by a spect-actor,
contravening the standard forum theatre practice in which only the 'oppressed' can
be replaced by a spect-actor. In this way, however, a 'natural' solution could be found,
closer to their own real life, and students could move from 'solidarity' to 'analogy' or
'absolute identity'. This is an example of how artists' competence and the relational
nature of the practice could introduce self-correcting changes to adapt the form to
the context. Had the story been told from the son's point of view rather than the
house-worker's, the students would have probably been able to identify with the
character in a closer way and see in the play a resemblance of their lives.

Moreover, the play is perceived as a theatre performance, requiring skill to
participate rather than an 'open space' for discussing problems. This may be due
to the students' lack of experience with forum theatre and the theatre in general.
Unlike other theatre groups, which work in workshop situations with a reduced
number of participants and for a long period of time, Aarohan adopted the street
theatre practice of giving a one off performance for large audiences (200–400). This
makes their theatre practice an excellent instrument for communication, like other
forms of street theatre, but is not necessarily the most suitable way to discuss real
life conflicts or to rehearse solutions, in particular because it takes time for audience
members to familiarize with the theatrical language and form. The interactive and
revolutionary power of forum theatre in this case seemed diluted.

The post-performance discussions and follow-up

During the first part of my fieldwork (December to January 2005) the performing group met after each *kachahari* for 'firing meetings' during which each artist had the opportunity to share their feelings and opinions about the performance with both colleagues and director. Firing meetings were moments of self-reflexivity that explored strengths, weaknesses, and ways to improve; they smoothed over occasional clashes and united the group. Cohesion and immediate mutual understanding are fundamental in an improvisation-based theatrical performance. But when the 'child labour play' started to be performed, these meetings became infrequent and eventually ceased altogether, under the pressures of the increased workload. Artists spoke with the director only if they had specific problems. Aarohan Theatre did not practise any form of follow-up activity to assess the impact of the performance. Actors point out that at the beginning of their experience with *kachahari*, they went back to certain schools to see if any transformation had taken place, but after a while they stopped doing this. And yet, when discussing an example of a 'successful' performance, actors refer directly to the follow-up. The group performed a play about drug addiction in a squatter's area. Suresh, an actor and a martial arts teacher, returned out of his own initiative, over the course of a year, to teach martial arts and theatre. He recalls that

> the performance was successful because a lot of audience participated
> and they tried to speak about their problems through theatre. We
> tried to do our best. Finally we arrived at some consensus on how
> to solve this problem. The play was successful in highlighting the
> issues. But how to solve them? And in the play I suggested to go
> there, personally work with the young people of the areas. And they
> said yes, please come and we started [he lowers his eyes and smiles].
> I went there and started a martial arts class with drug users. In the
> starting phase they were dangerous, and I gave them NRs 10, 20.
> They eat [the drugs] and then they came to the class [...] I spent
> some money. Slowly I increased the exercise and slowly, slowly
> they decreased the drugs. I went there every day from 6 to 7.30-
> 8 a.m. Then slowly they called me, 'teacher, teacher, guru, guru'.
> Then slowly they stopped using drugs in front of me, they started to
> respect me. One month passed, two months passed, in six months
> they quit drugs and they started to do more and more exercise.[33]

Follow-up is routine practice with other theatre groups using forum theatre techniques. For example, Adrian Jackson from Cardboard Citizens, a London-based theatre company, claims that in order to naturally and productively involve the audience, a forum piece should 'provoke and seduce' (2009, 44). As a result, his group has moved away from forum theatre as an 'event' towards an 'Engagement Programme' (Ibid.) in which, after the performance, the actors[34] discuss with the audience how they can follow-up the ideas suggested during the play. Afterwards, many participants start attending the workshops run by the company, or actors accompany the participants to one of the charities linked to the company so that their desire for change can be actualized, in order to 'extrapolate from rehearsal in the theatre to performance in real life' (Ibid.). Despite Aarohan Theatre group's decision not to do follow-up activities, some actors believe that one performance of *kachahari* was not enough to bring about the transformation advocated in the play. 'Theatre is only a weapon', comments an actor confidentially, '*Kachahari* is not only theatre, it is social work'.

Workshop-based *kachahari*: 'Construction workers' rights'

Let us move now to the second case-study in which the issue to stage is selected and explored during a workshop with actors by some representatives of the community where the play would later be performed.

In December 2004, during a forum theatre training for artists belonging to Aarohan and their partner groups led by Julian Boal[35] in Gurukul, Sunil conducted a workshop for 19 actors, 12 construction workers, and two trade union leaders as a 'practical'. They discussed problems the workers faced at their work place. The labourers had migrated from different parts of Nepal, and were of mixed age and ethnicity. Some had been working in the capital for many years. Others had recently migrated and were hesitant to speak about themselves, but the introductory games facilitated talking and being listened to. The group decided to perform a *kachahari* play about how employers exploited workers by not paying them wages and not providing them with health care when injured. The scripting process was collective through discussions between actors and workers, followed by improvisation. The place and time of performance were chosen strategically. The following day at 6 a.m., artists and workers met in Bhimsengola, a crossroad near a river where the labourers met in the morning and waited for middlemen to pick them up for daily jobs. The workers' bosses would also be present. Some of the workers rehearsed with the actors and performed the following day.

The play was an extraordinary event in comparison to 'every day' *kachahari* performances. It was recorded by the group cameraman and observed by both Julian Boal, who conducted the workshop, and by the other workshop participants. It was, therefore, staged as an example of how *kachahari* theatre was performed in Nepal.

Unlike in 'ordinary' performances Sunil conducted the forum as the *sutradhar*. The performance was followed by a discussion concerning the weaknesses and strengths of both technical and theatrical aspects of the play. Among the difficulties, artists highlighted the limited space available for the stage, the difficulty of hearing due to traffic noise, and the topic and power structures were not clear to all actors. Observers praised, instead, the powerful manner in which actors used to gather people – pretending to fight in the 'invisible theatre' style, the good structure and rhythm of the play, the excellent 'jokering', and the sincerity and friendliness of the actors. From an aesthetic and dramaturgical point of view the whole discussion was precise and revealing and the performance was regarded as successful. Yet, I believe it was also the power of the workers' participation in the whole process, the very specific social components tackled by the play, as well as the social interaction created by performing such a relevant play in that context, that made the performance powerful.

Four months later Bikram, a union leader who had himself taken part as an actor, revealed that the play had been successful to the point of bringing about desired changes in the workers' lives, such as having their bosses pay them a regular salary. Bikram said that through the performance they received new ideas on how to face their issues. They had already met before the play and discussed their problems, but they could not find a way out. The labourers were afraid of speaking. They felt the power was in the hands of the employers. In the play they were not afraid, they 'opened their hearts', said Bikram, miming the gesture with his hands. He added that when he came to Gurukul for the workshop, he realized they should not be afraid of any boss because what they were asking for were their rights; that is, that they should receive their wages on time. Bikram describes his experience in physical terms. Boal places a strong emphasis on the fact that oppression is embodied and that they can be perceived physically. Though development projects often emphasize the verbally-dialogic aspect of forum theatre, interaction, critical thinking, action, and fun, Boal has stressed the importance of a whole series of physical exercises and games that usually precede forum theatre.[36] In forum theatre the body plays a central role as the emphasis is placed on 'embodying' alternative actions and possible solutions, not just verbally articulating them. In this way the dramatic work becomes a 'rehearsal for life'. Boal believes that the body is 'one's most essential tool in transforming physical sensations into a communicable language and altering everyday space into a theatrical arena, or an aesthetic space' (1992, 3).

Bikram explained he had arrived in Gurukul with his friends; they were asked their names and some information about themselves, and then they talked about the problems they had with their bosses, and rehearsed the play. From Bikram's words, it became apparent that finding an 'audience' who actually listened to them and legitimized their claims had been an empowering experience in itself. He recounted that before the play the workers had been beaten, but after the performance the brokers were afraid because if not paid on time, the workers would perform the play again, in Bhimsengola, in front of the company building, or at their work place. The play, and the public exposure that it brought about, became a bargaining tool for the workers. It was not perceived as a 'mere' representation or *natak*, but rather as a 'real thing', with the 'real' consequences of making 'public' unpleasant truths. The *kachahari* play inserted itself in the wider process of conscienticization carried out by the union members who not only participated in the workshop and play but continued to maintain the link between the fictional and the real world after the *kachahari* was over. Workers and union leaders created a stronger bond through the play and created a group who continued to use theatre to make workers aware of their rights. After the play Bikram returned to see other stage plays; he loved the theatre, he said. What he liked about the *kachahari* was the fact that it was connected to life and helped with life. He also liked the fact that working class people had open access to forum theatre: 'People who are not affluent can see the play. The audience can interrupt the action to raise their problem, to show whatever they feel. People from every class can act'. He also pointed out that in contrast, proscenium theatre was only for people with higher income because NR 50 for each ticket was prohibitive for the workers.

Creating a *kachahari* through a workshop enhanced the topicality of the play presented, making it highly relevant to the audience. The boundaries between life and theatre could blur. Performance could be powerful because most of the audience had had experience of the situation portrayed. The workshop became a space in-between where transformation and awareness could start. Workshops could – usually, but not always – increase the familiarity and closeness between actors and community members that facilitated participation in the interactive part of the *kachahari*. Citizens' active participation in the frame helped the audience establish a stronger connection with the performers and the union movement became a container for the play, just like the CMDP was for the *loktantrik natak* in Chapter 3.

However, performing workshop-based *kachahari* was extremely time consuming. According to some artists, there is also increased uncertainty and the possibility of breakdown or obstacles to performance. Allowing community members to participate in the creation of the frame obliges actors to identify specifically with the content in ways they may not be familiar with. This is a way of handing over, at least partly, the means of artistic production to the audience and relinquishing control of the performance. When the conflict portrayed through theatre reflects and distorts a real life issue the risk of 'failing' may be high. Sunil recalled an instance in which, through a workshop, the actors realized that the real problem expressed by the students was the fact that the teachers beat them. However, when informed about the situation, the headmaster asked the actors to change the topic. The actors felt that the 'theatre of the oppressed' had turned into 'the theatre of the oppressor'. The theatrical experience strengthened rather than challenged the oppression. Oppressors may refuse to participate, but if they do, the possibility of triggering real-life resistance increases, as the case of Bikram confirms. Similarly, in a workshop that took place in Gurukul, Rajan felt that the *kachahari* would fail because the issue was very complex (nepotism and unequal opportunities in a martial arts club), and they were not sure the 'oppressors' would accept the invitation to even attend the play the following day. In fact, they did not and the *kachahari* performance was cancelled.

But how is 'failure' interpreted? The meaning of 'success'/'failure' in *kachahari* performances is central to the success of the theatre itself, and in some cases important to keep funding going. Success in terms of audience numbers and smooth performance of the play, like in the case of Devi's story, may not equal success in terms of topicality and audience identification, as in the case of the construction workers. Less controlled, artistically under-rehearsed and one off plays such as that performed in Bhimsengola can in fact bring about unexpected extraordinary outcomes but be extremely risky as described above.

Conclusion

Several considerations emerge when comparing issue-based *kachahari* with workshop-based *kachahari*. First, the workshop emerges as a central part of the forum theatre process. It is the moment when a group of community members can debate a shared issue, experiment with theatrical tools and games, and feel part of the planned performance. Boal defines the workshop as the place where contact between a community group and the actors starts (1998, 47). In Boal's model, workshops can be of different length: two hours, days, weeks, or months. But they are integral to the rehearsal of the play with the community participants. Let me cite Boal's definition of rehearsals:

> It should be understood that rehearsals are already a cultural-political meeting in themselves. Theatre will be the medium of the encounter, theatre will be enacted, but it is very important to be aware that it is the citizens who will be making the theatre, around their own problems, trying their own solutions. In this context, every exercise, every game, every technique is both art and politics (1998, 48)

Therefore the workshop-rehearsal is at the heart of Forum Theatre but in *kachahari natak* as generally practiced by Aarohan during the period of my fieldwork the workshop was removed. Conducting workshops with community groups and scripting plays with them was time consuming, and could give rise to a sense of responsibility deriving from the knowledge acquired during the performance that may bind artists in the post-performance. Workshop-based *kachahari* stretched theatre from the realm of artistic performance to that of social work. Issue-based *kachahari* brought it back to its starting place, where artists and audience are separated. The audience participation and agency was thus limited because non-artists could not choose a topic and create a script about it with the theatre group.

Second, the topicality of the performance facilitates the research for solutions that can work in real life. *Kachahari* theatre, as performed by Aarohan Theatre, changed from being mainly process-oriented (based on a specific problem shared by a well-defined community) into being product-oriented (artists select a topic in advance, prepare a frame for the forum theatre and then performed it in front of different audiences), thus losing specificity, topicality, and contact with community-based issues. Some artists noticed the changes and lost interest in *kachahari natak*. A former Aarohan member distinguished between the beginning, when doing *kachahari* was interesting and challenging because it was 'experimental' and involved coping with the 'unexpected', with the later stage when it became *bikase* (developmental). The metaphor suggests a similarity between professional street theatre and NGO project work. Another artist defined the new working style as 'commercial': in fact, what the group offered to the audience was a pre-packed performance in which the audience could only participate in a limited and guided way.

Third, the audience agency is affected by such technical choices. In fact, not only does the workshop within a specific community create an environment from which a burning issue can emerge and be rehearsed; the workshop also allows some of the community members to familiarize with the dramaturgical techniques and later spur other audience to take part to the forum theatre performance as the distinction between specialized artists and community members is less clear-cut. By presenting a 'product' rather than a 'process', and allowing the audience to re-script the narration only from the critical point in which the *sutradhar* entered, artists maintained the means of theatrical production.

Fourth, the group's decisions not to engage into post-performance activities with the audience or repeated performances in the same communities prevented *kachahari natak* from becoming a bridge between the fiction rehearse during the play and real-life possibilities for changes. *Kachahari natak* became more a once off experience within the out-of-the-ordinary world of theatre rather than an instrument embedded in everyday life.

Doing social theatre with communities can become an all-compassing, full-time job. Aarohan actors talked about the limits of a theatre group's involvement with social action and community work. Were they supposed to keep in contact with the community? Were they supposed to provide links with NGOs who could help the community face the problems discussed in the plays? For Sunil, the group should do theatre, and only theatre. He was rather firm in his conviction, and this derived from his previous experiences in which community theatre became a comprehensive activity that did not leave the group time to focus on stage productions. Other actors remarked that Gurukul could draw attention to a problem, and thus help in this way, but not get involved practically to solve it. Sunil reminded his actors that promises have to be fulfilled, and it is easy to create hopes with theatre. But hopes can easily turn into disillusionment. He emphasized the fact that artists should constantly think about their limitations as a theatre group. They can help by giving theatre skills and scripts, but nothing beyond this. Theatre according to Sunil needs boundaries and limits. Yet, performances generate a great deal of information and knowledge about a problem, and knowledge triggers a sense of responsibility and different kinds of expectations as Suresh's personal long-term involvement with landless children demonstrates. While not willing to become a service-delivery 'NGO' or to raise NGO-type expectations in order to remain a theatre group, Aarohan streamlined *kachahari* in a way that nonetheless recalls the secure and controlled environment of planned development. By partly losing *kachahari's* methodological creative and liberating capacity, Aarohan safeguarded its professional identity.

Endnotes

1   For literature on theatre and development communication, see Epskamp (2006) and Mda (1993).

2   Interviewed in March 2005.

3   Ibid.

4   I use the general term 'development message' to indicate various issues like family planning, sanitation, drinking water, and environmental protection that often constituted the topic of street plays.

5   Artists kept NR 100 for themselves and left NR 50 to develop the village club the group belonged to.

6   The interface between actors-audience and the social distance that separated them is explored in Mottin (2007).

7   Heaton Shrestha reports similar metaphors: donor's money is likened to *heroin, aphim khayo* (it has eaten opium) (2006a, 28).

8   Hand drum used in Nepali folk music.

9   The role of the *sutradhar* appears both in top-down street theatre and in *kachahari* theatre: in the first the character is close to a narrator that comments upon the story; in *kachahari*, the *sutradhar* becomes a 'facilitator' who attempts to activate the spectators.

10 *Kachahari natak* is the Nepali version of Boal's forum theatre, see paragraph below.

11 A civil war affected Nepal between 1996–2006 between the Maoist revolutionaries and the state. In the next chapters, when analysing Maoist cultural performances, the Maoist term 'People's War' will be used instead.

12 Puskar Gurung remembers having a session of forum theatre training with teachers from London in 1999.

13 Other informants told me about a forum theatre workshop organized by the British Council around 2000 but I could not track down more information.

14 In MS publicity material *kachahari* is also referred to as 'conflict theatre' but during the period of my fieldwork this definition was not in use.

15 Rajkumar, interview, December 2004.

16 Interview, December 2005.

17 What will happen to the knowledge produced during the performance will be discussed later.

18 The different flow of information reflects the difference between 'instruction' (from the Latin in-struire, meaning 'putting in') and 'education' (e-ducere, meaning 'taking out). But where does the knowledge acquired in the performance go? Who benefits from it? Both issues will be taken into account later on in the description of the performance production.

19 During a trip to Nepalgunj, I met a local group that did not know anything about Forum Theatre but practiced a very similar form that ended with questions addressed to the audience in a dialogue between artists and spectators. The group leader said they had seen this form in India.

20 Breed (2009) observes that in post-genocide Rwanda, any form of public 'telling', including theatre, could lead to a public act of incrimination, turning the 'theatre of liberation' into a 'theatre for incrimination.'

21 The frame is the script performed until the critical moment when the *sutradhar* stops the play to ask the audience how to move ahead.

22 Like many city-based theatre groups, Aarohan is linked to theatre groups based in different regions in Nepal, called 'partner groups'. They are linked through a partnership to the main group and perform shows in their local areas and are financially supported by the donors linked to the main group.

23 Interviewed in November 2004.

24 *Sutradhar* translates the roles usually referred to as Joker in the Theatre of the Oppressed literature. The word *sutradhar* is commonly employed in Nepal in mainstream message-oriented street theatre to indicate a mediator or facilitator. His/her role is to facilitate the audience understanding of the 'message'. The role of the *joker* in forum theatre, on the contrary, should be a critical one (Schutzman and Cohen-Cruz, 2008). This cultural adaptation of the role blurs the critical difference between forum theatre and message-oriented street theatre. The *sutradhar* existed also in Sanskrit theatre; he was the director and stage manager (Iravati, 2003).

25   It was actually performed at least until August 2007, and then went on well into 2008 too.

26   Kirstine is a development advisor who worked with the group through the partnership with an INGO.

27   This was the nickname of one of the boys working in the Gurukul canteen.

28   The concept comes from the two ideograms used in Chinese language to translate the word 'crisis': 'danger' and 'opportunity' (Boal, 2006, 129).

29   Interview, July 2012.

30   Mani, informal conversation, January 2004.

31   The play was performed in private schools of the Kathmandu area.

32   These are the categories I used in my questionnaire.

33   Interviewed in July 2006.

34   The actors in the company are ex-homeless and they often perform in hostels and day centres where the audience is composed of homeless. Therefore, audience and actors have a strong, shared experience.

35   Julian Boal is Augusto Boal's son. He is a leader of Theatre of the Oppressed workshops as well as one of the founding members of the Centre for the Theatre of the Oppressed in Paris.

36   Image theatre is one of these, in which the human body is used as a tool to represent feelings, ideas, and relationships. The participants 'sculpt' others or use their own body to represent and reflect on a situation or an act of oppression. Image theatre exercises are often employed before forum theatre to create trust and provide 'visceral cues' (1999, 3) about the themes that are being investigated.

5

Activism not Development Work

Explorations in Tharu *kachahari natak*

A arohan and political cultural workers are specialists in their own artistic work, as theatre and political art full-time professionals. Research on how the Kamlari Natak Samuha, one of Aarohan partner groups, used *kachahari natak* in their social movement provides a comparative view from the grassroots. Before detailing how the Kamlari Natak Samuha worked, I will introduce Aarohan's network across the country. In 2005, Aarohan had 12 partner theatre groups, very diverse in motivations, working conditions, members' age, type and frequency of performance, and history.[1] Partner groups usually associated with Aarohan because they received training or co-performed in Aarohan's productions: for example, Aarohan members carried out follow-up field visits to some groups that received training in *kachahari natak* in order to support and advise local members on how to make their theatrical work more effective. Once trained, the groups would obtain project work by themselves through local NGOs or be commissioned street plays to perform as part of the project work secured by Aarohan through international donors. What in my opinion was most important, however, was that local groups could find in Gurukul a meeting and reference point. Very often actors travelling to the capital for their personal occupations stopped in Gurukul to update the group with local news, exchange views with Sunil and the other actors and to share problems and satisfactions. Gurukul had therefore become a place where 'theatre work' was considered important, the centre for a community of peers spread all over the country. I will introduce four groups to exemplify their such diversity. The Mithila Natyakala Parishad (MINAP) was one of the oldest theatre groups in Nepal. Established in Janakpur in 1979, the group was a centre for Mithila culture, gathering writers, musicians, and artists. Their actors engaged in both proscenium and street theatre. Shristi Natya Samuha from Dharan started as a proscenium theatre group in 1995. The group then performed *kachahari* theatre to strengthen the link with their local community, tackling issues like environmental problems, drug addiction, and alcohol, both through NGO projects and out of their own initiative. The group was facing a huge problem: continuity. Its members were mostly young, only three of them had been working for 10 years, and many artists were compelled to quit acting to study or work. What affected their continuity was also the lack of resources: the group didn't have any office or rehearsal room. The Taranga Sanskriti Parishad was a cultural group established in 1994 in Hetauda. Founded by local artists, singers and actors, Taranga was soon well appreciated by funding agencies for their artists' ability to mix educational messages and entertainment. They 'specialized' in HIV-AIDS, which had become, by the time I met the group, their single topic. The group was very popular and toured on monthly basis performing both along highways and in urban areas. They worked in partnership with Aarohan and on independent projects. The artists involved in the 2004 campaign were engaged full-time and lived off the income they received from their street theatre performances. NGO and INGOs usually employed street theatre to provide communities, illiterate, and marginal groups[2] in particular, with top-down basic information to raise awareness about HIV-AIDS, STI family planning or trafficking, as a form of behaviour change communication. Taranga's artists helped the audience fill post-performance questionnaires and got paid after handing them to the NGO that employed them. For the NGOs getting feedback was important to understand if the audience enjoyed the play, understood its language and acting style. Although assessing the level of the audience's knowledge before and after the play was difficult, they considered it effective as usually 3-5 people visited their STI clinic after every street play. For example, the HIV-AIDS NGO privileged simple and direct scripts, using conversational rather than scientific language. The street play performed by Taranga in 2004 was simple, based on real-life experiences. What was stressed by advisers was that the message had to be direct so that the audience could easily understand. It was also considered essential that the presentation be interesting and humorous so that the audience could have fun while watching the play. Comic actors were popular, and sought after when NGOs recruited theatre groups: the NGO of the first example appreciated the acting of Mr Kumar from Taranga because as soon as he started talking, people laughed. The Saipal Samuha from Humla was a new partner that undertook *kachahari* training in 2004 in Gurukul. The group members used to spend the winter working in Kathmandu and then returned to Humla over the summer. Although they were really interested in *kachahari*, two years after the training they had not managed to perform any and were still looking for funding. Aarohan artists explained that unless groups start performing and working without funds, NGOs would not trust them and give them project work. Some group members were also interested in showing their own 'local culture', e.g., Deuda dance, in Kathmandu and in 2005 they managed to perform at the theatre festival organized by the Academy. The group leader was also a poet and hoped to have his work translated into English.

Local groups approached Gurukul with different expectations, such as receiving training, getting funding for their own street theatre or cultural performances, gaining visibility, and getting access to foreign funding in particular when they perceived not being able to speak English as a barrier. Such expectations were not always met.

This chapter provides a close-up on how a local organization employed theatre and how it linked to the global development network. After providing a background on how the Kamlari Liberation Movement evolved through the work of a grassroots NGO, SWAN (Society Welfare Action Nepal), I will focus on how dramatic forms enabled activists[3] from the Kamlari Natak Samuha (Kamlari Theatre Group) – a theatre group associated to SWAN – to challenge the *kamlari* practice both in local and national/international arenas through *kachahari natak* and proscenium theatre. Yet, in order to appreciate theatre within the Kamlari Liberation Movement it is necessary to unpack how activists frame their social development work as well as their own place within it. First, despite receiving funding from international donor agencies, SWAN activists conceptualize their work as activism (*abhiyan, andolan*) not as 'development work'. This questions the apparent opposition between international development and social movements as mutually excluding pathways to social change clearly explored and challenged by Fujikura (2013). Second, ethnographic analysis of applied theatre practices problematizes the role of arts in development (Prendergast and Saxton, 2009; Prentki and Preston, 2009; Thompson, 2003). Rather than stopping at the self-expressive power of theatre (Clammer, 2015) or dismissing it as a ritual of development (Ahmed, 2002; Munier and Etherton, 2006), this case-study will strengthen this book's claim that theatre needs to be analysed through the context in which projects develop, through the artists' identities, their motivations and networks and, moreover, through the claims that activists can raise through theatre activities, even if only for the limited period of time during which projects are implemented.

In conclusion, I will argue that through the *kamlaris'* voices and movements, both in dramas and in street protests, art bridged the silences of community and policy. Instead of assuming that the arts can inherently provide spaces for agency through self-expression (Clammer, 2015), I argue that it is when art, and theatre in the specific case, is appropriated that the social actors involved can re-think and re-orient their own lives. In fact, the activists' focus on what they believe is 'real', that is their 'real work', 'real feelings', 'real pain', and 'real tears' shared through dramatic performances is perceived as a powerful means to raise awareness, galvanize, and empower their community and assert their own agency within the development discourse. This way of understanding *kachahari natak* seems to offer a way between the top-down, politically engaged work of the Maoist cultural activists and the participatory but ultimately vicarious experience mediated by Aarohan professional artists.

The *kamlari* practice

Among Tharu[4] communities of the western rural districts of the Tarai (Dang, Banke, Bardiya, Kailali, and Kanchanpur), girls from 6–16 years of age are sent as *kamlari* to work in landowners' houses or to well-off families in the cities. The *kamlari pratha* (practice) is considered as a remnant of the *kamaiya* system. *Kamaiya* indicates a form of male bonded labour that existed in western Nepal and was officially abolished by the Nepali Government in 2000 after a liberation movement that freed more than 16,000 labourers (Fujikura, 2001; 2013). Fujikura (Ibid.) highlights that while most of the *kamaiya* were Tharu bonded labourers, many of whom had lost their land and were displaced in the 1950–60s when migrants from the hills settled after the eradication of malaria; the word is also used to indicate people who work under a landowner with different types of annual contracts. *Kamlaris* are female bonded labourers. Girls are sent away from home as *kamlari* for different reasons such as their parents' debts, because it is requested by the landlord in order to give the parents land to sharecrop. Some other families were said to assign their daughters as *kamlaris* because it was perceived as common practice; the girls' mothers having been a *kamlari* before them. Parents received between NRs. 4000–5000[5] a year from assigning their daughters as *kamlari* and hoped the girls would get food, clothes, and an education, which was rarely the case. Former *kamlaris* did not conceptualize their experience as 'work' but as 'life': they would normally use the Nepali phrase *kamlari basne*[6] that can be translated as 'to live as a kamlari'. For example, Manjita, a former *kamlari* remembered that 'whatever work they gave, it had to be done. No matter if it was 2am or if I was sick. I had to do whatever work they gave. If I was sick, they said it was a lie'. She had to leave the kitchen 'when the rice started to cook' and she still carries that bewilderment 'I asked myself why, who am I? I was very puzzled, why was I being treated like an animal? I still ask myself sometimes.' With the eyes of a nine year old, she remembers the fascination of travelling for the first time by bus to the landlord's house with her father. That excitement would turn into desperation when she wanted to leave, but neither did she know where her house was, nor did she have any money. Beyond hard work, violence, abuse, and torture, the condition itself was described as one of total lack of any agency or control over one's life.

SWAN and the Kamlari Liberation Movement

SWAN is a Tharu community-based organization established by a group of young people in 1994 in Lamahi, Deukhuri Valley, Dang district (western Nepal). Krishna Chaudhary, a school principal by profession and the chairperson of SWAN, remembers that after finishing his studies, he decided to start SWAN together with some friends because they felt outraged by the gender disparity that led boys to school while their sisters became *kamlari*.[7] He describes this urge as a 'desire deep-seated in their hearts since childhood'.[8] They therefore started community work trying to persuade parents not to send their daughters away. Despite their commitment, the group soon recognized they were limited by lack of resources as the girls' parents described their problems, in particular poverty: 'We talked', explains Krishna 'but our talk was empty as we could not provide any support, not even a rupee'.[9]

SWAN then linked up with Friends of Needy Children (FNC), a Kathmandu-based NGO that in 2000 started the 'Indentured Daughters Program' (IDP) in Dang-Deukhuri, in collaboration with Nepal Youth Foundation (NYF), a US donor agency, to eradicate the *kamlari* practice. Contrasting conceptualizations and representations of this practice co-existed both on the media and among NGO staff and activists. *Kamlariya* is at times represented as a 'tradition', as a '*kusanskar*' (negative cultural practice) in Tharu 'culture', at times explained as a result of poverty and backwardness. Some of SWAN activists are critical of how the practice was represented by INGOs/NGOs run by mostly upper caste staff, as they believe that such representations dehumanized Tharu landless people and concealed oppressive power relations that led to indented labour. An activist explained that when

> the landlords made pressure to the poor people; there is no way out, they are bonded; there is big pressure, they made everything tight, no ideas, no way out, what to do; they must send their children, it's not culture [...] sending your daughter is not culture, this is discrimination. It's because they [NGO staff] did not understand Tharu, the poor, that they say this is culture.[10]

According to the activists there were two main reasons fuelling the *kamlari* practice. First of all poverty: many Tharu landless families relied on the small annual income they got from the girls for their survival. Second, the normality of the practice:[11] when I first met the group in 2005, having *kamlaris* working at home was not only well-accepted, it was also considered as a measure of status. SWAN activists lamented that even human rights advocates, journalists, lawyers, and NGO staff kept *kamlaris* in their homes while working against child labour in the public. To tackle poverty, the activists started income-generating activities, e.g., giving the families a piglet, to compensate them of the amount lost if their daughters would return or remain at home and go to school instead of becoming a *kamlari*. Scholarships would also support former *kamlaris* in their education after returning to their villages. To symbolically change the public perception of this practice, the activists engaged in extensive awareness raising and advocacy campaigns where street theatre assumed an increasingly prominent role among other means including wall-newspapers, posters, radio drama, radio programmes, and rallies, and as the project developed year after year, documentaries broadcast on national TV, media (documentaries, short films) produced for international audiences.

During the early years the internal conflict between the Maoists and the state (Hutt, 2004; Lawoti and Pahadi, 2010; Lecomte-Tilouine, 2013) intensified and the area where SWAN's and their partner organizations operated was under Maoist control. At the time the Maoist party did not allow development work to continue and many development projects had to stop. To be able to carry on working in the villages, in 2004 SWAN had to register with the Bhattarai[12] faction of the Maoist party by paying NR 10,000. Nonetheless, in April 2005 Krishna was kidnapped and very severely beaten by the Prachanda faction of the party after some cadres interrupted a street theatre performance and warned the organization to stop their development work.[13] There was a clear clash between the way in which SWAN and the Maoist party conceptualized the *kamlari pratha*. Once freed, Krishna contacted the district Maoist commander through village representatives of the Maoist government to explain SWAN's activities and to show that they were also fighting against poverty and discrimination. The Maoists seemed unhappy with SWAN's community work because they claimed that *kamlari/kamaya* issues were political and not just social and for this reason they claimed that they should be fought through their People's War, not through theatre and development projects. Somehow the Maoists felt that the NGO was invading their sphere of competence and this undermined their power. Once Krishna managed to clear the issue with the district leader, he got permission to resume the *kamlari* theatre and scholarship projects but not the micro-finance ones or campaigning for land reform. In the meantime, in 2005, PLAN Nepal entered a partnership with SWAN to further support their activities.

The *kamlari* projects resumed in the winter of the same year, just before the Maghi festival 2006 (Fig. 5.1, photo by the author). Maghi (Maghe Sakranti) is the most important festival for Tharu communities. It marks the beginning of the Tharu New Year and falls on the first day of the Nepali month of Magh (January-February). Maghi festival also marks the moment in which all the plans, agreements, and labour contracts for the New Year are renewed and people who work far away or abroad

Figure 5.1: *Kamlari* rally in Lamahi, 2006

return home to see their families. During this holiday fathers also make agreements with brokers to send their daughters out of the village to work as *kamlari*, renew the contracts, and receive the annual payment for their work. During Maghi, artists performed *kachahari natak* both in the villages and in official programmes organized by the NGOs around the local *mela* (festival) in Lamahi.

Following the People's Movement and the re-establishment of democracy in May 2006, INGOs and NGOs activities against the *kamlari* practices surged as a result of the opening up of the public space in which different oppressed communities could raise their voices against the government. Other organizations then got involved in the campaign and its activities increasingly moved from Deukuri/Dang to Kathmandu. After FNC/NYF submitted a petition in September 2006, the Supreme Court of Nepal directed the government to abolish the system and to allocate a budget for the rehabilitation of the former *kamlaris*. The activists, understanding their limitations, thought it was the state's responsibility to support the former *kamlaris* in their return to ordinary social life. The campaign therefore continued, culminating in a big demonstration in Kathmandu in 2009 when more than 600 former *kamlaris* sat in protest demanding the government to release the rehabilitation budget and to abolish the practice. By then the campaign had escalated to international level, other organizations got involved in what transformed into an anti-slavery campaign and a delegation of former *kamlaris* visited ministries and international human rights groups.

2010 marked the establishment of the Freed Kamlari Development Forum

(FKDF) in Lamahi, an NGO led by former *kamlaris* and an important shift in the movement leadership, well outlined by the protagonists of the struggle. But first, I will explain in some more detail why SWAN got involved against the *kamlari* practice. SWAN's mission was twofold: fighting against the *kamlari* practice and for land reform. While the first issue was taken up and funded by development agencies, land reform was progressed only by the activists separately, on voluntary basis. With the establishment of the FKDF, SWAN refocused on land rights but found no donor partner to support its actions. SWAN activists believe that from the legal point of view there is no difference between *kamaya* and *kamlarya* – both are related to bonded labour, but they explain that the liberation movement led by BASE (Fujikura, 2013), that brought up the plight of *kamayas*, did not improve the lives of the *kamlaris* whose works was equated with 'housework'. The movement against the *kamaya* practice led to its abolition in 2000. However, this was perceived to have caused a backlash and led itself to an increase in the number of girls sent to work as *kamlari*. SWAN activists believed that at that time NGOs were aware of the 'pain suffered by *kamlari* girls' but they were not confident that bringing this issue up would have been successful, and thus 'kept the *kamaya* and the *kamlari* issue separate'.[14] Krishna points out two main hurdles, age and gender: as young girls, *kamlari* would not be able to speak by themselves or organize a protest movement. To elaborate on a metaphor used by Krishna, Tharu educated men 'took the issue on their shoulders' and started a movement on behalf of their younger sisters and daughters whose voices could not be heard. They liaised with a wide network of national and international organizations but with the establishment of the FKDF, both SWAN and FNC let former *kamlaris* took the lead of 'their' movement as they did not need to be 'carried' anymore. Man Bahadur Chhetri, FNC project manager who spent more than a decade working in western Nepal on this issue, explains that '[n]ow they are at the front. We help from the back. We give technical and emotional support, but they do their own way now.'[15] Man Bahadur believed that the socio-political context had changed and if former *kamlaris* spoke directly about their problems, without external mediation, they would indeed be listened to.[16] Throughout more than a decade of activism, more than 11,000 *kamlaris* were 'liberated' by the two organizations, more than 7,000 were attending school (formal, informal, or vocational trainings), some had opened their own business, and others got married and settled with their families. The activists were also keen to emphasize that throughout this period former *kamlaris* also 'got education' and developed leadership skills that allowed them to manage the NGO, interact with different publics (ministers, national and international media) and run advocacy campaigns. Some of the girls have become 'role models', and films and books have been produced on their life stories (Chaudhary and Schwaiger, 2011).

But the promises made by the government did not actualize. The funds allocated were not distributed, and thus the movement continued, acquiring more and more visibility. In 2012, the activists explained the importance of strengthening the legislation. If there was a specific law against the kamlari practice making it illegal, it would have been easier for them to pursue the exploiters. At that time they had to file cases using 'sometimes the kamaya act, sometimes the child labour act, sometimes the trafficking act'.[17] The suspicious death of Srijana Chaudhary,[18] a 12 year old kamlari in Kathmandu in March 2013 revived the movement (Himalayan News Service, 2013). From 28 May 2013, an umbrella organization, the United Committee for the Elimination of Kamlari Practice (UCEKP) organized street protests in Kathmandu through sit-ins, demonstrations, and Taraibandha.[19] Images of girls being hit by the police appeared in national and international media. On 18 June, the government officially abolished the kamlari practice.

Why theatre in an activist movement?

SWAN employed street theatre in their advocacy intervention to raise awareness against the practice both among kamlari's parents living in the villages, to persuade them not to send their daughters away, as well as to connect to national and international groups. They worked through the Kamlari Theatre Group, an activist theatre group linked to SWAN. The group enlisted former kamlaris as artists, and other activists, mostly farmers, in the male roles. The director of the group, Dhaniram Chaudhary, one of the founders and vice-president of SWAN, is the son of former kamlari, a farmer by profession, an actor, street theatre trainer and organizer of street theatre performances. Tracing the social networks within which the activists operate provide an insight to understand how the activists were grounded in the local community. For example, Dhaniram and other male members of the Kamlari Theatre Group were also members of the Deuna Bebri Cultural Group, a local cultural group performing Tharu songs and dance to show and preserve 'Tharu culture'. While the two groups had different agendas, at times they collaborated. Unlike professional or semi-professional theatre groups who are commissioned by NGOs to produce and perform street plays within development projects, the Kamlari Theatre Group performed exclusively against the kamlari practice in their own district, Deukhuri-Dang Valley. Occasionally, in 2005, they performed a more 'aestheticized'[20] stage version of the same story in Kathmandu, in collaboration with Aarohan Theatre Group to expose the problem to potential city employers and to attract the attention of the international community, which for their campaign was very important, as we will see later. It is on these two forms of theatre that I will now focus my analysis.

Starting from the activists' identities, I will elaborate on how activists perceive the role of theatre in their movement and on how the aesthetic differences between the theatre performed in the village and the stage 'cultural and social translation' of the same story staged in Kathmandu allowed the group to reach different audiences.

The Kamlari Theatre Group staged both street theatre and *kachahari natak* in Deukuri Valley since 2004. Som Paneru[21] from FNC explained that when in 2004 former *kamlaris* returned to their communities after being rescued, members of his organization thought that it would have been very powerful to communicate with local communities through street plays in which former *kamlaris* acted out their past experience so that the parents of *kamlaris* could experience first-hand what their daughters were going through. Nine former *kamlaris* were sent to Kathmandu for training. Once they returned, they developed a plot based on their own personal experience as well as on interviews with parents, brothers and sisters in law, who seemed to play a crucial role in sending girls away. They tried to understand their circumstances and pressures. The group did not fix scripts in writing nor were there fixed roles. Both depended on the availability of the artists and on their life cycle. For example, few of the activists that performed regularly in 2005 were still performing or involved in theatre in 2012; many had in fact married or had taken up different jobs. There was, however, strong continuity in the plot and methodology and in the activists' lived experiences that provided coherence to the performance through time. In the early, most intense period of their local campaigning, the group met twice a month – when necessary – for rehearsals and performed *kachahari* about once a week, on Saturdays, when the activists were free from agricultural work or school. All the theatre activists were volunteers and only received snacks after performing. The performances intensified before Maghi festival in mid-January.

The group followed the standard *kachahari* performance structure made of three parts: an introductory session to attract audience, a dramatic frame illustrating the issue and an interactive forum with the audience to unpack the problem and try out solutions. Tharu songs and dance introduced the *kachahari*. 'Official' performances during cultural programmes or performances in the bazaars displayed a wide range of 'cultural items' such as Tharu dresses, jewellery, and decorations. In the villages, artists often performed without the traditional dress or jewels, according to the time that they could dedicate, as their identity was already established. The *kachahari* dramatic part (frame) narrates the reasons why a girl is sent as *kamlari* – e.g., the mother is sick and does not have money to buy medicines – in a simple, realistic, concise and straightforward way (Fig. 5.2, screenshot from documentary courtesy of FNC).

Activists believed the frame should not be longer than 15 minutes or the audience would lose interest. The frame would also show the heavy workload the

Figure 5.2: Documentary produced by FNC (screenshot)

girl does in the landlord's house, her sufferance and powerlessness. The girl would ask to go home but she would be denied. The frame ends with this climax and the joker (*sutradhar*) enters with a question: what can the *kamlari* do? In the forum, which the activists consider the most important part of the performance, audience members could give suggestions, replace the actors, search and try out ways to allow the *kamlari* girl to return home and study. During the forum the activists would also try to persuade the parents not to renew the contracts for their daughters and discuss with them alternative ways of supporting their households, and inform them about SWAN's development projects. While acknowledging that Tharu *kala sanskriti*[22] is in 'danger' and they should struggle for it as much as they are doing against the *kamlari* practice and for land rights, SWAN activists also believe that *kala sanskriti* – in this case the songs and dances in the drama – reached people's innermost parts, creating a reaction from inside.[23] Activists believe that theatre goes straight into the heart (*mutu*) of the audience in ways that speeches fail to. Activists include both street theatre and *kachahari natak* into what they call *kala sanskriti* (cultural art) that includes also Tharu songs, dance, traditional clothes and jewellery. It seems that they incorporated dramatic techniques in their pre-existing repertoire to a degree that they were not perceived as external, 'development-like' adjuncts. I will delve into the external/internal metaphors further as this seems the way through which activists made distinctions between 'development work' and what they are engaged in, and thus fundamental to understanding the unique way in which theatre is used.

The second arena in which *kachahari* was performed was during official NGO programs, in particular around Maghi. Maghi festival 2006 was significant as it represented the moment in which the group resumed its theatrical activities after being halted by the Maoists. It also shows the challenging conditions under which activists were working, the links to the community, and the allegiances to funding agencies, as the following extract from my fieldwork notes exemplifies:

Lamahi, 13 January 2006 - The mela space in Lamahi bazaar is very colourful. Lots of stalls set up by women's group showing improved stove, new irrigation systems, local products, honey, biscuits, etc. As we walk through the park, waiting for the audience to take their place, PLAN Nepal project manager explains how the whole programme is organized by village youth clubs. Youth clubs are active in the area but now PLAN is working on their capacity building giving them financial resources. In Deukhuri Valley there are around 12 youth clubs and three children's clubs. Members of these clubs started preparing for the programme two weeks earlier, getting the stage ready, contacting the cultural groups for the song and dance performances, and spreading information in the villages. Dhaniram was very active around the stage; he was one of the organizers. Once everything was in place, well after 12 pm, the programme started. All the guests were greeted and called to sit on the huge concrete stage permanently built on one side of the park. Two rows of cushions, SWAN written with a felt tip pen on all of them, indicated that there would be many guests. To my surprise, I'm also called to sit there. The stage is full of decorations. At the back, two huge FNC banners remind people that girls should study not work. The programme begins in the usual style, never ending official speeches by different authorities, politicians, representatives of women, community, and environment groups. No matter what their speeches were about, all of them, at a certain point mention the '*kamlari* problem' and thank FNC and SWAN for their work in the communities. A local leader of the Congress Party, for example, talks against the employment of young girls as domestic servants and emphasizes the importance of alternative income generation activities, he talks of the improved stoves just like those displayed at the entrance by the women's group that can help reduced the *kamlari* practice. He gives an example of how even in his own family they used to have a *kamlari* girl but now they are doing everything by themselves: they cook, wash, and have alternative energy resources. The audience is not huge in comparison to the crowd that would turn up later for the cultural programme. Different youth clubs present their dance performances: Nepali dance with traditional costumes and dances based on the latest Hindi film songs. The audience greatly appreciated. While introducing the groups, the MC from time to time proudly states slogans against the *kamlari* practice and in support of children rights. Since most of artists of the Kamlari theatre group also belong to Daunabebri Sanskriti Samaj, they first perform a Tharu dance: Dhaniram and Krishna play the *madal* while Deepa and Sita dance. The *kachahari* play is also preceded by a Tharu folk song and dance. The stage is about 1.5 metres high which is not ideal for interactive and participatory theatre. The audience carefully follows the development of the story but during the forum nobody offers any suggestion to solve the problem. Dhaniram, the joker asks for help; he goes beyond himself and jumps down the stage, approaching the audience with a mike but it doesn't work. He only manages to get a few suggestions from some of the organizers and helpers who were working around the stage and then he decides to finish off the play quickly. Thulo Shiva was quite disappointed, she said the plays at the villages were so good, this was not the right kind of space. Clearly the audience had come to spend a joyful Saturday afternoon and to 'watch' whatever kind of programme. They did not seem to care too much about what was happening to Sano Shiva, who was performing the *kamlari* role, or about how to get the money to bring her back to her village, they were not willing to 'participate'. It was the first time the group performed in such a context and the performance was considered a sort of failure. We don't stay there for the end of the programme, the activists ask me to accompany them at the SWAN office where they change clothes and get ready to go home. [...] Lamahi, 14 January 2006 - The day starts very early. I spend the night at Chandrama's house and we get up at 4 am to get ready to walk to the Rapti River for a ritual bath in its freezing cold water. [...] After having breakfast, we get ready for the rally. SWAN volunteers coordinated the rally and were proud that all went smoothly and more than 1,000 girls had turned up, with banners, wearing traditional Tharu dresses or school uniforms and chanting slogans to abolish the *kamlari* system. The afternoon was busy with another official programme, this time in Gorahi, in the nearby district of Dang. The group had been invited to perform at 2 pm. The bus journey from the Lamahi bazaar is interrupted by frequent police check posts. The atmosphere on the bus is joyful, Dhaniram sings a song while the musician from Deuna Bebri play the *madal*. Some people are sleeping, probably tired from the early morning bath. All the female activists are already wearing their traditional costumes for the performance. It's a sunny day in the hills of western Nepal, too warm for my Kathmandu *kurta surwal*. Slowly we reach the check post at the entrance of Gorahi. Dhaniram tells the soldiers we're artists and we're going to perform in a cultural programme. A soldier nods and lets us move on. At Gorahi main *chowk* the driver stops the bus, talks with some people on the road and then crosses the highway, taking a tiny road on the opposite side. The market was really quiet. All the shops and restaurants were closed, few people walking around, the police patrol festival day. There is another check post. The road is completely blocked by a horizontal wood bar and there are soldiers on both sides. Dhaniram gets off and moves towards the army post. After talking for a few minutes he comes back. We all have to get off and walk to the hall as the bus can't cross the check post and has to be parked nearby. The actors are not happy at all but we take our bags including some props, two plastic buckets, a broom, a bag with bottles and another bag with the men's costumes. After walking under the scorching sun we reach a big militarized courtyard. The hall rented by FNC is attached to the CDO, which is heavily patrolled. At the check post gate the soldier is supposed to check all the bags but when the artists say they contain props, he lets us in. The doors of the hall where FNC is holding their programme are open, although it's 2.30 pm the meeting is still going on and we have to wait for it to finish. The *kachahari* will take place after. I peep in from the main door. The room is packed with former *kamlaris* wearing their traditional Tharu dress. One girl is sharing her experience on the mike. Facing the audience, there is a long row of guests including the American donor and her photographer with an FNC manager from Kathmandu. I feel really tired. I sit outside with the activists, only after having asked the soldier for a place where I could have the battery of my video camera recharged. Time passes, the activists get bored. We talk about Maghi; we have some more *dhikri* (made of steamed rice flour), the typical food prepared in the morning for the day. We sit in the sun as Shiva is still feeling cold and weak. The meeting seems never ending. It's almost 4 pm, I'm feeling hungry, I had only some rice early in the morning. I ask Dhaniram if we have time to get some food; he says that the meeting is still carrying on so the performance won't start soon. I go with Chandrama *didi* and Bhawana, her little daughter, to look for some food. No shops around; there is only a small tea shop near the check post. Chandrama *didi* is not happy. She thinks it's not really clean but we have no choice, we're all hungry, there is not much time and all the shops are shut. We sit and have some chowmein. While we are eating we see a long line of women walking past the window. We pay quickly and start running back. When we arrive, all the Kamlari group stands around a circle.... at least they have not started, we comment. When I reach the circle I ask what happened. Thulo Shiva tells me that there is a street theatre group from Gorahi that is playing now, they are also connected to FNC, her group will play afterwards. We are all waiting again. The performance is almost a déjà-vu: a rich lady is mistreating a young girl working as *kamlari*, the only difference lies in the skirt. Tharu women of Dang Valley wear plain white skirts while in Deukhuri the skirts are colourful. Gun in their hands, the army stand behind the audience mostly composed of former *kamlari* and NGO staff. When the play finishes the audience stands up and leaves. There is not going to be any other performance because it's too late. The activists call me to walk back with them, the NGO delegation leaves quickly, I don't have the time to greet them. Dhaniram calls the group to go quickly back to the bus. Once on the bus, there is not much talking, everybody is tired because of the long way and sleep. We leave Gorahi, heading back to Lamahi without having performed the play. In Lamahi we all go to a hotel for *nasta* (snack) made of *samosa* and *tarkari*, except for Thulo Shiva, she is tired and sick. Nobody talks about the performance.

As a global dramatic structure (Cohen-Cruz and Schutzman, 1994; Schutzman and Cohen-Cruz, 2006), forum theatre went through a process of adaptation and appropriation when employed and spread through trainings by Nepali artists (see Chapter 4). In 'global' Forum Theatre – turned *kachahari natak* in Kathmandu, turned into a different localized form of *kachahari natak* in Deukhuri, artists innovated and localized it by bringing in Tharu stories, dance and songs in Tharu language. Folk/ethnic songs and dance themselves are quite flexible. 'Sajan' is one such Tharu songs. It tells about a young married woman who longs to return to her native home for a religious festival but her relatives cannot go and fetch her, according to the Tharu tradition, because they are working in the fields. In everyday life 'Sajan' is usually sung for entertainment during everyday activities, e.g., working in the fields, doing house-work, tending cattle. But as I said earlier, activists also sing 'Sajan' at the beginning of *kachahari* and during other cultural programmes organized by NGOs. Moreover, this song was also used as the musical leitmotif of a stage version of the *kamlari* stories that ran for a week in April 2005 in Kathmandu for urban and international audience, showing an example of how local artistic knowledge/culture is transfigured into the global set.

'Kamlari. A story prepared from memories of tears', directed by Sunil, is a collective creation of Aarohan Theatre and the Kamlari Theatre Group. The Kamlari Theatre Group lived in Gurukul for a month and during a workshop with Aarohan artists, funded by a donor agency linked to Aarohan, the activists engaged in a creative process that was similar to that which leads to *kachahari* dramas: no written script, the scenes were rehearsed from lived experience and agreed upon, but artists could later modify their lines to make them fit better.

In comparison to the street theatre produced for local audiences, this process of 'translation' expanded the exploration of Tharu identity rooted in the land, their sense of dispossession and exploitation leading only at the end of the play to the departure of Shiva, the main female character as *kamlari*. This was achieved by focusing on what activists call Tharu farmers' 'culture', expressed through different performative means: sketches of daily activities in the fields and at home, enactment of religious rituals, and Maghi celebrations with songs and dance are all politicized when re-contextualized on stage. In this process of aestheticization of Tharu everyday life in terms that were visually appealing to an urban audience, the Tharu song 'Sajan' set the mood and linked the scenes. In contrast, the poem 'Kamlari', which was specifically created by the poet Shrawan Mukarung after interacting with the artists during the rehearsals, critically and reflexively exposed the exploitation of landless Tharus. The extract below provides an example of how the song 'Sajan' – in the background – blended into the poem 'Kamlari' recited by Aarohan Theatre director, reinforcing the visualization of the farmers' life struggles.

> Oh Lord!
> Oh great knower!
> Oh supreme being!
> This tree did not belong to them
> This soil, field and path
> This jungle, brook, birds and songs
> They did not belong to them
> This house, yard and well
> Mother, father and sky
> They did not belong to them
> I was this tree
> This tree did not belong to them

I wonder – today this tree
How could it have become theirs?
How could I have become theirs today?

Another example of the stage aesthetcization of Tharu culture is represented by the play's climax, when the *kamlari*, Shiva, the same female actor that played the role of the *kamlari* in the village *kachahari* at that time, is not allowed to go home for Maghi. Unlike the 'local'/*kachahari* version, in the stage version Maghi festival is conjured up as a memory through the Tharu stick dance (Fig. 5.3, screenshot from video by the author).[24] In the end, Shiva would collapse under a huge *nanglo*,[25] a symbol of her heavy work that marks the end of the play (Fig. 5.4, screenshot from video by the author). The spontaneous post-performance talks outside the theatre hall, the TV and newspaper coverage replaced the structured forum of the village.

Figure 5.3: *Kamlari* play performed in Gurukul: stick dance

Figure 5.4: *Kamlari* play performed in Gurukul: Shiva succumbs under heavy work

What emerges from these performances is a local-global exchange and interaction that creates a tension. First, in the villages of Deukhuri Valley, it is the assumed 'global' format of *kachahari* with its forum that allows for the exposure of the *kamlaris'* painful experience, that I will discuss in the last section. Second, in Kathmandu, it is the landless Tharu cultural identity and social exploitation visually essentialized, politicized, and materialized onstage through the reproduction of rituals, daily activities, songs and dances that acquires a prominent role in both expressing the farmers exploitation and in attracting, entertaining, and engaging with an urban, mostly upper class audience. Third, Aarohan's international experience with what in Nepal is defined as 'western drama' allowed for the transaction of the cultural elements in forms that were recognized and appreciated in both contexts thus allowing for the *kamlari* struggle to acquire national and international visibility.

Activism not development work

So far we could argue that *kachahari* is simply 'development theatre'. The song 'Sajan' or the Tharu stick dance can be considered items of indigenous artistic knowledge, a variation of the indigenous technical knowledge that the development discourse appropriated since the 1980s to render programmes more participatory. In many theatre-for-development projects, artists from a different place enter a community, create a story with some of its members and collect songs and dance to give the performance a local flavour. In this way, performance art is packaged, objectified, and frozen. But the process seems reversed here and it is linked to how the activists perceive their own work as a movement (*andolan*) rather than 'development'. Besides, what appears is also a strategic appropriation of forms that are well-accepted in the development discourse into which Tharu activists reposition their artistic knowledge. In this way, the activists manage to enroll both local and international audiences in their movement. Activists consider the engagement of both as necessary to change the perceptions of the *kamlari* system. In fact, SWAN activists believe that it is because of the pressures created by the international community on the Nepali Government, aided by the focus provided by their activism, that their movement has been successful in starting to change the government policy.

Similarly, the performance of SWAN/*kamlari* identity during street demonstrations is also intriguing. It displays a mixture of Tharu 'traditional' cultural elements, e.g., songs, dances, drums, dresses, jewellery and NGO visual paraphernalia such as caps, jackets with logos, and campaign slogans (Fig. 5.5, photo courtesy of FNC). Activists perceive all of this as central for their movement: activists claimed

Figure 5.5: *Kamlari* rally in Kathmandu

that if they had not gone to Kathmandu in big numbers – in 2009, 600 former *kamlaris* were taken to Kathmandu to pressurize the government, but even in local rallies the activists display themselves en masse – and 'showed' their culture, they would not have been noticed. In other words, SWAN activists believe that they needed to show themselves strong, clear and 'distinct' in order for the *kamlari* issue to be considered in the public sphere: in the same way as the problems faced by the *kamlari* needed to be 'shown' to the parents through theatre in the village for them to feel their daughters' pain. This position raises questions: does this point to a 'normalization' of the development discourse and its degree of cultural penetration in the country? Is this a social movement phrased in NGOs' performative language? Or has 'development culture' become part and parcel of contemporary Tharu culture and Nepali contentious politics? Rather than assessing whether SWAN activists have been co-opted into mainstream development discourse or whether they appropriated it, it is worth exploring a bit further how they conceptualize their work within the development discourse.

SWAN activists make it clear that they are involved in campaigning and activism (*abhiyan*), in a movement (*andolan*) not in 'development work'. They distinguish between 'outside' vs. 'inside', Dhaniram is very clear. He explains:

> We are not working for someone, we are not doing project work. We are not working for money. We have worked for our community. This thing has come from our brain (*mastishkako kura ho*) since we were children, and what we got from outside was only the support. It is because of this that we managed to do a lot of work. If we had worked by ourselves we could not have been successful because we only had the effort.[26]

They give two reasons. First, according to the activists, what SWAN received was only the financial support to back a community work that they had already started without money, and neither external staff was involved, nor were things from outside brought in. This point is particularly interesting within the perceptions of development in Nepal as something coming from 'outside' (see Lietchy, 1997). Second, SWAN activists believed they were not doing 'development work' because they noticed that projects are shifted when the local conditions become challenging for NGOs. SWAN activists are proud of having carried on with with their work throughout the People's War. They only stopped some of their programmes for five months after Krishna was kidnapped. Krishna himself explains that during the People's War many NGOs closed their projects and left:

> But we wore a white piece of cloth, it's called *kappal* and it is worn at the time of dying. We tied it on our forehead and we said we are even

ready to die for these children but we won't leave. We stayed here because we work for our people, for these *kamlari*. The more the war threatened us, the more we raised our voices for the liberation of the *kamlari*, from village to village. In many villages NGOs could not even enter for fear of the Maoists. But starting from the villages, waiving our flag, we moved in a rally, we took the children to the government centre, in a successful rally. We were close with the inside. We were not there for project work.[27]

Activists feel that decision-making had never been in the hands of donor organizations. Some members felt they have been the agents who decided how to direct the movement from the beginning to fight against an inequality they painfully co-existed with since their childhood. What emerges clearly is that Tharu activists feel that in order to be successful a social movement needs to be rooted in the local community but at the same time glean support and resources from national and international communities. SWAN members do not see any contradiction between calling themselves activists and receiving funding from NGOs, working through their network, relationships or through their cultural languages and contrasting discourses. But the reverse is also true. In this way, indigenous aesthetics not only condensed ethnic identity in portable forms, easily understood by local audiences and similarly exchanged within development project politics, but 'development' *kachahari natak* was re-contextualized and performed during Maghi festival along with Tharu dance and songs in local cultural programmes, as I observed in 2006.

The Kamlaris' real dramas in both Kathmandu and Dang

Scarry (1985) describes the invisibility of the physical and psychological pain of people who may sit close to us. Such remoteness may not disappear even after its verbal expression. While parents knew that the *kamlari* work was hard, the girls' mothers had experienced it, others assumedly 'didn't know' what happened to the girls after they reached the landlord's house. The girls returned home for Maghi but when their parents asked them, many say they were afraid to speak: 'so after lying to our fathers we sat in silence' Manjita explains. Besides, in certain Tharu households, the social distance between fathers and daughters was such that even pronouncing the father's name would be considered as a sin, let alone share one's pain with him.

In this context, *kachahari* allowed for the direct display of the *kamlaris'* pain and parents could understand the suffering of their daughters, without exposing the protagonists themselves. Krishna believes that in comparison to other awareness-raising means, through drama 'what the audience see reaches their soul' people understand immediately, 'from inside'. The *kachahari* performed by the Kamlari

Theatre Group is not 'acting' according to Krishna. He thinks that it is because the young activists had experience themselves the 'real *kamlari* pain' that they can play that role, and

> they would not have been able to play the role empty. They would have cheated. Cheating and playing a role are different things. They had carried that pain before for real. They had already performed a real drama in their lives and thus had no problem in playing the role [...] they showed real real acting.

Shiva, the lead character in both plays, describes the interplay between reality and drama: 'When I remembered the pain that I suffered, tears came. It was easy to cry. It was easy to make people cry too... While playing and playing, it was real. It was easy to do theatre.' Performance enabled pain to move out of the personal, to enter a realm of 'shared discourse' that is wider, social and political. If the acting is real, so are the tears or the joy experienced while dancing. And they are a measure of the actual sharing. 'People cried as if it was real, not drama', says Shiva.

Kabeer (2005) argues that to be disempowered means to be 'denied choice', while empowerment entails the ability to make choices, which are conditioned not only by the existence of alternatives but also by the visibility of such alternatives. By making alternatives visible to parents, daughters, and wider social actors in both the Dang Valley and Kathmandu, I argue that the theatre 'affected' the perception of the *kamlari* practice both at local and global level. Similarly, donor funding opened up new networks and possibilities for SWAN activists to raise their issue nationally and internationally, and to advocate for change.

Conclusions

This chapter explored how theatre could strategically essentialize Tharu cultural identity and how *kachahari natak*, as a synthetic and transient performance practice merged local and global aesthetics, facilitating the exposure of the *kamlari* system among diverse audiences, and simultaneously revealing the *kamlaris'* pain in a changing encounter.

The global-local divide collapses in SWAN and the Kamlari Theatre Group's activism as they see the enrollment of the international community as necessary for the success of their movement and imbue their indigenous aesthetic knowledge with 'global' dramatic forms. By placing themselves outside the mainstream development discourse and identifying themselves as activists, but while simultaneously working through the development channels, resources and networks, Tharu art-activists symbolically forward their cultural critique.

The *kamlari* voices and movements on stage are perceived as powerful because they are 'real' not an 'empty role'. A dramatic actor cannot replace a social actor in this form of representation: SWAN activists believe that social change requires direct action and cannot be mediated, no change can be obtained vicariously. *Kamlaris'* 'real' voices and movements contributed to the social movement for their liberation. There is diversity of forms across the local-global trajectory, but continuity of sensations and feelings. One artist said that through cultural art (*kala sanskriti*) people's mind is 'diverted and may even change'. Similarly, SWAN activists conceive their work as 'real work' because of the close bond with their community and because of a strong motivation that emerged from their heart, and their lives. Activists distinguish between what comes from 'inside' and what is 'external'. But these two trajectories are not mutually exclusive. *Kachahari* theatre is incorporated into the community's *kala sanskriti*. In the same way, the development network and the resources made available through it allowed SWAN activists to fulfill their dream. With this account, however, I do not mean to conflate SWAN activists' narratives with the narratives of NGO and INGOs that collaborated with them. Divergences remain, and some are fundamental. First, participant observation showed that the relationships between members of different organizations working in the Lamahi-Kathmandu-global context network changed from 2005 to 2012. Second, the politics of representation of the *kamlari* issue and liberation movement on media and NGO literature is revealing but deserves separate exploration: for the moment, we could argue that by entering the development world SWAN activists partially lost the power to represent themselves and worked within the theoretical framework of international development agencies. For example, Krishna explains the *kamlari pratha* as agricultural exploitation and suggests a political solution, claiming that land reform would stop the practice: if landless Tharu had land to cultivate they would not depend on landowners anymore. In contrast, Som Paneru from NYF believes that what he learnt in 13 years of work is that 'social change is brought by civil society and NGOs' and that distributing land is not feasible and that without a proper housing policy the problem would not be solved.[28] SWAN activists could employ the 'special' of theatre only during the period it was useful for their advocacy campaign and then moved on to their own 'ordinary' professions, unlike Aarohan artists who were striving to turn the 'special' into an 'ordinary' profession, as we will see in Chapter 7.

Endnotes

1   For details about Aarohan partner groups in 2005 see Ghimire (2004, 12).

2   Their target groups were internal migrant workers, porters, trekking porters, small street-based shopkeepers, construction workers and small garment workers.

3   I will use the term 'activist' to indicate members of the NGO SWAN and will problematize this later on.

4   The Tharu are an indigenous group (*adivasi/janjati*) whose identity and origins are rather contested (Guneratne, 1998, 2002; Krauskpff, 2003, 2009; McDonaugh, 1997; Maslak, 2003). The Tharu are broadly divided into several groups – Rana, Kathariya, Kochila, Mahotani, Deokhura and Dangaura – based on territorial, cultural and linguistic differences. In 'Many tongues, one people' Guneratne argues that while there is an instrumental aspect to the refashioning of Tharu identity as a single ethnic group in modern Nepal, Tharus have indeed discovered a commonality they were previously unaware of and the label has become reified. The Tharus' solution to explaining their difference is 'to posit an original unity and then argue that underdeveloped conditions in the Tarai, especially its infrastructure, left them ignorant about their ethnic kin and produced the cultural and linguistic variation that exists today' (2002, 7). The activists with whom I worked did not assign particular meaning to these subcategories. In contrast, they distinguished between Tharu who owned land and were in powerful positions and landless Tharu.

5   In 2006, when this research started the amount was considered as the equivalent of the price of a piglet or a goat.

6   Interviews and conversations with group and community members during my fieldwork in Deukhuri Valley and in Kathmandu were carried out in Nepali language, with translations from Tharu language when required.

7   Gender roles as perceived by parents affected not only girls' access to education but also their workload within the household. While Tharu girls are usually expected to help with household chores, e.g. cooking, caring for younger siblings, cleaning, collecting firewood, taking care of goats, boys are free to go to school and hang out with friends. Such a disparity is portrayed in street theatre plays and in the *kachahari* frame.

8   Interviewed in January 2012.

9   Ibid.

10 Interviewed in January 2012. Reflections on the politics of representation would deserve more space than is available in this chapter. Just to add another brief example, the name of SWAN and of its members appear on newspapers in Nepali language while they disappear in English language national newspapers that mentioned mostly national and international partners (FNC/NYF) and their staff.

11 SWAN activists emphasize that explaining the practice in terms of caste would not do justice to the complexities of their experience. Landlords are both Brahmin, Chhetri, and Tharu. They remember that in the past landlords used to be Tharu but because of modernization, migration from the hills and increase in wealth, the practice spread, involving members of other castes as well.

12 In late 2004, early 2005 the relationship between the two Maoist leaders Prachanda and Baburam Bhattarai became tense because of divergences over power. Bhattarai was first expelled and then reinstated in the party.

13 Cultural activities within development projects occupied a gray zone during the harshest phases of the People's War and many street theatre projects had to stop in areas controlled

by the Maoist party. Unlike the example given above, some artists who performed for NGOs in another district in western Nepal reported that they had to stop performing in villages because their development street theatre performances were confused by villagers with the Maoist cultural programmes.

14 Interviewed in January 2012.

15 Interviewed in January 2012.

16 The outcome of this movement should be understood against shifts in power relation/ discourse both locally and internationally. First, the shift of the global development discourse towards rights and advocacy legitimized a stronger presence of former *kamlaris'* voices internationally. Secondly, power within Tharu communities is traditionally held by men (Maslak, 2003; Bjork and Guneratne, 1999; Guneratne, 2002). Thus the activists' struggle against the *kamlari* system represents a strong gender and cultural critique that also impacted on their personal lives. However, both issues deserve a separate paper to be thoroughly explored.

17 Man Bahadur Chhetri, interviewed in January 2012.

18 The girl was found dead with severe burning in her employer's house. The protestors demanded further investigation.

19 A strike blocking the traffic in the Tarai.

20 For 'aestheticized' I do not only mean more 'artistic' but also more 'sensitized' (Rockhill, 2004), as I will make clear in the conclusion.

21 Interviewed in May 2005.

22 The phrase can be translated as 'cultural art', but in daily conversations it includes not only Tharu dance and songs but also other elements that define Tharu identity such as their musical instruments, dress, jewellery, etc.

23 I will elaborate more on the metaphor outside/inside in section 4.

24 Traditional Tharu dance.

25 A flat, round tray made of bamboo.

26 Interviewed in January 2012.

27 Interviewed in January 2012.

28 *The Kathmandu Post*, 2013.

6

A Cultural Army for a Cultural Revolution

Maoist cultural programmes and revolutionary theatre[1]

I want to put forward a short commitment (*pratibaddhata*). This is not only mine. This is the commitment of our whole Samana Battalion cultural movement. I take the commitment to fulfill the dream of the martyrs. [...] We, cultural workers, want to give you our commitment. In this coming storm, we will also, at any cost, play our role. This commitment we put in front of you. What we are singing in front of you people, these all are your own songs, including your pains, your tears, your happiness. Through these songs we can stop the hidden royalist system from raising their head and to stop them we will go to Singha Durbar and to the Royal Palace with harmoniums and guitars. Then, if it does not work, we will join the PLA [People's Liberation Army] to enter Narayanhiti [Royal Palace]. This is our oath. You may wonder, 'how can you reach Narayanhiti?' You can see it in our banner, Samana Cultural Battalion, Battalion means warriors, cultural war, cultural army, cultural fighters. We are not only cultural workers. We don't want to be only artists. Political people and intellectuals say that artists should be independent, they should not have any political affiliation, they should not be attached to politics. But we say we are artists and we want to join politics. We want to sing the songs of the people. Politics is a way to free suffocated people. We, artists, want to do the same. This is our commitment as artists.[2]

The Maoist revolutionary cultural programmes represented another type of performance for social change available to Nepali audiences in those transitional years. Catchy melodies, colourful dresses, traditional steps broken by classical mudras suddenly turning into clenched fists: since the beginning of the People's War in 1996, Maoist cultural troupes travelled the country offering villagers engaging politico-cultural programmes; after the People's Movement in 2006, they also performed in the cities and in the capital. The first 'Cultural Battalion', Madhya Samana Battalion 6 was formed in October 2006. It included the four 'cultural companies' of Central Nepal, Sen Chyang Cultural Company, Anekot Cultural Company, Shiva Sharada Cultural Company, and Chunu Shilpa Cultural Company. The battalion was subsumed under the cultural section of the party, Akhil Nepal Jana Sanskitik Mahasangh (All Nepal People's Cultural Federation). Maoist cultural groups were active in each of the 75 districts of Nepal. Furthermore, 13 cultural groups were linked to each of the Maoist Federal States, and 11 were connected to their ethnic fronts (Sharma, 2004, 41–42). Samana Parivar is the historical cultural group associated to the party's central committee. Cultural groups were also present within the PLA and other workers' organizations although they performed as a leisure activity.

Towards the end of the war, around 1,500 artists were engaged full-time in composing songs, dance, and drama, which were performed during public political meetings to entertain and educate the audience between the speeches of the party leaders. Cultural programmes were also organized for fundraising (Fig. 6.1, photo by the author). The cultural troupes' repertoire was regularly created to match the development of the political situation. The task of the party's artists is twofold. During public programmes, they aim at getting the people's support for the revolution. During the party's internal meetings, they criticize the leadership whenever they fail, according to them, to follow the people's desires. The Maoist cultural front produces both literary works including magazines, novels, drama, and poetry as well as performance art such as dance, theatre, and songs that circulate through tapes, CDs, and videos. Only the latter will be considered in this chapter.

Figure 6.1: Final scene of the cultural programme staged at the Nepal Academy in September 2006

After briefly outlining the role of art in revolutionary theory and situating revolutionary artists within the party strategy, I will detail how Maoist cultural programmes can be conceptualized as both political rituals and popular culture. In the end of the chapter I will describe how the artists' position changed at the end of the War and the beginning of the professionalization of their activities.

Revolutionary aesthetics

Cultural work plays a relevant role in Leftist popular movements. Songs, dance, dramatic performances, and cinema have been employed to popularize Communist ideology in China (Mao, 1960; 1967; Lang and Williams, 1972), Peru (Starn, 1995), Chile (Morris, 1986), Cuba (Moore, 2006) and Nicaragua (Judson, 1987). The cultural front of the Communist movements[3] that developed in Nepal in different historical periods was steered by Mao's ideas on art and literature outlined in the Yan'an Forum, known in Nepal since the 1950s (Onesto, 2006, 136). According to Mao's thought, a Communist party requires 'three magic weapons' to capture political power: the Party, as a strong, disciplined organization; armed struggle, e.g. the PLA, guerrilla fighting under the party's direction; the united front, e.g. sister organizations and ethnic fronts to strategically broaden the party's support base and develop armed struggle. The cultural front, Akhil Nepal Jana Sanskitik Mahasangh (All Nepal People's Cultural Federation), was one of these fronts, including, among others, the women's association, several unions (e.g. students, teachers, farmers, etc), and ethnic fronts. Maoist cultural work evolved from the underground progressive cultural movements described in chapter three. Activists could easily access the works of Marx, Engels, Lenin, and Mao, as well the translation of revolutionary novels such as Maxim Gorky's 'Mother', Yang Mo's 'The Song of Youth', produced by the Soviet and Chinese cultural centres in heavily subsidized editions, mostly through the school circuits (Gellner and Karki, 2007, 383–8; Adhikari, 2014, 6). The Naxalite movement in India was also a source of inspiration but so was the Chinese Cultural Revolution: Agni Sapktota, a Maoist leader, remembers being moved by the patriotic songs and dance of the Chinese cultural groups that were performing for the road construction workers (Chaulagain and Khandel in Adhikari, 2014, 4). There is continuity between the ideas fostering the cultural front of the Jhapa Communist Movement in the 1970s and the cultural work of the Maoist groups in the 1990s. Grandin (1994, 175) points out that while remaining within the musical genre of modern or folk songs broadcast by Radio Nepal, progressive songs introduced innovations both in content and interaction with villagers. A Maoist commissar[4] explains how progressive singers inspired them along the same lines, although they would then develop the genre further:

They travelled from village to village against the Panchayat system to make people aware and get them to stand up. [...] Their thinking was that songs should not be about *'saila and maili'*, or *'kancha and kanchi'* [that is 'love songs'] but should be about the people'.[5]

Communist parties went through various splits but the core message of progressive songs remained the same. De Sales (2003) describes the circulation of four cassettes by Raktim Parivar (Family of Blood) in a Magar village in Rukum in 1994, well before the beginning of the People's War. Raktim Parivar is a cultural movement established by Jeevan Sharma in 1986 and in the early 1990s associated to the Nepali Communist Party Masal, a Maoist faction; by 2001, they had released 11 cassettes and 10,000 copies of a booklet with the song texts were published every year. By 2009 Raktim Parivar had produced more than 40 albums containing approximately 10 songs each. Grandin (2005, 28) observes that de Sales's (2003) study of Raktim Parivar's rhetoric shows elements of the Panchayat year's progressive songs like realistic description of people's lives, reference to nature, anticipation of the day of change, and also localizing songs by mentioning specific places and events. The presence of 'blood' represented a new development. My analysis of a sample of Maoist songs produced across the war period shows that these rhetorical elements continued to be important and are enriched by references to specific campaigns that brought to the audience new political directions through cultural productions.

At the beginning of the People's War cultural activists were caught and killed, publications were closed and the cassettes of the songs were seized from the market. Cultural activities continued in spite of being banned (Baral, 2007). 1999 marked the first national convention of Akhil Nepal Janasanskritik Sangh (All Nepal's People's Cultural Association), which aimed at promoting the work of the cultural teams. This coincided with a period of state violence and repression, the Operation Kilo Sierra 2 (Thapa and Sijapati, 2003, 90-94; Karki and Seddon, 2003, 23), and in many places writers and artists were captured and disappeared. In other places they were imprisoned, like Rishi Raj Baral, the editor of the revolutionary literary magazine Kalam and Krishna Sen[6] (Baral, 2007). Cultural families mobilized in different parts of the country, e.g., Maila Lama's Sailung Parivar campaigned in eastern Nepal, and so did Garjan Parivar and Chomolungma along Kshitij Parivar was active in Lumbini, Jaljala Parivar in Rolpa, Sisne Parivar in Rukum; Ichchhuk Parivar and Chuli Parivar were also active locally. During the middle period of the War, Hitman Shakya and Purna Gharti developed cultural activities in western Nepal through Pratirodh Pariwar. Samana Pariwar, reorganized and coordinated by Khusi Ram Pakhrin and Maila Lama, conducted the 'Mechi to Mahakali Cultural Defensive Movement' that was a cornerstone in the expansion of Maoist cultural activities (Ibid.). At the time, the fundamental work of publication and distribution of cassettes and song booklets was done both at central and local levels (Ibid.).

According to Mao, revolutionary art and literature are subordinate to politics because only politics concentrates the needs of the class and the mass, but they are nonetheless important, like 'cogs and wheels' in the revolutionary cause (Mao Tse-Tung, 1967, 13). Aesthetics was not a central concern in the writings of Marx and Engels (Moore, 2006, 10; Williams, 1977; Long and Williams, 1972). Strongly deterministic readings of Marxism included art in the ideological superstructure. As part of the intellectual life, it was deemed to be conditioned by material circumstances, following Marx's dictum that 'social being determines consciousness' (Marx, 1859). In contrast, less deterministic views stress the interconnectedness of ideological forms with the economic system, because art has the potential to intervene in the socio-economic context by spurring the audience to adopt certain attitudes and practices.[7] In this way, 'culture' as artistic performance can affect 'culture' as a system of meanings and practices. Maoist artists' narratives reveal a concept of culture that is indissolubly linked to politics, as a commissar was keen in pointing out the first time I interviewed him:

> Because we are Communist, in our understanding the point of view to see everything is class. Seeing the development of society, every political revolution is a cultural revolution in itself. And in culture the genre that directly affects people is literary art (*sahitya kala*). Literary art reflects the reality of a society. It also heightens awareness and provides support to society. That's why, in our 10 year experience of people's war, [we have realized that] to fight against the injustice and oppression done upon the people, presenting our ideas in artistic ways, through opera, drama, dance and revolutionary songs, motivates people more than a 5 hour speech by a leader. They give the awareness to go forward and rebel. Although other ways can be powerful, art and literature are more powerful. [...] When we presented our pains, our sorrows, the reality of war through art, people could easily understand. They could easily follow and appreciate their liberation war[8]

The commissar continues his explanation emphasizing the relation between war-culture, culture-art and thus war-art:

> When we started our People's War the battle war and the drum (*madal*) war went together. Pen war and bullet war. The pen supported the war and the war made the pen revolutionary. When these two things went together, the war was not only of bullets and guns but also of thoughts and pens. When Krishna Sen Ichchhuk, a magazine editor and Nepal's

top literary person, became a martyr in the name of progressive [writing] (*pragatisil*), the soldiers who beat him to death said that a pen was more powerful than thousands guns because one bullet from one gun can kill only one army soldier, it kills one enemy, but his pen was killing thousands of soldiers at once (Ibid.).

For Maoist artists distinctions are clear-cut and consequential: because there are two classes in society, the oppressor and the oppressed, the bourgeois and the proletariat, there are also two cultures, 'bad culture' and 'good culture'.[9] As a result, while art that simply mirrors the social reality without questioning it can be defined as 'bourgeois art', 'revolutionary art' has to spur people to change society, defining art, as Brecht claims, 'not as a mirror held up to nature but a hammer with which to shape it'. It is the conflation of ideology in culture and art that makes every political revolution simultaneously a cultural revolution.[10]

A leader of an ethnic liberation front associated to the CPN(M) emphasizes the relation between art and politics, defining art as a vital part of an individual, and thus a privileged and 'natural' means of political expression:

> We don't accept the bourgeois view that art and music are the ornaments of the country. We are not ready to accept this. Art and literature are body parts of the country, inseparable organs of the nation. To protect nationality (*rashtriyata*) we need art. We need talent. That's why we say that art is not like an ornament to be worn when you feel like, and put into the garage when you don't. This can't happen. That's why today we are taking this music to create a relationship with the government.[11]

In unintended ways, the leader's metaphor echoes Bourdieu's concept of artistic habitus. Questioning the Romantic view of the artist as a charismatic individual, independent and disinterested in his work, Bourdieu brings the artist back into the power rules of the cultural field. Therefore, both the ability to be creative and the practice of being creative are seen as effects of the individual artists' habitus – the embodied structure developed out of the individual's history, and their social and historical contexts (J. Webb, T. Schirato and G. Danaher, 2006). I will revisit this issue later in relation to the artists' multiple roles.

Revolutionary performance

Representational practices have the power to reorganize the sense of self, to build alternative perceptions of possible futures and be the engines of social transformation. They can contain dreams and visions. Artistic performances do not simply provide an aesthetic experience. As symbolic performances they 'make it possible for there to be a consensus on the meaning of the social world, a consensus which contributes fundamentally to the reproduction of the social order' (Bourdieu, 1990, 166). Extending Bourdieu's view, artistic experience can create a climate of consensus to subvert the social order itself. What Bourdieu suggests is that symbols, in the form of creative presentations, actually construct society by providing people a specifically social and visible experience of identification that is publicly recognized.

Artistic performances were used in different ways before, during and after the People's War. Maoist artists draw on artistic performances to communicate with the audience, to create a sense of inclusion, to energize the PLA, to popularize Maoist ideology, spread political education, mobilize support and legitimize their political claims. Cultural programmes also provide a platform for personal expression of often shared life experiences. These objectives are achieved through the particular structure of cultural programmes, as I will outline below.

What immediately distinguishes Maoist performances from other artistic performances for social change is their strict connection with the party's political agenda and structure. Cultural groups depend on the party for political organization and thought, while remaining independent in the creative and practical organization of their work. In this sense, cultural performances cannot be conceptualized as 'products' to be offered to an audience, a commodity, but rather as a process of interaction through which the link between the party and the audience is created and sustained. The comparison with street performances for social change is intriguing. A commonly perceived limitation in certain street plays (Epskamp, 2006; Mottin, 2007) is the disjuncture between the artists as specialists and the audience, as well the lack of follow-up activities which results in the reduction of the power of theatre to achieve social transformation. The plays thus become more of a show than a form of social intervention. As party members, Maoist artists are backed by a strong organizational structure, which embodies the message that they convey. Any person in the audience wishing to follow their message can find an institutional apparatus that sustains their choice.

During political mass meetings, cultural programmes usually start 2–3 hours before the arrival of the political leaders and then continue between the leaders' speeches. Artists anchor cultural programmes in a performative style. They introduce the songs and provide the audience with links to wider political issues, in the same style described by Manjul earlier. The audience, the artists and the party are symbolically joined in a single voice by revolutionary rhetoric. Artists become the spokespersons of the imagined temporary community that is established through the performance. A crescendo of cross-references[12] plays within introductory speeches like an incantation: plain speaking is enriched with quotations from Maoist poems, which in turn change into revolutionary songs (Figs. 6.2–6.5, photos by the author).

Figure 6.2: Leaders of the Cultural Section of the CPN (Maoist) head a rally in Chitwan, October 2006

Figure 6.3: Leaders sing the 'Internationale' with raised clenched fists at the opening of the cultural programme, Chitwan 2006

Figure 6.4: Some members of the audience also raise their fists and sing along

Figure 6.5: Dancers wear Chinese-style martial art costumes during the song 'Today the epoch says'

By skillfully alternating different rhythms of speech, use of repetitions and catchy phrases, and variations in the intensity of voice, the audience's attention is aroused and sustained. For example, the Sen Chyang commander opened his introductory speech in 2006 by citing a poem written by Krishna Sen:

> Oh rulers
> We won't accept your autocracy and orders
> However you spread the orders
> No matter how you suppress
> If you can take control of the senses
> Keep the truth in jail
> But, oh, dictator
> Against your cruelty and self interest
> We will keep raising our voice
> We will keep raising our voice

Ladies and gentlemen, I recited few lines from Pratibadhata, 'Commitment', in fact while reciting the poem I'm feeling very sad.

This is the pain of all of us and of all our martyrs, our Krishna Sen Ichhuk, our great master of literature, the heart beat of the people. Everybody believe that if you put him in our eyes he will not hurt you [he is a very good person] and a very talented warrior, he's not in front of us now. I read his poem Pratibadhata. From the blood of all our cultural martyrs like him the very talented, our Samana Sanskritik Battalion was born.[13]

Anchoring not only takes place in live programmes but also in recorded MCs and VCDs. For example, the party cultural leader Ishwar Chandra Gyawali introduced the revolutionary songs performed by Sen Chyan Cultural Group in 'Voices of Hope' (*Asthaka Swarharu*). This is an example of the integration of artistic production within the party image-construction and celebration project. According to Bourdieu, culture is both 'unifying' (1990, 7) and 'divisive', distinguishing between those who share the same ideals and those who do not.

Cultural productions create symbols of 'us' as communities, as revealed in the following lyrics:

Look towards the mountains, a new beautiful world is being born
This is our Nepal, this is lovely Nepal
This is our Nepal,
Look towards the mountains, a new beautiful world is being born
As the snow falls in winter, injustice surrounds us
In the country of Everest, we practice Malemabaad[14]
The thought to change the world, born and heightened
That is Prachandapath, the great Prachandapath, the great Prachandapath
Look towards the mountains, a new beautiful world is being born
(From 'Voices of Faith')

Therefore, cultural programmes can be conceptualized as political rituals that create particular kinds of communities, 'communities of feelings' (Berezin, 2001, 93), intense experiential moments of shared identity that extend beyond live performance through the use of popular media such as VCDs and cassettes. The structure of cultural programmes is repetitive, opening in the same way with the singing of the 'Internationale', clenched fist raised to symbolically connect to revolutions across the world, followed by a moment of silence to commemorate the martyrs. As performance, Maoist cultural programmes not only make visible the imaginings of people who share the same ideology, they also emotionally enact their sense of belonging. In other words, cultural programmes are both representational and performative.

The content and organization of cultural programmes changed during the stages of the People's War, and after April 2006. The evolution of revolutionary performances can be traced through the analysis of the songs, dance, and drama over a decade. But that would require a paper of its own. Placed chronologically, artistic productions offer a meta-commentary of the development of the wider political struggle. This is how the commissar explains how they actively involved and motivated audiences at the beginning of the People's War:

> When we were underground, after 2052 *Falgun* 1ˢᵗ [13 February 1996, the day in which the People's War was launched] we went from village to village at night. We could not walk during the day. We called people and sang for them, playing *madal* with a small voice, sometimes playing bells and glasses:
>
> Wake up farmer, your right has been ravished
>
> Your blood and sweat are mixing with the soil
>
> Without holding a gun on the shoulder good days won't come for the poor
>
> Without fighting this war, people's culture will never come in this country
>
> We had to go at night, in the houses, closing the doors, and we used to sing like this. Therefore people's war and cultural war went together.[15]

During the People's War artistic presentations centered on themes of sacrifice, courage, and struggle. In fact, the same images and rhetorical devices run through revolutionary songs, poems, drama, memoirs, and wider literature. Analysing poems and diaries, Lecomte-Tilouine (2006, 2010) describes 'martyrdom as generative sacrifice' in Maoist's ideology. Death becomes asymmetrical: one's own warriors death is noble, heroic and sustains the struggle of the living; the death of the enemy is scorned (Ibid.). Not only that: the death of Maoist martyrs is creative and produces other warriors. The self-sacrifice of the martyrs is creative also because it passes their dreams on to the living who are left with the commitment of writing about the martyrs to give them immortality (2010). Lecomte-Tilouine explains that:

> [m]artyrdom acquired a strong power of attraction in that it fundamentally asserts that anyone, whether illiterate, poor or of the lowest status, is of 'priceless' value, and can contribute to the magnificent project of changing the order of things by putting his or her life at stake (Ibid., 2).

Here is an example from one of the songs that I have analysed:

Hundreds of new braves have been born in the time of struggle

The fearful disappear in the floods of the People's War

The braves have united and fight in the harshness

They are moving ahead, removing obstacles

With their death, the braves keep living era after era

(Written by Purna Gharti, from 'Songs presented during the great People's War')

In contrast, in autumn 2006 performances dealt with the advent of peace and republic. This is how the commander introduced his party's political turnaround in a public meeting:

> The journey of the rebels started in 2052 *Falgun* 1st, the road of blood. Samana Parivar has walked the road of blood for a decade, Samana Parivar, the artists belonging to CPN (Maoist). Now they are in your cities, in your villages. For a decade they have been singing songs of bombs, weapons, revolution, sacrifice, tears. But now we are singing songs of peace because it's the people's desire. [...] Respecting Nepali people's feelings and desires, our party CPN (Maoist), with deep feelings of responsibility, now comes out to campaign for peace, a journey towards peace. Our Samana Parivar, our people's artists are leaving all the songs of weapons to sing songs of peace and also revolution because the feelings and desires of the 19 day people's movement have not yet been fulfilled.[16]

The commander's announcement during a public cultural programme becomes a form of 'behaviour heightened' (Schechner, 1993, 1) that has the power to legitimize political choice while enacting it on stage. In a way, Maoist cultural productions represent the symbolic creative side that contrasts against the destruction generated by the armed struggle. But the post-April 2006 performances also validated the People's War, and served to guide the audience through the different stages of the subsequent political struggle.

Though the backbone of cultural programmes are dances and songs, dramas, satire, opera and comic sketches appeared too. For this purpose, I have analysed a play performed during the Campaign for Republic 2006 (*Ganatantra Abhiyan*) as a case-study from which I select short extracts. The play 'After Understanding' (*Bujhepachhi*) consists of three scenes set respectively in Kathmandu, in a rural village, and in the Royal Palace. It opens with a girl moaning in the streets during a demonstration. She has been injured and cannot see her friends around. When one of them arrives to help her run away, they comment about the popular movement and the value of sacrificing their own life for the betterment of the country. They also recount to each other how one of their comrades was killed. The second scene is set in a village chowk, where people stop and exchange views regarding the future of the country. News about the death of the boy during the demonstrations reaches the village and provokes reactions from villagers. Rumours of the upheaval also echo inside the Royal Palace in the third scene. The king and queen are still unable to foresee the possibility of their demise. In the background, popular slogans in favour of a republic intensify.

Unlike the plays devised by the Naxalite revolutionary cultural groups with villagers in India,[17] this and other plays performed by Maoist cultural groups in Nepal were based only on the collective work of the troupe rather than a collaboration with villagers. In this case, the cultural group commissar scripted most of the text. It was later modified according to the group's suggestions during rehearsals. Such plays were prepared for performance rather than for spectator/audience involvement. Like for Aarohan, scripting plays remained the domain of the 'specialists' and did not extend to the audience. The play was staged both outdoors and indoors during public meetings organized by the party as part of its political campaign. Let me quote a section from the first scene. The actors used costumes and few props. In this scene, the girl injured in the opening scene (A1) meets her comrades who come to help her (A2, A3, A4 and A5). The girl character links the initial reporting of the demonstrations with their subsequent description to the comrades that were not present.

(Sound of a bullet blasting)

A3:   Did you hear the blast of a bullet?

A2:   Yes I did.

A3:   Friend.... [approaching the injured girl]

A1:   The sound of a bullet.... After taking my friend ..... the police left... and he was killed by the bullet. Another friend has become a martyr....

A4:   If our young people are ready to let their blood flow, what can a meaningless bullet do? I don't feel any fear inside myself. I'm not going to leave this movement... as long as the people's good days haven't come, the sun of justice hasn't risen and these totally pitch dark nights are not finished, my friends......

A5:   You said right, the sacrifice of the brave will not leave the world silent. Rather, the flame of fire shining so brightly will give birth to lakh of braves. And we'll fight to make this black rule fall.

A3:   Oh friend, when the people made of steel go ahead to climb the top of the mountain to fulfill the martyrs' dream, who can stop them? If somebody attempt to stop [them], then they will be compelled to live inside the rotten black rule, my friend.......

A5:   We should not live in the night, my friends. When the rulers reach their last stage, they shoot bullets showing their cowardice. When power enters people's heart, a different light is enlightened which gives me the fire to fight, my friend.

A1:   I have lost my hand... my blood flowed... I don't have any regret towards anybody. But if this black rule will continue, then there will be regrets for all those who desire justice....

A4:   First of all, we should treat the wounded, the movement has lessened ... the police have gone to their camps.

A3:   You are right, let's move away quickly.

In this section, the dialogue mixes realistic descriptions with Maoist jargon and metaphors. The conversation evolves once again around the theme of martyrdom mentioned earlier. The king's government – and in general non-Maoist forms of governance – is described with metaphors linked to the semantic field of 'darkness', such as 'pitch dark nights', or 'nights' in opposition to the 'light', such as 'flame of fire shining so brightly', 'a different light is enlightened which gives me the fire to fight', 'the sun of justice' brought by Maoism and by Maoist combatants. This is how the same metaphor is used in a song

> With a beautiful picture of the horizon
> We people's army come smiling as red rays
> We have come filling sad people's hearts with happiness
> We have come spreading light in those dark villages
> We have come crossing floods and thunders
> We have come fulfilling martyrs' dream
> (From 'A Beautiful Horizon', in 'Voices of Hope')

The phrase 'let blood flow' recurs both in songs and in the commander's anchoring of the cultural programmes to describe the sacrifice of the rebels to fulfill the dreams of the martyrs:

> He is not dead, he has become a candle of faith

Blood has not flown, it has become the flame of fire
(From 'He is not dead' in 'Voices of Hope')

Apart from the extended use of Maoist metaphors, both the language and the staging of the play were very simple and realistic, recalling the aesthetics of agit-prop street theatre. However, more than acting out roles, like Kamlari theatre activists, Maoist cultural workers re-enacted their own lives. Most of them in fact had real-life experiences of war. Nepali theatre artists regarded Maoist acting as amateurish in comparison to professional performances. However, despite being aesthetically simple, Maoist performance is based on direct personal experience of struggle, which made them specialized and 'professional' in their own field. Such practical competence, akin to the 'feel for the game' (Bourdieu, 1990, 66) of *loktantrik natak* performers or *kamlari* theatre artists is what emotionally involves the spectators. Their acting is empowered by their energy, their enthusiasm and the fact that they 'play' themselves as dramatic and social actors, as cultural workers and activists. Their strength therefore comes from the immediacy, topicality and the emotional response,[18] which songs, dance, and dramas trigger in the audience. Emotions seem to be at odd with Maoist rhetoric. Although Prachanda (2001) highlights the role of cultural programmes in involving the masses both ideologically and emotionally, 'sentimentalism' is often disparaged, as in the opening of the play 'After Understanding':

A2:   I'm also injured. Police are coming after us.....

A1:   Police? And where are the other friends?

A2:   Our friends are moving ahead, they are demonstrating.

A1:   Leave this place quickly. Don't stay here. These human ghosts/ beasts won't leave you here. Go quickly.

A2:   How can I go, leaving you here alone...

A1:   Listen, in this time cheap sentimentalism (*sasto bhavukta*) will bring you only more loss. Go fast

A2:   This is not cheap sentimentalism, my friend. Police are coming. Let's move from here.

A1:   Look, I've lost lots of blood [lots of my blood has flooded], I will not live ...

A2:   Friend, what are you saying? You have to live, the country needs you.... Stand up, friend, stand up.

One could argue that the cultural programmes may just be a way of 'preaching to the converted' (Dolan, 2005, 65). Yet, as Holly Hughes (Ibid., 48) suggests, political 'conversion' is unstable. People are never blindly converted to anything. Ambiguity and doubt are always present. Cultural programmes therefore provide coherence through the use of a common shared language that facilitates the renewal of faith required to sustain political identity.

Revolutionary performances as popular culture

Debates on popular culture are usually concerned with mass-media, magazines, TV, cinema or cyber-culture. However, Maoist cultural programmes can be conceptualized as a form of popular culture for different reasons. The troupes' organization, described in the introduction, shows clearly that Maoist cultural programmes have wide diffusion. Each team performs an average of 2–4 programmes a day during campaigning periods and 10–15 shows a month for the rest of the year.

Like street theatre, Maoist cultural programmes are free and therefore reach a wide audience. Moreover, the large number of cassettes, CDs and videos produced and sold, contributed to locating revolutionary performance within popular culture. For example, Sen Chyang Cultural Group, a federal team established in 2004 and working in the Kathmandu area, by 2008 had already produced four cassettes: '21st Century People's War' (2004, 3,000 copies), 'We are in War' (in Tamang language, 2005, 3,000 copies), 'Voices of Faith' (in Nepali, Bhojpuri, and Thami languages, 2006, 10,000 copies), 'People going to War' (in Tamang language, 2007, 10,000 copies), 'The Sacrifice will never Die' (in Nepali language, 2008, so far 10,000 copies but the production will be increased). Every federal and ethnic troupe had already produced or was in the process of producing its own cassettes and CDs.

Live performances are the foundation for the popular videos available in every bazaar. Revolutionary songs, compete with pop music and can be heard during leisure time, bus trips, weddings, and other kinds of celebrations among Maoist sympathizers.

But how do they differ from 'mainstream' Nepali culture? Marxist debate on art often centres on the relationship of revolutionary works with traditional forms (Lang and Williams, 1972).[19] As we have seen before, cultural programmes are a well-recognized 'old' format that has been adopted and adapted by Maoist troupes. Similarly, revolutionary songs and dance themselves are deeply rooted in the Nepali folk tradition and represent variations and developments from 'old' forms. Since the songs' melody is usually inspired by folk songs while the lyrics are created anew, audiences find the tunes familiar and thus become instantly involved. While some lyrics are clearly hymns to the party's policies and leaders, praising Prachanda

Path and the 'red people' through Maoist jargon, others describe the oppressions and pains faced by villagers and cannot be distinguished from other songs sung by progressive non-party artists.

Songs are often accompanied by dance. At times, 'revolutionary movements' like raising a clinched fist are mixed with traditional folk or Bollywood-like dance steps. Dancers wear costumes typical of different ethnic groups, as well as Chinese martial art-like suits and military dresses to match movements inspired by martial art or military actions. For example, the song 'Parading' (2006) performed by Sen Chyang is accompanied by a military style march characterized by regular, emphatic beats and is introduced by spoken military commands. Dancers wear combat dresses and the movements of military drills are transformed into a dance. Yet, as soon as the introduction ends, the sounds of the *madal* and the harmonium start and the song loses its threatening tone. It resembles other sweet folk songs, in stark contrast with the outfit of the dancers and the lyrics about the arrival of the PLA. The 'Nepali' flavour of Maoist art is immediately evident.

Dancers often wear a Maoist red band with a white star on their forehead. A red band across the chest indicates the name of the cultural group. Hammer-and-sickle Communist flags and guns were used at times as props. The peace agreements, especially the ban on displaying weapons in public affected Maoist dance as well. In early September 2006 'Parading' was performed indoor with fake weapons. In an outdoor performance the following October, the guns had to be replaced by sticks. In 2007 and 2008 weapons were not used any more. According to the artists, there was no longer any need to display arms.

The rhythms of the songs and dance are usually very energetic and appealing, and it is not unusual to see spectators standing up from the ground to dance. Even during political meetings I heard spectators calling *nach, nach* (dance) in the middle of a complicated speech full of Maoist jargon, making it obvious which of the two forms the audience preferred. Entertainment plays an important role in the success of the cultural programmes.

By making reference to different areas, costumes, languages and dancing styles found throughout the ethnic groups of Nepal, cultural programmes also create and make visible a 'national'[20] culture, unifying diversity through and into Maoist ideology:

We are Madhesi [from the plains], we are Pahadi [from the hills],
We are Himali [from the mountains], we are Nepali
One caste, one class, all Nepali
Wake up Nepali, to build a new Nepal

Unite Nepali, to build a new Nepal
(From 'The Flame of Revolution')

About 200 artists lost their lives during the 10 year armed struggle. Artists often quote two episodes when whole cultural teams were killed by the armed forces: seven artists from Anekot Cultural Group died in Kavre (1999) while 11 died in Palwang, Rolpa (2000). Cultural groups are named after martyrs. For example, Sen Chyang comes from the names of Krishna Sen and Chyangba Lama. For the artists, songs and drama performed during cultural programmes are also a cathartic expression of the grief caused by the loss of friends and relatives, and are reflections upon personal experiences:

> When the ridge opens across the mountain
> When the rhododendron blooms in the hills
> I wish I were absent-minded while I remember him/her
>
> While the storm blows and cuts the clouds
> While the heaven of evils falls down
> I wish I could run and call him/her
> When the ridge opens across the mountain
>
> While the whole world is rising
> While the flame of revolution is dazzling
> I wish I could hum a song for him/her
> When the ridge opens across the mountain
>
> (Written by Mohanlal Chand, from 'Songs presented during the great People's War')

Artists in fact bring on stage the scars that the years of war left on their bodies: an artist lost hearing as the result of a bomb blast and was dependent on an aid, another could not memorize the song lyrics anymore following shell shock that left him unconscious for a long period and had to sing from a piece of paper where he would jot down the words that he often created himself. Therefore, Maoist cultural presentations cannot be confined to the genre of political propaganda. As representations of life experiences, they can be included in the wider field of 'witness art'[21] and for this reason they represent another form of contemporary Nepali popular culture.

Revolutionary artists

What partly characterizes a hegemonic culture is the monopoly of the means of production and representation. The role of 'symbolic depiction' and/or 'speaking for' is the domain of leaders, experts and artists. The peculiar identity of Maoist artists need to be considered at this point because of their role in advancing their 'cultural war' against what they conceive as hegemonic bourgeois culture.

Maoist artists often stress their closeness to the villagers that characterized the War period. At that time, mobilization work was carried out in the villages far from the urban areas, which were under the control of the Nepali army. However, during the first stages of the war, a commissar explained that villagers were usually scared of Maoists so cultural programmes were occasions through which artists not only conveyed political thought but also built trust. Songs were used to establish a connection with the audience and to communicate with them. In order to persuade the villagers that they were their friends, artists helped them in their daily work and were hosted by them in return, as a commissar recalls:

> We listened to them [villagers] after eating rice. We helped them with their chores, building their houses. We gave medicine to sick people. If we had food we shared it with them as well. We helped farmers plough the fields, and helped with work inside and outside the house. So people came to think that Maoists are good people, and the Maoist party is good [...] At that time we did programmes. I sang songs. And after listening to my songs, people commented that the songs were 'so sweet' (*kati mitho git*), and then I talked, and then again I sang. I had a guitar. Now I can't play the guitar because my fingers have been damaged in a bomb blast... People listened and relaxed, and then I talked political and ideological things, about the war, why we had to go into war. We tried to convince them, and they were convinced.[22]

Yet, this picture is complicated by narratives of the dangerous predicament in which villagers found themselves in: on one side the Maoist rebels seeking shelter, on the other the police accusing the villagers of siding with the revolutionaries and offering food and shelter (see the problem in staging a *kachahari* play on this topic discussed in Chapter 4, p. 128). Pettigrew (2013, 112) writes that women of a Gurung (Tamu) village refused to send teenagers to singing and dancing events organized by the Maoists for fear that they may join the party as they 'evoked both fear and fascination'. The commissar's description, however, gives hints about the organization of the cultural programmes as well as the activists' tasks. The role of the cultural workers consisted in singing songs and entertaining people, but also explaining the songs' messages, the reasons of their struggle, listening, and engaging in discussions with the audience, as well as living with them. He continues:

> I was also *sena* [PLA soldier]', we were artists, we were also in the army, we had to do everything by ourselves [he smiles while raising

both hands, to emphasize that there was no other possibility], political leader, cultural member, organizer... (Ibid.)

Artists therefore mediate between the party and the masses, had multiple roles and formed a close bond with people in the rural areas. This connection with the audience emerges as crucial in the artists' narratives. The artists' way of life and work allowed them to establish close bonds with the inhabitants of rural areas. Moreover, unlike some city-based artists who traveled in the hills during the Jhapa Movement (Chapter 2). Artists, coming from a similar background to the villagers, gave voice and dignity to poor people's life experiences while feeling appreciated by the party:

> This is the main thought: we were born in huts, we are people from remote areas, who suffered from injustice, violence, corruption, oppression, very discriminated communities. Our community is Tamang, we are oppressed by caste, we are also an oppressed class. Only high-class people are active in society and seeing all this we got knowledge that we should fight against this. Then we got involved. Our aim was to be active politically, but what the party said was that if your ability is in music, in writing, in going to war you should follow it. Some people have principally the capacity of explaining, ours is of singing, writing, playing instruments. If you have this ability, you will work in this area. The party gave us this responsibility and in these 10 years we worked in this area.[23]

Artists often claim that they are amateurs, despite their popularity. In a public meeting a commissar was apologetic about their shortcomings due to the inexperience of the artists. The distance between artists and audience is thus reduced, as they make no claim to having any special status. On the contrary, what is often emphasized is the fact that the cultural groups are the medium through which the people's voice is amplified and diffused. At the same time, there is a constant appeal to the audience for support for the Maoist campaign. While claiming a shared identification with the audience, artists convey political strategies. However, since the party's entry into mainstream politics, artists in Kathmandu have been taking performance classes, committed to increasing their professionalism.

Bourdieu highlights how class relations are mediated through symbolic struggles. Maoist artists, as 'symbolic producers', legitimize particular definitions and classifications of the social world. They:

> hold a specific power, the properly symbolic power of showing things and making people believe in them, of revealing, in an explicit, objectified way the more or less confused, vague, unformulated, even unformulable experiences of the natural world and of the social

world, and of thereby bringing them into existence (Bourdieu in Swartz, 1997, 220).

Maoist artists therefore embody both the power of intellectuals and the persuasiveness of performers.

Because of the direct contact with the grassroots, artists acquire direct experience and knowledge which then allow them to raise critiques with their political leaders during internal programmes. The commissar explains that criticism, while remaining constructive and friendly, works at three different levels: first within the self, then within the organization, and thirdly it becomes class struggle. For example, after the Chunwang meeting (2005) the party was on the verge of splitting. Artists produced many songs and dramas[24] that depicted the situation and called for unity:

Let's walk together, friends
Let's struggle together, friends
And preserve the class love inside the heart.
(Hitman Shakya)

Another instance regards dramas performed in 2007 which depicted the urban-centric attitude of the leadership and satirized their living styles: political leaders' big cars and expensive clothes were contrasted against the frugality of lower party cadres. Similarly, artists set the politicians' struggle for state power against what they felt was an urgent concern among the people: knowing the whereabouts of the disappeared. In 2012 criticism towards the Maoist leadership became overt for the first time, sharply criticizing the faction of the party led by Prachanda and Bhattarai in a movement that caused a split in the party. A leader of the People's Cultural Federation estimated that about 90 per cent of the *janakalakar* (people's artists) joined Mohan Vaidya's new party.[25] Artists therefore also embody a visionary role that allows them to be simultaneously both inside and outside the party.

Revolution as life

September 2007, in the camp where Sen Chyang and the Newa groups live. We reached the camp in Godavari at around 8.30 pm. The camp is set up in an occupied, empty government building. We travelled back on the usual crammed bus, full of artists and followers both inside and on the top of the bus. There are PLA who had not found a proper place yet as well as others in charge of the security. Everybody is tired after the cultural programme. For a programme starting at 3 pm, artists have to be there by 12 pm, to set up the instruments and entertain the audience before the beginning of the political speeches. When the programme takes place in an equipped space like Khula Manch, the artists change their costumes and wait either in the rooms attached on the backstage or in tents set up for the purpose on the back. After returning to Godavari, the cadres in charge of the kitchen realize there is no food to cook. They have to go out and look for some. 'Magne' (asking for) as they said. In the meantime, some artists go to sleep in the dormitories. Others watch TV. Time passes but there is no call for dinner. In one of the bedrooms that host the TV, a group of artists watch a Nepali movie, a pirated DVD with a horrible sound and faded colours, and complain about its bad quality. Others talk, or sleep. The commander is also sitting with us, watching the film. At around 11 pm, he is called for a meeting. He has not eaten yet. He gets up unwillingly, and comments, very annoyed 'Kasto jivan ho yo, sangharshako jivan!' (What kind of life is this life of struggle!) He said he would be back but he did not return. At around 11.30 I go to sleep. Few people remain to watch TV. Rice is not yet ready. A slogan painted on the wall of the building that functioned as camp in Godavari said 'sangharsha euta jivan ho': 'struggle is a way of life'. But what kind of life is it? This is an all-encompassing slogan that reminded me of the 'theatre as life' ideal that guided the opening of Gurukul.

Cultural groups usually gathered around 50 artists, even though they did not perform all at the same time. Moreover, since I researched the groups in a transitional period, PLA members first and Young Communist League cadres later, often lived in the same premises. Most of the artists belonging to the group I worked with in 2006 were very young, from around 16 years to mid-20s. Leaders, in contrast, were in their 30s. During the first period of traveling with the group, the commander guessed what he thought were my questions regarding the age of the artists, especially girls. He explained that they came from villages where they would not have been able even to go to school, thus suggesting that joining the party was a better option. Some cadres that I met explained that they joined the cultural group out of a commitment towards revolution; some had parents or relatives in the party and followed their family choices. Others joined simply out of a passion for dancing and singing. One artist told me that at first she did not understand much about the party but afterwards she learned about it.

The concept framing the group is that of a 'family' (parivar), like in the theatre. Members in fact, alternated the appellative 'comrade' with the more common 'dai/

bhai' (brother) or *'didi/bahini'* (sister) when calling each other. Members of each cultural group shared the residential space in the camp and moved together by bus according to the location of the cultural programmes. Artists – both male and female – were involved in shifts in the kitchen while everyone washed their own plates. In the camp, there were separate male and female dormitories. On some occasions, higher ranking cadres had a single room with a bed rather than a mat on the floor, suggesting the existence of a hierarchy. Moreover, unequal resources could be noticed among the different cultural groups themselves: some had good quality blankets, others lacked enough. Some groups had a TV set, others did not. When I asked for explanations, an artist belonging to the group that had the fewest material facilities explained that the difference depended upon the commanders' ability in fundraising. Some groups, I was told, were financially supported by affluent people. However, the same artists belonging to the less resourced group, remarked that the group was well-managed by the leadership and was very egalitarian. In fact, according to them, artists from *janajati* (ethnic) backgrounds were not discriminated against.

Being a full-time artist in a Maoist cultural group thus emerges as an all-embracing commitment. Maoist 'culture', as well as the shared objective of struggle, certainly function as a powerful glue to hold different people together. Maoist culture dictated norms regarding daily practices, as for marriage (against polygamy, dowry and preference for sons), gender roles (Onesto, 2006), festivals, fashion, body display and relationship attitudes. The artists' degree of adherence to such rules varied throughout the different stages of my fieldwork. For example, in 2006, female artists were not supposed to wear earrings or nose pins or clothes other than simple *kurta-surwal* (long tunic with loose pants) or pants and shirt. They told me the commanders would scold them if they refused to obey; but they were free to wear what they liked when they went home for holidays. Much more freedom appeared between 2007 and 2008 when female cadres not only started to wear jeans, but also lip-gloss and sunglasses when going out of the camp. If in 2006 artists mostly listened to revolutionary songs in their free time, in 2008 commercial pop cassettes powerfully entered not only the camp but also the artists' discussions and style models for their productions. For example, in 2008 one of the most talented dancers of the group I worked with, as well as one of my key collaborators, left the party and the cultural group because of disagreement. The general mood among the artists was low as they felt the party was not taking care of their needs or providing them with opportunities to improve their lives. They felt that during campaigning periods their art was useful but once campaigning was over, they were left hanging on. Many of them had dropped school when they joined the party during the war and they felt unable to compete with their peers who in the meantime had completed their studies and had more opportunities. Contradictions emerged. For example, despite having heralded Maoist culture for six years as a member of a cultural group, the female cadre who left the group started to dance in a casino in Kathmandu for a living. All in all, dancing was what she was good at.

The shift to the capital affected the cultural programmes aesthetically. When performing in the villages during the People's War, artists narrated that they were not concerned with make-up or look in general. After settling in Kathmandu and performing in popular halls like the Nepal Academy or City Hall, they felt the need to improve their artistic skills and become more 'professional'. This led them to attend music, singing, and dance classes. One example is interesting as it expresses the degree of internal contradiction. In 2007, artists performed at the Nepal Academy for a fundraising programme. The usual discussions that took place the day after, mainly to share problems and find ways of enhancing the performance, centred on the make-up of the lead female actor. How should Maoist artists present themselves in the city? A strong group, mainly composed of men, vehemently criticized her and other actors for using intense make-up. She explained that 'they were not in the jungle anymore' and they had to fit in with Kathmandu audience's expectations so they needed to follow the common practice of applying heavy make-up for stage lights. The group opposing her claimed they should not follow such 'bourgeois culture' but, rather, change it.

While having changed throughout the different stages of the revolution, the identity of Maoist artists is complex. Research with the cultural groups started in 2006, that is when they had already entered the cities and their working strategy had already changed. Artists lived in camps and travelled together to the various venues where they had to perform. In 2008, one commissar believed that after they settled in Kathmandu, they had lost contact with the grassroots and therefore, for the Constituent Assembly election campaign, they felt the need to 'go back to the people' again and campaigned in the villages around the Kathmandu Valley. However, the professionalization of the artists continued. Once the Maoist party entered the government, and the need for campaigning diminished, many cultural workers joined other sectors of the party. A former commissar of a cultural group explained that during the war she sang because she was asked to, but she did not consider her voice good enough to become a professional singer. Despite shifts due to campaign priorities, dedication to social transformation requires full-time commitment, which is hard to sustain over time among all members, especially after leaving the underground and coming into contact with the urban and the bourgeois 'culture' of Kathmandu. In 2008, the commissar of the group I worked with, talked about the challenges of living in small, closed group. He needed new experiences as he had spent the previous four years with his group members. His concerns seemed similar to those that emerged in the Gurukul theatre community. The young group members' worries about their future, including their artistic aspirations and social pressures to settle and get married, were not dissimilar to those of some Gurukul artists, as I will detail in the next chapter.

Conclusion

In this chapter I have tried to show how the Nepali Maoist revolutionary performance can be viewed as the latest adaptation and evolution of Marxist cultural practices into local folk and political forms. Political songs, dance, and drama represent much more than a cultural 'show'. Artists frequently use the word *pratibaddhata* to describe their activities. A *pratibaddhata* is a strong commitment. Not only does it bind the speaker to the words they utter, but it also seeks commitment from the community of listeners who attend the programme. As both representational and performative practices, cultural programmes have become political rituals in which messages are spread and where the emotional link between the party and the audience is constantly renewed and strengthened. However, because of the diffusion of both live programmes and artistic performances through media, Maoist cultural production is also well on its way to establishing itself as a new form of popular Nepali culture. Maoist cultural programmes in fact represent an adaptation and expansion of 'traditional' practices, as well as a new form of artistic 'witnessing' during a critical historical moment.

I chose to present this discussion about cultural programmes through the voices of the commander and the commissar because of the artists' unique position inside the party and within the party's political project. The key to the political functioning of the cultural programmes is that the performers are simultaneously artists, intellectuals, organizers, activists, guerrillas, leaders and visionaries. According to Gramsci, intellectuals are the 'agents' of ideological practice. Gramsci conceived ideology[26] as a battlefield, as a practice involving continuous struggle. As ideological transactions (Kershaw, 1992), performances become the terrain for the creation of an 'ideological unity' (Mouffe, 1979, 184) which, according to Gramsci, is crucial to the establishment of a new hegemony.[27] Maoist cultural programmes tackle the moral, emotional and intellectual dimension of political struggle that at the same time bears practical consequences. During the People's War, cultural programmes were crucial to creating and maintaining the 'ideological unity' and the public sympathy necessary to fight the physical war.

While the Maoist cultural organization was not tied to the parameters established by funding or by the desire of exploring new forms of theatre, they faced the dilemmas of changing from being political activists into political artists once they stabilized themselves in Kathmandu and focused on enhancing their artistic skills. Over time, the constraints and the necessity of bonding presented by the underground was removed, internal strains began to manifest themselves, at times threatening the unity of the group and the morale of the performers, widening the gap between the group and the grassroots. The urban environment of Kathmandu produced different responses among the members of the troupe, some feeling the need to adapt their political message to the new circumstances, even to the point of altering some aspects of their performance ethos, such as simplicity of presentation, and turning to forms that were closer to what they would have previously called 'bourgeois' art.

Endnotes

1   This chapter is a revised and expanded version of Monica Mottin, 'Catchy Melodies and Clenched Fists. Performance as Politics in Maoist Cultural Programs', in *The Maoist Insurgency in Nepal. Revolution in the Twenty-First Century*, edited by M. Lawoti and A. Pahadi, 52–72, Routledge, reproduced with permission.

2   Commander, public speech, translated from video recording by the author, October 2006.

3   The Community Party of Nepal was established in 1949. For an account of the frequent splits in the Communist party and the merging of the CPN (Maoist) see Seddon and Karki (2003), and Rawal (2047 BS).

4   I have conflated various voices into those of the 'commander' and the 'commissar' to protect the identity of my research participants. Each Company and Battalion had a double leadership, a commander with mainly organizational tasks and a commissar in charge of political education.

5   Interviewed in October 2006.

6   Artists remember Krishna Sen as a '*mahan sahid*' (great martyr). Krisha Sen Ichchuk was the editor of the pro-Maoist daily Janadisha and former editor of the weekly *Janadesh*. Repeatedly arrested and kept in jail through fake charges, Sen was tortured and killed in police custody in 2002; Revolutionary Worker # 1160, 2002; Li Onesto, 2002).

7   Marxism is not a unified and fixed theory. Different positions regarding the relation between art and society coexist (Lang and Williams, 1972; Solomon, 1979).

8   Interviewed in October 2006.

9   Lecomte-Tilouine (2006) interestingly pointed out that although praising dialectics, Prachandapath seems to be based upon binary oppositions between oppressor-oppressed, feudal-proletariat, reactionary-revolutionary and in the military context, unjust-just wars. Binary oppositions work strongly also in art. Revolutionary art is contrasted to bourgeois art, and linked to the other dualistic oppositions resulting from class struggle. I think it is worth reflecting upon how much such a dualism can be the result of a 'Nepalization' – via the

ideology of development – of Marxism, rather than a mere 'reduction' of Marxist dialectics. Dual thinking has been widely documented by Pigg (1992; 1993) who analysed how the ideology of development has created a series of dichotomies along those of 'developed' and 'underdeveloped'.

10 Parallels between the Chinese Cultural Revolution and the Cultural Revolution advocated by CPN (Maoist) could be intriguing but risk being misleading in such a short space. Suffice it to say that the socio-historical conditions are very different. While in China the Cultural Revolution was implemented at mass-scale by a party in power, in Nepal it is promoted by a revolutionary party mainly among its followers. As for daily practices, the Cultural Revolution in Nepal brings about changes in marriage-related practices (against polygamy, dowry, preference for son), gender roles (Onesto, 2006), festival celebration, fashion, body display, relationship attitudes. As for the cultural sector, a leaflet (November 2005) indicated, among others, the necessity of making government institutions and other media organizations 'progressive', closing 'vulgar third grade cinema halls', dance restaurants, and massage centres, creating special days to celebrate the People's War, and creating people's literature and art.

11 Public speech, videorecorded, September 2006.

12 See Hutt (2012) for how similar rhetorical elements appear in Maoist memoirs.

13 Public speech, video-recorded, October 2006.

14 Malema is an abbreviation of Marxism (ma), Leninism (le) and Maoism (ma).

15 Interviewed in November 2006.

16 Public speech, video-recorded, October 2006.

17 George Kunnath, personal communication, 2004.

18 In the last three decades emotions had no place in the rationalistic, structural, and organizational models that dominated academic political analysis and were previously associated to irrationality (Goodwin, Jasper and Polletta, 2001). My research aims to add to the recent trend (Ibid) reincorporating emotions into research on politics and social movements. Audiences in fact, are not to be regarded as passive receivers of the performances. Audiences identify with emotions and representations that touch them.

19 Mao (1967, 5) believed there is no such thing as art above politics or art free from 'politics'. All works of art have a political character and serve one kind of politics or another as they forward a particular view of how society is or should be. Mao also rejected the general assumption that popular forms of art are technically and stylistically inferior to the 'sophisticated' dominant ones (Ibid, 1967). He spurred artists to live among the peasants to understand their problems better (Ibid). For Mao old literary forms should not be rejected but infused with new content (Pen-Yu, 1967).

20 Debates over 'national' culture in Nepal are widespread. The Maoist modality of 'displaying' cultural diversity is similar to the government practices during the Panchayat years and afterwards. The context and the process of the performances, as well as the composition of the artistic groups, vary substantially.

21 Behar (1996, 27) suggests that in traumatic situations life stories can play the role of witnessing. She argues that witnessing merges with the genre of testimonio literature and cites I, Rigoberta Menchu as an example of how personal narratives can help the wider community of readers to come to terms with their shared painful reality. Extending this concept, Maoist

cultural/artistic productions may fulfill both an internal therapeutic function (for the party artists) and an external witnessing role (for the wider audience).

22 Interview, September 2007.

23 Interview, October 2006.

24 See Stirr (2013) for an analysis Khusiram Pakhrin's *giti natak* or opera, 'Returning from the Battlefield'.

25 A thorough assessment was difficult to carry out as I conducted follow-up research in June-August 2012, soon after the party split, so some members were still uncertain of which affiliation to take.

26 Ideology has been defined in different ways as 'false consciousness' or as a 'system of ideas'. Mouffe emphasizes how Gramsci rejected 'epiphenomenalist conceptions which reduce it [ideology] to mere appearances with no efficacy' (1979, 185) while pointing out the material existence of ideology as practice.

27 Gramsci defines hegemony not as imposition or domination but as a process of internal coherence.

7

The Ordinariness of the Special

Towards the professionalization of theatre work

Despite playing around with the blurred boundaries between onstage representations of life and real-life performative acts, setting performances in non-traditional, real-world locations, or by using participatory and interactive dramaturgical techniques, the theatrical performances that have been discussed so far are usually characterized by a time and space separation from everyday life. They occur in specifically defined places such as cultural programmes, theatre halls, community spaces, schools or streets that are temporarily occupied. At the end of the play or programmes the 'boundaries' and the 'roles', which may have been reversed during the performance, are reinstated. Aarohan artists are professionals and they remain the 'specialists' of the theatre. For the audience the performance represents 'an experience' (Turner, 1986)[1] and remains 'special' because of its intensity. However, for theatre workers who 'make' theatre and live in and through theatre, theatre is indeed very much embedded in everyday life, in its concerns and struggles. The dramatic metaphor is reversed: 'theatre is life', artists often repeated in Gurukul, but what did a life fully dedicated to the theatre look like in mid-2000s Nepal?

This chapter explores the development of Aarohan Theatre Group as an organization, including artists' motivations to turn their passion for theatre into a full-time job and their efforts to strengthen and define their professional identity. Studies in the field of the anthropology of organizations suggest that institutions are shaped by official and informal rules which are monitored and controlled by leaders through 'conscious disciplinary process' and division of labour (Morgan 1990 cited in Gellner and Hirsch, 2001, 3). Organizations are represented as having a specific 'identity', a 'shared governing ethos' (Ibid. 4). They also work in relation to the wider context that 'provide[s] them with the aims they pursue and set the limits to the way they may operate' (Ibid.). But how is identity and meaning negotiated within a theatre group trying to become an organization? Anthropological studies have questioned monolithic understandings of organizations (Hilhorst, 2003; Mosse, 2005a; Long and Long, 1992; Gellner and Hirsch, 2001). Studying organizations requires first understanding their internal diversity, and second, locating them culturally and historically. Like an NGO, a theatre company is a multi-faceted organization where different notions, identities and opinions co-exist, compete, and sometimes clash. For that reason, this ethnographic account needs to be considered as a situational, time-bound description of a stage in the process of the development of Aarohan Theatre as an organization.

Fieldwork for this research coincided with a particular moment of transition in the establishment of Gurukul as an institution and the transformation of Aarohan Theatre Group into a regularly working professional company. Contradictions and instability are inevitable in many processes of creation. The group's first years of 'learning and experimenting' with forum theatre (2000–04) have been reconstructed through interviews. My own participant observation took place when forum theatre was more systematically adapted to the local working environment that coincided with a period in which the theatre itself as a genre was being promoted and acquired increasing audience attention. Between 2004 and 2006, Aarohan artists were engaged in several fronts. First, they gave continuity to the performance of artistic stage dramas at Sama Theatre Hall in Gurukul. Second, they performed *kachahari natak* based on social issues in the streets and schools of Kathmandu as part of development projects. Third, they staged *loktantrik natak* on a voluntary basis during the public programmes for democracy and peace. I argue what is most important is that Aarohan artists were engaged in constructing and 'performing' their own identity, producing a historical change in theatre practice, and showing that acting, however 'special', could indeed be a respectable and rewarding profession. For this reason the first part of this chapter discusses the actors' social status, drawing extensively on personal narratives to explain how the institutionalization of the theatre group can be seen as a practice aiming to stabilize artists' identity.

From stigma to glamour: Routes to Gurukul

Although the origin of theatre is regarded as divine, the social position of performers in ancient Indian theatre was ambiguous (Iravati, 2003; Gupta, 1991). By forcing nymphs and singers to move down from heaven to earth and marry mortals, King Nahusa is said to have first established theatre (Gupta, 1991, 96). Yet, according to Bharata, actors mocked some holy sages and were cursed with the loss of their status, becoming Sudras. Similarly, Manu[2] condemns the profession, prohibits Brahmins from becoming actors and even from accepting food from actors (Baumer and Brandon, 1981, 363). Manu grouped actors with wrestlers and boxers, while actresses were considered courtesans (Ibid.). Yet, artists were often dialectically linked to powerful people, such as kings or dramatists. The powerful despised performance artists but were at the same time attracted by them and required them to enhance their prestige.

Beyond mythology, the ambiguous status of the actors' profession, despised on the one hand, yet indispensable for various reasons, including ideological legitimation through performances of power-validating narratives, is evident in the practical experience of contemporary South Asian popular theatre artists (Seizer, 2000; 2005; Hansen, 1992; Mehrotra, 2006). In Nepal, artists from lower castes were traditionally responsible for the singing and dancing at Hindu religious rituals and festivals. However, these occupations have progressively transformed. For example, the Damai are a caste of tailor-musicians who perform in a musical ensemble called the *pancai baja*, which includes shawms, drums, cymbals, and trumpets. They are responsible for creating an auspicious atmosphere during religious rituals, weddings, and secular processions (Tingey, 1994). Members of the Gaine caste play the *sarangi*[3] to entertain villagers narrating the joys and pain of everyday life (Weisethaunet, 1998), while Badi women traditionally entertained high-caste audiences with their dance (Cox, 1992).[4] Amatya (1983) argues that with the end of the Rana rule in 1951, the performing arts gradually lost their caste-restricted rigidity and were opened up as a paid profession. Although descendants of some traditional musicians have indeed now become professional musicians, the background of most senior theatre artists is just the opposite. They are mostly Bahun-Chhetri and were introduced to theatre at school and university (Onta, 1997; Rijal, 2007), as well as during village festivals. This suggests that the profession of theatre artist does not grow out of local caste and ethnic traditions, but is rather emerging as the domain of high-caste, middle class elite. In this it resembles Nepali literature (Hutt, personal communication). The en masse conversion of traditional caste-specific performers into theatre actors suggested by Amatya did not occur. Most of the artists performing in theatre do not come from families having performed art as their caste occupation. Moreover, many of my research participants rejected 1951 (the end of Rana rule) as a significant date in this regard. Instead, professional theatre artists amongst my research participants, in their 40s or 50s, identify the theatre that was popular among university students in the 1980s as their reference point (Chapter 2). In summary, present-day theatre artists professionally connect themselves far less to folk drama than to a theatre with palace origins, 'vernacularized', 'villagized' and politicized by Balkrishna Sama, as well as the politically activist street and stage theatre that emerged during the Panchayat period. Traditional performers and theatre artists seem to belong to two different categories. In contrast to folk performances where roles are strictly scripted and caste-based (Toffin, 1999), in modern theatre no such family heritage exists and so far involvement in the theatre does not stretch beyond two generations within the same family. Yet, despite actors' appealing for an 'intellectual' stage tradition, theatre is commonly associated with popular street theatre and finds inspiration in folk performance.

Contemporary Nepali theatre is in no way disjoint from traditional rituals and folk performances. Many proscenium plays in fact incorporate ritual and folk cultural elements. For example, Aarohan Theatre's 'Dreams of Peach Blossom' displays Newari dance and songs, 'Fire in the Monastery' presents Buddhist rituals and shamanic practices, and even translations of world classics like 'A Doll's House' are often produced as cultural translations where plots are adapted and situated in Nepal, incorporating cultural and folk elements. Most importantly, many artists, originally from rural areas, reveal that they had been fascinated by the traditional performances that they attended during festivals in their native villages but were also attracted by the cinema and 'filmy songs'. As a result, they entered theatre productions at school and in local cultural groups which would then lead to choosing theatre as a profession. Starting from the life narratives of theatre artists from Gurukul and including experiences gathered while researching theatre in Kathmandu and the Tarai, this section focuses on how artists encountered the theatre and traces some of the routes that brought many of them to the capital and to Gurukul.

The appeal of the rich popular performance traditions seems to be an element that cuts across generations. The living heir of Balakrishna Sama's acting tradition: interviewing Prachanda Malla means plunging into a Kathmandu that I could only imagine. Always generous in sharing stories over a cup of Nepali tea, Prachanda Malla thus remembers when the theatre captured him and later was brought to the great actor's house:

> My uncle, Khadgamon Malla, sang and played the harmonium when I was a child, in a room, while he was worshipping. He had a very beautiful voice. We were very much attracted by him when he sang, closing his eyes. We used to go and listen to him. And listening to those songs I also got interested in singing. I started singing with my uncle too. People said that my voice was very sweet when I was a child, beautiful. My friends, my uncle, my brothers, my relatives and my father said so. They said 'you have a sweet voice, you must sing' and so I started. In those days I loved watching the plays in which my friends were acting, plays performed during our festivals like Indra Jatra, Gai Jatra, eight day plays. We made costumes and masks like cows. They wore caps upside down, torn caps and made up different characters. They created comic make up, plots. Dialogue was also

funny. The plays didn't have a Nepali outlook though, like dialogue, heavy sets, it looked like Parsi theatre.[5]

But Prachanda's passion for the theatre quickly got out of hand and his family could no longer cope with him:

> My interest was more in drama than in studying. My parents were worried for me. They heard me delivering dialogues in my room. They were also hurt that I was not studying well. I usually went to dance and see plays secretly at night, coming back late. Then in 1952 one morning my brother took me to the emperor of drama Balkrishna Sama. He was a playwright, actor and director. I lived in Indrachok (Guchhatole) and Balkrishna Sama's house was in Gyaneshwar. My brother told him: 'this is my brother, he delivers dialogues in his room. Morning, evening, afternoon, he goes to see plays and listens to songs, that's why he doesn't study. If you take him for drama, his life will take some direction. Otherwise, he will be ruined'. Then Balkrishna Sama laughed and said 'Looking at his face, he does not seem suitable for drama, and he also has a small body'. And then said: 'He will do, send him from tomorrow'.[6]

Moving to Balkrishna Sama's palace in the 1950s to learn theatre meant moving into a totally different social context but Prachanda remembers the great actor and playwright in affectionate terms:

> my brother taught me that there are many differences between the palace and our house, and therefore I had to speak accordingly. The next day I went to him and I didn't use any royal language, I didn't say 'Hajur', I said 'Namaste' and he asked me to sit in a very polite and respectful way. He used to respect everybody, his wife, son, grandchildren and servants. Respecting everybody was very rare in Nepali society. I learnt that there.[7]

Set in a different part of Nepal and thirty years later, Anil's life narrative presents similarities. Originally from Sunsari district, Anil describes his childhood fascination for the theatre and how it differed from the theatre he would find later in Kathmandu:

> In my village there were lots of Jagar dances, a Dalit caste. At that time my uncle worked in a German project, he worked in Germany for many years. So many German friends went there. We had many fields and the Jagars worked there. My uncle organized Jagar dance programmes when his friends came to the village, from 8–9 pm to 1,

2, 3, 4am. I enjoyed that a lot and wondered 'what is this?' From then I started to enjoy this field. There were *mela* (festivals) in the village, like the Koshi mela, and there was theatre. We also ran to India to watch dramas... we had 10-20 rupees, watch the drama, then went back. We were scolded and beaten, stayed quiet for two days and then again, we set off. I started doing theatre in 1981. There is a great difference between the theatre we do here and theatre there. Theatre in the village was like Ramlila,[8] with instruments, live singing. It was like *gitinatak* (musical theatre). Actors would sing, dance and also deliver dialogues. It was religious drama, there was Ravan, Krishna, Ram... . Now it's different. I find lots of differences between the drama they did at that time and dramas we do now, like the difference between the earth and the sky. That was like *nautanki*, the real theatre is what we do today, which we are doing now.[9]

Anil clearly separates contemporary Nepali stage drama from folk drama and *nautanki*.[10] His distinctions reveals a lot about a hierarchy of theatrical genres where folk drama was perceived as inferior to stage theatre as mentioned earlier. However, it was 'village' theatre that attracted Anil and led him to proscenium theatre. Anil describes himself as a very naughty child. A single son of landowners, he was sent to study away from home, to Nepalganj, to Bardiya, to Kanchanpur but nothing seemed to calm him down so he was admitted to Bijay Memorial School in Dilli Bazar, in Kathmandu. In the capital, Anil met Sunil Pokharel:

One day maybe seeing my activities, my uncle, Sitaram Pokharel, asked me 'would you like to act in a play?' I said yes. He said 'come with me, I'll take to a person, he's also from Biratnagar'. He introduced me to Sunil Pokharel. One day I was going to the market to buy vegetables. I lived in Kamal Pokhari at that time. I was holding the bag and walking. Sunil dai was coming from another side. Sunil dai was going to the RNA [Royal Nepal Academy], for rehearsals, he asked me 'Would you play in a drama?'. I was puzzled, he again asked 'do you want to play in a drama?' This was in 1982 when he called me to the Academy. I brought the vegetables home and went to the Academy. Then he introduced me to Ashesh Malla, and afterwards I acted in 'From Street to Street' (*Sadakdeckhi Sadaksamma*). I got the role of a beggar, a very beautiful role.[11]

Aruna is one of the two female artists of Gurukul's first batch, with Sarita. Aruna is also originally from the Tarai.[12] She started acting when she was 13, having been

attracted to the theatre by the dramas that were performed during the festival of
Dasain in her village near Janakpur:

> My father came from the hills, from Dolakha. He has a conservative
> mindset, old fashioned. My mother is from Darjeling, Dehra Dun.
> She studied up to 10th class, so she doesn't have that kind of thinking.
> When I was studying in grade 7, in our village there was the culture
> of playing drama during Dasain festival on the day of *tika*.[13] I liked the
> plays very much. At the end of the plays, actors were congratulated and
> talked in good manner. Seeing that, I felt the desire to act. I started 13
> years ago. When I was in grade 7 my maternal uncle, a little far related,
> called me and I played in a drama for the first time in Lalgardh. At that
> time I was very afraid and I forgot all the dialogue. I went on stage
> wearing a *sari*, at a very young age, and fell down from it. It was made
> of wood, adding 7 beds together. I fell down from that. They made
> me stand up, closed the curtain and opened it again. I forgot all the
> dialogue. They asked one person to go near the sofa and to suggest
> the dialogue and then I did it. The play was 'The Minister' (*Mantriji*)
> it was about corruption. The ministers used to take a lot of money
> from people, they put girls to prostitution and married many wives.
> They gave the money they got from corruption to their many wives.
> I was the second wife of the minister. We did the play. The next day
> everybody said it was very good. I was really worried I was not doing
> well, I forgot all the dialogue, but they all said I did well. Since then
> I got interested and the next year I did it again. Each year there was
> a different topic. The second year I did a play about the Nepali men
> who work abroad, about *lahure*. It was very good and I liked it a lot.[14]

In Aruna's village the annual drama was organized by the library, established
with the funding collected by the villagers during Tihar's *Deusi* singing. After many
youths involved in the library moved out of the village to work, the responsibility
of organizing the play shifted to the local youth club. Aruna met Sunil Pokharel in a
training that he delivered at Lalgadh Leprosy Hospital and she started travelling to
perform street theatre on development issues. She remembers that Sunil had trained
another two groups in Dhanusha district during the same period, and about 15 in
other districts. But the route that would take her to Gurukul would be unpredictable.
Aruna kept performing street theatre for another three years, while studying in
college. She could not take many exams because she was busy with drama. As a
result, her father got very upset with her and she was sent to Kathmandu to stay with
an aunt. She continues:

It was 1997-98 and I joined Patma Kanya College. It went well in the
first year. I didn't know many people so I didn't do theatre in the first
year. My *fupu* (aunt, father's sister) didn't like *natak*. I went to college
after preparing food and I cooked also when I came back. Then one
friend of mine told me that her friend did natak. I went to the office
of that group called Munas in Koteswhor. They did street drama for
projects, not many, once or twice a month. There were no rehearsals.
We did a single ticket programme and there I played a role. My aunt got
very angry. I left my aunt's house and I phoned my father: 'I don't want
to stay in my aunt's house' and he said 'so you have to do some other
work'. I got work in a project of street theatre by Himal Social Welfare
Organization about HIV in Kathmandu, Bakhtapur and Lalitpur. Its
office was in Kupondole and the branch was near Koteshwor. They
wrote the script and gave it to me. I studied that and I re-arranged
it a bit. They liked it. We got together and did rehearsals. We played
it and it was good. I did it for 2 years but on and off. Though, I only
worked there regularly for 6 months. At that time I joined Paribartan
Nepal. They taught drama, dance, beautician skills. ... It is in Putali
Sadak. I went there also for learning dance and they knew that I played
drama, *sadak natak* (street theatre). I worked there for one and a half
years. They sent me to the National Theatre to train. I studied there
for 4 months, acting classes, though it was for 1 year. Sunil Sir taught
there the previous year, Gurukul wasn't open. He went there searching
for actors for a radio drama in Radio Nepal. After doing a reading,
Sunil Sir told me that there was a radio drama for 2 years, I agreed.
After doing the recording of 2 parts he asked me if I wanted to stay in
Gurukul for 2 years.[15]

Originally from a village in Morang, Kamal encountered theatre through a street
play performed by Aarohan.

I was studying in grade 9, in my village. Once Aarohan Biratnagar
came to the village to do street theatre. This was my first experience of
theatre and I wanted to do the same. I was from the village so I didn't
know what to do. I told them I also wanted to play in theatre. They told
me that I could play the joker because I did caricatures. I liked that. So
I did the character of the *Tarai bhasi* (Tarai dweller) who doesn't speak
Nepali very well. I did the caricature and I made them laugh.[16]

Kamal then started acting in comedies during Dasain in his village. They collected
beds from different houses and used bed covers for the curtain. With a mike and a

petromax (kerosene lamp), the stage was ready for a night performance. After passing the School Leaving Certificate (SLC), Kamal moved to Itahari, a town nearby. He studied there for two years, continuing to offer comedy sketches during welcome parties in his college. But he felt that studying there was not good for him so he asked his father to go to Kathmandu for computer training. Once in Kathmandu, Kamal explains that he did nothing for a year, he did not even do the training. He just stayed in his room, listening to music and singing. Then a friend of his elder brother's asked him to play in a drama produced by Jayatu Sanskritam,[17] and students from the Sanskrit Chhatrabas (Sanskrit College), in Durbar Marg, to commemorate the anniversary of the movement. A friend suggested that he should join the Cultural Corporation but the admission time was over. The year after he did:

> I attended the interview. There were Sunil Sir and Ashesh Malla. I felt I was from village and I didn't have any resources. There was nobody there for me. I attended the interview and then went straight back to my village. Afterwards I called my friends and they told me my name was in the second position, the first was Bhola. At the time I didn't know Bhola. Bhola came from a different group and place. I told my father I was going to Kathmandu for a one year acting course. I took the course at the Cultural Corporation. When the course finished there was no work. Where to work? I worked with Birendra Hamal for about one year, in MArt.[18]

At MArt Theatre, Kamal met Sarita, Rajan, Rajkumar – who had also taken an acting course at the Cultural Corporation and Saugat. Saugat's way into the theatre was rather similar. Saugat remembers that since he was 7–8 years old, he watched lots of movies, listened to songs, and danced whenever possible, at religious festivals, marriages, at home, or at school. Nobody taught him. Ramlila, based on the *Ramayana*, was performed in his village every year at Dasain and Tihar. Plays were performed every night for 5–6 days, from 10 pm till 4–5 am. Villagers would collect money or sell crops and arrange the performance that included artists of all ages. Saugat performed three times in the Ramlila and also performed in comedies at school. He also went to Kathmandu for a computer course though, as soon as he arrived, he started to look for jobs in the cinema. He was 16 years old. Saugat explains a form of cheating that was common at the time: he would fill the casting forms, and pay some money, but then the casting organizers would run away with the money. He was cheated three times. Afterwards a friend introduced him to a film director based in Kathmandu who was connected to the Pune Institute in India. Saugat invested all the NRs. 10,000 he had taken from home for the computer course to pay his acting classes. He then got a small role in the director's first film.

After that he was once more 'going here and there', until he saw the MArt Theatre notice board, near where he lived. He knew about Birendra Hamal, MArt Theatre's director, because he was a film hero and acted in many serials, but Saugat had never met him in person. So he went to see him:

> I went there and he was not there the first time. Rajkumar, Rajan and Sarita were talking. I asked for Birendra Sir. He was not there. I waited for some time. After Birendra Hamal returned, I told him I wanted to work. I had just finished training. 'OK, then, if there is work I will tell you', he said. I would then go there regularly. They became my friends.[19]

Saugat then joined the production of a performance that was presented at the-then RNA:

> Kamal and I got small roles in a new drama. He had just graduated from the National Theatre training. We played and after that I did many performances from Birendra Hamal. Two, three ballet dances, and seven or more dramas. I learnt a lot there. And then Anup Baral was directing 'Ask the Yogi about his Caste' (*Jat Sodhnu Yogiko*). Birendra Sir was playing the role that I am playing now.[20] But he couldn't play because of his own work. I think he had shooting for a serial. The opening was coming nearer and nearer. Everyone was in trouble. What to do? Who could do the main role? It was very difficult. Birendra Hamal said 'I have a student, I think he can do it'. It was a very big problem for them because it was a very big role to do, an important role. And he took me there. There were another 5 or 6 people there to audition. They told me to read, the others tried too. They selected me. I did the role. It was a very nice play.[21]

Afterwards, Saugat continued to perform in plays directed by both Sunil Pokharel and Anup Baral. As mentioned earlier, Bhola met Kamal, Suresh and Yubaraj at the year-long acting course ran by the Cultural Corporation. Originally from Hetauda, Bhola also remembers how he got involved in the theatre:

> When I was at school people organized plays in the villages. We went far to watch them, and we liked to play too. When I was in class 7 there were cultural programmes during Dasain. I got the chance to do a play named 'Stupid Patient' (*Murkha Birami*). Everybody liked it, and the interest increased. Every year we staged a play in the village. Also during Krishna Jatra there were plays. They were religious plays, about Lord Krishna. I played and everybody liked it. Then I played

a teleserial named *Hamro Ban, Hamro Sanrakshan* (Our Forest, Our Protection). After that, the chairman of Taranga Sanskritik Parisad called me and I played there. There was also Namuna Sankritik Kalakendra where I did lots of plays. They were different. With Namuna I did 4-5 stage dramas and with Taranga I did street theatre. I did more than 500 plays with them. Then we established a new group named Chorus Kalakendra. We did 4-5 plays there too. It was after doing those plays that I came to know about the Cultural Corporation. I applied, I did the interview, I passed. Then I came to Kathmandu, and stayed one year in Kathmandu. During this learning period I met Sunil Sir, and after meeting Sunil Sir I played with Anup Baral and since then I am still in Gurukul.[22]

In the village, youth mostly learned theatre by themselves though Bhola remembers a teacher, Rajendra Banya, who taught him dance and 'a little bit of drama'. But Bhola brought to Kathmandu his experience of participating in politically committed cultural programmes, organized by what he calls 'democratic people'. Bhola's uncle, a Maoist leader, also wrote and performed plays during festivals, and Bhola went along.

> One of my brothers wrote plays on political issues and directed, during festivals. There were songs and dramas. Many villagers came to watch the drama for the whole night, political singers like Ramesh. I also sang the song 'Sitting in the Shadow of the Simali' (*Simali Chaya Ma Basi*)[23] with my uncle. Once our uncle did one play in a place named Mawaldap. In that play there was one landlord who used to cheat the people from the village. While we were performing the play people who didn't like democracy threw stones and made us run away. Before acting I sang. I was studying in class 5-6 [13-14 years old], my uncle used to act, sing [progressive] songs. There were lots of incidents like that. After democracy, I also did political plays. Before coming to Gurukul I did political theatre and then I started to work on social issues.[24]

In contrast, Suresh's passion for the theatre emerged in Kathmandu. Suresh arrived in Kathmandu from Salyan to study in a college in 1996. He had participated in folk performances at school, but nothing like 'the theatre', he says, and was not particularly impressed. He was more interested in martial arts. In fact he was a renowned martial artist in his district. With hindsight, he explains that when he was in his village, he did not think that theatre could be 'a kind of work, a profession'. So he moved to Kathmandu, trained at the National City Stadium in the morning and attended college classes during the day. But the civil war that started in his home areas affected him. He explains:

> Suddenly I missed my family. I lost communication with my family. Where is my mother? Where is my father, my brother? Where am I... Suddenly I felt these problems, and in 1997-98 I took up a job, a government job actually... near Kathmandu, Bhaktapur, Sano Thimi.[25]

Suresh had a government job, was making a good income, had professional development opportunities and good relationships but was not happy. After three years he left his job, went back to college and to martial art training. Then a chance encounter with the popular artist Hari Bansha Acharya changed his life:

> I was in Kathmandu with my father. At that time, I was living in Gattekulu, near Maiti Devi. Incidentally, I was living in front of Hari Bansa Acharya's house. One day I was walking in the street. I looked a little bit handsome, I was tall, I was a bit different at that time. I was a national martial artist. A bike stopped in front of me and the man said '*Bhai* (younger brother), can you come to my home tomorrow morning, 7-8am'. I was surprised and asked my father 'What to do? Hari Bansa Acharya invited me to his house, maybe I did a mistake'. My father said 'if you are right, don't worry, you can go'. And I went there, he was at home. The first question was 'are you interested in acting in films?' I was surprised and I said 'I have no money, I don't have good contacts, and I don't know anything about cinema'. He said 'Don't worry, I will manage everything for you because you look good, you have a good behaviour and I have been watching you for long'. I said OK, I will talk to my father. I talked to my father and he said 'OK, go if you want'. The next day I went there and I said I would try. He sent me to the National Theatre for the one-year course.[26]

At this point Suresh crossed paths with Kamal, Bhola, Yubaraj, and Sunil, with whom he started to collaborate for street plays, stage performance, and radio dramas. In contrast to traditional performance practice that is caste-based and passed on from one generation to the next (Toffin, 1999), what emerges from actors' narratives is the importance of places like the National Theatre/Cultural Corporation and Royal Nepal Academy in providing training. Though limited, they importantly helped create a network of theatre practitioners. A second important element arising from the artists' life narratives is a pattern of conflict with their families: parents are rarely happy with their children embarking on a theatrical career because of the low status and the financial insecurity of the profession. Caste matters too. Most of the actors involved in modern theatre that I interviewed belong to Bahun-Chhetri families. Aarohan Theatre is an interesting example in this regard. Sunil Pokharel believes that the caste composition of contemporary Nepali theatre can be explained by the fact that, especially in the past, Bahun-Chhetri had more access to education, which provided the link to theatre performed at school and university. According to Sunil, theatre also offered young people from strict Brahmin families a space of freedom. There is, therefore, a substantial difference between performing by birth and by choice: acting by choice involved a departure from family expectations and a degree of rebellion. When the second intake of Gurukul students was selected, the management on purpose provided seats to artists coming from non Bahun-Chhetri backgrounds. While the first batch of students encountered Sunil through informal networks in the capital, street theatre workshops, the Cultural Corporation and Royal Nepal Academy, the second batch of students was recruited through Aarohan's network of partner groups from different districts. In particular, Aarohan tried to recruit *janajati* students to address the bias evident in the group, and to enrich their performance expertise.

Despite social changes that had taken place over the previous 25 years, especially in big cities, that made it easier for young people to choose an acting career, Nisha believed the stigma still existed, the connotation may have changed somewhat, measured by the standards of education and the commensurate and desirable careers that could be pursued, rather than the effects on caste status. Nisha explained:

> Still now, people think that this profession is not good, for girls and for boys because if you have nothing to do, or if you could not study further and you are weak in studies, then you just jump into theatre because in theatre you don't need anything. This is what people still now think, though slowly it's changing.[27]

It is useful at this point to detail the contrasting pressures that artists faced in pursuing their careers by further drawing on the life narratives of some of Aarohan Theatre artists, in particular Kamal, Aruna, Rajkumar, Nisha and Bhola.

In rural areas artists were often mocked at. Kamal[28] remembers that when he started doing theatre in his village in Morang (eastern Nepal), people teased him, addressing him 'hero, ehh hero', with contempt. Kamal was taunted, 'Oh, he's a dancer, show us a dance!' Artists explain that since good dancers sometimes show girlish behaviour, people would mock them. Acting and dancing were perceived synonymously. The stigma could go as far as making it difficult for male actors to find a wife. Actors had to travel a lot and were often far from their own home. For this reason, partners may become suspicious. This distrust adds to the financial insecurity usually associated with the profession, which is the main worry for parents. For example, when Kamal met the father of the woman who would become his wife, he was asked about his job. Kamal replied that he was an actor, but his future father-in-law rephrased his question, 'For food, what do you do?' Therefore, while enjoying recognition and success in the capital, actors from rural areas would have to cope with a different identity when returning home. An urban-rural divide in attitudes was clearly discernible.

Despite being well-established on the media both as an actor in Gurukul and as a journalist, Yubaraj also initially felt similar unease. It was only with the establishment of his own theatre group, Shilpi, in 2007 that people managed to frame his profession properly:

> Now I can say proudly what I'm doing. Many people don't ask now 'but what are you doing', it's a little bit solved… my father and mother in law had a hard time at the beginning: what was their son in law doing? It was fine with them but they had a hard time to convince others. When the neighbours would come together they would say 'oh my son in law is in the US', 'my son in law is an engineer' they had fixed jobs. … Now they see my picture, my name. Now I think the neighbours also understood what I'm doing so they don't ask anymore.[29]

Unlike some artists who were supported by their families, Yubaraj explains that he was helped only the first year he was in Kathmandu, when he received rice and lentils from home. Afterwards he had to support his acting career through freelance journalism. He declares with pride that he wrote more than 1,000 articles, earning extra NR. 5,000 to add to the NR. 5,000 wage he received in Gurukul.

Rajkumar's story is different. From Nuwakot, Rajkumar desired to act since adolescence, but was vehemently opposed by his family. Before joining Gurukul, he had asked his parents for NR 2,000 to stage a play and start a theatre group in his area. He spent NR. 800 for the rehearsal room, NRs. 500 for travelling and the rest for food. Rajkumar's intentions did not materialize the way he had anticipated, as he had not properly managed the expenses. Moreover, many extra expenses arose. The initial 10 people working for the play became 25 by the end of the project, bringing in more bills and mouths to feed. 'It was so horrible, my parents hated me' Rajkumar remembers,

> somehow I lost my relationship with my parents. After that they also told me to leave the country, otherwise to do something else here, but not theatre. In my heart there was a pain, about this NR. 10,000 loss.[30]

Despite the hardship, Rajkumar returned to Kathmandu and looked for other jobs, but kept theatre as his central focus. He believed his parents' concerns went beyond the financial problems usually associated with theatre, resting also on caste practices. Though he is now a renowned theatre artist and travelled to different countries to perform, yet

> they are suggesting that I leave this job, they don't like it...I can't really say what the matter is but I can imagine that in our culture... we can't use leather things. The *madal* (drum) is made of leather. It comes from buffalo. It's illegal for a Brahmin to touch it. So, culturally, we're not allowed to do theatre. The other thing is that the state of theatre is very bad. Nobody is earning a lot of money, and becoming well off through theatre. At present, if you are educated, and you can't earn money, it's not good. So they are still suggesting that I leave. I'm not interested in showing them my performances. They have never come here...[31]

If acting is not considered a good profession for men, mainly because of economic instability, it has been an even harder choice for women, especially in rural areas, because of the social stigma attached to it. Theatre was, and still is, in many villages, considered as an 'entertainers' domain. It is linked to the courtesans of the Rana palaces on the one hand (Chapter 1), and on the other with *nautanki*, the travelling Parsi theatre troupes, whose erotic plays attracted a mainly male audience. Sunil explains that:

> In the Tarai, there was a famous form called *nautanki*, from India. Academically, it was Parsi theatre. *Nautanki* was from Uttar Pradesh, somehow they merged. They were professional theatre companies, travelling theatre companies. They used to come from India, they were second, third-grade touring *nautanki* companies. Then a dance, a bit erotic, and then the audience offered some money and they announced: 'Mr Phalano gave 20 rupees to Miss Bala' or something like that. And then this Miss Bala, the actress, did suggestive moves to the rhythm. And then 'Thank you' [bowing] [laughs]. At the end they tried to encourage the erotic in the audience based on some myth or hero. That is theatre in the Tarai. So you can understand why people react in that way.[32]

Basanta recounts that when he started acting in Biratnagar in the early 1980s, theatre was not regarded as 'good' for women. Doing theatre in fact requires interacting with men and often having to return home late at night after rehearsals. He explains that because of the strict social rules that prevented young boys and girls from meeting, theatre was sometimes used as a 'platform' where meetings could actually take place. Once again the peculiar space occupied by theatre becomes evident, a place where social rules can be bent. Some senior actors believe that the theatrical space was 'misused' as a cover for romantic engagements by young people. Basanta remembers that sometimes just a month after being involved in theatre the youth got married, and so a negative impression of the theatre and the theatre people circulated within the community. Sunil points out that theatre was a space of freedom and it was common for young boys and girls who had grown up in a very strict environment not to have the necessary skills for coping with so much liberty.

As a result, male artists had to strike compromises with the families of the actresses through complex negotiations mediated by cultural practices. For example, Sunil recalls that when Basanta and Badri Adhikari went to speak with the families of actresses performing in Aarohan in the 1980s, they had to assume entire responsibility for the girls: 'the parents of the girls used to say "if something happens, ... you have to marry her"'.[33] They had to agree. Parents would allow daughters to attend rehearsals if actors assured protection, that is, if the girls were not only going to be regarded as actresses but also as ritual 'sisters'. Basanta remembers that during Tihar, he had to visit many houses to receive Bhai Tika[34] and thus renew the fraternal bond with the female actors of his group: 'Tika is powerful for human beings...' he explained, 'they did not believe me, they believed in tika'.[35] The 1980s were in fact characterized by a shortage of actresses. This affected both the choice of theatre productions and the dramaturgy. Ashesh Malla, playwright and director of Sarwanam, reveals how the absence of female characters in his early plays was not at all the result of a deliberate choice but a necessity.

However, the stigma attached to female artists' profession not only changed historically, but was also dependent on location and social background. For example, the street theatre group in which Aruna initially performed, staged between 60–90 plays per month, two to three plays a day. They returned home once a month. They performed, ate, and then walked to the next village. The group included 10 members, only 2 of whom were female. Aruna remembers that people in her village did not like her profession because 'boys and girls stay outside their homes, play drama together and may get married'. She remembers it was very difficult to perform in the Tarai. Aruna remembers:

> Their girls don't speak a lot ... and have to cover their face with the sari if you go there to play drama it's a bit bad. They didn't give us the rooms, they kept us outside and we had to sleep outside. But in some villages they called the girls and they said that they should be like Aruna. It was a bit difficult. Now it's less.[36]

Aruna points out that they were aware of villagers' prejudices and avoided talking openly with boys to prevent gossip. Aruna remarks that if a girl behaved 'badly', if she acted in dramas and then got married, let alone married someone from a different caste, 'the road' for other girls doing theatre would be blocked. Families would refuse to give their daughters permission to join theatre groups.

However, the story of Nisha, a leading theatre artist,[37] provides one exception. Born in a Bahun-Newar family in Kathmandu, Nisha started acting in Aarohan when she was very young, following her sisters. Nisha explained that her family had always supported her artistic career. She attributes this to the specific background of her family. Her mother is a Newar and being so is, according to her, more open-minded. She was given permission to enter an inter-caste marriage with a Brahmin. Besides, artists frequently gathered in her family home to perform. Nisha's marriage to Sunil certainly facilitated the continuation of her career. Sarita and Pramila too, also from Kathmandu, had been supported by their families in their choice, thus emphasizing an urban-rural difference in the acceptance of the profession.

Marriage is often the reason why female artists of Hindu backgrounds are compelled to leave the stage and remain at home. Families and husbands are still considered as the bearers of traditional Hindu values, which do not regard women's presence on stage positively. Aruna attributes her own capacity for remaining on the stage after marriage to the fact that her husband is also an actor in Aarohan, and that his family is related to Sunil's. What emerges from the actors' narratives is therefore their struggle to change existing social stigma around their profession.[38] They feel this is achieved whenever their work allows them to sustain themselves financially, when it is publicly recognized by the media, or legitimized by tours abroad. Yet, some female actors remark that often male actors are the first who endorse and reinforce such stigma towards their own profession. While on stage, male actors are keen to portray and question gender discrimination and talk in a very open and progressive way. However, when the time of choosing a life partner comes, they seem to prefer women outside the theatre world. Questioned directly, Sunil jokingly notes 'there is a famous saying by my teacher in Delhi: 'you would like a very advanced girlfriend and a very domestic wife.'[39]

What emerges from interviews extended outside Gurukul is that theatre appears to be a male-dominated world, a space in which decision-making power, directing, and producing plays is gendered, like in many other countries. If marrying male actors give female actors social security and allow them to continue their work in the theatre, it alternatively allows others to note that family relations impinge upon casting and fair competition among female artists. For example, some directors may tend to select their own wives or girlfriends for the main roles, neglecting the high skills of other artists. In addition, female artists are usually paid less than male artists with the same experience and popularity. Despite championing equality and staging plays that herald women's rights,[40] daily practices indicate strong gender discrimination within the theatre world itself. Nepali theatre had not reached a level of professionalism which can ensure fair competition and a diverse range of opportunities. The wider context also makes it harder for female artists not backed by networks to prove their professional qualities. For different reasons, such as lack of training and a shortage of financial resources, theatre productions are still often 'family productions'. The joint effort of husband, wife, and relatives in the theatre assures working continuity and provides sustainability to many artistic projects.

Shared dreams: The foundation of Gurukul

Foundation myths are at the heart of organized groups, be they nations, dynasties, empires (Rippin and Fleming, 2006) or religious groups (Michael, 1983). Similarly, business foundation myths lie at the heart of corporate culture. Although organizations may not consciously refer to these archetypal myths, these can be used as a lens through which to study organizational claims to legitimacy and autonomy in pursuing their agendas. In this section, I will first unpack some of what I define Gurukul foundation myths that emerged from actors' narratives; in particular, I will focus on the the establishment of Gurukul as a struggle to make theatre socially acceptable and ideas of a dream/vision behind such choices. It will then contextualize the teaching 'tradition' within which the theatre school inserted itself. Reviving a traditional, 'pre-western' style of education, with specific roles and practices, was not without consequences.

The establishment of Gurukul can be understood as a sort of recovery of the wild. The forest is a particularly powerful symbol, the location of the ascetic, of the transcendent, but also of the wild itself, of the uncivilized. In the case of Gurukul, what was symbolically carried out was a 'purification' of the forest. Rajkumar recalls that the tiny hill where Gurukul would be established was at first desolate, 'just a structure and a forest, a place for drug users'. So, the actors themselves cleaned the place, put in sanitation, fixed the house, added a canteen, and turned the building into a theatre hall dedicated to Balkrishna Sama. The theme of purification reminds the actors' effort to 'sanitize' the 'theatrical genre', make it acceptable to society, and turn acting into a respectable profession. This is ritually evident during the Bhai Tika practices carried out by actors to safeguard actresses' sexuality, as mentioned in the earlier section.

Another recurrent narrative emphasized risks and struggles that can be associated with a sort of journey into the unknown aimed at bringing a stigmatized artistic form back into society. Bamboo, metal, lights, bricks, and cement, were all bought on credit. Not knowing the outcome of the project, the group agreed to rent the land for three years. Different artists recall that the group managed to pay the early expenses by donations from well-wishers and friends, or by credit. The mayor of Kathmandu, Keshav Sthapit offered to pay for the rent of the land for the first six months. The actors used the money they earned from a radio serial to build the centre and pay the scholarships. Six months later, the mayor lost his position and the group's funding was cut. Rajkumar remembers the months of hardship that followed: 'no scholarships, no food, no money to pay the land rent'. Because of financial difficulties, the group turned to street theatre. Some NGOs commissioned projects that helped the group survive. Sunil pawned his wife Nisha's jewellery and used the money to pay the rent. Actors themselves collected their personal savings to support Gurukul. After six months, Sthapit became mayor of the capital again and continued helping them. The group entered a partnership with a Danish INGO, and survival became easier. They also started performing proscenium plays at Sama Theatre Hall with great dedication, 'even when only two people were in the audience'.[41] 'We had nothing but crazy minds' comments Rajkumar with pride.

The third narrative *topoi* can be associated to the common foundation tale of the dream/vision. In this case, the dream has a particular connotation: it is an eleventh hour dream. Nisha recounts that the hardships of the 1990s, the economic problems, and criticism the group had received, the lack of audience and thus the forecast of a grim future had made Sunil feel depressed. Nisha remembers she was also disheartened, and they thought about moving to the US where her sister was living. At the very last moment, when Nisha had already submitted the certificates for their visa, Sunil asked her to give him another two years so that he could try to open a theatre school. Nisha remembers Sunil saying:

> 'If I succeed ok, if I won't, then I will do whatever you would like'. I said ok, because for many years I followed him, and supported him in what he said. And two more years were nothing in comparison. So I said ok, let's see for two years. We got this place [Gurukul], we called the students and said let's see for two years. They also wanted to jump. If we succeed ok, if we won't we will go back to what was there before. But it's not happening.... God is with us. The situation is now good.[42]

But Gurukul was a dream not only for Sunil. Many of the artists/students who accepted what they describe as a 'challenge' left their jobs and invested their whole life in the group. Sunil had met most of the first intake of students at the acting course run at the Cultural Corporation. If Nisha describes the establishment of Gurukul as a jump into the unknown, a leap of faith, the actors' response was like the response to a 'call' from their guru. They left what they were doing to follow Sunil.

Rajkumar quit his work in Nuwakot District. He was performing street plays for a local NGO. The group was getting NR. 3,000 a play, which allowed them to survive, but acting was becoming difficult because of the intensification of the civil war. Rajan and Kamal left their jobs in commercial offices. Anoj was an accountant at a hotel and left his job to take up Aarohan's administration. Mani did not have to leave his job and was still holding a government post, but managed to get enough free time to rehearse and participate at workshops, meetings, and performances. The other actors were not then working permanently.

The group's formation is portrayed almost in religious terms, as a leap of faith towards Sunil's vision, inspired by its own passion and inner call to theatre. The risks were justified because they were building a new 'profession' as well as renewing theatre art in Nepal. Artists' narratives about the beginning of Gurukul are full of the emotion, the enthusiasm, the pride and the contradictions that accompany the manifestation of a collective dream through risks and personal challenges. The artists of the first intake remember with nostalgia and affection the initial period of struggle, which created a cohesive group, strengthened by the communal system. While listening to the tales of the first intake of students, Pashupati, a student from the second, regrets having missed that closeness and sharing of experience with senior actors.

The second issue of this section concerns the organizational model of the theatre school. As the brochure in Fig. 1 and Fig. 2 highlights, Gurukul's structure is an adaptation of the traditional system of the *guru-kula*. *Guru-kula* means 'the house of the guru'. The word *guru* comes from Sanskrit. '*Gu*' signifies 'shadow/darkness' while the syllable '*ru*' means 'the person who disperses it'. Therefore the *guru* is the person who disperses darkness (Antze, 1991; Prickett, 2007:26). In ancient India it was the locus of artistic apprenticeship, both in dance and music (Antze, 1991; Prickett, 2007). In fact, the student was customarily incorporated into the household of the *guru* so that they could live in constant one-to-one contact with the teacher and thus learn as much as possible by practice and imitation (Antze, Ibid.). For example, Kalakshetra, the dance school founded in Chennai by Rukmini Devi in 1936 was devised according to the principles of the *guru-kula*. It was a boarding school where students and teachers lived and worked together for a minimum of four years. While undergoing training, they served the teacher (Antze, 1991; Zarrilli, 2000). Antze reveals that for most of the contemporary dance students the *guru-kula* belongs to an idealized past as a long residence with the *guru*, more than a few months, is not feasible in contemporary society (Ibid.). The *guru-kula* presumes a specific apprenticeship style named *guru-shishya parampara* (*guru*-disciple tradition) that will be explained in the next section. During the two-year course offered by Gurukul, the students lived in the hostel inside the compound, and ran the centre themselves. They were taught by local artists and visiting teachers from abroad who conducted workshops at the school.[43] Rajkumar explains that Gurukul was inspired by the National School of Drama in Delhi, that Sunil attended, 'but they have holidays', he adds, 'there are no holidays here'. Sunil in fact tried to overcome the problem of having to pay for rehearsal rooms and halls, not having a stable group of artists and the lack of specific theatre training that were perceived as barriers for the development of theatre in Nepal. What he had in mind was, in Rajkumar's words, 'a school and theatre hall where students can live in theatre day and night to develop theatre in Nepal', an all-encompassing experience. The year-long training offered by the Nepal Academy was not considered enough as it comprised only one and a half hours a day, 'it has to be the whole of your life here', explains Rajkumar. The first intake of students started in 2002. The second started in the summer of 2004 and finished in 2006. The school had a loose curriculum and during my fieldwork was in the process of getting affiliation for a graduate course in theatre from a Nepali university. Gurukul offered students different classes:[44] acting, yoga, martial arts, music and *charya* dance.[45] The morning started very early. At 4.45 the alarm clock rang. The female students whose room I shared usually wished to sleep over but Pashupati was very precise and keen to start. At 5 o'clock we would meet in the courtyard and go for a morning run, usually to Pashupatinath Temple and back. We could see Kathmandu waking up. On the way to the temple, cleaners were sweeping the road while on the way back, the street tea vendors in Purano Baneshwar Chowk were already in full activity. Martial arts, yoga, *charya* dance, acting classes would follow one after the other, with a few minutes between for breakfast in the canteen: *anda* toast (fried eggs and toast), *chana* (cheakpeas) and *roti* (flatbread) with tea. Some classes were taught continuously, others took place intermittently. The classes were taught by renowned teachers, Anup Baral volunteered acting classes while Chandra Man Munikar was the *charya* dance *guru*. Late mornings and afternoons were often dedicated to *kachahari* performances, workshops or rehearsals of stage dramas. The core of the teaching was de facto practice-based through the endless hours of rehearsals of the plays.[46] The *guru-kula* system was modernized and adapted to Gurukul. A major departure from the tradition consisted in the fact that only the students lived inside the school while the teachers and married senior artists lived in private houses outside the compound, thus breaking with prescribed commonality.

Life in Gurukul was spartan. The main building was basic, with no hot water or central heating that made it humid during the freezing cold winter and the monsoon season. We had to wear winter puffer jackets all day and wear wool caps while sleeping. We used to have showers during the warmest hours of the day and sit in the sun to warm up and dry the hair. Simplicity also brought lots precious moments of sharing. I still cherish the memory of the long chats, squatting around fire lit in the courtyard, while warming hands over it. Discipline was a typical feature of the *guru-kula*. In Gurukul there were no written regulations. I came to know most of the rules by observing practice. Discipline with regard to movement, to the body – particularly with regard to the female artist's 'image', and to male-female interaction was most evident. Since the management[47] was responsible for the security of the students, artists could only leave the compound after having received permission from either Basanta or Sunil. They were required to mark their exit and entrance times on a register. While male artists seemed to have more freedom, female artists from the first intake were seldom allowed out in the evening. The political instability of the period also required extra caution. Some rules were aimed at safeguarding artistic performance. For example, everybody had to be inside the compound by 9 pm, and lights had to be switched off by 10 pm. Tacit rules governed the permissible interactions between actors. Although jokes and teasing were common, I was told that it was not good for male and female artists to sit and talk with one another for a long time in the open space of the courtyard. Similar rules governed the internal space of the dormitories. The atmosphere was very friendly and all the artists seemed to be rather comfortable with the mixed gender situation and simultaneously respectful of the privacy of each other's spaces.

Female artists were prohibited from wearing revealing clothes, and in the first stage of my residence in Gurukul, a tacit dress code forbade the wearing of jeans and T-shirts. The reason was first of all practical. While rehearsing and doing other kinds of work in the compound, loose clothes like track-suits or *kurta surwal* (long tunic with loose pants) were regarded as more comfortable. Yet, female artists were careful not to wear tight or sleeveless tops, they justified it saying that 'Sunil Sir did not like it', which was another way of saying that it was not socially acceptable. *Kurta surwal* was also the proper dress required to perform *kachahari* in the streets or in schools and communities. Artists came from different backgrounds and some found it hard to comply with Gurukul's rules. For example, one day an artist from a well-off family showed me her new pair of sandals. She put them on and started to walk as if on a catwalk in her bedroom. Then she bitterly commented the she would never be able to go out and wear them, so she has to do it inside the room. At home, in fact, she enjoyed much more freedom than in Gurukul. The situation was hard for her. Such restrictions would disappear in the later stage of fieldwork, from 2006 onwards.

For the first period of my fieldwork the internal space of the theatre in Gurukul could be conceptualized as a highly regulated and 'controlled space'. In order to challenge traditional social taboos against the theatre, and to allow for male and female artists to live and work in the same space, Gurukul management established conservative rules governing both relations and attitudes. Their strict control over artists' bodies and interactions was not dissimilar to the dictates of 'traditional' Hindu society. In fact, it was the artists' identity and profession that they were constructing and trying to make acceptable to the dominant paradigms of society.

Let me sum up the key points raised in this section. The foundation of Gurukul represented a key moment in the lives of senior artists. It was also a turning point in the students' lives as joining the group inevitably meant challenging both their families' and their cultures' general distrust of theatre. The foundation of the school was considered a struggle, but the prize at stake was the following of their inner passion: making theatre their life. The school system was inspired by a traditional institution, the *guru-kula*, and adapted to the local environment. Regulations governed the communal life in Gurukul, particularly with regard to the body, as if in an attempt to legitimize theatre by playing into the values of the Hindu society that condemned it. Living and working together created a strong emotional bond between the group members and their place. The next sections will detail how theatre knowledge was passed on, how the group developed into a theatre organization, and how this impacted on artists' daily lives.

Tradition and modernity in the theatre

The concept of *guru* and the sacredness of the stage are two important elements linking traditional folk performance to contemporary theatre. Performing on a stage is still respected as a religious act in ritual folk performances. There is a temple in Patan dedicated to Nrittyaswor or Nrityanath,[48] the god of dance, music, and drama. An image of the god appears on the *torana* (archway) of the temple, dancing with 16 hands. Inside the temple there are abstract representations of the god, stones and holes, as well as a *madal* on each side of the room containing the god. Every day, devotees come to make *puja* (worship), offering food and flowers. Satya Mohan Joshi, a Newar intellectual, academician and performer, emphasizes that central to the understanding of theatre in Nepal is the god of dance and the *dabu* or *dabali*, that is an open-air stage, that has hosted public performances since the sixth century CE (Chapter 1).

Many theatre artists transferred the 'sacredness' from the *dabu* to the modern stage. For example, the theatre hall is seen as a 'temple'. Gurukul established a strict policy for managing the theatrical space. Before the beginning of any show spectators were advised both by a speaker, and through a written notice outside the entrance, to switch off their mobile phones[49] and restrain from eating or drinking. The atmosphere in Gurukul was very different from other halls such as the Nepal Academy where spectators would talk aloud, move around, enter late, or just come in and go out of the hall at any time during a performance.[50] In Gurukul, once the show started the doors were closed, and there was no more communication between the world of theatre and the outside. The audience was expected to remain in total silence for the whole duration of the performance. Such a strong exercise of authority over the audience in the name of the theatre brings modern Nepali proscenium theatre closer to the strict separation between artists and audience that characterizes mainstream western theatre.[51]

Before entering any kind of stage, be it a platform in the street or a hall, starting a rehearsal, cleaning the stage or performing, artists would habitually bend, touch the stage with their right hand and then bring their hand to the forehead and the chest as a sign of respect and worship. The platform, in fact, represents the god. Satya Mohan Joshi highlights that traditionally the first performance, dance or drama, must be 'sung' in the name of Nrittyaswor. Only then can any programme start.[52] The following is the prologue of the song to the god of dance:

> I am just coming for refuge,
> Protect me and give me the nine sentiments[53]
> Allow me to treat these so that [I will be] a good actor/performer
> (Ibid.)[54]

Satya Mohan Joshi also remarks on the importance of some of the 'rules and regulations' transmitted from guru to student. Bowing to the guru, bowing to the platform/stage, bowing to Nrittyaswor, imploring 'I am just at your feet, protect me, teach me, whatever I may learn to be a good artist', and the observation of *puja* at the openings are all important rituals. According to Satya Mohan the link between the artist and the divinity is strong. The artist must respect these 'ethical rules', which are 'important for the morality' of the actors in order to achieve a connection with the divine. The rules apply only during the performance. Should the artist 'misbehave or not conduct [himself] well, we say the man will turn into a madman' comments Satya Mohan. Satya Mohan explains that rules such as bowing to the *guru*, to the platform, and performing puja are still followed by the artists of the Nepal Academy.[55] An image of Nrittyaswor was established in a corner of the basement of the Academy where the artists practice.

In Gurukul, a *puja* (worship) was carried out at the opening of any performance and actors would take *prasad* (sacred food received after worship). It was also common practice before any show to light incense sticks and take them backstage and onto the stage itself to worship the gods and pray for a good performance. Artists sometimes place their hands over the holy smoke coming from the incense and bring them to their eyes. Part of the pre-performance ritual also involved shaking each other's hands and wishing 'best of luck', in a more secular way.[56] Saraswati Puja and Guru Tika on the last day of Dasain, are two occasions that are used to renovate the link between theatre artists and the gods, and to strengthen the theatrical community through traditional practices. The second, in particular, started in 2005 and has since become a central event in the artistic community. The last day of Dasain is fixed for the Guru Tika (Fig. 7.1, photo by the author). Senior artists – actors, playwrights, teachers, dancers – gathered for a public ceremony in Gurukul. Younger artists would pay them respect

Figure 7.1: Senior artists are honoured in *Gurukul* during *Guru Tika* day

and in return be ritually blessed with a *tika*. Photographic portraits of artists and playwrights of the past were removed from the internal halls of Gurukul and placed in the yard in a public display of reverence governed by hierarchies of age and status.

Literature on Indian classical dance and music is helpful to understand the *guru's* practical role in the arts. In traditional teaching, the *guru-shishya parampara*, 'guru-student (line of) tradition' suggests a particular relationship (Antze, 1991; Prickett, 2007). The *guru* is more than a preceptor for the student, like a second father because he gives birth to the artist in each of his or her students. The *guru* is placed at a higher level than a parent, at the same level as a god, and thus revered accordingly (Antze, 1991). The role goes beyond the transmission of knowledge and invests the human development of the students (Antze, Ibid.). The relationship is based on love, devotion and reverence (Ibid.). For example, Ravi Shankar places three central ideas at the heart of the Indian music tradition: the *guru, vinaya* that is 'humility tempered with love and worship' and *sadhana*, which means practice and discipline involving 'complete faithfulness to the *guru's* tradition and absolute obedience to his instructions in art and life' (Antze, 1991, 31). All in all, the *guru-shishya parampara* results in an intimate yet hierarchical rapport rather than a meeting of friends or equals (Ibid.).

Theatre groups usually apply these rules in different ways. In Gurukul for example, Sunil, considered as the *guru*, did not want his artists to bow down to him or touch his feet as some senior artists and directors still welcome. Nonetheless the core spirit of the relationship remained as habitus from actors' previous artistic experiences. This was renewed in public ceremonies and practiced in daily interactions. Although the term *guru-shishya parampara* was never mentioned in Gurukul, hierarchy was expressed in several ways both through forms of address and services to the teachers. Seniority also appears as another important signifier in the relationships among artists, marked by the appellatives of 'Sir' and *dai/didi* (elder brother/sister). Within Gurukul, only Sunil and Basanta were called 'Sir'. Anil, another senior member of Aarohan who lived outside Gurukul but often engaged in projects was addressed as *dai* (elder brother) although he was only a few years younger than Sunil. Among artists, the spirit was collaborative, open and friendly. Gurukul's artists addressed their older peers through kinship idioms as *dai/didi* (older brother/older sister).

Hierarchies in Gurukul were therefore established through seniority and knowledge. Although framed as a modern organization, Gurukul centred upon a mixed form of leadership, traditional and charismatic. The *guru* is indeed a traditional authority,[57] legitimized by his link to an artistic tradition (Antze, 1991; Prickett, 2007). Although Sunil did not inherit his role as traditional artists had done but constructed it through study, practice, and hard work, he was publicly recognized as an authority in his field and belonging to a specific tradition, along the line of those artists that were venerated during *guru tika* day. Charismatic authority does not appear in a vacuum but grows out of pre-existing forms of traditional or legal authority, which creates the boundaries, norms, and social structure. The traditional role of the *guru*, opened the way for Sunil's charismatic leadership. In fact, Sunil exercised leadership through the respect for his knowledge, in the form of 'mastery' sanctioned by the NSD diploma and 25 years of experience, and 'seniority', which included also a certain amount of awe. Frequently artists shared with me their desire of talking openly to Sunil but simultaneously admitted their incapacity because of this perceived structural difference. They also shared their deep happiness whenever the director started personal conversations with them.

Artistic authority and seniority were highly recognized and respected in Gurukul. Whenever a senior artist approached the thatched gazebo under which actors and students used to sit and chat, the juniors were always ready to stand up and offer their seat. Such ceremonial practice was highly significant of the person's social status. Sunil explains that a *guru* deserves respect:

> If Dinesh Adhikari comes here, he is a poet, I have to leave and offer my chair saying 'please sit here' and it's very impolite that he is standing and I am sitting... because I am a teacher too, there is a privilege for me to decide about a few things and say 'no'. And because of respect for the teacher, even if you don't agree, you do it.[58]

Authority was internalized and situational. While being Gurukul's *guru*, Sunil paid respect to his own masters in a 'traditional way', thus placing himself in a lower hierarchical position to his teachers. In traditional teaching, in fact, asking questions or disagreeing could be perceived as a challenge to the *guru*'s authority and knowledge (Prickett, 2007). There was diversity in the perception of the *guru* role, depending on artists' different ages, experiences, and social background. For example, an artist explained that 'father' and '*guru*' were the 'same' in Hindu culture, although he would define the relationship between *guru* and student 'professional-traditional' rather than simply traditional as a lot has changed in comparison to the past. In a purely professional environment he would have no problem raising questions directly, unlike with his *gurus* because his *gurus* 'made him the artist he is now'. He explains that both his father and his *guru* know that he drinks alcohol, but he would never drink 'in front of their face' out of respect even though some of his colleagues have no problems doing so. While respect towards the *guru* remained unchanged and was shared by all artists, the forms through which such respect was shown to the *guru* varied.

Institutionalizing the theatre group

The years 2005–07 were significant for Gurukul's organizational development. In its 25 year history, Aarohan Theatre expanded from a loose meeting point of artists, working sporadically together for specific theatrical productions, into a stable group based in a specific location with the creation of Gurukul in 2002–03. At the beginning of 2004, partnerships with INGOs (Jan 2004-Jan 2007) provided both funding for street performances and for strengthening the administration and supporting theatrical activities. The project focused on institutional capacity-building achieved through strengthening the organizational structure of the group, defining more precisely the staff roles and responsibilities, developing strategic plans, and networking with local theatre groups. Sunil continued to lead as artistic director. Basanta resigned from his job at the Home Ministry (early 2004) to occupy a full-time position as chief administrator (*Thul Daju*),[59] supported by Anoj who lived and worked in Gurukul as an unpaid volunteer. Yubaraj was assigned a place in the office and was responsible for networking with local communities, follow up activities and media (described as *Saathi*). As a small organization, Aarohan's actors had to work as 'generalists' rather than as 'specialists'.[60] They had to act, on stage and in the streets, and also run the other departments, such as lighting, library, stage management, etc. Individual actors were responsible for the supervision of different departments. The position of *guru* was more clearly defined, but even that was in a continual process of negotiation. The purpose was to make the group financially self-reliant and develop theatre methodologies for social change and democracy.

On the artistic side, since the beginning of 2005, a partnership with the National Theatre of Norway allowed the group to perform 10 *kachahari* plays a month, adding to the 4–7 commissioned by MS Nepal. External support also meant a significant increase in material facilities, technical resources, and making international exchanges available to the group. For example, the group received stage lights sufficient for two halls, 'Light Design', 'Art Management' and 'Directing' workshops facilitated by Norwegian specialists, the possibility of having a play directed by a Norwegian director in Nepal, a month-long workshop in Norway offered to a Nepali artist, and a generator to prevent performance interruptions during the frequent power cuts that afflicted the capital. From February 2005, the group started performing stage plays regularly (Chapter 3) and received an overwhelming response from the audience. Throughout 2005–07, the group experienced a significant increase in technical skills, logistical resources with the construction of a second hall, publicity, marketing, and production management. Regular stage work continued along with *kachahari natak*, as well as voluntary political theatre performances for public assemblies. This progression radically increased workloads for artists who were engaged in performing, advertising the plays, and working in the organization and management of the school, doing partner group follow-ups and performing voluntarily in the cultural programmes for democracy.

Despite conflicts inevitably arising in community life, sharing the same space strengthened the friendship that linked the actors and that was evident on occasions like birthday parties or weddings celebrated inside the compound and theatre hall. The group members also shared each others' problems. For example, the management tried to devise strategies to keep the group together and help actors face their family's pressures to marry. In a meeting in December 2004 the management suggested that the artists get married and bring their partners to Gurukul, allowing them to attend the two year course and start working with Aarohan. Artists considered it a very important opportunity because all their families were pressing them to marry. However, the proposal was perceived as benefitting male more than female artists since women traditionally would have had to move to their husbands' house after marriage, and probably quit the theatre. Soon afterwards one of the artists married and his wife joined the Gurukul training. However, coming from a village in western Nepal, she felt uncomfortable with the theatre. She quit the course and began training in a field that she preferred. Subsequently, other artists married but none of their wives joined the group. The effort to encourage actors' partners' membership in the school, by recruiting through family connections rather than interest, did not work.

At the end of 2004, the tight organizational rules started to be perceived as limiting. Pressed by obligations to move ahead with their own lives, getting married, caring for children, the scholarship offered by Gurukul seemed inadequate for many artists. Exclusivity of work, necessary to focus completely on Gurukul's productions, was also perceived as a barrier. According to some artists, they could have earned NR. 1,500 extra a month – to add to their NR. 5,000 month scholarship – if they could work outside four days a month. What artists asked the managers in December 2004 was to give them one day off a week, so they could work outside. This was later allowed, but artists had to give 10 per cent of their wages to the group. Exclusive focus on Gurukul created a closure to the outside world that became unbearable for the whole group, including the management themselves. In February 2005, both the director and the artists lamented their inability to lead a private life separate from their professional life and they decided to fix Sunday as their day off. More freedom of movement or dress was achieved, but the in-built hierarchy that sustained the organization remained. Unlike in the traditional *guru-kula*, life and theatre started to separate. What seemed in theory an ideal situation, that is, the merging of life into the theatre, led in practice to a trap. The 'special' could not be sustained on the long run and a division between personal life and work in theatre had to be re-established. The group's institutionalization and work streamlining put in place new representations of leadership, the roles and positions inside the group became more defined to increase the representation of efficiency but did not change relations in practice.

Some artists found a room outside the compound and went to Gurukul just for 'work'. Most of the artists ate in their own rooms. The conviviality experienced in the first period reduced. Few people ate at the canteen in the summer of 2007 when I returned. The atmosphere of community that I had experienced in late 2004 was slowly disappearing. The distance between life and theatre increased further. The risk of reviving tradition is that of reproducing the unequal power relations embedded in them (Hashmi, 1989). We can therefore suggest that what was being put under test in Gurukul was the *guru-kula* tradition as a foundation of a modern organization. Examples from India show how this practice is changing. For example, a student's unconditional deference to a *guru* is perceived as problematic in contemporary society (Prickett, 2007). A dance student reported that his 'intolerance to serfdom' led to his professional isolation (Rajan cited in Prickett, 2007). As a result, private *gurus* and some institutions have started introducing pedagogical and organizational changes (Prickett, 2007). A distinction is being drawn between the role of a '*guru*' providing the student with a holistic experience (spiritual, emotional and physical) and that of a 'teacher' who just teaches dance steps (Rajarani cited in Prickett, 2007, 35). The preference for the second model suggests a wider shift in the arts from the domain of 'religion' to that of the 'secular' and professional.

Another aspect needs to be considered to understand the challenge to the tradition. Those years of political upheaval had dramatically raised people's material and artistic expectations. The pace of real change, however, seemed much slower in external politics as it was in Gurukul. Gurukul was not a community of equals to start with due to pre-existing age, gender, ethnicity and class differences and thus even benefits could not increase equally quickly.

New trajectories

Nepali theatre in Kathmandu profoundly changed and flourished since the conflict-ridden and transitional period between 2005–08 when Aarohan started to showcase plays on a regular basis. Gurukul closed down in 2012 as a result of an unsustainable increase in the rent of the land on which the school was built, highlighting once again how the survival and development of any independent theatre group depended on the existence of accessible performance spaces. The Gurukul decade spurred extraordinary interest in the theatre and planted seeds that would develop after the end of the civil war. Although Gurukul closed, other theatre groups managed to find stability through owning their own performance spaces. In the end of 2006, Rajan and Yubaraj left Gurukul to establish Shilpi Theatre with other young artists and to develop their own, different understanding of social and political theatre. As Yubaraj explains, their 'dream was becoming bigger and bigger'. It could therefore not be contained in Gurukul anymore. Rajan then left Shilpi and established Mandala Theatre with Dayahang Rai in 2009; in 2012 they started building their own theatre hall in Anamnagar. After having rented a space for the first years, Yubaraj also had his own hall, 'Gothale Theatre' built in Battisputali. 2012 also saw the opening of Sarwanam's theatre hall and Dramatic Arts Centre in Kalikasthan. Village Theatre led by Bimal Subedi also established its own theatre hall in Lazimpat. All these spaces were conceived as multi-arts centres, with rehearsal halls available for renting, libraries, cafes, and hosting art exhibitions and film screenings. All the four groups, together with the Actors Studio established by Anup Baral in Jhamsikhel also offer acting training and workshops. Aarohan as a group led by Sunil Pokharel still stages theatrical productions, although an alternative site to rebuild Gurukul has not been found yet. The impact of the experience and preparation offered by Gurukul can still be perceived in the work and accounts of its former members. A close-up of the work of Yubaraj and Suresh who have developed in individual and different ways the legacy of Gurukul will be revealing, with particular reference to the structure of their theatre groups and the type of *kachahari* theatre that they produce.

Yubaraj feels that the period spent in Gurukul was a fantastic opportunity to experience new styles, techniques, forms. There, he could develop not only his acting skills but also focus on communications and publishing. At that time, in fact, Yubaraj was also doing freelance journalism, writing mostly on arts. From an organizational perspective, Shilpi had a core group of seven full-time members and administrative staff, and hired artists based on the need to do both theatre within development projects and stage productions.[61] As Shilpi's artistic director, Yubaraj experienced some of the contextual difficulties already faced by the Gurukul management. Yubaraj talked about the challenge of keeping artists through a profession that still does not offer a guaranteed salary. Yubaraj explains that he tends to rely on and hire trained artists that have both experience and commitment, often former Gurukul friends such as Kamal, Pasupathi, Saraswati, and Bhola. In terms of leadership, Yubaraj explains that he would not like Shilpi to be a one-man hierarchical organization as is the case with most theatre groups in South Asia. Shilpi is a fairly structured group in which all members share the artistic and financial responsibilities of their projects. But leadership is relational and also based on perceptions: Yubaraj observes that as the group director, at times he was given the authority to take decision, and outsiders often contacted him instead of the person who had specific responsibilities in the group. Moreover, individual members preferred certain fields, e.g., willing to only act, and he recognized that it was difficult to get the same level of commitment from all artists.

In a way that resembled Gurukul, Shilpi was engaged both in proscenium and social theatre. Yubaraj's conceptualization of theatre had changed though. After he left Gurukul, he studied theatre in Denmark for two years and being exposed to an international context shifted his vision. While continuing to be interested in political theatre and on how theatre can vehiculate ideas of social change, the more entertainment-based productions that he experienced in Europe allowed him to deepen his artistic skills. Yubaraj explains:

In my theatre, I want to cut out the tears, not putting 'ashu' (tears),
When I watch other plays I can see if they move or if they don't. In
some plays I see many problems like killing, murdering, firing, I see
them but they don't help me to act….so that's my vision…I want to
do entertaining theatre, cutting the tears out, putting the situations,
and making the audience realize. [62]

He felt that to be powerful and challenge the audience both his proscenium and street theatre plays needed to be led by the 'theatrical': the political or social message should come through the art rather than be expressed directly through emotions. In comparison to the other experiences analysed in the previous chapters, Yubaraj reclaims the power of the artist, even when performing theatre for social change and *kachahari natak*:

I always say to my friends, even if someone offers to do a play about
condom or clean water, lets make it theatre first, don't worry about
convincing the NGOs. Same thing in a *kachahari* play, bringing the
issue is like propaganda, but my point is we don't need to follow
Augusto Boal. He was living in specific circumstances and he
practiced in these circumstances. We have another mentality, even his
son cannot follow his ideas always, why should we? We take his ideas
but we use them in another way, in a totally different situation, but I
think we destroyed Forum Theatre. If Augusto Boal saw this he would
say 'what are you doing?'[63]

Rather than working through workshops with specific communities, Yubaraj in fact prefers to build a frame through workshops with artists in his own hall in Kathmandu and then perform the same play in different locations. Besides establishing contacts with partner groups in different districts of Nepal, Yubaraj also engaged in donor-funded weeks long *yatras*,[64] in the style of the early street theatre of the 1980s. Not having to spend time training and working with communities allows Yubaraj to develop his very rich stage repertoire. Unlike Boal, who insisted on the fact that everyone can make theatre, Yubaraj redraws the boundaries of his hard-earned profession, and explains 'if you see, most Forum Theatre groups are not artists, they are social activists, for me to do forum theatre you need to be an actor and a director'.[65]

Rather different is the trajectory followed by Suresh. He left Gurukul in 2008 because he needed to earn more for his family: while in Gurukul, Suresh got married, moved into a flat outside the school, had a son and as he grew up, the NR. 5,000 monthly scholarship was not enough to live on. After doing some community theatre for different NGOs, having the chance of travelling to nearly 60 districts, and training groups in Forum Theatre, Suresh established Space, his own theatre group in 2010. Suresh explains that the mission of the group was twofold, doing both stage and street theatre. Yet, since the beginning he almost exclusively focused on performing *kachahari* theatre in schools and giving training. Interestingly, through Space, Suresh was able to actually practice *kachahari* in the form that he thought most effective and he had already tried to experiment with in Gurukul: through long-term engagement with communities, e.g., producing a frame through workshops with children over six weeks. In this way students were in the position of choosing the topics that were relevant to them, such as caste discrimination, water, while also learning theatre skills that would allow them to express their experience:

> Our organization is really using Forum Theatre. First day warm up, introduction, entertaining things; on the second day the children share their problems, what type of issues they have. Third day, they choose the major issue and the fourth they rehearse the issue, the fifth again they rehearse and in the sixth week they perform. In the performance there may not be quality because they are not professional actors, but through the play they raise the problems, and we are planning to ask the people [audience] these are the problems raised by children, if they are your problems, how can they be solved? It is really good.[66]

Suresh believes that it is actually possible to change society through theatre. In fact the group also moves beyond the aesthetic space in which the children perform and try connecting the schools with government offices, NGOs, and organizations to facilitate the change advocated through the theatre. This recalls Boal's idea of breaking down the barrier between actors and audience, what Yubaraj, in contrast, tries to redefine. Suresh explains that:

> you have to think about the problem, you don't say it's a performance, it is theatre. If you think, it's life, and you can feel you and I as a part of this problem, then you can solve it; otherwise just performance and back doesn't work.

He explains further:

> when I go to the community, no one can tell that I am an actor. They trust me like a son, like a friend. And when I work with children I go like this, I don't go there as an actor, 'I am famous, I have so much experience'. I never go like this. I say, 'ok, if you are interested, I have some games, I have some techniques', because we are all Nepalese, we are all friends, we can talk through the process, and slowly we talk.

And you know, in every programme, after the programme I have a very good relationship with them ...[67]

Shilpi and Space present differences in organizational development: while Yubaraj tried to structure his group around a core group of artists who would take ownership of the organization, Space seems to be less structured and works with a group of 10 artists engaged on individual project basis. The diversity of Shilpi and Space also exemplifies the tension between social engagement and aesthetics, highlighting how difficult it still is to reconcile both in contemporary Nepal, in which creative work is still development-dependent and precarious.[68]

Conclusion

This chapter outlined the development of Aarohan theatre group into an organization and its attempt to professionalize theatre. This process involved opening of a theatre community and the establishment of two theatre halls, the creation of the first private theatre school in the country, the production and staging of regular proscenium theatre plays, the development of a theatre audience that would follow the productions and would be interested in buying cultural work, the organization of national and international theatre festivals, marketing the performances, the delineation of more specific organizational roles and structures, and the continuation of development theatre through *kachahari natak* performed by Aarohan group itself, as well as by their partner groups. The group also regularly invited college students for matinee performances to nurture their future audience.

In short, the heroic mission of resurging Nepali theatre and 'sanitizing' the acting profession by making it not only respectable but also a potentially remunerative job was accomplished and the signs of its success started to be seen within the period of my fieldwork.

Many radical theatre groups at a certain stage of their evolution felt a need for stability, expressed through the building of stable theatre halls or in the engagement in productions close to the establishment or the neoliberal market (Van Erven, 1988; 1992; Afzal-Khan, 1997, 2005; Barucha, 1998). In an interview Safdar Hashmi talks about the different jobs he and his actors had to do for a living while doing political theatre, and about the family pressure he was starting to feel (van Erven, 1992, 155). When they started, most of the group were unmarried but in the late 1980s [1988] they had to support their families. For this reason he felt the need to transform his group into a professional company and establish a workers' cultural centre where a repertory company could perform and train other groups. He was planning to work for TV and cinema for a couple of years in order to get the necessary money.

His experiences reflected many of the problems felt by Aarohan in the attempt to professionalize the group.

One way in which Aarohan tried to achieve stability was through the opening of Gurukul and the institutionalization of the theatre group. However, the institutionalization of the group also increased the distance between leadership and the artists, widened everyone's expectations, which led either to acceptance of the organizational limits or to their departure from the community. Many of the artists with whom I talked in 2007 revealed their intention of looking for jobs or scholarships abroad to widen their experience. In 2004 most of them could not consider leaving Gurukul as the place felt like 'home'. The private space in Gurukul, the space of the actors, also changed: at first it was a controlled space; it later became more open. But despite the rules governing space in Gurukul became looser, some artists decided to move out or take rooms outside whilst maintaining their membership, suggesting that the place transformed from a 'home' into a 'work place'. The audience space inside Gurukul changed as well: from being free, or just NR. 25 for undifferentiated seating, it later became regulated and structured. The premieres of stage plays were reserved for guests on an invitation basis and the ticket prices varied from NR 25 for students in defined areas of the hall, to NR 50, 100 or 500 according to the position and the event. While fully embedded in the economics of everyday life, and slowly turning acting in theatre into a respectable and sought after job, in Gurukul theatre retained the 'special' attached to it while at the same time introducing changes that would make acting in theatre sustainable, like an 'ordinary' profession.

Endnotes

1 'Mere experience is simply the passive endurance and acceptance of events. An experience, like a rock in a zen sand garden, stands out from the eventness of passing hours and years and forms what Dilthey called a 'structure of experience' (Turner, 1986, 35).

2 Manu Smriti (Laws of Manu) is a work of Hindu law, containing rules and codes of conduct for individuals and communities. Some of these laws codify the Hindu caste system. It is usually dated around first century CE.

3 A musical instrument similar to a violin.

4 Most of the literature available focuses on Badi women as commercial sex workers and just mentions their role of entertainers in passing. The shift from dancers to sex workers is said to have taken place in the last 50 years as a result of socio-political changes (Pigg and Pike, 2004).

5 Interviewed in November 2006.

6 Ibid.

7   Ibid.

8   The Ramlila, literally 'Rama's play', is a folk re-enactment of the life of Rama through song, narration, and dialogue, see Kapur (2006).

9   Interviewed in December 2005.

10   Folk theatre performance popular in the North of India, see Hansen (1992).

11   Ibid.

12   Aruna was in her mid 20s when this research was carried out.

13   Mark on the forehead created by the application of powder or paste on ritual occasions as a blessing. The colour of the tika depends on the ritual and culture, e.g. on Dasain tika is vermilion.

14   Interviewed in December 2005.

15   Ibid.

16   Interviewed in January 2006.

17   The Jayatu Sanskritam Movement was initiated in July 1947 by students of Tindhara College, demanding democracy and the inclusion of modern subjects in their curriculum. The initiators were sent into exile in India by the Rana rulers.

18   Ibid.

19   Interviewed in January 2006.

20   At the time of the interview, the play, an adaptation of Vijay Tendulkar's work, was being restaged in Gurukul, see page 93.

21   Ibid.

22   Interviewed in December 2005.

23   A progressive song composed by Jivan Sharma from Raktim Parivar.

24   Ibid.

25   Interviewed in January 2006.

26   Interviewed in July 2012.

27   Interviewed in November 2005.

28   In his mid 20s at the time of fieldwork.

29   Interviewed in July 2012.

30   Interviewed in January 2006.

31   Ibid.

32   Interviewed in November 2006.

33   Interviewed in November 2006.

34   Bhai tika is celebrated on the fifth and last day of Tihar. Brothers and sisters bless each other. Sisters offer food and bless brothers with a garland of flowers to wish them a long life. They then apply a seven-colour tika on their foreheads to thank them for their protection. Brothers, in turn, bless their sisters with tika and offer them a gift.

35   Interviewed in October 2005.

36   Interviewed in October 2005.

37 In her mid 30s at the time of fieldwork.

38 Film acting was usually considered a more prestigious profession because there were more financial rewards. Yet, very often film female actors appeared on screen and in newspapers (like *Saptahik, Kamana*) in scanty dresses and overtly sexual poses, in contrast to theatre actresses. This leads to the assumption that the restraints on theatre are due more to economic than moral reasons.

39 Interviewed in November 2006.

40 For a gender analysis of two plays, Gopal Prasad Rimal's 'The Graveyard' (*Masan*, 1945) and Abhi Subedi's 'Fire in the Monastery' (*Agniko Katha*, 2004) see Gurung, 2011; Sharma (2011) instead analyses Nepali theatre representations of some stigmatized categories, including women, windows and women with disabilities.

41 Rajkumar, informal conversation, November 2004.

42 Interviewed in November 2007.

43 Even in India the *guru-kula* has evolved (Antze, 1991). Even the traditional and rigorous *kathakali* training is transmitted in modern institutions like Kerala Kalamandalam to full-time students who live in the institute in a very simple manner and receive a subsistence stipend rather than on one-to-one basis (Zarrilli, 2000, 69).

44 Courses stopped in 2006.

45 Charya dance is a Newar classical dance form.

46 Three students left the school because of several personal reasons. A common dissatisfaction, however, was that they felt they were not learning what they expected from Gurukul's structural organization.

47 By 'management' I mean the group of senior artists who shared the highest responsibilities within the group during the period of my fieldwork, that is Sunil Pokharel, Nisha Sharma Pokharel and Basanta Bhatta.

48 The god is also called Nateshwori/Natyashwori, in Newari its name is Nasadyah. In the literature (Hoek, 1994), Nasadyah is indicated as god of dance and music.

49 This was very unusual practice at the time where mobile phones normally rang in the most diverse situations, during meetings, during the shooting of films, and during formal and informal conversations. Answering was usually not considered rude. Conversely, during rehearsals artists' mobiles rang all the time thus suggesting that real-life was indeed part of the theatre.

50 Like in many cinema halls in the periphery. Similarly, musical performances and religious ritual usually do not require hushed silence.

51 See Abbing (2002) for more on the sacredness surrounding the theatre in the west.

52 Interviewed in October 2006.

53 He indicates 'humour, pathetic, marvellous, and the movements' (Ibid.).

54 Satya Mohan Joshi sang in Newari language and then translated himself into English.

55 Interviewed in October 2006. Similar rituals are performed also in the world of cinema: *puja* is carried out before shooting films, and whenever an actor enters the set for the first time he/she bows to the camera, which is considered as a god, touching it with the forehead and then bowing again while rising up. It is also necessary to bow in such a ceremonial way to the

director and the cameramen, waiting for their blessing. Some actors bow to the director at every meeting, until the director touches their heads, although many directors are less formal and do not require this practice.

56   Similar informal rituals characterize western theatre as well.

57   See Mines and Gourishankar (1990) for other forms of traditional authority, 'big men' in this case, in South Asia.

58   Interviewed in November 2006.

59   Official title of the position in the project.

60   The terms come from an 'Arts management' workshop hosted in Gurukul in February 2005. It was sponsored by the Oslo National Theatre and run by its art manager.

61   Interviewed in July 2012.

62   Interviewed in 2012.

63   Ibid.

64   One of these *yatras* is described in a documentary produced by the group in 2012, 'A journey into theatre'.

65   Interviewed in 2012.

66   Interviewed in January 2012.

67   Interviewed in 2012.

68   See cross-cultural comparative examples in Umney and Kretsos (2015), Abbing (2002).

8

Conclusions

A day will come when our societies will know again those hours of creative effervescence in the course of which new ideas arise and new formulae are found which serve for a while as a guide to humanity.

Durkheim, 1976, 427–28

One feeling guided my experience of doing fieldwork in Nepal in those strange times of swift political change: that transformation seemed to move like a vortex, and there seemed to be no permanency. One day you could wake up isolated from the whole world, and the political scenario could turn upside down, what the king said, was not what he meant. Once I asked one of my research participants if I could quote a controversial remark. They were surprised. 'Why not?' adding that if I would ask the same question the day after, they may change their mind and give a totally different answer. There seemed to be no certainty beyond present visibility. And even what was visible sometimes seemed a fleeting representation of something else – one among a myriad possible representations. For this reason, I think, performance, and theatrical performance in particular, well interpreted the mood of the time. A piece of theatre is a multi-vocal, multi-spatial representation that leaves open as many possible interpretations as there are spectators. It does not entail a long-term commitment, and you cannot easily fix it. But for the same reasons, theatre could also create subtle emotional threads, bring back memories of the past, and sustain dreams and hopes. The perception of such a fast change did not correspond with the pace of actual change: imagination and expectations moved quickly, the changes in the material realities were slower and such a gap caused disillusionment.

In this concluding chapter, I am going to draw parallels between the different performances that I have documented, namely *loktantrik natak, kachahari natak,* and Maoist cultural programmes to understand what an aesthetics of theatre for social change would entail and what we can learn from comparing theatre in development with theatre in social and political movements. I will then discuss the tension between professionalism and activism in the arts. I will assert that despite *kachahari natak* becoming less participatory in Aarohan's adaptation, Aarohan artists were themselves rehearsing for their own lives when they practicing it in this way. They were led by their own aspirations and passion, just like political and social activists. What was at stake was the development of Nepali proscenium theatre as well as their professional identity.

The emergent aesthetics of theatre for social change

So, what type of aesthetics of theatre for social change emerges from a comparative analysis of *loktantrik*, *kachahari* and revolutionary theatre? Below is a summary of the 'conditions of performance', including pre-performance (nos. 1–2), performance (nos. 3–4) and post-performance (nos. 5–9):

Table 8.1: The conditions of performance

	Aarohan *loktantrik*	Aarohan *kachahari/* workshop	Aarohan *kachahari/* issue-based	Maoist theatre	Kamlari *kachahari*	Space *kachahari*
1. Workshop	No	Yes	No	No	No	Yes
2. Topicality	Yes	Yes	Yes/No	Yes	Yes	Yes
3. Spectators' agency during performance	No	Yes: on the critical moment when the play is stopped by the *sutradhar*	Yes: on the critical moment when the play is stopped by the *sutradhar*	No	Yes: on the critical moment when the play is stopped by the *sutradhar*	Yes: on the critical moment when the play is stopped by the *sutradhar*
4. Repetition in the same community	Yes/No; a play is usually not repeated but artists perform similar plays in other events within the political movement	No	No	No; plays are performed across different locations during a campaign; different campaigns may return to the same community	Yes/No but the district where they perform is well defined and they can go back to the same village	Yes

	Aarohan loktantrik	Aarohan kachahari/ workshop	Aarohan kachahari/ issue-based	Maoist theatre	Kamlari kachahari	Space kachahari
5. Location and Context	Citizen-led social movement mass meetings	Community	Created for a performance	People's War and political mass meetings	Created for a performance	School and local community
6. Follow-up activitities	Not by theatre group but the movement continues	Not by theatre group; dependent on community members	No	Artists are party members, both artists and activists	By NGOs linked to the theatre group	Yes
7. Membership	Yes: artists participated as citizens	No: no connection between artists and audience	No: no connection between artists and audience	Yes: similar ideology and background	Yes: same ethnic group, community and background	Yes: same school and village
8. Degree of involvement	Occasional	Part-time	Part-time	Full-time	Part-time	Part-time
9. Funding	Voluntary	INGO	INGO	Self-organised in relation to the Party	INGO	INGO

Source: Author's compilation

Activists and theatre workers use theatre to bring people together, to establish a dialogue with communities, to mediate and open discussions, to share information and raise awareness. Topicality appears to be central in activating involvement and agency from the spectators. The pre-performance workshop usually constitutes the moment when artists can get first hand experience of the burning issues that members of a community wish to reflect upon through theatre. The standardized *kachahari* on child labour presented by Aarohan in many schools skipped this phase. While nonetheless facilitating reflection and raising awareness of child labour among school children, the embodied component of oppression that is usually confronted by replacing the character on stage was not directly challenged:

the creative shift between reality/play and onstage/offstage was not triggered. Activist theatre, be it Aarohan's *loktantrik natak*, the Kamlari's *kachahari natak* or the Maoist cultural work also pre-packaged performance, as no workshop took place with the communities. However, because of the fusion of players' social and dramatic roles, and the context in which theatrical performances took place, these were not isolated events but connected to wider campaigns. The audience that attended *loktantrik natak* performances or Maoist cultural programmes could find in the plays elements that could trigger reflections upon their own personal lives. They could also find a structure through which to channel, in case, the enactment of the scripts performed on stage in real life once the performance was over. Art-activists and political cultural workers were part of and had a stake in the communities of imagination that they helped conjure up through their theatre. Yet, if the topic represented onstage is very close to the actor's and the audience's real lives, for instance, construction workers demanding their rights, citizens invoking democracy or activists demanding the abolition of the *kamlari* practice, the stage is not a neutral or safe space. The representation becomes political, conflict can escalate rather than be resolved (Chapter 5). If there is no close identification between characters, topic and audience, and power structures are not directly challenged, discussions can indeed take place freely and openly but the transformative power of the aesthetic space is diluted. This book questioned the assumption of the performance space as a universal safe arena where social problems can be debated and hypostasizes that the world of reality and that of representation are not autonomous at all. It is in fact its interconnectedness that makes the aesthetic space a political space, neither neutral nor 'safe' but precisely for this reason a space of possible transformation and social change.

Relationality, intended as establishing relationships or channels that can facilitate the real-life actualization of the opportunities explored through the aesthetic space is another important aspect that this book considered. The use of participatory techniques such as forum theatre may facilitate the audience involvement. However, what happens to the knowledge co-produced during the performance? The context of the performance, the follow-up activities, the artists' identities, and membership, the funding system through which they are produced, the support of organizations associated to wider political and social movements, do affect the possibilities of following up on the suggestions rehearsed on stage. Professional artists in fact discussed about their role, and solved the tension in different ways. While Aarohan practiced both workshop an issue-based *kachahari*, Shilpi opted for not carrying out workshops with communities and focused on refining their theatrical art as a means to convey social messages; Space, in contrast, chose to spend time sharing their theatrical skills with communities and helping them connect with organizations in the post-performance.

Boal explains that theatre can be a 'rehearsal for revolution' where oppressed people can explore strategies for resistance. 'Within its fictitious limits the experience is a concrete one' (Boal, 1979, 140) for the participants and the cathartic[1] effect is avoided. The drama creates a place where it should be 'legal'[2] to see one's imagination acted out. As the performance develops, play and reality blur. According to Boal, 'the practice of these theatrical forms creates a sense of incompleteness that seeks fulfillment through real action' (Ibid., 142). The audience are not just 'spectators' of the performance but 'spect-actors' who act out their ideas on stage. The play is therefore open-ended, unfinished, opposite to the finished forms of 'bourgeois theatre' (Ibid., 142). The examples explored in this book suggest that technique alone is not enough. The aesthetically simpler and technically less participatory methods used by the Maoist troupes or the *kachahari* performed by non-professional community groups – such as the Kamlari Natak Samuha – both backed by organizations that could in practice support the spectators in changing aspects of their own lives, were perceived by activists as extremely powerful in opening possibilities for social transformation. Maoist critique of bourgeois theatre is carried out on a different level. By using a very simple and traditional form of drama recalling bourgeois theatre in structure, based on a realistic reproduction of lived experiences on stage, Maoist artists created an environment in which, though spectators do not become 'actors' on stage, they could take action after the play was over by following the party. Guns were real guns and they could be held against the oppressors as Boal's peasants wished. Actors were not only actors but had multiple roles: they were actors, party members and rebels. Maoist drama, directly calling people to join their struggle, was backed by a structure that allowed the spectators moved by the play to continue their 'revolution' in real life. Similarly, the former kamlari artists performing in Deukhuri were the living example that the practice could be stopped.

It is worth discussing this issue of context and the politics of the performance a bit further. Participation in a performance does not only mean sharing the aesthetic space but involves sharing the social space as well, including common problems, feelings, hopes, opportunities, and desire for change. It also means belonging to an environment that can support the actualization of the different world envisioned onstage. Spectators may have become actors during the *kachahari* play and the play may have become a 'rehearsal for revolution,' but if the spectators are not in the position to achieve the changes they wish by themselves, the play remains a one off 'special' show. Yet, while Maoist drama offers the possibility of continuing in real life the 'rehearsal' vicariously experienced through the performances, the kind of script that is offered seems to be only 'one' such possibility: that is the script presented by the play, by the actors, by the party. Revolutionary theatre uses the same methodology as bourgeois theatre, replicating the division between actors and audience on stage, but conveys a different political message. Although this message is top-down and unidirectional, actors were in a social position that allowed them to share the 'responsibility' of their message with the audience.

A question now arises about the superior aesthetic quality of the forum theatre offered by professional artists. Cultural workers and theatre workers alike are aware of the limitations of repetitive, sloganist, and overly message-orientated theatre. However, scripting and playing onstage a story that re-enacts moments of artists' personal lives, as in the case of the *kamlari*, *loktantrik natak* or Maoist theatre, imbues the performance of a power and strength that purely 'representational' plays may not always have. Dramas built through direct knowledge and experience of marginalization and oppression become 'loaded' representations. I think that it is the 'something behind' that makes the difference between performance as representation and performance as an enactment of the artists' real life and that differentiates the 'aesthetic power' of the activists from the 'aesthetic skills' of the professionals. Interestingly, in different contexts artists talk about 'real' feelings shared with the audience. Sarita explains that when they make theatre they try to 'catch the reality of life'. 'If we manage to catch the reality of life', she continues, 'the audience will feel themselves on stage, they will be touched, they will think and speak'.[3] When describing the Kamlari actors' competence deriving from having lived through the pain of indentured labour, Krishna also makes a distinction between showing the 'real pain' vs. playing a 'role empty' (Chapter 5). Aarohan's artists too talk about 'doing theatre from the heart' when performing theatre for democracy, once again emphasizing a direct connection between their real life and its stage representation (Chapter 3). The constant reference to the reality of the representation brings again back Taussig's elaborations on mimesis in relation to sympathetic magic (1993, 56). What makes a representation powerful is not the 'faithfulness' of the copy, likeness is not enough, but the magic of 'contact'. In other words, the 'reality of the representation' matters, things that once were in contact are 'impregnated' with power. Artists that once lived – experienced contact – with specific situations embody the reality of the experience and this comes through in their representation. Their 'cultural performance' overlaps with their personal 'social performance' which extends beyond the stage, encompassing real life.

The relation between 'aesthetic power' vs 'aesthetic skills' brings forward another tension, and not necessarily an opposition, that between professionalism and activism, or the professionalization of activism. Because of a lack of state subsidies and supportive cultural policies, contemporary proscenium theatre grew alongside development theatre, favouring the interaction of established theatre artists with activists. Aarohan artists' struggle to stabilize acting as a profession required also establishing limits to development theatre and their involvement with communities to safeguard time for stage production and not to turn into social workers. The whole aesthetics of theatre for social change is premised on instability because of the constant need to adapt and respond to shifting and diverse realities. The intensity and the all-encompassing personal effort required for such is difficult to sustain in the long run. For many artists that I met in the field, including Tharu social activists or Maoist cultural workers theatre represented a 'special' moment in their lives, linked either to youth or to framed periods of engagement, e.g. a time-limited project work or campaigning. Both the Kamlari Theatre Group and the Maoist cultural groups had frequent turnovers as artists moved on with their lives, often into paid work that could sustain their families. Aarohan theatre workers, the specialists of cultural performance were trying to bring theatre into the realm of social performance, making it not only a form of social intervention but also a worthy form of livelihood, though at the time of fieldwork it was for many still sustained by passion and other side jobs. I hope this book has shown that beyond evaluations of theatre in development, stage success and the celebration of political change by social mobilization, inspired by cultural performance, lie the real life and aspirations of the 'theatre-makers' that go beyond the 'special' events that they create.

Endnotes

1 In *The Rainbow of Desire* (1995) Boal reshaped the meaning of catharsis.
2 The universal validity of the stage as a safe and legal place for social experimentation has been challenged in Chapters 4 and 5.
3 Focus group, 21 December 2004.

Bibliography

Abbing, H. 2002. *Why Are Artists Poor? The Exceptional Economy of the Arts.* Amsterdam: Amsterdam University.

Acharya, B. 2009. *Adhunik Nepali Natak* (Modern Nepali Theatre). Kathmandu: Sajha.

Adams, V. 1998. *Doctors for Democracy. Health Professionals in the Nepal Revolution.* Cambridge: Cambridge University Press.

Adhikari, A. 2014. *The Bullet and the Ballot Box. The story of Nepal's Maoist Revolution.* London and New York: Verso.

Adhikari, K. R. 1996. 'Naming Ceremonies as Rituals of Development', *Studies in Nepali History and Society* 1 (2): 345–64.

Afzal-Khan, F. 1997. 'Street Theatre in Pakistani Punjab. The Case of Ajoka, Lok Rehas, and the Woman Question', *The Drama Review* 41 (3): 39–62.

————. 2005. *A Critical Stage. The Role of Secular Alternative Theatre in Pakistan.* Kolkata and Delhi: Seagull.

Ahearn, L. 1999. '"A Twisted Rope Bind my Waist": Locating Constraints of Meaning in a Tij Songfest', *Journal of Linguistic Anthropology* 8 (1): 50–86. 2001.

Ahmed, S. J. 2002. Wishing for a World without "Theatre for Development": Demystifying the case of Bangladesh, *Research in Drama Education: The Journal of Applied Theatre and Performance* 7 (2): 207–19.

————. 2003. 'Carya Nritya of Nepal. When "'Becoming the Character'" in Asian Performance is Nonduality in 'Quintessence of Void"', *The Drama Review* 47 (83): 159–82.

Allen, M. (ed.). 1994. *Anthropology of Nepal. People, Problems and Processes.* Kathmandu: Mandala Bookpoint.

Amatya, S. 1983. *Some Aspects of Cultural Policy in Nepal.* Paris: UNESCO.

Anderson, B. 1983. *Imagined Communities: Reflections on the Origin and Spread of Nationalism.* London: Verso.

Anderson, M. 1971. *Festivals of Nepal.* London: George Allen and Unwin.

Ankersmit, F. R. 1996. *Aesthetic Politics. Political Philosophy beyond Fact and Value.* Stanford: Stanford University Press.

Andrejevic, M. 2003. *Reality TV: The Work of Being Watched.* Lanham, Md.: Rowman and Littlefield Publishers.

Antze, R. J. 1991. 'Apprentiship. Oriental examples', in *A Dictionary of Theatre*

Anthropology: the Secret Art of the Performer, edited by E. Barba and N. Savarese, 29–33. London: Routledge.

Anushil. 2006. 'Gaungaunbatautha', *Himal Khabarpatrika* (21–28 April).

Arce, A., and N. Long. 2000. 'Reconfiguring Modernity and Development from an Anthropological Perspective', in *Anthropology, Development and Modernities. Exploring discourses, counter-tendences and violence*, edited by A. Arce and N. Long, 1-32. London: Routledge.

Arendt, H. 1958. *The Human Condition*. Chicago: Chicago University Press.

Aryal, K. and U. K. Poudel (eds). 2006, *Jana Andolan II: a Witness Account*, Kathmandu: Informal Sector Service Centre (INSEC).

Askew, K. M. 2002. *Performing the Nation. Swahili Music and Cultural Politics in Tanzania*. Chicago and London: University of Chicago.

Auslander, P. 1994. 'Playing Boal', in *Theatre, Therapy, Activism*, edited by Jan Cohen-Cruz and Mady Schutzman, 124–33. London and New York: Routledge.

———. 2008. *Theory for Performance Studies. A Student's Guide*. London and New York: Routledge.

Aziz, B. N. 2001. *Heir to a Silent Song. Two Rebel Women of Nepal*. Kathmandu: Centre for Nepal and Asia Studies.

Babbage, F. 2004. *Augusto Boal*. London: Routledge.

Babcock, B. 1978. *The Reversible World: Symbolic Inversion in Art and Society*. Ithaca, N.Y.: Cornell University Press.

Bakhtin, M. 1981. *The Dialogic Imagination: Four Essays by M. M. Bakhtin* edited by M. Holquist. Austin: University of Texas Press.

Baltutis, M. 2011. 'Advertising Royalty: Popularizing the Monarchy for Kathmandu's Middle Class', *South Asian Popular Culture* 9 (2): 191–204.

Banham, M., J. Gibbs and F. Osofisan (eds). 1999. *African Theatre in Development*. Bloomington and Indianapolis: Indiana University Press

Baral, R. R. 2007. *Sangeet ra Saundarya* (Music and Aesthetics). Kathmandu: Progressive Literary Study Forum.

Barba, E. 1995 [1993]. *The Paper Canoe. A Guide to Theatre Anthropology*. London and New York: Routledge.

Barba, E. and N. Savarese (eds.). 1991. *A Dictionary of Theatre Anthropology: the Secret Art of the Performer*. London: Routledge.

Barber, K. 2000. *The Generation of Plays: Yoruba Popular Life in the Theatre*. Bloomington: Indiana University Press.

Barber, K., A. Richard and J. Collins.1997. *West African Popular Theatre*. Bloomington: Indiana University Press.

Barker, H. 1989. *Arguments for a Theatre*. London: Calder.

Barucha, R. 1983. *Rehearsals of Revolution: The Political Theatre of Bengal.* Honolulu: University of Hawaii Press.

————. 1998. *In the Name of the Secular. Contemporary Cultural Activism in India.* Oxford: OUP.

————. 2000. *The Politics of Cultural Practice. Talking through Theatre in an Age of Globalization.* London: The Athlone Press.

Bateson, G. 1972. *Steps towards an Ecology of Mind.* New York: Balantine Books.

Bathia, N. 2004. *Acts Of Authority/Acts Of Resistance: Theater and Politics in Colonial and Postcolonial India.* Ann Arbor: University of Michigan Press.

Baudrillard, J. 2005. *The Conspiracy of Art.* New York: Semiotext(e).

Baumann, R. 1977. *Verbal Art as Performance.* Prospect Heights: Waveland Press.

————. 1992. *Folklore, Cultural Performance and Popular Entertainments.* New York and Oxford: OUP.

Baumer, R. Van M. and Brandon, J. 1981. *Sanskritik Drama in Performance.* Honolulu: University of Hawai'i Press.

Beeman, W. O. 1993. 'The Anthropology of Theatre and Spectacle', *Annual Review of Anthropology* 22: 369–93.

Behar, R. 1996. *The Vulnerable Observer: Anthropology that Breaks Your Heart.* Boston: Beacon Press.

Bell, J. 1998. 'Louder than Traffic: Bread and Puppet Parades', in *Radical street performance*, edited by J. Cohen-Cruz, 271–81. London and New York: Routledge.

Bennet, S. 1997. *Theatre Audiences. A theory of Production and Reception.* New York: Routledge.

Berezin, M. 2001. 'Emotions and Political Identity: Mobilizing Affection for the Polity', in *Passionate Politics. Emotions and Social Movements*, edited by J. Goodwin, J. M. Jaasper and F. Polletta, 83–98. Chicago and London: The University of Chicago Press.

Berkoff, S. 1989. *I am Hamlet.* London: Faber and Faber.

Bharucha, R. 1998. *In the Name of the Secular. Contemporary Cultural Activism in India.* New Delhi: Oxford University Press.

Bhatta, C. G. 2007. 'Civil Society in Nepal: In Search of Reality', *Contributions to Nepalese Studies* 34 (1): 45–57. Available at: http://www.thefreelibrary.com/Contributions+to+Nepalese+Studies/2007/January/1-p5289 (accessed on 10 August 2009).

Bhattarai, B. 2005. 'Censored: Nepal's Press under King Gyanendra's Regime', *Studies in Nepali History and Society* 10 (2): 359–401.

Bial, H. (ed). 2004. *The Performance Studies Reader.* London: Routledge.

Bjork Guneratne, K. 1999. *In the Circle of the Dance. Notes of an Outsider in Nepal.* Ithaca: Cornell University Press.

Boal, A. 1979. *Theatre of the Oppressed*. London: Pluto Press.

————. 1992. *Games for Actors and Non-Actors*. London and New York: Routledge.

————. 1995. *The Rainbow of Desire*. London and New York: Routledge

————. 1998. *Legislative Theatre*. London and New York: Routledge.

————. 2006. *The Aesthetics of the Oppressed*. New York: Routledge

Borgstrom, B. E. 1980. 'The Best of Two Worlds: Rhetoric of Autocracy and Democracy in Nepal', *Contributions to Indian Sociology* 14 (1): 95–129.

————. 1982. 'Power Structure and Political Speech', *MAN* 17 (N.S.): 313–27.

Bourdieu, P. 1990. *The Logics of Practice*. Cambridge: Polity Press.

————. 2003. Participant objectification, *JRAI* 9 (N.S): 223–39.

Bourgault, L. M. 2003. *Playing for Life. Performance in Africa in the Age of AIDS*. Durham: Carolina Academic Press.

Brandon, J and M. Banham. 1997. *The Cambridge Guide to Asian Theatre*. Cambridge: Cambridge University Press.

Brecht, B. 1964. *Brecht on Theatre. The Development of an Aesthetics*. London: Methuen Drama.

Breed, A. 2009. 'Participation for Liberation or Incrimination?' in *Applied theatre reader*, edited by T. Prentki and S. Preston, 148–54. London and New York: Routledge.

Brook, P. 1968. *The Empty Space*. London: Penguin Books.

Burghart, R. 1987. 'Gifts to the Gods: Power Property and Ceremonial in Nepal', in *Rituals of Royalty: Power and Ceremonial in Traditional Societies*, edited by David Cannadine and Simon Price, 237–70. Cambridge: Cambridge University Press.

————. 1993. 'The Political Culture of Panchayat Democracy', in *Nepal in the Nineties*, edited by M. Hutt, 1–13. New Delhi: Oxford University Press.

————. 1996. 'The Conditions of Listening: The Everyday Experience of Politics in Nepal', in *The Conditions of Listening. Essay on Religion, History and Politics in South Asia by Richard Burghart*, edited by C.J. Fuller and J. Spencer, 300–18. Delhi: OUP.

Burke, K. 1945. *Grammar of Motives*. New York: Prentice Hall.

Burstow, B. 2008. 'Invisible Theatre, Ethics, and the Adult Educator', *International Journal of lifelong education* 27 (3): 273–88.

Byam, D. L. 1999. *Community in Motion. Theatre for Development in Africa*. Westport: Bergin & Garvey.

Cannadine, D. and S. Price (eds). 1992. *Rituals of Royalty: Power and Ceremonial in Traditional Societies*. Cambridge: Cambridge University Press.

Caramitru, I. 1996. 'Ion Caramitru in Conversation with Christopher Barron and Maria Delgado', in *In Contact with the Gods? Directors talk Theatre*, edited by M. Delgado and P. Heritage, 55–66. Manchester and New York: Manchester University Press.

Carlson, M. 2004. *Performance. A Critical Introduction* (second edition). London and New York: Routledge

Carmody, J. 2002. 'The Comfort of Crisis', in *Theatre in Crisis? Performance Manifestos for a New Century*, edited by Maria M. Delgato and Caridad Svich, 22–24. Manchester: Manchester University Press.

Castaneda, Q. E. 2006. 'The Invisible Theatre of Ethnography: Performative Principles of Fieldwork', *Anthropological Quarterly* 79 (1): 47–76.

Centre for Investigative Journalism 2004. *People in the 'People's War'*. Lalitpur: Himal Association.

Chaudhary (Tharu), B. R. 2011. 'A Study on Free-Bonded Labourer (Mukta Kamaya) in Nepal., Master's Thesis. Graduate School for International Development and Cooperation, Hiroshima University.

Chaudhary, U. and N. Schwaiger. 2011. *Sklavenkind: Verkauft, Verschleppt, Vergessen – Mein Kampf für Nepals Tchter*. München: Knaur

Chuck, M. 1999. 'Performance Studio Workshop. Igoboelerin East', in *African Theatre in Development*, edited by M. Banham, J. Gibbs and F. Osofisan, 61–78. Bloomington and Indianapolis: Indiana University Press.

Clammer, J. 2015. *Art, Culture and International Development. Humanising Social Transformation*. New York: Routledge.

Clifford, J. 1988. *The Predicament of Culture. Twentieth-century Ethnography, Literature, and Art*. Cambridge and London: Harvard University Press.

Clifford, J. and G. E. Marcus. 1986. *Writing Culture. The Poetics and Politics of Ethnography*. Berkeley and Los Angeles: University of California Press.

Cohen, A. 1993. *Masquerade Politics: Explorations in the Structure of Urban Cultural Movements*. Berkeley: University of California Press.

Cohen-Cruz, J (ed.). 1998. *Radical Street Performance*. London and New York: Routledge.

Cohen-Cruz, J. and M. Schutzman (eds.). 1994. *Playing Boal. Theatre, Therapy, Activism*. London and New York: Routledge.

Cole, C. 2001. *Ghana's Concert Party Theatre*. Bloomington: Indiana University Press.

Cook, B. and U. Kothari. 2001. *Participation: The New Tyranny?* London: Zed Books.

Conquergood, D. 1982. 'Performing as a Moral Act: Ethical Dimensions of the Ethnography of Performance', *Literature in Performance* 5 (2): 1–13.

———. 1995. 'Of Caravans and Carnivals: Performance Studies in Motion', *The Drama Review* 39 (4): 137–41.

Cornwall, A. 2002. 'Making Spaces, Changing Places: Situating Participation in Development'. *IDS Working Paper 173*. Brighton: Institute of Development Studies.

Counsell, C. and L. Wolf (ed). 2001. *Performance Analysis*. London and New York: Routledge.

Cox, T. 1992. 'The Badi: Prostitution as a Social Norm among an Untouchable Caste of West Nepal', *Contribution to Nepalese Studies* 19 (1): 51–71.

Crapanzano, V. 1986. '"Hermes" Dilemma: The Masking of Subversion in Ethnographic Description', in *Writing Culture. The Poetics and Politics of Ethnography*, edited by James Clifford and George E. Marcus, 51–76. Berkerley and Los Angeles: University of California Press.

Da Costa, D. 2010. Introduction: Relocating Culture in Development and Development in Culture, *Third World Quarterly* 31 (4): 501–22.

Dahal, D. R. 2001. *Civil Society in Nepal: Opening the Ground for Questions*. Kathmandu: Centre for Development and Governance.

Davis, C. 2002. 'Dabali: A Brief History of Nepal's Theatre in Transition'. Mime Journal, 22: 92–103.

———. 2003. 'Dreams of Peach Blossoms: Cultural Memory in as Nepali play', *Asian Theatre Journal* 20 (2): 179–90.

———. 2009. 'Decade of Dreams: Democracy and the Birth of Nepal's Engaged Stage', 1980-1990, *Asian Theatre Journal* 26 (1): 94–110.

———. 2010. 'Dramas of Disillusionment: Nepal's Theatre 1990-2006', *Asian Theatre Journal* 27 (1): 23–39.

Debord, G. 1997. *La Società Dello Spettacolo (The Society of Spectacle)*. Milano: Baldini and Castoldi.

Delgado M. and P. Heritage (eds.). 1996. *In Contact with the Gods? Directors Talk Theatre*. Manchester and New York: Manchester University Press.

Delgado M. and C. Svich (eds.). 2002. *Theatre in Crisis? Performance Manifestos for a New Century*. Manchester: Manchester University Press.

Des Chene, M. 1996. 'In the Name of *Bikas*', *Studies in Nepali History and Society* 1 (2): 259–70.

Diamond, E. (ed.). 1996. *Performance and Cultural Politics*. New York: Routledge.

Diamond, E. 1996. 'Introduction', in *Performance and Cultural Politics*, edited by Elin Diamond, 1–12. New York: Routledge.

Dixit, K. M. 1996. 'Foreign Aid in Nepal: No Bang for the Buck', *Studies in Nepali History and Society* 2 (1): 173–86.

———. 2006. 'People Power in Nepal', *THTonline*, 8 May.

Dixit, K. M. and S. Ramachandran (eds.). 2002. *State of Nepal*. Kathmandu: Himal Books.

Dolan, J. 2005. *Utopia in Performance. Finding Hope at the Theatre*. Ann Arbor: University of Michigan Press.

Durkheim, E. 1976 [1915]. *The Elementary Forms of The Religious Life*. London: Allen and Unwin.

Dwyer, K. 1982. *Moroccan Dialogues*. Baltimora and London: John Hopkins University Press.

Edmondson, L. 2007. *Performance and Politics in Tanzania. The Nation on Stage*. Bloomington and Indianapolis: Indiana University Press.

Emigh, J. 1996. *Masked Performance. The Play of Self and Other in Ritual and Theatre*. Philadelphia: University of Philadelphia Press.

Endelman, M. 1995. *From Art to Politics. How Artistic Creations Shape Political Conceptions*. Chicago and London: University of Chicago Press.

Epskamp, K. 1989. *Theatre in Search of Social Change: The Relative Significance of Different Theatrical Approaches*. The Hague: Ceso Paperback No. 7.

————. 2006. *Theatre for Development. An Introduction to Context, Applications and Trainings*. London and New York: Zed Books.

Evans, R. 2010. 'Cultural Expression as Political Rhetoric: Young Bhutanese Refugees' Collective Action for Social Change', *Contemporary South Asia* 18 (3): 305–17.

Fabian, J. 1990. *Power and Performance: Ethnographic Explanations through Proverbial Wisdom and Theatre in Shaba, Zaire*. Madison: University of Wisconsin Press.

Fernandez, J. W. 2001. 'Creative Arguments of Images in Culture, and the Charnel House of Conventionality', in *Locating Cultural Creativity*, edited by John Liep, 17–30. London: Pluto Press.

Fernandez, J. W. and M. Taylor Huber (eds.). 2001. *Irony in Action. Anthropology, Practice, and the Moral Imagination*. Chicago: University of Chicago Press.

Firth, R. 1980. Review, *MAN (N.S.)* 15 (2): 387–89.

Fischer-Lichte, E. 2005. *Theatre, Sacrifice, Ritual. Exploring Forms of Political Theatre*. London and New York: Routledge.

————. 2008. *The Transformative Power of Performance. A New Aesthetics*. London and New York: Routledge.

Fortier, M. 1997. *Theory/Theatre. An introduction*. London: Routledge.

Forum for the Protection of Human Rights (FOPHUR). 1990. *Dawn of Democracy, People's Power in Nepal: Photo Documentary of the Movement for Restoration of Democracy from February to April 1990*. Kathmandu: Forum for the Protection of Human Rights.

Foucault, M. 1967. *Of Other Spaces*. Available at: http://foucault.info/documents/heteroTopia/foucault.heteroTopia.en.html, accessed on 5 June 2008.

Freire, P. 2004. *La Pedagogia degli Oppressi*. Torino: EGA Editore.

Friedman, J. 2001. 'The Iron Cage of Creativity: An Exploration', in *Locating Cultural Creativity*, edited by John Liep, 46–61. London: Pluto Press.

Friends of Needy Children (FNC). 2061. *Annual Progress Report 2061-2062.* Kathmandu: Nepal.

Friends of Needy Children. 2011. *Kamlari Movement for Sustainable Rehabilitation.* Kathmandu: Nepal.

Fujikura, T. 2001. Emancipation of Kamayas: Development, Social Movement, and Youth Activism in Post-Jana Andolan Nepal, *Himalayan Research Bulletin* XXI (1): 29–35.

————. 2013. *Discourses of Awareness: Development, Social Movements and the Practices of Freedom in Nepal.* Kathmandu: Martin Chautari.

Fuller, J. C. and V. Benei (eds.). 2001. *The Everyday State and Society in Modern India.* London: Hurst & Company.

Gautam, B. 2007. 'Nagarik Andolan: Bhram ra Yatayat' (Civil Society Movement: Journey and Transportation), *Naya Patrika,* 27 August.

Gaventa, J. 2006. 'Finding the Spaces for Change: A Power Analysis', *IDS Bulletin* 37 (6): 23–33.

Gell, A. 1998. *Art and Agency: And Anthropological Theory.* Oxford: OUP.

Gellner, D. N. 1997. 'Ethnicity and Nationalism in the World's only Hindu State', in *Nationalism and Ethnicity in Nepal,* edited by David N. Gellner and Joanna Pfaff-Czarnecka, 3-31.

Gellner, D. (ed). 1999. 'Religion, Politics, and Ritual. Remarks on Geertz and Bloch', *Social Anthropology* 7 (2): 135–53.

————. 2003. *Resistance and the State: Nepalese Experience.* New Delhi: Social Science Press.

Gellner D. and E. Hirsch (eds.). 2001. *Inside Organizations: Anthropologists at Work.* Oxford: Berg

Gellner, D., J. Pfaff-Czarnecka, and J. Whelpton (eds.). 1997. *Nationalism and Ethnicity in a Hindu Kingdom. The Politics of Culture in Contemporary Nepal.* Amsterdam: Harwood Academic Publishers.

Gellner, D. and K. Hachhethu (eds.). 2008. *Local Democracy in South Asia. Microprocesses of Democratization in Nepal and its Neighbours.* Delhi: Sage.

Gellner, D. N. and M. B. Karki. 2007. 'The Sociology of Activism in Nepal: Some Preliminary Considerations', in *Political and Social Transformation in North India and Nepal: Social Dynamics in Northern South Asia,* edited by H. Ishi, D. Gellner and K. Nawa, 361–93.

Gellner, D. and D. Quigley. 2008 [1999]. *Contested Hierarchies. A Collaborative Ethnography of Caste among the Newar of the Kathmandu Valley, Nepal.* Oxford: Oxford University Press.

Geertz, C. 1980. *Negara. The Theatre State in Nineteenth-Century Bali.* Princeton: Princeton University Press.

————. 1983. *Local Knowledge: Further Essays in Interpretive Anthropology.* New York: Basic Books.

————. 1988. *Works and Lives: The Anthropologist as Author.* Stanford: Stanford University Press

George, D. 1995. 'Theatre of the Oppressed and Teatro de Arena: In and Out of context', *Latin America Theatre Review* 28 (2): 39–54.

Ghimire, R. 2005. 'Jantaka Gayak' [People's Singer], *Nepal,* 6 Kartik 2062 (Sunday, 23 October): 74–77.

Ghimire, Y. 2004. 'Yo Ho Jana Rangamanch' (This is People's Theatre). *Nepathya* 6: 12–13.

————. 2007. 'Pracharbadi Natak'. *Kantipur,* (21 July).

Giacche', P. 2004. *L'altra Visione Dell'altro. Una Equazione tra Antropologia e Teatro.* Napoli: L'Ancora del Mediterraneo.

Giri, A. 2005. 'Andolan ka Gayak', *Samaya* (June 20): 55.

Giroux, H. A. 2005. *Border Crossing: Cultural Workers and the Politics of Education.* New York and Oxon: Routledge.

Gledhill, S. 2000 [1994]. *Power and its Disguises. Anthropological Perspectives on Politics.* London: Pluto Press.

Goffman, E. 1990 [1959]. *The Presentation of Self in Everyday Life.* London: Penguin Books.

Goodman, N. 1978. *Ways of Worldmaking.* Indianapolis: Hackett Publishing Company.

Goodwin, J, J. Jasper and F. Polletta. 2001. *Passionate Politics. Emotions and Social Movements.* Chicago and London: The University of Chicago Press.

Gramsci, A. 1971. *Selections from the Prison Notebooks,* edited and translated by Hoare and Geoffrey Nowell Smith. London: Lawrence & Wishart.

————. 1975. *Quaderni dal Carcere,* edited by V. Gerratana. Torino: Einaudi.

————. 2005. *Selections from the Prison Notebooks.* London: Lawrence & Wishart Ltd.

Grandin, I. 1993. 'Music as Message', *Himal* 6 (6): 24.

————. 1994. 'To Change the Face of the Country. Nepalese Progressive Songs Under Panchayat Democracy', *Journal of South Asian Literature* 29 (1): 175–89.

————. 2005. 'Music under Development: Children's Songs, Artists, and the (Panchayat) State', *Studies in Nepali History and Society* 10 (2): 255–93.

————. 2011 (1999). *Music and Media in Local Life. Music Practice in a Newar Neighborhood in Nepal.* Kathmandu: Mandal Book Point.

————. 2017. 'Mobilising Meanings: Local Cultural Activism and Nepal's Public Culture', in *Political Change and Public Culture in Nepal,* edited by M. Hutt and P. Onta. New Delhi: Cambridge University Press.

Grieve, G. P. 2004. 'Forging Mandalic Space: Bhaktapur, Nepal's Cow Procession and the Improvisation of Tradition', *Numen* 51 (4): 468–512.

Grotowski, J. 1968. *Towards a Poor Theatre*. New York: Simon and Shuster.

Guneratne, A. 1998. Modernization, the State and the Construction of a Tharu Identity in Nepal, *The Journal of Asian Studies* 57 (3): 749–73.

———. 2002. *Many Tongues, One People. The Making of Tharu Identity in Nepal*. Ithaca and London: Cornell University Press.

Gupta, C. B. 1991. *The Indian Theatre*. New Delhi: Munshiram Manoharlal Publishers Pvt. Ldt.

Gurung, A. 2011. 'The Changing Ethos of Women in Nepali Theatre', in *IMAP Reader: A Collection of Essays on Art and Theatre in Kathmandu*, edited by S. Uprety and R. Piya, 1–16. Kathmandu: Himal Books.

Hachhethu, K. 1990. 'Mass Movement 1990', *Contributions to Nepalese Studies* 17 (2): 177–201.

———. 2007. 'Political Leadership in Nepal: Image, Environment and Composition', *Contributions to Nepalese Studies* 34 (1): 25–45.

Hachhethu, K and D. Gellner. 2010. 'Trajectories of Democracy and Restructuring of the State', in *Rutledge Handbook of South Asian Politics*, edited by P. Brass, 131–46. London and New York: Routledge.

Hallam, E. and T. Ingold (eds). 2007. *Creativity and Cultural Improvisation*. Oxford and New York: Berg.

Handelman, D. 1998 [1990]. *Models and Mirrors. Towards an Anthropology of Public Events*. New York: Berghahn Books.

Hansen, K. 1983. 'Indian Folk Traditions and the Modern Theatre', *Asian Folklore Studies* 42 (1): 77–89.

———. 1992. *Grounds for Play: The Nautanki Theatre of North India*. Berkeley: University of California Press.

———. 2003. 'Languages on Stage: Linguistic Pluralism and Community formation in the Ninenteenth-Century Parsi Theatre', *Modern Asian Studies* 37 (2): 381–405.

———. 2005. *The Parsi Theatre. Its origin and development by Somnath Gupt*. New Delhi: Seagull Books.

Harding, F. N.d. 'Theatre for Development'. London: SOAS Offprint 4870.

———. 1998. *African Theatre for Development. Art for Self Determination*, edited by K. Salhi, 5–22. Exeter: Intellect.

———. 1999. 'Fifteen Years between Benue and Katsina Workshops, Nigeria', in *African Theatre in Development*, edited by M. Banham, J. Gibbs and F. Ofisan, 99–112. Bloomington and Indianapolis: Indiana University Press.

Harper, I. 2003. 'A Heterotopia of Resistance: Health, Community Forestry and

Challenges to State Centralization in Nepal', in *Resistance and the State: Nepalese Experience*, edited by D. Gellner, 33–82. New Delhi: Social Science Press.

Hashmi, S. 1989. *The Right to Perform. Selected Writings of Safdar Hashmi*. Delhi: SAHMAT.

Hastrup, K. 1995. *A Passage to Anthropology. Between Experience and Theory*. London and New York: Routledge.

———. (ed). 1996. *The Performers' Village. Times, Theories and Techniques at ISTA*. Copenhagen: Drama.

———. 1998. 'Theatre As a Site of Passage: Some Reflections on the Magic of Acting', in *Ritual, Performance, Media*, edited by F. Hughes-Freeland, 29–45. New York and London: Routledge.

———. 2001. 'Othello's Dance: Cultural Creativity and Human Agency', in *Locating Cultural Creativity*, edited by J. Liep, 31–45. London: Pluto Press.

———. 2004a. *Action. Anthropology in the Company of Shakespeare*. Copenhagen: Museum Tusculanum Press.

———. 2004b. 'Getting It Right: Knowledge and Evidence in Anthropology', *Anthropological Theory* 4 (4): 455–72.

Haugerud, A. 2004. 'The Art of Protest', *Anthropology News* 45 (8): 4–5.

———. 2005. 'Intentions, Innovations, Ideas. Leave No Billionaire Behind: Political Dissent as Performance Parody'. Available at: http://www.princeton.edu/prok/issues/1-1/inventions.xml (accessed on 28 October 2007).

Heathcote, S. 2009. 'Drama as a Process for Change', in *Applied Theatre Reader*, edited by T. Prentki and S. Preston, 200–06. London and New York: Routledge.

Heaton Shrestha, C. 2001. *'Our Differences Don't Make a Difference': Practicing Civil Society in Nepal's Non-Governmental Sector*. PhD dissertation. SOAS, University of London.

———. 2002. 'NGOs as *Thekadars* or *Sevak*: Identity Crisis in Nepal's Non-Governmental Sector', *European Bulletin of Himalayan Research* 22: 5–36.

———. 2006a. 'Representing INGO-NGO Relations in Nepal: Are We Being donor-centric?' *Studies in Nepali History and Society* 11 (1): 65–96.

———. 2006b. '"They Can't Mix the Way We Can". Bracketing Differences and the Professionalization of NGOs in Nepal', in *Development Brokers and Translators: the Ethnography of Aid and Agencies*, edited by D. Lewis and D. Mosse, 195– 216. Broomfield: Kumarian Press.

Heaton Shrestha, C. and R. Adhikari. 2010. 'Antipolitics and Counterpolitics in Nepal's Civil Society: The Case of Nepal's Citizen's Movement', *Voluntas* 21: 293–316.

———. 2011. 'NGOization and De-NGOization of Public Action in Nepal: The Role of Organizational Culture in Civil Society Politicality', *Journal of Civil Society* 7 (1): 41–61.

————. 2014. 'Struggling on Two Fronts during Nepal's Insurgency: The Citizen's Movement for Democracy and Peace and the Meanings of Civil Society', *European Bulletin of Himalayan Research* 42: 39–74.

Hilhorst, D. 2003. *The Real World of NGOs*. London and New York: Zed Books.

Himalayan News Service. 2013. 'Kamlaris in Capital City in Quest of Justice', 28 April.

Hobsbawm, E. and T. Ranger (eds). 1983. *The Invention of tradition*. Cambridge: Cambridge University Press.

Hoek, B. Van der. 1990. 'Does Divinity Protect the King? Ritual and Politics in Nepal', *Contributions to Nepalese Studies* 17 (2): 147–55.

————. 1993. 'Kathmandu as a Sacrificial Arena', in *Urban Symbolism*, edited by P.M. Nas, 361–77. Leiden: Brill.

————. 1994. 'The Death of the Divine Dancers: The Conclusion of the Bhadrakali Pyakham in Kathmandu', in *Anthropology of Nepal. Peoples, Problems and Processes*, edited by M. Allen, 374–404. Kathmandu: Mandala Book Point.

Hoem, I. 2004. *Theatre and Political Process: Staging Identities in Tokelau and New Zealand*. New York: Berghahn Books

Hoftun, M., W. Raeper and J. Whelpton. 1999. *People, Politics & Ideology. Democracy and Social Change in Nepal*. Kathmandu: Mandala Bookpoint.

Hughes-Freeland, F. (ed). 1998. *Ritual, Performance, Media*. London and New York: Routledge.

————. 2007. 'Charisma and Celebrity in Indonesian Politics', *Anthropological Theory* 7 (2): 177–200.

Hughes-Freeland, F. and M. M. Crain (eds). 1998. *Recasting Ritual. Performance, Media, Identity*. London and New York: Routledge.

Hutt, M. 1991. *Himalayan Voices. An Introduction to Modern Nepali Literature*. Delhi: Motilal Banarsidass Publishers.

————. 1993. 'The Nepali Literature of the Democracy Movement and its Aftermath', In *Nepal in the Nineties*, edited by Michael Hutt, 82–97. New Delhi: Oxford University Press.

————. 1997. *Modern Literary Nepali. An Introductory Reader*. New Delhi: Oxford University Press.

————. 2002. 'Rup Chand Bista', in *Censorship. A World Encyclopedia*, edited by D. Jones, 246–47. London and Chicago: Fitzroy Dearborn Publishers.

————. 2004. *Himalayan 'People's War': Nepal's Maoist Rebellion*. London: C. Hurst and Co.

————. 2006. 'Things That Should Not Be Said: Censorship and Self-censorship in the Nepali Press Media, 2001-02', *The Journal of Asian Studies* 65 (2): 362–92.

————. 2012. 'Reading Nepali Maoist Memoirs', *Studies in Nepali History and Society* 17 (1): 107–42

————. 2013. 'The Disappearance and Reappearance of Yogmaya: Recovering a Nepali Revolutionary Icon', *Contemporary South Asia* 21 (4): 382–97.

Hutt, M. (ed). 1993. *Nepal in the Nineties*. New Delhi: Oxford University Press.

Hutt, M. and P. Onta. 2017. *Political Change and Public Culture in Nepal*. New Delhi: Cambridge University Press.

Jackson, A. 2009. 'Provoking the Intervention', in *Applied Theatre Reader*, edited by T. Prentki and S. Preston. London and New York: Routledge.

Jan Sanskritik Mahasangh (People's Cultural Federation). Unpublished. *Mahan Janyuddha Pratinidhi Githaru* (Songs Presented during the Great People's War).

Jasper, J. M. 1999. *The Art of Moral Protest. Culture, Biography, and Creativity in Social Movements*. Chicago and London: University of Chicago Press.

Jha, P. 2014. *Battles of the New Republic. A Contemporary History of Nepal*. London: Hurst & Company.

Jowett, G. S. and V. O'Donnell. 2006. *Propaganda and Persuasion*. London and New Delhi: Sage Publications.

Judson, F. 1987. 'Sandinista Revolutionary Morale', *Latin American Perspectives* 14 (1):19–42

Kabeer, N. 2005. Gender Equality and Women's Empowerment: A Critical Analysis of the Third Millennium Development Goal, *Gender and Development* 13 (1): 13–24.

Kapferer, J. 2007. 'The Arts and State Power', *Social Analysis* 51 (1): 1–12.

Kapur, A. 2006. *Actors, Pilgrims, Kings and Gods. The Ramlila at Ramnagar*. Seagull Books: London.

Karki, A. and B. Bhattarai (eds). 2003. *Whose War? Economic and Socio-Cultural Impacts of Nepal's Maoist-Government Conflict*. Kathmandu: NGO Federation of Nepal

Kershaw, B. 1992. *The Politics of Performance. Radical Theatre as Cultural Intervention*. London and New York: Routledge.

————.1999. *The Radical in Performance. Between Brecht and Baudrillard*. London and New York: Routledge.

Kertzer, D. 1988. *Ritual, Politics and Power*. Yale: Yale University Press.

Khanal, S. 2007. 'Committeed Insurgents, a Divided State and the Maoist Insurgency in Nepal', in *Contentious Politics and Democratization in Nepal*, edited by Mahendra Lawoti, 75–94. Kathmandu: Bhrikuti Academic Publications and Sage Publications.

Kidd, R. n.d. 'Theatre for Development': Diary of a Zimbabwe Workshop'. London: SOAS Offprint 473.

Korvald, T. 1994. 'The Dancing Gods of Bhaktapur and their Audience', in *Anthropology of Nepal. Peoples, Problems and Processes*, edited by M. Allen, 405–15. Kathmandu: Mandala Book Point.

Krauskopff, G. 2003. 'An "Indigenous Minority" in a Border Area: Tharu Ethnic

Associations, NGOs, and the Nepalese State', in *Resistance and the State: Nepalese Experiences*, edited by D.N. Gellner, 199–243. New Delhi: Social Science Press.

————. 2009. 'Intellectuals and Ethnic Activism: Writings on the Tharu Past', in *Ethnic Activism and Civil Society in South Asia*, edited by D. N. Gellner, 241–68. New Delhi: Sage.

Krauskopff, G. and M. Lecomte-Tilouine. 1996. *Célébrer le pouvoir. Dasai, une Fête Royale au Nepal*. Paris: CNRS éditions.

Kropf, M. 2003. 'In the Wake of Commercialized Entertainment: An Inquiry into the State of Masked Dance-dramas in the Kathmandu Valley', *Contributions to Nepalese Studies* 30 (1): 53–103.

Kunnath, G. J. 2006. 'Becoming a Naxalite in Rural Bihar: Class Struggle and its Contradictions', *The Journal of Peasant Studies* 33 (1): 89–123.

Klaic, D. 2002. 'The Crisis of Theatre? The Theatre of Crisis!' in *Theatre in Crisis? Performance Manifestos for a New Century*, edited by Caridad Svich and Maria M. Delgado, 144–59. Manchester: Manchester University Press.

Kirby, M. D. 1987. *A Formalist Theatre*. Philadelphia: University of Pennsylvania Press. Iravati. 2003. *Performing Artists in Ancient India*. New Delhi: D.K. Printworld.

Lakier, G. 2000. 'The Myth of the State is Real: Notes on the Study of the State in Nepal', *Studies in Nepali History and Society* 10 (1): 135–70.

————. 2007. 'Illiberal Democracy and the Problem of Law: Street Protest and Democratization in Multiparty Nepal', in *Contentious Politics and Democratization in Nepal*, edited by M. Lawoti, 251–72. Kathmandu: Bhrikuti Academic Publications and Sage Publications.

Lamsal, J. N. 2006. 'A Journey from Text to Visuality in Abhi Subedi's *Fire in the Monastery*'. MA Dissertation, Central Department of English, Tribhuvan University, Kathmandu.

Landi, R. J. 1993. *Persona and Performance. The Meaning of Role in Drama, Therapy and Everyday Life*. London and Bristol: Jessica Kingsley Publishers

Lang, B. and F. Williams (eds). 1972. *Marxism & Art. Writings in Aesthetics and Criticism*. New York: David McKay Company Inc.

Lawoti, M. 2005. *Towards a Democratic Nepal: Inclusive Political Institutions for a Multicultural Society*. New Delhi: Sage Publications.

Lawoti, M. (ed). 2007. *Contentious Politics and Democratization in Nepal*. Kathmandu: Bhrikuti Academic Publications and Sage Publications.

Lawoti, M. and A. Pahadi (eds). 2010. *The Maoist Insurgency in Nepal. Revolution in the twenty-first century*. New York: Routledge.

Lecomte-Tilouine, M. 2004. 'Regicide and Maoist Revolutionary Warfare in Nepal: Modern Incarnations of a Warrior Kingdom', *Anthropology Today* 20 (1): 13–19.

————. 2006. 'Kill one. He becomes One Hundred': Martyrdom as Generative Sacrifice in the Nepal People's War', *Social Analysis* 50 (1): 51–72.

————. 2010. 'Martyrs and Living Martyrs of the People's War in Nepal', *South Asia Multidisciplinary Academic Journa* , Thematic Issue 4, Modern Achievers: Role Models in South Asia. Available at: http://samaj.revues.org/index3018.html.

————. 2013. *Revolution in Nepal: An Anthropological and Historical Approach to People's War.* Oxford: Oxford University Press.

Lefebvre, H. 1991. *The Production of Space.* Oxford: Blackwell.

Lemert, C. and A. Branaman (eds). 1997. *The Goffman Reader.* Oxford: Blackwell.

Levy, R. I. and K. R. Rajopadhyaya. 1990. *Mesocosm: Hinduism and the Organization of a Traditional Newar City in Nepal.* Berkeley: University of California Press.

Li, T. M. 1999. 'Compromising Power: Development, Culture and Rule in Indonesia', *Cultural Anthropology* 14 (3): 295–322.

Lidke, J. 2006. 'Devi's Dance: The Interweaving of Politics, Mysticism, and Culture in Kathmandu Valley', *International Journal of Hindu Studies* 10 (1): 35–57.

Lietchy, M. 1997. 'Selective Exclusion: Foreigners, Foreign Goods, and Foreignness in Modern Nepali History', *Studies in Nepali Society and History* 2 (1): 5–68.

————. 2003. *Suitably Modern: Making Middle-class Culture in a Consumer Society.* Princeton: Princeton University Press.

Liep, J. (ed). 2001. *Locating Cultural Creativity.* London: Pluto Press

Linds, W. 2006. 'Metaxis: Dancing (in) the In-between', in *A Boal Companion. Dialogues on theatre and cultural politics,* edited by J. Cohen-Cruz and M. Schutzman, 114–24. New York: Routledge.

Lukes, S. 2005. *Power. A Radical View.* London: Palgrave Macmillan.

Long, N. and A. Long (eds). 1992. *Battlefields of Knowledge. The Interlocking of Theory and Practice in Social Research and Development.* London and New York: Routledge.

Madison, D. S. and J. Hamera. 2006. 'Performance Studies at the Intersections', in *The SAGE Handbook of Performance Studies,* edited by D.S. Madison and J. Hamera, xi–xxv. New York: Sage.

Malla, P. 1980. *Nepali Rangmanch* [Nepali Theatre]. Kathmandu: Royal Nepal Academy

————. 2009. *Kantipurko Rangmanch* (Theatre of Kathmandu). Kathmandu: Aarohan Gurukul.

Manjul. 1988. *Samjhanaka Pailaharu: Giti Yatrako Samsmaran* (The Footsteps of Memory: Memoir of a Musical Journey). Kathmandu: Ananda.

Mao Tse-Tung.1960. *On Literature and Art.* Peking: Foreign Language Press.

————. 1967. 'Talks at the Yenan Forum on Literature and Art', *Peking Review* 22: 5–18.

————. 1972. 'On Literature and Art', in *Marxism and Art: Writings in Aesthetics and Criticism*, edited by B. Lang and F. Williams, 108–19. New York: David McKay.

————. 1972b. 'On The Correct Handling of Contradictions among the People', in *Marxism and Art: Writings in Aesthetics and Criticism*, edited by B. Lang and F. Williams, 120–25. New York: David McKays.

March, K. 2002. *'If Each Comes Halfway': Meeting Tamang Women in Nepal*. Ithaca: Cornell University Press.

Marcus, G. E. 1995. 'Ethnography in/of the World System: The Emergence of Multi-sited Ethnography', *Annual Review of Anthropology* 24: 95–117.

————. 1998. *Ethnography through Think and Thin*. Princeton: Princeton University Press.

Marx, K. 1859. *A Contribution to the Critique of Political Economy*. Available at: https://www.marxists.org/archive/marx/works/download/Marx_Contribution_to_the_Critique_of_Political_Economy.pdf, accessed on 20 February 2008.

Maslak, M. A. 2003. *Daughters of the Tharu. Gender, Ethnicity, Religion, and the Education of Nepali Girls*. London and New York: Routledge.

Maskarinec, G. G. 2000 [1995]. *The Rulings of the Night. An Ethnography of Shaman Oral Texts*. Kathmandu: Mandala Bookpoint.

McDonaugh, C. 1997. 'Losing Ground, Gaining Ground: Land and Change in a Tharu Community in Dang, West Nepal', in *Nationalism and Ethnicity in a Hindu Kingdom. The Politics of Culture in Contemporary Nepal*, edited by D.N. Gellner, J. Pfaff-Czarnecka, and J. Whelpton, 275–98. Amsterdam: Harwood.

Mda, Z. 1993. *When People Play People: Development Communication through Theatre*. London: Zed Books.

Mehrotra, D. P. 2006. *Gulab Bai. The Queen of Nautanki Theatre*. New Delhi: Penguin Books.

Meyerhoff, B and J. Ruby. 1982. 'Introduction', in *A Crack in the Mirror: Reflexive Perspectives in Anthropology*, edited by J. Ruby, 1–34. Philadelphia: University of Pennsylvania Press.

Micheal, R. B. 1983. 'Foundation Myths of Two Denominations of Virasaivism: Viraktas and Gurusthalins', *The Journal of Asian Studies* 42 (2): 309–22.

Miller, R. 2000. *Researching Life Stories and Family Histories*. London: Sage.

Mines, M. and V. Gourishankar. 1990. 'Leadership and Individuality in South Asia: The Case of the South Indian Big-man', *The Journal of Asian Studies* 49 (4): 761–86.

Mohan, D. 2004a. 'Jana Sanskriti's Theatre and Political Practice in Rural Bengal. The Making of Popular Culture', *South Asian Popular Culture* 2 (1): 39–53.

————. 2004b. 'Reimagining Community: Scripting Power and Changing the Subject through Jana Sanskriti's Political Theatre in Rural North India', *Journal of Contemporary Ethnography* 33 (2): 178–217.

————. N. A. 'From Alienation to Healthy Culture: The Particularity of Jana Sanskriti's use of "Theatre of the Oppressed in Rural Bengal"'. Available at: www.janasanskriti.org/jsforwebsiteonto.doc (accessed in May 2008).

Monclair, P. 2009. 'Altogether Now? Reconsidering the Merits of Participation of Child-Rights Theatre', in *Applied Theatre Reader*, edited by T. Prentki and S. Preston. London and New York: Routledge.

Moore, R. D. 2006. *Music and Revolution. Cultural Change in Socialist Cuba*. Berkeley and Los Angeles: University of California Press.

Morris, N. 1986. 'Canto Porque es Necesario Cantar: The New Song Movement in Chile, 1973-1983', *Latin American Research Review* 21 (2): 117–36.

Mosse, D. 2004. 'Is Good Policy Unimplementable? Reflections on the Ethnography of Aid Policy and Practice', *Development and Change* 35 (4): 639–71.

————. 2005a. *Cultivating Development: An Ethnography of Aid Policy and Practice*. London: Pluto Press.

————. 2005b. 'Anti-social anthropology? Objectivity, Objection and the Ethnography of Public Policy and Professional Communities'. Malinowski Memorial Lecture.

————. 2015. 'Misunderstood, Misrepresented, Contested? Anthropological Knowledge Production in Question', *Focaal* 72 (10): 128–37.

Mottin, M. 2007. 'Dramas of Development: Theatre for Development or the Development of Theatre?' *Studies in Nepali History and Society* 12 (2): 321–47.

————. 2010. 'Rehearsing for Life: Theatre for Social Change in Kathmandu, Nepal', PhD Thesis. London: SOAS University of London.

————. 2010. 'Catchy Melodies and Clenched Fists. Performance as Politics in Maoist Cultural Programs', in *The Maoist Insurgency in Nepal. Revolution in the Twenty-first Century*, edited by M. Lawoti and A. Pahadi, 52–72. New York: Routledge.

————. 2017. 'Protests, Space and Creativity: Theatre as a Site for the Affective Construction of Democracy in Nepal', in *Political change and Public Culture in Nepal*, edited by M. Hutt and P. Onta. New Delhi: Cambridge University Press.

Mouffe, C. 1979. 'Hegemony and Ideology in Marxism', in *Gramsci & Marxist Theory*, edited by Chantal Mouffe, 168–204. London: Routledge & Kegan Paul.

MS Nepal. 2003. 'The Power of Theatre. Uses of Theatre for Conflict Transformation, Empowerment and Social Change', report from a workshop of Asian People's Theatre Groups. MS Nepal.

Mundi, S. 2000. *Cultural Policy. A Short Guide*. Strasbourg: Council of Europe Publishing.

Nepathya, issues from 2005 to 2007, Kathmandu: Gurukul.

Munier, A. and M. Etherton. 2006. 'Child Rights Theatre for Development in Rural Bangladesh: A Case-study', *Research in Drama Education: The Journal of Applied Theatre and Performance*, 11 (2): 175–83.

Nepal Youth Foundation. 2004. *Kamlari* (documentary).

Nicholson, H. 2009. *Theatre and Education*. London: Palgrave Macmillan.

Obeyesekere, R.1999. *Sri Lankan Theatre in a Time of Terror. Political Satire in a Permitted Space*. New Delhi: Sage publications.

Onesto, L. 2002. 'Killing the News. Censorship and Jailing of Journalists under the State of Emergency', *Revolutionary Worker* 1160 (28 July 2002). Available at: http://www. lionesto.net/articles/onesto/nepaljournalists.htm, accessed on 10 August 2009.

——. 2006. *Dispaches from the People's War*. Pluto: London.

——. 2007. 'The Evolution of the Maoist Revolution in Nepal in an Adverse International Environment', in *Contentious Politics and Democratization in Nepal*, edited by M. Lawoti, 120–42. Kathmandu: Bhrikuti Academic Publications and Sage Publications.

Onta, P. 1996a. 'Ambivalence Denied: The Making of Rastrya Itihas in Panchayat Era Textbooks', *Contributions to Nepalese Studies* 23 (1): 213–54.

——. 1996b. 'Creating a Brave Nepali Nation in British India: The Rhetoric of Jati Improvement, Rediscovery of Bhanubhakta, and the Writing of Bir History', *Studies in Nepali History and Society* 1 (1): 37–76.

——. 1997. 'Activities in a "Fossil state"': Balakrishna Sama and the Improvisation of Nepali Identity', *Studies in Nepali History and Society* 2 (1): 69–102.

——. 2002. 'Critiquing the Media Boom', in *State of Nepal*, edited by K.M. Dixit and S. Ramachandaran, 253–69. Kathmandu: Himal Books.

——. 2006. *Mass-media in Post-1990 Nepal*. Kathmandu: Martin Chautari.

Orioli, W. 2001. *Teatro come Terapia*. Cesena (FC): Macro Edizioni.

Passetti, E. 1996. *Conversazioni con Paulo Freire. Il Viandante dell'Ovvio*. Milano: Elèuthera.

Pettigrew, J. 2013. *Maoists at the Hearth: Everyday Life in Nepal's Civil War*. Philadelphia: University of Pennsylvania Press.

Pettigrew, J. S. and S. Shneiderman. 2004. 'Women and the Maobadi: Ideology and Agency in Nepal's Maoist Movement', *Himal Southasian* 17 (1): 19–29.

Pfaff-Czarnecka, J. 1997. 'Vestiges and Visions: Cultural Change in the Process of Nation-Building in Nepal', in *Nationalism and Ethnicity in a Hindu Kingdom. The Politics of Culture in Contemporary Nepal*, edited by D. Gellner, J. Pfaff-Czarnecka and J. Whelpton, 419–70. Amsterdam: Harwood Academic Publishers.

Pigg, S. L. 1992. 'Inventing Social Categories through Place: Social Representations and Development in Nepal', *Comparative Studies in Society and History* 34 (3): 491–513.

——. 1993. 'Unintended Consequences: The Ideological Impact of Development in Nepal', *South Asia Bulletin* XIII (1&2): 45–58.

——. 1996. 'The Credible and the Credulous: the Question of "villagers" beliefs in Nepal', *Cultural Anthropology* 11 (2): 160–201.

Pigg, S. L. and L. Pike. 2004. 'Knowledges, Attitudes, Beliefs and Practices', in *Sexual Sites, Seminal Attitudes: Sexualities and Masculinity in South Asia*, edited by Sanjay Srivastava, 271–99. New Delhi and London: Sage.

Pink, S., L. Kurti and A. I. Afonso (eds). 2004. *Working Images. Visual Research and Representation in Ethnography*. London and New York: Routledge.

Plastow, J. 2009. 'Practising for Revolution? The Influence of Augusto Boal in Brazil and Africa', *Journal of Transatlantic Studies* 7 (3): 294–303.

Pokharel, S. 2004. 'Kachahari Natakko Katha' (The Story of Kachahari Natak). *Nepathya* 6: 8–11.

Pottier, J. 1993 (ed). *Practising Development: Social Science Perspectives*. London: Routledge.

Prachanda. 1991. Second National Conference CPN (Maoist). Available at: http://www.massline.info/nepal/cpnm_spc.ml.htm, accessed in February 2007.

Prendergast, M. and J. Saxton. 2009. *Applied Theatre: International Case Studies and Challenges for Practice*. Bristol: Intellect.

Prentki, T. 1998. 'Must the Show Go On? The Case for Theatre for Development', *Development in Practice* 8 (4): 419–30.

Prentki, T. and S. Preston. 2009. *The Applied Theatre Reader*. London and New York: Routledge.

Prentki T. and J. Selman. 2000. *Popular Theatre in Political Culture. Britain and Canada in Focus*. Bristol and Portland: Intellect.

Prickett, S. 2007. 'Guru or Teacher? Shishya or Student? Pedagogic Shifts in South Asian Dance Training in India and in Britain', *South Asian Research* 27 (1): 25–41.

Pavis, P. (ed). 1996. *The Intercultural Performance Reader*. London and New York: Routledge.

———. 2003. *Analyzing Performance. Theatre, Dance and Film*. Ann Arbor: University of Michigan Press.

Raeper, W. and M. Hoftun. 1992. *Spring Awakening. An Account of the 1990 Revolution in Nepal*. New Delhi: Penguin Books.

Rai, S. 2060 B. S. 'Jantaka Git: Nirantara ra Sandarbhikata'. *Sramik Khabar*, 5–9 Cait.

———. 2060 B.S. 'Kasari Suru Bhayo Jangiti Gayanko Parampara (How the Tradition of People's Songs Started)'. *Sramik Khabar*, 12–16 Cait.

Raj, P. A. 2001. *'Kay Gardeko?' The Royal Massacre in Nepal*. New Delhi: Rupa & Co.

Ramachandaran, S. and K.M. Dixit. 2002. *State of Nepal*. Kathmandu: Himal Books.

Raj, P. 2006. *The Dancing Democracy. The Power of the Third Eye*. New Delhi: Rupa Publication.

Rana, S. P. 1999. *A Chronicle of Rana Rule*. Kathmandu: P.Rana

Rawal, B. 2047 B.S. *Nepalma Samyabadi Andolanko: Adbav ra Bikash* (Communist Movement in Nepal: Rise and Development). Kathmandu: Pairavi Prakashan.

Ripping, A. and P. Fleming. 2007. 'Brute Force: Medieval Foundation Myths and Three Modern Organisations' Quests for Hegemony', *Management and Organisational History* 1 (1): 51–70.

Rijal, S. 2007. 'Modern Theatre in Nepal: A Need for Aesthetic Acculturation', *Studies in Nepali History and Society* 12 (1): 25–53.

Rockhill, G. 2004. 'Translators Introduction', in *The Politics of Aesthetics*, edited by J. Rancière. London: Continuum.

Rosaldo, R. 1986. 'From the Door of His Tent: The Fieldworker and the Inquisitor', in *Writing Culture. The Poetics and Politics of Ethnography*, edited by J. Clifford and G.E. Marcus, 77–97. Berkeley and Los Angeles: University of California Press.

Routledge, P. 2010. 'Nineteen Days in April: Urban Protest and Democracy in Nepal', *Urban Studies Journal* 47 (6): 1279–99.

Ruby, J. 1982. *A Crack in the Mirror: Reflexive Perspectives in Anthropology*. Philadelphia: University of Pennsylvania Press.

Sales, M. de. 2003. 'Remarks on Revolutionary Songs and Iconography', *European Bulletin of Himalayan Research* 24: 5–24.

Salhi, K. (ed). 1998. *African Theatre for Development. Art for Self Determination*. Exeter: Intellect.

Samana Parivar. 2006. *East Tour*, VCD 1 and 2, unpublished.

Sax, W. S. 1995. *The Gods at Play. Lila in South Asia*. New York and Oxford: Oxford University Press

Scarry, E. 1985. *The Body in Pain. The Making and Unmaking of the World*. New York and Oxford: Oxford University Press.

Schechner, R. 1987. 'Victor Turner's Last Adventure', in *The Anthropology of Performance*, edited by Victor Tuner, 7–20. New York: Performing Arts Journal Publication.

———. 1988. *Performance Theory*. London: Routledge.

———. 1993. *The Future of Ritual. Writings on Culture and Performance*. London and New York: Routledge.

———. 2002. *Performance Studies. An Introduction*. London: Routledge.

Schechner, R. and W. Appel (eds). 1990. *By Means of Performance. Intercultural Studies of Theatre and Ritual*. Cambridge: Cambridge University Press.

Schechner, R. and V. Turner. 1985. *Between Theatre and Anthropology*. Philadelphia: University of Pennsylvania Press.

Schutzman, M. and J. Cohen-Cruz (eds). 2006. *A Boal Companion. Dialogues on Theatre and Cultural Politics*. New York and London: Routledge.

Scott, J. 1985. *Weapons of the Weak: Everyday Forms of Peasant Resistance*. Yale: Yale University Press.

———. 1990. *Domination and the Arts of Resistance. Hidden Scripts*. Yale: Yale University Press.

Seddon D. and A. Karki (eds). 2003. *The People's War. Left Perspectives*. Delhi: Adroit Publishers.

Seizer, S. 2000. Roadwork: 'Offstage with Special Drama Actresses in Tamilnadu, South India', *Cultural Anthropology* 15 (2): 217–59.

———. 2005. *Stigmas of the Tamil stage. An Ethnography of Special Drama Artists in South India*. Durham and London: Duke University Press.

Sen Chyang Cultural Company. 2006. *Asthaka Swarharu (Voices of Faith)*, MC.

———. 2006. *Campaign for Republic*, VCD 1 and 2, unpublished.

———. 2008. *Mardeina Balidan Kahilyai* (The Sacrifice Will Never Die), MC.

Sengupta, A. 2006. *Tehelka*, 3 June.

Shah, S. 2008. *Civil Society in Uncivil Places. Soft State and Regime Change in Nepal*. Washington DC: East-West Centre.

Shah Yatri, K. 2006. *Theatre Artist Hari Bahadur Thapa*. Kathmandu: Jyotipunja Sign Theatre.

Shank, T. 2002. 'Collective Creation', in *Re:direction*, edited by Rebecca Schneider and Gabrielle Cody, 221–35. London: Routledge.

Sharma, P. 2011. 'Stigma in Nepali Theatre: A Political Representation', in *IMAP Reader: A Collection of Essays on Art and Theatre in Kathmandu*, edited by S. Uprety and R. Piya, 70–91. Kathmandu: Himal Books.

Sharma, S. 2004. 'The Maoist Movement: An Evolutionary Perspective', in *Himalayan 'People's War'. Nepal's Maoist Rebellion*, edited by M. Hutt, 38–57. London: Hurst & Co.

Sharrock, J. 2007. 'Nepali Blogging and Democracy', *Studies in Nepali History and Society* 12 (1): 55–94.

Shrestha, A. P. 2000. 'Protest Poetry: The Voice of Conscience', *Contributions to Nepalese Studies* 27 (2): 259–67.

Shrestha, N. 1993. 'Enchanted by the Mantra of Bikas: A Self-reflective Perspective on Nepalese Elites and Development', *South Asia Bulletin* XIII (1–2): 5–22.

Shrestha, P. 2005. 'Hami Bise Nargachijasteita Ho Ni!' *Himal Khabarpatrika* (31 July): 58–59.

———. 2006. 'Janandolanma Kabi, Kalaakaar Rashrashta Janata Sangai', *Himal Khabarpatrika* (29 April–14 May): 66–69.

Skinner, D., D. Holland and G.B. Adhikari. 1994. 'The Songs of Teej. A Genre of Critical Commentary for Women in Nepal', *Asian Folklore Studies* 53 (2): 259–305.

Skinner, D., A. Pach III and D. Holland. 1998. *Selves in Time and Place. Identities, Experience and History in Nepal*. Boston: Rowman and Littlefield.

Slusser, M. S. 1982. *Nepal Mandala: A Cultural Study of the Kathmandu Valley*. Princeton: Princeton University Press.

Smith, D. 1998. *The Dance of Siva*. Cambridge: Cambridge University Press.

Snellinger, A. 2005. 'A Crisis in Nepali Student Politics? Analyzing the Gap between Politically Active and Non-Active Students', *Peace and Democracy in South Asia Journal* 1 (2): 18–43.

―――. 2007. 'Idealized Forms: The Parameters of Student Movements in Nepal', in *Contentious Politics and Democratization in Nepal*, edited by M. Lawoti, 273– 98. Delhi: Sage Publications.

Solomon, M (ed). 1979. *Marxism and Art. Essays Classic and Contemporary*. Detroit: Wayne State University Press.

Srampickal, J. 1994. *Voice to the Voiceless. The Power of People's Theatre in India*. New Delhi: Manohar.

Stanislawski, K. S. 2005[1936]. *Il Lavoro Dell'attore Su Sè Stesso*. Roma: Laterza.

Stanton S. and M. Banham. 1996. *Theatre. Cambridge Paperback Guide*. Cambridge: Cambridge University Press.

Starn, O. 1995. 'Maoism in the Andes: The Communist Party of Peru-Shining Path and the Refusal of History', *Journal of Latin American Studies* 27 (2): 399–421.

Steinmann, B. 2006. 'Le Maoisme au Nepal', Lectures d'une Revolution. Paris: CNRS Edition.

Stirr, A. 2008. 'Dohori in the New Nepal', *World Literature Today* 82 (1): 30–34.

―――. 2010. 'Singing Dialogic Space into Being: Communist Language and Democratic Hopes at a Radio Nepal Dohori Competition', *Studies in Nepali History and Society* 15 (2): 297–330.

―――. 2012. 'Changing the Sound of Nationalism in Nepal: Deuda and the Far West', *South Asian Popular Culture* 10 (3): 237–83.

―――. 2013a. 'Class Love and the Unfinished Transformation of Social Hierarchy in Nepali Communist Songs', in *Red Strains: Music and Communism outside the Communist Block*, edited by R. Adlington. Oxford: Oxford University Press.

―――. 2013b. 'Tears for the Revolution. Nepali Musical Nationalism, Emotion, and the Maoist Movement', in *Revolution in Nepal: An Anthropological and Historical Approach to People's War*, edited by M. Lecomte-Tilouine. Oxford: Oxford University Press.

St. John G. (ed). 2008. *Victor Turner and Contemporary Cultural Performance*. New York and Oxford: Berghahn Books

Stupples, P. 2014. Creative Contributions: The Role of the Arts and the Cultural Sector in Development, *Progress in Development Studies* 14 (2): 115–30.

Subedi, A. 2001. 'Nepali Theatre: An Overview', *Mandala* 1: 2–5.

―――. 2001a. 'Revitalizing Asian Performing Arts', *Mandala* 1: 8–12.

―――. 2001b. 'Indigenous Theatre: Question of Survival', *Mandala* 2: 2–8.

————. 2001c. 'Folk in Urban Space: Unique Tradition of Newari Theatrical Performance', *Mandala* 2: 12–16.

————. 2001d. 'Heritage of Nepali Theatre', *Mandala* 3: 3–12.

————. 2002a. 'Nepali Theatre at this Stage', *Mandala* 4: 13–15.

————. 2002b. 'Travel as Theatre in Nepal Mandala', *Contributions to Nepalese Studies* 29 (1): 173–83.

————. 2006. *Nepali Theatre as I See It.* Kathmandu: Aarohan-Gurukul.

Subedi, P. 2011. 'Bringing the Playwright Home versus Sending the Audience Abroad: Nepali Theatre Adaptations of A Doll's House and The Just (Assassins)', in *IMAP Reader: A Collection of Essays on Art and Theatre in Kathmandu*, edited by S. Uprety and R. Piya, 59–69. Kathmandu: Himal Books.

Swartz, D. 1997. *Culture and Power. The Sociology of Pierre Bourdieu.* Chicago and London: University of Chicago Press.

Tamang, S. 2005. 'Civilising Civil Society: Donors and Democratic Space in Nepal', *Himal South Asia* 16 (7): 14–24.

Taussig, M. 1993. *Mimesis and Alterity. A Particular History of the Senses.* New York and London: Rutledge.

Taylor, D.1999. 'Making a Spectacle: The Mothers of the Plaza de Mayo', in *Radical street performance*, edited by J. Cohen-Cruz, 74–85. London and New York: Routledge.

Thapa, B. B. 2011. 'A Study on the Nexus between Theatre for Social Change and Donor Agencies', in *IMAP Reader: A Collection of Essays on Art and Theatre in Kathmandu*, edited by S. Uprety and R. Piya, 37–58. Kathmandu: Himal Books.

Thapa D. and B. Sijapati. 2003. *A Kingdom Under Siege. Nepal's Maoist Insurgency, 1996 to 2003.* Kathmandu: The Printhouse.

Thapa, Deepak (ed.). 2003. *Understanding the Maoist Movement of Nepal.* Kathmandu: Centre for Social Science and Development.

The Kathmandu Post. 2013. 'Monday Interview. 500 Kamlaris are Still Held Captive by Top Police and the Powerful', 4 August.

Thompson, J. 2005. *Digging Up Stories: Applied Theatre, Performance and War.* Manchester: Manchester University Press.

Thompson, J. 2003. *Applied Theatre: Bewilderment and Beyond.* Bern: Peter Lang.

————. 2009. *Performance Affects. Applied Theatre and the End of Effect.* London: Palgrave Macmillan.

Tilly, C. 2008. *Contentious Performances.* Cambridge: Cambridge University Press.

Tingey, C. 1994. 'The Pancai Baja: Reflections on Social Change in Traditional Nepalese Music', in *Anthropology of Nepal. People, Problems and Processes*, edited by M. Allen, 423–33, Kathmandu: Mandala Bookpoint.

————. 1994b. *Auspicious Music in a Changing Society: The Damai Musicians of Nepal.* London: School of Oriental and African Studies.

Todd, N. 1974. 'Ideological Superstructure in Gramsci and Mao Tse-Tung', *Journal of the History of Ideas* 35 (1): 148–56.

Toffin, G. 1992. 'The Indra Jatra of Kathmandu as a Royal Festival: Past and Present', *Contributions to Nepalese Studies* 19 (1): 73–92.

————. 2008 [1999]. 'The Citrakars: Caste of Painters and Mask-Makers', in *Contested Hierarchies. A Collaborative Ethnography of Caste among the Newar of the Kathmandu Valley, Nepal*, edited by D. Gellner and D. Quigley, 240–63. Oxford: Oxford University Press.

————. 2008. 'Royal Images and Ceremonies of Power', *Rivista di Studi Sudasiatici* III: 145–80.

————. 2010. *La Fête-Spectacle. Théâtre et Rite au Népal*. Paris: Éditions de la Maison des sciences de l'homme.

————. 2012. 'A Vaishnava Theatrical Performance in Nepal: The Katti-Phyaka of Lalitpur City', *Asian Theatre Journal* 29 (1): 126–63.

————. 2013. *From Monarchy to Republic. Essays on Changing Nepal*. Kathmandu, Vajra Books.

Tordis, K. 1994. 'The Dancing Gods of Bhaktapur and Their Audience', in *Anthropology of Nepal. People, Problems and Processes*, edited by M. Allen, 405–15. Kathmandu: Mandala Bookpoint.

Trevino, A. J. (ed). 2003. *Goffman's Legacy*. Lanham: Rowman & Littlefield Publishers.

Turner, V. 1969. *The Ritual Process. Structure and Anti-Structure*. New York: Aldine de Gruyter.

————. 1974. *Dramas, Fields and Metaphors: Symbolic Action in Human Society*. Ithaca: Cornell University Press

————. 1982. *From Ritual to Theatre: The Human Seriousness of Play*. New York: Performing Arts Journal Publications.

————. 1986. 'Dewey, Dilthey and Drama: An Essay in the Anthropology of Experience', in *The Anthropology of Experience*, edited by V. Turner and E. M. Bruner, 33–44. Urbana and Chicago, University of Illinois Press.

————. 1987. *The Anthropology of Performance*. New York: Performing Arts Journal Publication.

Turner, V. and E. M. Bruner (eds). 1986. *The Anthropology of Experience*. Urbana: University of Illinois Press.

Tyler, S. 1986. 'Post-modern Ethnography: From Document of the Occult to the Occult Document', in *Writing culture. The poetics and politics of ethnography*, edited by J. Clifford and G.E. Marcus, 122–40. Berkeley and Los Angeles: University of California Press.

Umney, C. and L. Kretsos. 2015. '"That's the Experience": Passion, Work Precarity, and

Life Transitions among London Jazz Musicians', *Work and Occupations* 42 (3): 313–34.

Upreti, B. J. 2008. 'Dispute Settlement at the Local Level: Observations and Lessons from Nepal', in *Local Democracy in South Asia. Microprocesses of Democratization in Nepal and its Neighbours*, edited by D. Gellner and K. Hachhethu, 150–74. New Delhi: Sage Publications.

Upreti, P. R. 1992. *Political Awakening in Nepal – The Search for a New Identity*. New Delhi: Commonwealth Publishers; New Delhi: Sage Publications.

Uprety, B. 2016. 'Presenting the Absence: A Contrapuntal Reading of the Māita in Nepali Tīj Songs', *Journal of International Women's Studies* 17 (1): 39–61.

Uprety, S. and R. Piya (eds.). 2011. *IMAP Reader: A Collection of Essays on Art and Theatre in Kathmandu*. Kathmandu: Himal Books.

Van Erven, E. 1988. *Radical People's Theatre*. Bloomington and Indianapolis: Indiana University Press.

———. 1992. *The Playful Revolution: Theatre and Liberation in Asia*. Bloomington and Indianapolis: Indiana University Press.

———. 2001. *Community Theatre. Global Perspectives*. London and New York: Routledge.

Vegati, A. 1995. *Gods, Men and Territory: Society and Culture in the Kathmandu Valley*. New Delhi: Manohar.

Wasserstrom, J. N. 1991. *Student Protests in Twentieth-Century China. A View From Shanghai*. Stanford, Stanford University Press.

Webb, J., T. Schirato, and G. Danaher. 2006. *Understanding Bourdieu* London: Sage Publications.

Weisethaunet, H. 1998. *The Performance of Everyday Life: The Gaine of Nepal*. Oslo: Norwegian University Press.

Whelpton, J. 2005. *A History of Nepal*. Cambridge: Cambridge University Press.

Widdess, R. 2006. 'Musical Structure, Performance and Meaning: The Case of a Stick-Dance from Nepal', *Ethnomusicology Forum* 15 (2): 179–213.

Williams, R. 1977. *Marxism and Literature*. Oxford and New York: Oxford University Press.

Wilmore, M. 2008. 'Urban Space and Mediation of Political Action in Nepal: Local Television, Ritual Processions and Political Violence as Technologies of Enchantment', *The Australian Journal of Anthropology* 19 (1): 41–56.

Wiltshire, B. 1982. *Role Playing and Identity. The Limits of Theatre as a Metaphor*. Bloomington: Indiana University Press.

Wood, E. 2001. 'The Emotional Benefit of Insurgency in El Salvador', in *Passionate Politics: Emotions and Social Movements*, edited by Jeff Goodwin James M Jasper and Francesca Polletta, 267–81. Chicago: University of Chicago Press, .

————. 2006. *Insurgent Collective Action and Civil War in El Salvador*. Cambridge: Cambridge University Press.

Wortham, S. 2001. *Narratives in Action. A Strategy for Research and Analysis*. London and New York: Columbia University.

Yarrow, R. 2001. *Indian Theatre. Theatre of Origin, Theatre of Freedom*. Richmond: Curzon Press.

Yong, K. H. 2007. 'The Politics and Aesthetics of the Place-names in Sarawak', *Anthropological Quarterly* 80 (1): 65–91

Zarrilli, P. B. 1995. *Acting (Re)Considered. A Theoretical and Practical Guide*. New York: Routledge.

————. 2000. *Kathakali Dance Drama. Where Gods and Demons Come to Play*. London and New York: Routledge.

Zournazi, M. 2002. *Hope. New Philosophies for Change*. London: L.W.

Index

Maoist revolutionary cultural programmes, 182–187
  in cassettes, CDs and videos, 196
  live performances, 196
  Maoist artists, 198–201
  Maoist modality of 'displaying' cultural diversity, 197, 207n20
  outfit of dancers, 197
  as popular culture, 196–198
  revolution, as life, 201–205
  revolutionary performances, 187–196
  rhythms of songs and dance, 197
'marked' performance, 3

mimesis (imitation), 4

Mithila culture, 158

Mithila Natyakala Parishad (MINAP), 158

ML (Communist Party of Nepal - Marxist Leninist), 41

Mukarung, Shrawan, 173

Nachghar (National Theatre), 53

Nahusa, King, 210

Narayan, Bekha, 41

National School of Drama (NSD), 15

National Theatre, 58

National Theatre (Rastriya Nachghar)/ Cultural Corporation (Sanskritik Samsthan), 11

Naxalite movement in India, 184

Naxalite revolutionary cultural groups, 193

Nepal Academy, 58

Nepal Academy (Pragya Pratishthan), 11

Nepal, Kamal Mani 20, 103,106–109, 135, 138, 216-217, 221-222,

Nepali Bhasa Prakashini Samiti, 40

Nepali civil society, 78

Nepali Communist Party Masal, 185

Nepali Congress, 62n20

Nepali theatre(s), 7–12
  connection to political power, 7–8

created by 'teacher-dramatists and student-performers,' 10
history, 8
kings performed as actors on dabali or dabu, 8
Malla period (1200-1768), 8, 12
modern drama and theatre, 10
Ranas (1846-1950) period, 9–10
relationship between foreignness and, 15
Shah Kings period (1768-1846), 8

New Nepal (Naya Nepal), 26

NGO theatre, 121

Pakhrin, Khusi Ram, 185

Panday, Devendra Raj, 78

Pangeni, Badri, 80

Parajuli, Arjun, 80

Parsi theatre and performances, 9–11

Patnaik, Subodh, 53

People's Cultural Federation, 201

People's Movement, 2, 28, 33, 43

People's War, 61n3, 96, 127, 163, 176, 182, 185–186, 188, 191–192, 196, 204–205

Pokharel, Anil, 21–22,119, 125, 213-215, 234

Pokharel, Mani, 20, 125, 132, 145–146, 228

Pokharel, Nisha Sharma, 16,110, 221, 225, 227, 245n47

Pokharel, Sunil, 13–17, 20–21, 27, 32–33, 52–53, 55, 57–58, 60, 68–69, 89, 97, 119–120, 124, 150–151, 214–215, 218, 221, 239, 245n47

political situation of Nepal
  King Mahendra's take-over in 1960, 35–36
  levels of repression during Mahendra's rule, 35–37
  political resistance, 36–37
  state of emergency, 32–35